GEORGE GRANT:
A GUIDE TO HIS THOUGHT

George Grant (1918–1988) is widely regarded as one of Canada's most
influential philosophers and political theorists. His best-known work,
Lament for a Nation (1965), presented a radical reinterpretation of Canadian history and inspired a surge of nationalist sentiment across the
country. Along with Grant's other books, it addressed the major cultural shifts and dilemmas of our age, and introduced several generations of students to the basic questions of political philosophy.

This study aims to guide the reader towards a clearer understanding
of Grant's thought. Focusing on his six short books and some of his
most significant articles and speeches, Hugh Donald Forbes provides
both an introduction to and an overview of Grant's career and his
many contributions to the fields of political science, philosophy, religion, and Canadian studies. Throughout, Forbes sheds light on some
of Grant's more contradictory and complex ideas, and provides an
assessment of his impact on the Canadian political and cultural land-
scape. Forbes also relates Grant's work to that of three disparate and
controversial European thinkers – Martin Heidegger, Leo Strauss, and
Simone Weil – providing contexts and comparisons outside the strictly
Canadian framework in which he is normally situated. Comprehensive and lucidly written, *George Grant: A Guide to His Thought* is an
invaluable resource for students, general readers, and academic specialists alike.

HUGH DONALD FORBES is a professor in the Department of Political Science at the University of Toronto.

HUGH DONALD FORBES

George Grant

A Guide to His Thought

UNIVERSITY OF TORONTO PRESS
Toronto Buffalo London

© University of Toronto Press Incorporated 2007
Toronto Buffalo London
Printed in Canada

ISBN 978-0-8020-4318-4 (cloth)
ISBN 978-0-8020-8142-1 (paper)

Printed on acid-free paper

Library and Archives Canada Cataloguing in Publication

Forbes, Hugh Donald, 1942–
    George Grant : a guide to his thought / Donald Forbes.

    Includes bibliographical references and index.
    ISBN 978-0-8020-4318-4 (bound)   ISBN 978-0-8020-8142-1 (pbk.)

    1. Grant, George, 1918–1988.   I. Title.

    B995.G724F67 2007   191   C2007-901487-9

University of Toronto Press acknowledges the financial support for its
publishing activities of the Government of Canada through the Book
Publishing Industry Development Program (BPIDP).

This book has been published with the help of a grant from the Humanities
and Social Sciences Federation of Canada, using funds provided by the
Social Sciences and Humanities Research Council of Canada.

University of Toronto Press acknowledges the financial assistance to its
publishing program of the Canada Council for the Arts and the Ontario
Arts Council.

To the memory of
my father and mother

Contents

Preface   ix

Introduction   3

PART ONE: POLITICS

1 Nations and Necessities   19

2 Technology, Freedom, Progress   27

3 From Education to Indoctrination   35

4 Modern Liberal Theory   46

5 Varieties of Conservatism   59

6 Overcoming Nationalism   71

7 What Is Worth Doing?   79

PART TWO: PHILOSOPHY

8 Nature and History   87

9 Enlightenment and Nihilism   99

10 Platonic Political Philosophy   114

11 Theology and Politics   127

12 'Tyranny and Wisdom'   147

PART THREE: RELIGION

13 Making Sense of Religion   167

14 Discovering Simone Weil   180

15 Escaping the Shadows   191

16 'Faith and the Multiversity'   207

Some Further Reflections   223

Notes   233

Bibliographical Notes   281

Index   297

Preface

Some writers need to be introduced; others, such as George Grant, need to be followed up. He is not a difficult author who needs simplification (because hasty or unprepared readers would otherwise fail to make any sense at all of what is being said), but rather a deceptively simple one whose more difficult or challenging points need to be highlighted and spelled out, so that readers will not take away the argument they would prefer to hear rather than the one that Grant was making.

This book is directed to readers who are already acquainted with at least one or two of Grant's short books and who want some help in reaching a better understanding of his provocative claims. If it makes its way into the airport bookshops and persuades some unlikely converts to spend more of their time studying Grant's political and religious thought, I will be pleased, but I will not begin by trying to justify my own long-standing interest in Grant and I will simplify my task as a commentator by assuming a receptive audience. Anyone reading this book who has not already read something of Grant's writings would do well to put it aside for a time and to take up instead *Lament for a Nation*, a masterpiece of brevity and Grant's most impressive discussion of politics and philosophy. It demonstrates that Grant is an engaging writer, first of all, because of his strong and clearly expressed political opinions. No matter whether you are inclined to agree with his opinions or to reject them, you are never left in doubt about where he stood. Moreover, no one can read his best political writings, such as *Lament for a Nation* or *English-Speaking Justice*, without becoming aware of the power of his mind and the breadth of his knowledge.

Grant's renown has faded somewhat since his death in 1988, and some of his writings are naturally less timely now than when they first appeared, but the ongoing publication of his *Collected Works* is showing the range of his interests and making it easier to see more clearly the fundamental problems with which he was grappling. He discussed politics philosophically, in the light of general principles and on the assumption that we should strive to make our political beliefs consistent with all our other beliefs, on a host of different matters, since they are all more or less interconnected and interdependent. Needless to say, not all the opinions that we commonly entertain are really coherent, and Grant never claimed that he had himself escaped all the difficulties of his inherited beliefs. But it was his aim to help others to attain clarity by revealing some of the contradictions he saw in the thinking of those among whom he lived and whose opinions he naturally began by sharing.

As a philosopher, Grant stood apart from the academic philosophers of his generation. The questions that absorbed their attention – the rather technical questions of modern Anglo-American positivism or analytic philosophy – were not the ones that he regarded as most important. Grant's first book, *Philosophy in the Mass Age*, clearly shows his tendency to focus instead on the big political and religious questions that figure more prominently in popular discussions of philosophy and in its older classics than in the most recent professional literature. In fact, as this first book suggests, Grant was as much a theologian as a philosopher. He was never responsible for teaching students preparing for clerical careers, but his interests were theological as well as political and philosophical.

It is not my purpose to compare systematically Grant's contributions to our knowledge with those of his contemporaries. It is certainly legitimate to ask whether there is anything of value in his thought that cannot be found in the work of others – Arendt, Berlin, Gadamer, Habermas, MacIntyre, Nozick, Rawls, or any of the other outstanding moral and political philosophers of the twentieth century with whom he could be compared. To be frank, however, my own interest in him derives from less lofty preoccupations. I was irritated by the blessing he gave the founders of the NDP in 1961. Four years later I was provoked by his challenging critique of the nationalist credentials of Liberals like Mackenzie King and Lester Pearson. It seemed to me then, as it still sometimes seems to me now, that it would not be difficult to show how questionable were some of his historical and political judgments. His way of mixing opinions from left and right was intriguing, however, and it was obvious even then that he was drawing on some deeper sources than the intellectual traditions of our Progressive Conservative Party. My interest developed slowly from that starting point, moving, as this book will move, from politics through philosophy to religion. The more I read of Grant's books and articles the more I became aware of how extraordinarily challenging his ideas were and how poorly they are described by the usual labels.

In short, I have in mind readers who have already encountered Grant's work, who have found it engaging for some reason, and who, no matter whether they have been excited by the discovery of a sympathetic intellectual master (as I was) or irritated by political opinions they find offensive or incomprehensible (as I also was), have at least realized that there is something in his arguments and assertions that they would do well to consider more carefully. I will focus on Grant's best-known and most characteristic writings, his six books, and only when necessary cite his shorter or unpublished writings. For the books, I will cite the currently available editions rather than the original editions or the *Collected Works*. For the other writings up to 1969, I will give the original sources but cite the locations of the quotations or other references in the first three volumes of the *Collected Works*. The fourth volume, covering the period from 1970 to 1988, has not yet been published, so I will cite the original sources for published material from this period or the edited transcripts of the unpublished writings. For additional information about the different editions of Grant's writings as well as suggestions for further reading, please see the Bibliographical Notes at the end of this volume.

I have occasionally borrowed passages from earlier publications, namely, an article on Grant's political thought in the *Journal of Canadian Studies* in 1991 and a chapter on Grant and Strauss in *George Grant and the Subversion of Modernity*, edited by Arthur Davis and published by the University of Toronto Press in 1996.

Finally, I would like to thank the many people who have helped me during the writing of this book. It was suggested a decade ago by Ron Schoeffel, the indispensable editorial patron of the Grant publications from the University of Toronto Press. He has always been patient and encouraging, despite innumerable delays. My understanding of Grant and related matters has been shaped by conversations over many years with Edward Andrew, Clifford Orwin, Thomas Pangle, William Parsons, Jone Schoeffel, John Uhr, and the late Allan Bloom. I have had the good fortune to teach students who shared my interest in Grant, particularly James Farney, Michael Pratt, and Scott Staring. At an early stage of the project, I got some helpful advice about style and approach from my sons, Marc and Peter, who brought a non-academic perspective to what I was trying to do. While I was writing, Sheila Grant welcomed me into her home, gave me free access to her husband's library and papers, and was generous with her time and careful in answering questions. Access to Grant's unpublished writings was greatly facilitated by Arthur Davis, who willingly provides edited copies of material slated for publication in the *Collected Works*. The first version of the entire manuscript was read by Edward Andrew, Leah Bradshaw, Arthur Davis, Gerald Owen, and Henry Roper, and their comments have saved me from many errors and misjudgments. As well, I was the beneficiary of three excellent reports from anonymous reviewers engaged by the Press. One report in particular was a model of what every author hopes to receive: detailed comments from a very knowledgeable critic, favourably disposed but unsparing in pointing out deficiencies and generous in suggesting remedies. To all of the above, my thanks and, of course, my acceptance of responsibility for whatever faults remain.

Writing, being a solitary activity, imposes burdens on those who live with its distracted practitioners. In my case, these no doubt include some students and colleagues, but I owe a special debt of gratitude to my wife, Frauke Rubin, for her help and encouragement as well as her forbearance when it must have seemed that the project would never end.

GEORGE GRANT:
A GUIDE TO HIS THOUGHT

Introduction

George Grant was an unusual combination of public intellectual and cloistered scholar. As a young man, he made a strong impression on his contemporaries; in later life, he became a symbol of Canadian nationalism; and today, almost twenty years after his death, his major writings, though few in number and limited in scope, conforming to the conventions neither of popular nor of academic authorship, continue to engage readers and to provoke discussion.

Who was George Grant? What did he really think? What can we learn from him? He sometimes called himself 'a lover of Plato within Christianity,' but this description, though undeniably precise and to the point, raises such difficult questions that it is the wrong place to start when trying to grasp Grant's significance. When others try to define this significance, they usually focus on his politics rather than his philosophy or his religion. They say that he was somehow both a socialist and a conservative, straddling the usual distinctions between left and right. For a long time, 'Red Tory' has served as the quickest way to sum up his political thought, since it nicely suggests its paradoxical quality. Sometimes, more prosaically, he is said to have been a critic of modernity. He was too much of a conservative to share the hopes of most socialists, and too much of a socialist to find much common ground with most conservatives, but he sympathized with both the Marxist and the aristocratic critiques of modern urban industrial society. Like others beyond the left and right of established opinion, he entertained serious doubts about the basic ideas of the most influential modern social and political theorists. He gave voice to concerns about globalism, technology, and the environment long before it was fashionable to do so. However, what is most commonly said about Grant is that he was a nationalist: 'George Grant loved Canada and Canadians and hated America and Americans. He was a Canadian nationalist.' This grossly oversimplifies his political thinking (and is a caricature of Canadian nationalism), but it points to one important reason for the continuing interest among Canadians in someone who was not rich or much of a celebrity, who never held public office, and whose best-known book deals with an almost forgotten era in Canadian politics. By providing a sophisticated but unapologetically nationalist account of Canadian American relations, Grant's writings have helped a great many Canadians to gain a better understanding of their country and a freer relation to its history. His analysis of liberalism and conservatism clarifies the original meaning and the current significance of Canada's long-standing rivalry with the United States. Since the 1960s, his writings have introduced innumerable students in Canadian universities to some of the basic questions of political philosophy. To understand Grant is to understand much about Canada.

Grant's thought is not easy to understand, however. He knew that one way to engage good readers is to make them solve a few puzzles. To grasp the distinctive character of his political thought, one must put it in its philosophical context. And then to understand Grant's relation to political philosophy, one must see it in the context of his religious loyalties and convictions. In almost none of Grant's published writings are standard theological questions discussed directly, but no attentive reader of his most important works can fail to sense their importance for him. Admittedly, he was not at all a sectarian or evangelical writer. Nonetheless, a great part of Grant's appeal to his readers is his ability to restore a certain dignity to philosophical and religious positions that are implicitly denied serious consideration within our prevailing liberal and democratic language of politics and morality.

My purpose in this book is to provide some assistance to those who wish to read Grant with greater understanding. He offers a provocative – and for some, a convincing – perspective on Canadian and American politics. He relates politics and morality to philosophy and religion, leading his readers from their practical political preoccupations to a clearer understanding of their philosophical and religious origins. However, even those familiar with his most important writings about nationalism, liberalism, and political philosophy can remain quite unsure of the fundamental principles of his thought. It is easy to see that it has breadth and depth, but its unity can be elusive. I shall proceed by highlighting some key points or problems and then explaining what I think Grant meant or what the problem is. As already indicated, I have primarily in mind readers who do not need to be persuaded of Grant's importance, at least for Canadians, and who are already acquainted with at least one or two of his books. Starting from some easily overlooked points in the argument of his most widely read book, *Lament for a Nation*, I shall highlight the basic questions that were on Grant's mind when he was writing it. Eventually I will relate these to his earlier and later writings. But before saying anything more about the plan of the present book, let me provide a short account of Grant's life and times.

George Grant – his full name was George Parkin Grant – was born in Toronto in 1918. He was the youngest of four children, and the only son, of William Grant and Maude Parkin. They were descended from distinguished Maritime Canadian families. William Grant (1872–1935) was the only child (who survived to adulthood) of George Monro Grant (1835–1902), a Presbyterian minister and native of Albion Mines, Nova Scotia, who from 1877 until his death was the influential principal of Queen's University. Maude Parkin (1880–1963) was the second of five children of Sir George Parkin (1846–1922), a prominent public figure, originally from Salisbury, New Brunswick, who spent the last twenty years of his life in England. He began his illustrious career as a teacher in Fredericton and he later served for seven years as the headmaster of a private boys' school in Toronto, Upper Canada College, but it was as a spokesman for the cause of imperial federation that he gained prominence and the support of some influential patrons. From 1889 until his move to Toronto in 1895, Parkin travelled the world as a 'wandering Evangelist of Empire,' and from 1902 until his retirement (and knighthood) in 1920 he served as the first head of the Rhodes Scholarship Trust. Grant's father, William, was a historian with a particular interest in Canadian history. Before the First World War, he held teaching positions at Upper Canada College, Oxford University, and Queen's University. In 1916 he enlisted in the Canadian army and was immediately posted overseas, despite his relatively advanced age and two small children, with a third about to be born. Later that year, in France, he was seriously injured when he was thrown from a horse. He returned to Canada in 1918 to become the principal of Upper Canada College, as his father-in-law had been before him.

Grant himself attended Upper Canada College from 1927 to 1936 and then Queen's University, where he studied history and literature with the idea of later studying law and eventually embarking on a political career. In May 1939 he was awarded a Rhodes Scholarship for study at Oxford, and in October he travelled to England, even though war had been declared in September. He completed one year of study towards a law degree, before suspending his studies. During his high school and university years, he had thought of himself as a pacifist, and at Oxford he had become acquainted with a group of pacifists he greatly admired. In 1940, when he enlisted, it was in an ambulance corps, an alternative form of war service available to conscientious objectors, and not in the army or navy as his family desired and expected. During the heavy bombing of London from September 1940 until the spring of 1941, he was the warden of an air-raid shelter in Bermondsey, a poor district of factories and warehouses near the Surrey docks on the south bank of the Thames. On 17 February 1941, the shelter, a railway arch, suffered a direct hit and was 'smashed to ribbons,' with enormous casualties, including the deaths of several people with whom Grant had become close. The following months were difficult ones for him, and there is much that remains obscure about this period in his life. He had close family in London, and under their increasing pressure to abandon his pacifism, he decided to enlist in the merchant marine, still avoiding a combat role but not the dangers of the war.[1] He completed the enlistment formalities and was assigned a ship, then disappeared from London for two months. He worked for a time on a farm in Buckinghamshire, about fifty kilometres from Oxford, where he underwent a life-changing experience of which more will be said below. When he reappeared in London in January 1942, he was suffering from tuberculosis. With the help of his family he was able to secure passage to Canada in February and he spent the rest of the war in Toronto, at first being nursed back to health by his mother and then working for the CBC.

In this period of the life, Grant threw himself into the development of radio broadcasting as a way of educating the general public for the responsibilities of democratic citizenship. He wrote two pamphlets and a journal article on Canadian history and foreign policy and worked on some twenty radio scripts and 'study bulletins' for the CBC. Nothing about his enthusiastic involvement in adult education with a patriotic purpose suggested any basic change in direction. Nonetheless, when he returned to Oxford in 1945 to continue his studies, it was – to the surprise and consternation of his family – with a completely new purpose. His focus was now on theology and philosophy, and his goal was to write a thesis for the Oxford doctorate (the DPhil) and to become a university teacher. He sought the supervision of A.D. Lindsay, a highly respected scholar and political figure whom he had met in 1939. The topic of the thesis, suggested by Lindsay, was the thought of John Oman, a Scottish theologian who had died a few years earlier, after having directed the Presbyterian theological college in Cambridge for many years. The purpose of the thesis was to clarify Oman's treatment of the relation between the natural and the supernatural.

In 1946, through his involvement in the circle around C.S. Lewis, Grant met Sheila Allen, and they were married in 1947. Later that year they moved to Halifax, where Grant had secured an appointment in the Department of Philosophy at Dalhousie University. The Grants spent eleven years in Halifax. Their first child, Rachel, was born in 1948, and five more children were born before they left in 1960. They spent two academic years in England in the 1950s, the first, in 1949–50, to complete the thesis, and the second, in 1956–57, on a sabbatical leave.

Grant's students from this period testify to his amazingly engaging presentation of the problems and literature of philosophy. He was a natural teacher, it seems, with a genuine love for his best students. His openness or honesty, and his and Sheila's easy hospitality, won their affection and admiration, and several of them became lifelong friends. Grant also developed close friendships with some of his colleagues, particularly James Doull, whose understanding of ancient philosophy and Hegel's alternative to it made a deep impression on him.

Grant was emerging as a public figure during these years. As already noted, he had made some contributions to political debate in the 1940s, when he was working with the CBC, but it was probably the report he wrote on philosophy for his uncle Vincent Massey's Royal Commission on National Development in the Arts, Letters and Sciences in Canada (commonly known as the Massey Commission, which was appointed in 1949 and reported in 1951) that first brought him to the attention of a wider and more discriminating audience. Grant began his survey of the current state of philosophical studies in English Canada with the provocative declaration that 'the study of philosophy is the analysis of the traditions of our society and the judgment of those traditions against our varying intuitions of the Perfection of God.'[2] He went on to deplore the widespread tendency to assume that philosophy is a technical subject confined to specialists in universities rather than 'an activity necessary for all sorts and conditions of men – politicians and saints, artists and businessmen, scientists and farmers – if such men are to relate their particular functions to the general ends which society desires.' The academic philosophers, particularly in the Anglo-American countries, Grant claimed, were guilty of accepting and even promoting the false understanding of their subject as essentially a technique independent of the theological dogmas of faith. Grant concluded his assessment of the state of contemporary philosophy with the following statements: 'It is a great illusion that scepticism breeds thought and that doubt is the producer of art ... It is in the ages of faith that men pursue truth and beauty ... It would be impudence indeed in this essay to suggest how and when we Canadians will reach a fuller and more balanced intuition of God. It is not impudence however to point out that without such faith it will be vain to expect any great flowering of our culture in general and of our philosophy in particular.'[3]

Not surprisingly, some leading academics were offended by Grant's unflattering depiction of their easy-going secularism and complacent professionalism, and they hit back hard.[4] After all, the damaging aspersions had come, not from some venerable greybeard whose scholarly achievements and inveterate habits of cautious understatement might have made the negative judgments hard to dismiss, but from the scornfully argumentative young nephew of an influential public figure.

Grant's subsequent publications were in part defensive reactions to the stinging criticism directed at his royal commission essay. In the following year, for example, he wrote two articles for academic journals exposing the very questionable assumptions of two liberal and progressive thinkers, Bertrand Russell and Karl Popper, who were then in vogue. Their inflated reputations survived his forceful objections, which were easily brushed aside by the leaders of the profession in Canada, but Grant's unorthodox conservatism – his way of combining fidelity to religious traditions with antipathy to the domination of Canadian life by scientists and businessmen – was welcomed in other quarters, as shown by the frequency of his appearances on radio and television during the 1950s. The culmination of this phase of Grant's intellectual life was his 1958 series of radio lectures on 'Philosophy in the Mass Age,' which were published in book form in 1959 and which will serve below as a baseline for understanding his view of philosophy.

In the 1960s, Grant's circumstances were quite different from what they had been in the 1950s and so were his intellectual preoccupations. He and his family had moved to Toronto in 1960 so that he could take up the position he had been offered as the first head of the philosophy department of the new university, York, that was being built on the northern fringe of the city to accommodate its rapid growth and the anticipated increase in the number of young people who would be attending university in the future. The president of the university, Murray Ross, withdrew the offer, however, when Grant refused to accept the terms of the temporary relationship that had been negotiated between York and the University of Toronto so that the first few classes of York graduates could be awarded University of Toronto degrees. The purpose of the arrangement was to encourage good students to enrol in the new university. It gave the philosophy department at Toronto the right to choose the textbook in the introductory course that Grant had been assigned to teach, and this meant that he would have to use one written by a senior member of the senior institution – one that he found unacceptable. When Grant refused to budge and York's offer was withdrawn, it was impossible for him to return to Dalhousie and too late for him to find an alternative position elsewhere. He worked for a year as a consultant to the editors of the Encyclopedia Britannica and wrote a lengthy review of philosophical publications for the 1961 yearbook of the *Great Books of the Western World*, a related enterprise. The following year he returned to teaching, this time as the first head of a new Department of Religion at McMaster University in Hamilton. The department had been established to offer students the opportunity to study religion as an academic subject, like philosophy or sociology, and not just as theological training for a clerical vocation. It was a response to the growing interest among students in learning about religion without being confined to the formulas of any particular religion. It gave Grant the opportunity to design a 'great books' program with the focus on religion. He was able to teach the thinkers he found most interesting without having to deal with the expectations of either the professional philosophers or the professional theologians. He could offer classes on Plato and Augustine, or Nietzsche and Heidegger, or even Marx and Freud, for all of them could be regarded as in some sense religious thinkers. Grant's eclectic interests and unconventional approach to broad 'existential' questions fitted the rebellious spirit of the times and drew a large number of first-rate students to his classes. The department also provided a good context for Grant to explore in detail the thought of two important writers who had captured his attention, despite their low profile at the time – Leo Strauss and Simone Weil.

Grant is best known to most readers through his books from the 1960s, *Lament for a Nation* (1965) and *Technology and Empire* (1969). These are the works that earned him his enduring reputation as a nationalist, a Red Tory, and a critic of modernity. In them he deals more clearly and directly with politics than he had in his earlier writings about philosophy and education. His criticisms of secular liberalism and academic philosophy are still developed from a perspective of religious faith, but this source of his thought is now much less evident than it had been previously. Indeed, he may seem at times to be only a conventional socialist critic of capitalism and the Western alliance with no real interests beyond the practical controversies of the day. This is far from the truth, as I shall show later, but the burning questions of nationalism and imperialism tend to distract attention from the broader or more abstract questions of principle that provide the framework for these writings. Equally, however, Grant's practical preoccupations – the great issues of war and peace and domestic politics that he discusses in his best-known books – help to show the real significance of some fundamental questions of political philosophy.

In *Lament for a Nation*, Grant's most admired and most widely read book, he decried the loss of Canadian independence and sketched a philosophical justification for nationalist policies. He used a serious disagreement between the Canadian and American governments in the early 1960s to heighten awareness of the differences between Canadians and Americans. By praising a defeated prime minister, John Diefenbaker, for courageously resisting an American demand (they wanted the anti-aircraft missiles that Canada had purchased a few years earlier to be fitted with the nuclear warheads necessary for their assigned role in the existing integrated continental air-defence system), Grant dramatized the American commitment to 'technology and empire' and contrasted it with an earlier Canadian acceptance of a more traditional conception of what it means to be free.

Grant's contentions were, of course, controversial. Do we Canadians, with our colonial and imperial past and our ever-present technological interests and aspirations, really represent a different kind of politics and society? Many have pointed out that we too live 'the American way of life,' even if we live it a little more modestly, without as yet all the excesses that we see south of the line. Is it not just a matter of time, and really a very short time, before we too will have all that they have now? Do we not share the same fundamental values and pursue the same goals? Do we not share the same basic conception of the good life? Admittedly, an international boundary and two different governments, with their different policies, passports, and citizenships, will create some important distinctions between the two peoples, but can one seriously maintain that they mark a real difference of cultures or nationalities?

These challenging questions invite a simple but misleading interpretation of Grant's anti-American nationalism. Many have wanted to explain it away as a reflex induced by his ancestry. He was just the faithful scion of a British imperialist family, they have said. And not only had he inherited a grudge against the Americans, one could add, but their involvement in Vietnam, which was beginning to get a lot of attention in 1964, was sharpening his rivalrous antipathy. Along with many others in the 1960s and 1970s, Grant felt little sympathy with the American government's policy of bombing, burning, terrorizing, and defoliating Vietnam in a fruitless attempt (as it turned out) to impose its will on the Vietnamese people and to incorporate them in the American empire. Had he identified more strongly with that empire, perhaps he would have found some excuses for its violence in Vietnam. But must we assume that his opposition to it can have only an 'explanation' and not a justification? Further, could any reasonable justification be confined to criticism of a government and not bring into question the character or culture of the people they were governing? What is really being said by those who emphasize the similarities between Canadians and Americans? (Since we share so many vices, we should be the best of friends?) Grant was impatient with journalists and academics who personalize important political questions, but he might have spelled out his objections more clearly and observed the necessary precautions more carefully if simple-minded anti-Americanism had been as socially unacceptable among the Canadians of his generation as were many other irrational prejudices from the past that respectable Canadian society had already proscribed as beneath contempt.[5]

By the end of the 1960s, Grant was not just an admired teacher but also a prominent public figure. Each of his three small books had attracted far more public attention than do most books written by academics. He was certainly a more engaging figure than most academics, less narrow and cautious and colourless. On the surface, he was an odd mixture of the arrogance and pretensions of Canada's old anglophile elite and the rebelliousness of its counter-cultural youth. The economic and cultural nationalism of the 1970s – with its sometimes bitter debates about the role of multinational corporations in the Canadian economy, American faculty in Canadian universities, and Canadian-content regulations for radio and television – lacked strong leadership, and in

Grant it found one of its icons. He had dismissive critics, to be sure, but also a large following in the universities and beyond. When he appeared on television, he was now the person being interviewed rather than the one doing the interviewing. He became a fellow of the Royal Society in 1964 and also began to be awarded honorary degrees, receiving six altogether between 1971 and 1980. During the 1970s, however, Grant was actually moving away from direct involvement in practical politics. His two small books from this period, *Time as History* (1971) and *English-Speaking Justice* (1978), are of a distinctly less popular character than his earlier publications, even though both originated in invitations to give public lectures. The first, his Massey Lectures for the CBC, offers a brief but incisive introduction to the thought of Nietzsche and Heidegger; the second, his Josiah Wood Lectures at Mount Allison University and his most academic book, dissects modern liberal theory as represented by an influential Harvard philosopher, John Rawls. When Grant is known outside Canada, it is usually for this book about Rawls. The practical issue it highlights is abortion. Grant presents the mass acceptance of safe cheap abortions as evidence of the darkness that now surrounds justice. Regarding the famous decision of the United States Supreme Court that made abortion a woman's lifestyle choice, *Roe v. Wade*, he says that it has handed 'the cup of poison to our liberalism.'[6]

Grant was in some ways a more controversial figure in the 1980s than he had been earlier. The practical questions that had put him on the left side of public debate in the 1960s and 1970s were fading from view and the painful new issue just mentioned, abortion, had emerged, putting him distinctly to the right of the moderate and respectable consensus (that abortion, though never, of course, desirable in itself, is sometimes necessary for a woman's mental, physical, and social health). The old issue of Canadian independence flared up briefly in 1987 and 1988 because of the negotiations with the United States that resulted in the Free Trade Agreement (and eventually in the North American Free Trade Agreement with the United States and Mexico), but Grant's health was failing, and he took little part in the debate. He had moved back to Dalhousie in 1980 as a result of a bitter quarrel with some of his colleagues in the religion department at McMaster. His last book, *Technology and Justice*, was published in 1986. It contains a lengthy chapter, 'Faith and the Multiversity,' which may be regarded as Grant's testament. He died in 1988. He is buried in a small graveyard on the edge of a fishing village a short distance from Halifax, near a cabin where he and his family had spent many summers.

No short biographical account can convey an adequate impression of the larger-than-life quality of Grant's personality and career. Fortunately there is an excellent biography by William Christian and some valuable memoirs from former students and colleagues.[7] In this book I shall concentrate on Grant's writings and say almost nothing more about his life, not because I think that anyone's thought can ever be detached from their life, or because as a writer I think that nothing else really matters except writing, but because Grant's writings now provide the only possibility of a direct, unmediated access to the thought of the remarkable Canadian who has best revealed the pathos of Canadian nationalism and pointed beyond it.

Grant's most accessible writings deal with political and historical questions; five of his six short books are concerned primarily with such questions. I shall therefore begin by attempting some clarifications of his political thought. It stands on its own, needing little knowledge of other authors for its comprehension. A few of Grant's allusions to contemporary events do require some additional explanation, but the more important source of difficulties is likely to be his subtle and slightly deceptive rhetoric. Even in the 1960s, the basic argument of his most popular book, *Lament for a Nation*, was easily overlooked, so it will not be a waste of time, I suspect, to start with a review of some simple but fundamental points about nationalism and political necessity (chapter 1). The dark side of modern science and its mysterious character were themes in Grant's writings from the earliest years, even before he began using the word 'technology.' What he thought that overworked term really signified and how he understood its relations to politics and education are the topics of chapters 2 and 3, which provide the background needed for understanding his arguments about the foundations and shortcomings of modern progressive liberalism (chapter 4). Grant is often said to be a pessimistic writer, but he rejected this description, and it would be better, I shall suggest, to refer to his realism and his belief in necessity. What this means will be clarified by considering what he says about conservatism (chapter 5), the overcoming of nationalism (chapter 6), and the practical challenge now facing those of high ambition who are drawn to politics (chapter 7).

As we shall see, Grant's political thought cannot be separated from broader philosophical and theological questions. Parts Two and Three deal with this broader context of his claims, and in particular, with basic questions about reason and revelation. Unfortunately, Grant wrote relatively little that can be called primarily philosophical or theological rather than political, and the meaning of what he wrote will often remain obscure until its relation to the thought of three notoriously difficult and controversial writers is taken into account. These three are Martin Heidegger, Leo Strauss, and Simone Weil. Despite the difficulty of gaining access to their thought, they provide the best landmarks from which to take one's bearings when trying to understand Grant's distinctiveness or originality.[8] To begin to understand his affinity with any one of these outstanding thinkers is to penetrate well below the surface of what he wrote, not by tracing its 'sources,' which were far more diverse (above all, Plato and Augustine, but also Kant, Hegel, Oman, Doull, Sartre, and others), but rather by grasping its 'logic' or inner coherence.

Different readers will naturally prefer different comparisons, depending upon their backgrounds and sympathies, and those already familiar with one or another of the three major figures just mentioned are obviously in a different position from those equally unfamiliar with all of them. Grant himself praised all three, and especially Leo Strauss and Simone Weil. In what follows, much more attention will be paid to them than to Heidegger, even though one could reasonably think that Heidegger had the greatest impact on Grant and therefore deserves the most attention. The relative neglect of Heidegger in what follows, even though it may seem unjustified, is unfortunately unavoidable. The reasons for it will become clearer, I hope, as the discussion proceeds. For the present, it must suffice to say that Heidegger's thought is extraordinarily difficult to explain in any words but his own, and at length. Moreover, Grant wrote little and published almost nothing about Heidegger. So, in the five chapters of Part Two, I shall instead give primacy to Leo Strauss. In the 1960s Grant praised Strauss in the very highest terms. It seems clear that he never thought of himself as simply a disciple ('a Straussian'), but clearly he was deeply impressed by Strauss's understanding of the differences between ancient philosophy and modern thought. The affinity between Grant and Strauss is thus revealing but also easily misunderstood. Strauss's thought, though significantly easier to grasp than Heidegger's, is nonetheless not easily accessible, and many strange things are now said about it. Chapters 10 and 11 will deal directly and systematically with what Strauss taught, providing first a relatively brief overview and then a more detailed (too detailed perhaps for some readers) account of his early and fundamental analysis of philosophy and revelation. Chapter 12 will present

Grant's one extended discussion of Strauss, to clarify some basic points of agreement and disagreement. Chapters 8 and 9 – the first two chapters of Part Two – deal with Grant's most philosophical books, *Philosophy in the Mass Age* and *Time as History*, in order to establish the framework needed for any usefully brief comparisons with any of the three landmark figures mentioned above.

Grant was a religious as well as a political and philosophical thinker, but since he published almost nothing directly relevant (not even his Oxford thesis on John Oman), any attempt to clarify this side of his thought faces almost insurmountable obstacles. Again, I think the solution – in so far as there is a solution – lies in elaborating a comparison suggested by Grant himself. In both published and unpublished writings, he made clear the depth of his admiration for Simone Weil. The four chapters of Part Three try to throw some light on the reasons for this admiration and Grant's affinity with her thought. They provide, first of all, a brief, rather schematic account of how the ancient connection between Christian faith and philosophy or theology stood at the time that Grant began his studies (chapter 13), then a short outline of Simone Weil's life and writings and Grant's opinions about them (chapter 14), followed by sketchy summaries of some key points in her thought (chapter 15) and finally a more detailed discussion of Grant's last book, *Technology and Justice*, and in particular its longest and most important essay, 'Faith and the Multiversity' (chapter 16). The aim of this third part is to provide a few basic facts and some broad conjectures that may help anyone trying to advance in the direction Grant indicated.

The final section of the book, not really a chapter but more like an introduction in retrospect, attempts to recapitulate the main points of the earlier chapters in such a way as to encourage readers to return to Grant's writings so that they can form their own appreciation of their significance. The great source of misunderstanding of his thought, it should by then be clear, is the almost inescapable tendency to simplify it for the sake of classification and comparison. For example, one may be tempted to ask whether Grant was a conservative, a liberal, or a socialist – or if these familiar categories all seem too simplistic and too confining, to wonder whether he might not have been all three at once, a Red Tory, even if this term then requires as much clarification as the thought it was meant to clarify. At a higher level, perhaps, one may wonder whether Grant was or was not really a Straussian or a Heideggerian. And in what sense exactly was he a Christian?

The deeper problem here is the inherent insufficiency of conventional terminology, even the arcane jargon of sophisticated academic disciplines, for expressing unconventional thoughts in compact form without the loss of crucial detail. There is really no adequate shorthand for philosophy, theology, and politics. As Grant himself observed at the beginning of his most academic book, *English-Speaking Justice*, we have no language for the discussion of politics and morality but that of our liberal political tradition, and it puts almost inescapable constraints on what can be said about patriotism and religion without seeming to be fundamentally irrational or reactionary.[9] Simone Weil, in one of her finest essays, compared language to a prison cell which may be larger or smaller, depending upon the intelligence with which it is used, but which is never able to give adequate expression to more than a few of the many relations that must be seen simultaneously if one is to live in truth. 'So the mind [enclosed in language] moves in a closed space of partial truth, which may be larger or smaller, without ever being able so much as to glance at what is outside.' Only by escaping the constraints of explicitness can one begin to attain the knowledge of the whole that would be wisdom. 'The mind which is enclosed within language can possess only opinions.'[10]

The aim of this work is not to sift through Grant's opinions in order to assign him his proper place within the prison, but to help those readers who suspect that there may be something beyond its walls, even if it cannot be clearly or concisely stated, and who wish to avail themselves of Grant's assistance in finding what they seek. I hope that the plan of exposition or exploration that I have adopted is not needlessly indirect, and I hate to think that I may be accused of being a mystery monger, but I realize that my meandering, somewhat repetitive course may not agree with all readers. They should realize from the outset, however, that terms like nationalist, or social critic, or even Red Tory are at best pointers or blazes at the head of a trail that leads far from its starting point and that will eventually return the persistent explorer to that point with a new understanding of their meaning. Thus, to see Grant as someone who loved Canada and Canadians and who hated America and Americans may be a first step towards understanding what it was about him that attracted the interest of many of his contemporaries in Canada, and why his writings are never likely to have much appeal to Americans, but it is not at all to understand who he really was and why, almost twenty years after his death and forty years since the height of his celebrity, he still has devoted readers.

PART ONE

Politics

I often meet people of my generation who went to university in the 1930s, and who speak as if the institutions their children or grandchildren are now attending are really the same as those they went to. But this is simply an illusion. The names are the same, but they are such different places that they should have different names.

George Grant

George Grant's fate was to be a nationalist by birth and conviction in a nation dedicated to the overcoming of nationalism. No reader of his most widely read book, *Lament for a Nation*, can miss his longing for a more Canadian Canada, more distinct and independent, less like the United States and less subservient to its government. But no one can understand the argument of that book without becoming aware of his belief that such longings can never be satisfied, given the aspirations of Canadians and the paradoxical character, therefore, of our nationalism. We can best begin to understand his reasons for writing of the defeat of Canadian nationalism and the necessity of Canada's disappearance by focusing on his analysis of Canadian life and politics in the early 1960s. To see what the familiar descriptions of Grant – as a nationalist, a Red Tory, and a critic of modernity – are trying to capture or encapsulate, and the relation of these labels to the deeper themes of his political thought, we shall have to consider what he says not just about nationalism and Canadian politics but also about technology, freedom, education, liberalism, conservatism, and the universal and homogeneous state.

1 Nations and Necessities

Between 1959 and 1986 George Grant published six short books. The most widely read of these is undoubtedly *Lament for a Nation*, which appeared in 1965. Grant's reputation rests largely on this one book. It strikes most readers today as passionate and prescient – passionate because its author obviously had a deep commitment to Canada and a strong belief in its independence, and prescient because he could foresee, long before the free-trade agreements and the current 'war on terror,' how hard it would be for us to avoid becoming an economic, political, and cultural satellite of our powerful, domineering neighbour. But the book also strikes many readers as 'too pessimistic.' Grant seems to be saying that Canada is fated to disappear, as if by some mechanical necessity or play of forces that is compelling our annexation by the United States. Absorption into American politics and culture is the destiny that awaits us, he appears to suggest, no matter how hard we struggle to maintain our independence and even if we manage to retain some semblance of it. A make-believe sovereignty may not be too difficult to defend, he says, because the Americans may have no interest in forcing any humiliating formal incorporation on us. All they may really want is compliance with what they really want. 'A branch-plant satellite, which has shown in the past that it will not insist on any difficulties in foreign or defence policy, is a pleasant arrangement for one's northern frontier.'[1] But more than this is impossible.

Many readers who accept much of what Grant is saying about Canada's origins and the weakness of our political leaders in the past balk at his gloomy view of our future. 'Why so pessimistic?' they ask.[2] Even forty years ago, not all Canadians were dreaming the American Dream, and many fewer today seem to want to blend into American society.

Many more of us have a strong sense of Canadian identity and a distinct vision of Canada's future. This is not to deny that there are some ways in which Canada is being Americanized, and, as Grant said, some of our un-American characteristics are disappearing. Still, new distinguishing traits have developed, so there seems to be no reason why, with an effort of intellect and will, we cannot retain them indefinitely. The Americans may try to force us to conform to their way of doing things, internally and externally, but we can still maintain national policies such as bilingualism and publicly funded health care that set us apart. And obviously (as the current war in Iraq has shown) our foreign policy does not need to be a slavish imitation of theirs. By taking the lead in disarmament and peacekeeping, we have forged an independent tradition that is now expressed in our initiatives on human security and international law.

Moreover, despite its pessimism, Grant's *Lament* was in fact a rallying cry for Canadian nationalists. Many have pointed to the contradiction between its major thesis and its practical effect: by declaring the death of Canadian nationalism, Grant brought it back to life. (This should be the entry for Grant in any dictionary of accepted Canadian ideas.) By reminding Canadians of their conservative national traditions, at a time when the meaning of those traditions was fading in the glare of American power and prestige after the Second World War, Grant opened the way to giving Canadian nationalism a new meaning. He confronted the burning issues of the 1960s – the arms race, the spread of nuclear weapons, American imperialism, and the war in Vietnam – from a truly Canadian perspective, thereby foreshadowing a new attitude among Canadians generally. He gathered up the crucial elements of Canada's heritage and projected them into the future, showing a real possibility, even if it was one he himself denied. Thus, by demonstrating that we have had a fundamentally different past from the Americans (contrary to what liberals and continentalists were claiming), he showed that we can have a significantly different future: a Tory communitarian past contains the seeds of a progressive communitarian future.[3] Not even Grant himself said that we have to imitate every feature of American liberal capitalism. We remain free to create something better.

Many readers have taken this more hopeful and constructive message from Grant's 'implacably pessimistic' analysis of our history and politics. From this standpoint, his *Lament* exemplifies the kind of historical writing that, by praising the great achievements of the past, inspires future greatness, thus serving life better than would any merely anti-quarian research or dispassionate critical objectivity. What is called Grant's 'pessimism' can be attributed to his personality or personal circumstances or his painful wartime experiences, rather than to the situation he was describing. The dark colouring of his description can be separated, as it were, from its overall design. The pessimism does not invalidate what he says about American domination and the need for radical policies to meet the threat of cultural and political homogenization. Rather it goads the reader to fight for Canadian independence and a brighter future.

The fly in the ointment of this more optimistic, forward-looking interpretation of Grant's message is what he said, not about Canada's past or future, but about its *present*, more than forty years ago. The simplest and most memorable thesis of *Lament for a Nation* is as challenging today as it was in 1965, when the book was first published. Can we really say, as Grant is evidently saying, that Canada had already disappeared when the book was being written? Could 'the defeat of Canadian nationalism' that Grant laments – the loss of sovereignty he explains – have already happened before the book was published? This seems to be Grant's contention, but few readers are likely to give it much credence, at least not when it is stated so baldly.

The obvious and seemingly fatal objection to such a strange claim is that Canada still exists. We have not become part of the United States. We still govern ourselves, as we did a generation or two ago, and we remain formally as free as we ever were to adopt whatever laws and policies we think will best serve our interests. Indeed, in some respects we are more independent now that we were forty or fifty years ago. We now have our own flag, for example, and we no longer depend on the British parliament for the amendment of our constitution. Our national unity may be more secure than it was when separatism was a new movement in Quebec, full of promise and threat. To be sure, our economic life has gradually become more entangled with that of the Americans, and our sovereignty may have been more compromised than we would like by treaties such as the free-trade agreements (and certainly more compromised in practice than American sovereignty has been, because of their size and power). However, treaties put constraints on all the parties to them, and these have certainly not destroyed our economy and especially not our cultural industries, so vital for our national consciousness, for they are thriving. Our novelists, for example, are publishing more books than ever before and many of them have achieved international recognition. Margaret Atwood, Douglas Coupland, Mavis Gallant, Rohinton Mistry, Michael Ondaatje, Nino Ricci, Carol Shields, and many others are telling our stories, and the world is listening. Our music industry is booming. Canadians are among Hollywood's funniest comedians, brightest stars, and most creative directors. The production of romantic fiction is dominated by a Canadian multinational. Does it make any sense, then, to speak of Canada as having already disappeared?

The readers of *Lament for a Nation* may generally be divided between those who dismiss its opening claim about defeat and disappearance as totally unrealistic and those, on the other hand, who avert their eyes from the difficulty I have just indicated. The latter – Grant's more sympathetic readers – seem generally to assume that he was exaggerating to make a point. Canada has not literally *disappeared*, they are inclined to say, but it is gradually *disappearing*, being swallowed up by American culture and society, and unless we are careful it will really cease to exist altogether at some unspecified time in the future. Grant may seem to be bewailing a fait accompli, but he is really trying to show a trend and to project it into the future in order to warn us of a danger we should face and try to avoid. His lament, according to this interpretation, is really a call to arms. Canadian nationalists should become more aware than they have been of the danger of Americanization and they should 'stand on guard' for the economic and political integrity of their 'home and native land.'

Grant provides some justification for this qualified and relatively unproblematic interpretation of his position. (It is difficult to imagine that he did not have some inkling, as he was writing his *Lament*, of the impact it would have on its readers.) And yet the simpler, balder, bolder, less qualified, less easily accepted statement of his thesis – that Canada had already disappeared, even in 1965 – may take us more quickly to the heart of the most interesting problems the book raises. It may be the good reader's task, not to make Grant sound less challenging than he really was and more at home in the common sense of his time and ours, but to see more clearly how exactly he was dissenting from it.

Grant assumed that nations are to be understood by reference to their fundamental guiding intentions, and not just their objective geographic, demographic, linguistic, cultural, or genetic characteristics.

His political analysis rests upon the traditional assumption that a nation (or state or political system) is a partnership that must be understood primarily or fundamentally by understanding the purposes of the partners in forming the partnership. To be sure, nations grow 'organically' and 'historically'; the actions of their members illustrate various principles or laws of human behaviour; there may be little agreement among them about the best policies to pursue at any particular time; their customs and conventions can be understood (up to a point) without considering their fundamental purposes; and we certainly have to learn from Marx and Freud about the complexity and hiddenness of human intentions. But, having said all this, can we really understand a nation and its institutions without understanding what its members, and particularly its leading or directing elements, regard as good in life and the ends they are agreed on pursuing? The character of a partnership is determined fundamentally by the ends of the partners. As Grant says in an easily neglected footnote, 'national articulation is a process through which human beings form and re-form themselves into a society to act historically. This process coheres around the intention realized in the action' (13). Or as he says later, 'a society only articulates itself as a nation through some common intention among its people' (67).

The specific intention whose disappearance Grant lamented is one that we can plausibly attribute to the British and French Canadians of two centuries ago. They refused to become part of the American republic because they rejected the republican principles of individual liberty and popular sovereignty on which it had been established. Their common negative intention was rooted in two divergent political and religious traditions, one Protestant, the other Catholic, both difficult to describe briefly. Grant claims no more for the Loyalists and other British settlers in the Atlantic colonies and central Canada than 'an inchoate desire to build, in these cold and forbidding regions, a society with a greater sense of order and restraint than freedom-loving republicanism would allow.' Their distinctive conservatism, like the British conservatism from which it derived, was 'less a clear view of existence than an appeal to an ill-defined past' (68–9). The conservatism of the French Canadians, by contrast, was rooted in a more formidable tradition. 'During the 19th century, they accepted almost unanimously the leadership of their particular Catholicism – a religion with an ancient doctrine of virtue. After 1789, they maintained their connection with the roots of their civilization through their church and its city, which more than any other in the West held a high vision of the eternal' (74). These different conservatisms never became a conscious bond, Grant says, but they were sufficient for a limited practical cooperation. 'Both the French and the British had limited common ground in their sense of social order – belief that society required a high degree of law, and respect for a public conception of virtue. Both would grant the state much wider rights to control the individual than was recognized in the libertarian ideas of the American constitution' (67).

The intention Grant describes underlay the Constitution Act of 1791, our first constitution, and the British North America Act of 1867. It explains the desire of many Canadians in the past, including many leading politicians – reformers as well as conservatives – to maintain a connection with Great Britain as a country with ways of life from before the age of progress. But this basic conservative intention is clearly a thing of the past, and there is no need, given our main objective here, to review the events in Canadian history that mark its gradual disappearance. One can reasonably wonder whether Grant lays too much of the responsibility for its demise at the feet of Mackenzie King and C.D. Howe.[4] One can question whether it makes sense to blame these two politicians, or any particular individuals, for what, as Grant himself says and as we shall shortly see, was a very broad trend going back many years. For present purposes, it suffices to summarize what Grant says about John Diefenbaker.

Diefenbaker served as leader of the Conservative Party for a decade, from 1957 to 1967; he was prime minister from 1957 to 1963; and he is, of course, the hero of *Lament for a Nation*. Grant praises his sincere nationalism, his courage, and especially his loyalty to his embattled minister of external affairs, Howard Green. Diefenbaker and Green were old friends and political allies, both bred-in-the-bone Canadian conservatives of the kind once defined by opposition to the Jeffersonian republicanism dominant in the United States.[5] In the defence crisis of 1963 they refused to bow to the internal as well as external pressures to adopt the defence policy favoured by the American government. Their refusal was, in Grant's view, 'the strongest stand against satellite status that any Canadian government ever attempted' (12). Nonetheless, Diefenbaker was plainly a flawed hero, as Grant makes perfectly clear. He had become prime minister in 1957 on a wave of popular disgust with Liberal arrogance and he saw his destiny as reviving the Canadian nationalism that had been wasting away for twenty years under Liberal stewardship. But he failed completely to develop the economic and other policies that would have been necessary if nationalism were to be more than a romantic sense of historical continuity. His nationalism was mixed in a confused way with populism and free-enterprise ideology. Thus he failed to check the quickening slide in Canada's heartland towards cultural and economic integration with the United States. He succeeded only in alienating the business community, the civil servants, and the French Canadians in Quebec. Indeed, in his approach to questions of nationality and individual rights, he showed himself to be an American liberal rather than a Canadian conservative. He certainly desired an independent Canada, and he had a vague sense of the threat to nationalism implicit in the policies of his predecessors, but he had no understanding that Canada's existence depended on a clear definition of conservatism, and he sought no help from the intellectual community, as shown by the appointments he made to royal commissions and other advisory bodies. 'He acted as if friendship with public-relations men and party journalists was a sufficient means to an intellectual nationalism' (25).

Grant's account of Canada's problems raises no hopes, however, that Diefenbaker might have received any real help from Canada's more thoughtful conservatives, had he been willing to lend a more attentive ear. After all, who were these thoughtful conservatives? Canada was impossible precisely because a genuine, thoughtful, practical conservatism that would give Canada a distinct identity consistent with its origins was no longer possible. As Grant declared in one of the most frequently quoted lines from the book, 'the impossibility of conservatism in our era is the impossibility of Canada' (67). And Grant himself made it clear that he was offering no practical proposals for our survival as a nation. Canada's disappearance, he maintained, was a matter of necessity, because the necessity in question had nothing to do with any known physical forces or social or psychological mechanisms that might be amenable to some kind of nationalistic social engineering. Rather it was due to the deepest tendencies of our own thought. What Diefenbaker would have had to do, to revive Canadian nationalism as an alternative to American republicanism, was not (Grant is suggesting) *physically* impossible (as it may be impossible to remove a brain tumour surgically without doing fatal damage to the rest of the brain), but rather, in a sense, *unthinkable*. Following the examples of Castro and de Gaulle, he would have had to combine nationalism and socialism in such a way as to distinguish Canada from the capitalist liberalism of the United States. But neither he nor anyone else could do this, because no one who mattered could really believe that any kind of national socialism would be good.

To simplify and generalize, then, Canada has disappeared because of the modern assumptions about human good that Canadians and Americans share. Geography and language were not the causes of Canada's defeat, but rather the incomparably more powerful necessity that governs the development of political intentions. As Grant says in another easily overlooked footnote: 'Historical necessity is chiefly concerned with what the most influential souls have thought about human good. Political philosophy is not some pleasant cultural game reserved for those too impotent for practice. It is concerned with judgements about goodness. As these judgements are apprehended and acted upon by practical men, they become the unfolding of fate' (91).

To understand the necessity of Canada's disappearance – to understand what has disappeared and why – one must understand what the most influential political thinkers have thought about human good. Canada's disappearance must ultimately be attributed, not to any vices or other failings of this or that leader, nor to any inherently insurmountable challenges of size or diversity, but simply to our prevailing assumptions about human good. An older Canada has gradually given way to a newer Canada, and the old Canada has thus *disappeared* because of the aspirations of Canadians, who have shared – and the most thoughtful, the most thoughtfully – the common Western desire to build a better world. This is not, however, to say that the disappearance of Canada has been the result of a free and responsible choice as usually understood. It was not a choice we ever consciously made, nor is it one we can simply reverse. No real choice is involved until we can bring the relevant thoughts to clear consciousness. For when we are truly convinced of what is good, and not in doubt about it, are we any longer free to do what we think is not good? The Canadian nationalism whose defeat Grant laments was the victim of what we Canadians confidently regard as good.

2 Technology, Freedom, Progress

The dominant spirit of all modern societies, according to George Grant, is that of modern practical science. It provides the kind of knowledge needed to overcome the cruelty and stinginess of nature and to build a better life for all mankind. The attainment of this goal, it is generally believed, depends upon the careful investigation of natural processes together with their redirection to alleviate human suffering and to increase the enjoyment of life. In the past century, modern science has made spectacular advances – in nuclear physics, for example, and molecular biology. Its effects are all around us – cheap power, effective medicines, televised entertainment, and a host of similar things. The computerization of our society during the past generation provides many vivid illustrations of the impact that advances in arcane scientific disciplines (finite mathematics, solid-state physics, and so on) can now have on the way we live. Great hopes for human betterment have long been entertained in connections with advances of this kind. Great fears, too, are felt by some – admittedly – but for most North Americans, our increasingly scientific society is, as Grant said, no terra incognita into which we advance fearfully, but a kind of promised land which we have discovered by the use of calculating reason and which we can ever more completely inherit by the continued use of calculation. 'Man has at last come of age in the evolutionary process, has taken his fate into his own hands and is freeing himself for happiness against the old necessities of hunger and disease and overwork, and the consequent oppressions and repressions.'[1] This is what Grant variously calls 'the objective spirit,' 'the progressive spirit,' 'the drive to practicality,' 'the will to technology,' 'expansionist practicality,' 'the drive to unlimited mastery,' or simply 'technology.'

When discussing the manifestations of this modern spirit, Grant rarely makes any distinction between Canada and the United States. In fact, in the essay quoted a moment ago, 'In Defence of North America,' he insists on the deep spiritual affinities between the two countries. They are alike in two crucial ways, he says there, and these similarities explain why the technological or progressive spirit is so strong among their citizens.

First, the formative experience for all North Americans has been one of conquest. Both countries were peopled by European migrants driven from their homelands by adversity of one kind or another. They settled an empty, harsh land. 'The very intractibility, immensity and extremes of the new land required that its meeting with mastering Europeans be a battle of subjugation.'[2] The difficulties they faced and their success in establishing themselves in an alien environment have left a mark within our souls. We are inclined to accept as perfectly obvious what is in fact quite debatable, that humanity's relation to nature is one of struggle and conquest.

Second, the Europeans who first established themselves here and who came to dominate the intellectual and cultural life of most of Canada and the United States were Calvinists or Puritans, a mere 'fragment' of Europe's rich religious and political diversity. These Europeans themselves represented a break within Europe – 'a turning away from the Greeks in the name of what was found in the Bible.'[3] Their extraordinary emphasis on revelation, and the independence of their theology from a philosophy of natural order that would limit God's activity, opened them to the empiricism and utilitarianism of the new physical and moral sciences of the sixteenth and seventeenth centuries.

Grant describes this 'North American primal' – 'the meeting of the alien and yet conquerable land with English-speaking Protestants' – in order to explain the persistence among us of the belief that our increasing practical mastery of human as well as non-human nature is contributing to something of the highest value, namely, freedom. For mastery is thought to serve more than just power or profit; it means the overcoming of all the conditions that in the past have constrained the human spirit. The contempt expressed by some Europeans for North America shows how tempting it can be to see our society as barren of anything but the drive to mastery for its own sake. But this is a shallow view, Grant says, since it fails to appreciate the connections that our leaders in all walks of life make between technology and freedom. 'What makes the drive to technology so strong is that it is carried on by men who still identify what they are doing with the liberation of mankind.'[4] Mastery serves progress understood as increasing freedom.

Grant questions this conception of progress and the identification of freedom with technological mastery that underlies it. To understand how and why he does so is to understand what it really means to say that he is a critic of modernity. Grant's reasoning may be hard to grasp, however, for not only does 'freedom' have a confusing variety of uses in our language, but it is also hard to think what exactly it means in its most relevant use, in connection with moral responsibility. Some of the most interesting things Grant wrote, particularly in the 1950s, have to do with this problem. It will be best to approach it indirectly.[5]

Many people could of course *believe* that the development of technology was serving to increase human freedom, even though it might in fact be gradually limiting or undermining our freedom. Indeed, technology could be preparing or imposing a new form or forms of servitude. At least for a time, many people could experience these changes as liberation, even if they might appear, from a more distant perspective or with the benefit of deeper insight, as the very opposite of liberation, that is, the enslavement or destruction of mankind. The quest for freedom as we understand it could be like an addictive substance that eventually destroys the life of the addict. The dystopias one finds in science fiction make it easier to imagine this possibility.

Being able to *imagine* such grim possibilities is not at all the same, of course, as being able to *demonstrate* that we are fated to experience any of them. Grant did not claim psychic powers that enabled him to predict the future. To repeat the basic point of the previous chapter, his thesis about the defeat of Canadian nationalism was essentially an interpretation of what had already happened, not an attempt to predict what must inevitably befall us. And with respect to the future, much will obviously depend on what we try to do – the choices we make and how we understand our options, as that understanding is shaped by our use of words like 'technology' and 'freedom.'

The word 'technology,' which Grant used more and more frequently in his later writings to refer to the development of mass scientific societies of the kind that exist in North America, has a troublesome ambiguity which will be explained shortly. It is far less problematic, however, than 'freedom,' with its confusing variety of uses. Thus ordinary citizens have long been called free, while slaves and prisoners are not free (they are prevented by others from doing what they want). It is often said that people generally have more or less freedom – more or less personal autonomy and security of the person – depending upon the character of their government (whether it is limited rather than 'totalitarian' and respectful of human rights and the rule of law). Similarly, people are said to have more freedom when, through free and fair elections, they have a say in how they will be governed. (There can be freedom in collective action as well as in individual choice.) And the members of an affluent society can be called freer – because they have more choices and more opportunities to do what they want – than those trapped in poorer societies who have to spend all their time in back-breaking labour. (The freedom to starve is no real freedom.) Within any given society, therefore, those who are richer are also in a sense freer, so that economic growth can increase freedom, as can the redistribution of income, at least for those who benefit from it. 'Freedom,' in these uses, is close to being a synonym for 'power' – the ability to do what one wants, despite the potential opposition of others – but the term can also refer to something more elusive than power and more like constraint.[6] People sometimes talk of being enslaved to their passions and of the freedom they enjoy after they have mastered them. In a more contemporary idiom, we can speak of being paralysed by our hang-ups: we are not free to do what we want because of our guilt or our internal conflicts. Addicts exemplify another kind of unfreedom whose source seems to be internal rather than external (political status, economic circumstances, and the like). What exactly do we have in mind when we use 'freedom' in these more extended senses? Does it have anything to do with what Grant had in mind when he questioned the identification of technological mastery with freedom? Often he seems to be suggesting that the development of technology necessarily entails the spread of a simplistic, one-sided understanding of freedom as being able to do whatever one wants. But what else could freedom really mean at bottom? The challenge is to grasp how a broader understanding of freedom might make sense.

In one of his finest early essays, 'The Uses of Freedom: A Word and Our World,' Grant related our understanding of freedom, not to our market economy or liberal-democratic government, but to our general circumstances as North Americans. Along the lines already sketched, he emphasized that we are the descendants of pioneers who opened up a large continent just as scientific technique could combine with abundant natural resources to produce immense wealth more widely distributed than ever before in history. This experience has encouraged the concentration on the external that Grant calls the objective spirit. 'The word freedom has come to mean for the majority the opportunities afforded to realize an increasing number of objective desires. The world of the motor car and the thirty hour week, the economy of organized obsolescence and high returns for the salesman and the technician, the society of public technical education and social equality, the personal life of sexual fulfilment and ever more diversified and simpler popular entertainment, this is what generally we mean when we say we live in a free society. Freedom for man is the ability to get what he wants. This vision of freedom finds in our society its ever fuller incarnation.'[7]

Freedom, on this account, can be said to combine a simple, self-centred hedonism (getting or doing what one wants) with a more selfless dedication to increasing our collective power to change the world (so that all are more and more able to satisfy an increasing number of objective desires). The immediate problems here have to do with the difficulty of knowing what we really want and with justifying whatever formal or informal restrictions there are on what we allow ourselves and others to do.

In 'The Uses of Freedom,' Grant raises some basic questions of moral philosophy and psychology. Let me spell out in my own words some questions that are only implicit in what he wrote. What is it that we really want to do? Can we really be happy simply doing what we like, more or less on impulse, and – assuming we are not entirely selfish – helping others to do what they would like? Or do we have to reflect on our desires in order to clarify what we *truly* desire? Do we have to make an effort to know ourselves, not just our hang-ups, but our *nature*? More broadly, can we be satisfied with the modern account of reason as an instrument of our desires? (David Hume put the point provocatively when he said that reason 'is and ought only to be the slave of the passions, and can never pretend to any other office than to serve and obey them.'[8]) Is there no real knowledge apart from the observations and calculations that show us how to change the world, the better to satisfy our various desires? But if there is such 'unscientific' knowledge, who can claim to have it? Should anyone, because of such knowledge, have a right to limit the freedom of others to do what they want?

Grant came to believe that our thinking about such questions is being deeply affected by technology in a more insidious way than is generally recognized. In later writings he criticized the common assumption that technology can be understood simply as a collection of practical techniques – a set of instruments, procedures, devices, or tools – that we can use, in our freedom, for whatever ends we choose. This is the assumption underlying the tendency to speak of technology as itself a tool like a hammer or saw or knife – something outside ourselves that we can use well or badly. It is the understanding implicit in the frequently heard injunctions that we must, of course, use technology only for good and must not allow it to undermine our values. But technology, for Grant, was *not* just a tool or instrument, the use of which leaves the user unchanged. Rather, as will be explained more fully below, it is fundamentally a way of knowing and relating to the world and other people. It is the 'objective' way of grasping our environment as something outside ourselves for our use. Thus the triumph of the technological spirit during the past three or four centuries, particularly in North America, is closely linked to a new understanding of what it is to be human. This new understanding is hardly visible, however, for not only is it inconspicuously woven into the texture of innumerable distinct activities, but it directs men's minds to the objective world – to the world of objects whose laws we can discover and whose processes we can therefore more and more easily adapt or adopt to our own advantage – thus turning them away from the mind itself, or human subjectivity. When dealing with human beings, it encourages an 'objective' approach, that is, the treatment of them as objects to be manipulated by careful calculation. This manipulation may normally be for their own advantage or improvement, of course, as in better child-rearing or in some modern forms of psychotherapy or the cure of souls. Perhaps it is only in rare circumstances that it is directed to the advantage of others, in running corporations and bureaucracies, for example, or in advertising or government propaganda, but it may still have undesirable consequences, even when used with the best of intentions.

Our increasing concentration on the 'objective' means, necessarily, an increasing neglect of the 'subjective,' what Grant calls 'the freedom of the spirit,' and the ways in which we come to know it. Freedom understood 'objectively' – as our increasing ability to change the world – could ultimately mean the disappearance of the belief that there is anything to know that does not lead to such changing. If genuine knowledge must be 'objective,' as could be assumed, would this assumption not imply that there can be no *knowledge* of the freedom of the spirit? In 'The Uses of Freedom,' Grant highlighted this negative implication of the increasing acceptance of the objective understanding of freedom. 'This view of freedom appears most clearly in a negative form, that is in the dying out on this continent of personal relations, art, philosophy and prayer. For these activities have respectively less and less to do with changing the world. If there is freedom to be gained from them, it is not a freedom to manipulate the world. And so these activities are in decay. Personal relations are seen as serving ends beyond themselves; art is turned into making life pleasant. Linguistic analysis and petitionary prayer become the archetypes of thought and desire.'[9] Consequently, Grant suggests, the future promised by our worldly reformism and democratic hedonism may not be the benign, pacified society that the early advocates of individual liberty, constitutional government, and the conquest of nature promised and that the leaders of our society still expect. In 1956 Grant ventured a prediction: 'In the next years, if we are not destroyed by war, we will watch the domination of the elite by the pleasures of personal power and the domination of the more submissive by the pursuit of those less strenuous pleasures which alleviate boredom. As thought about our proper end disappears, the busy specialists and the lazy whom they serve, will, almost without thought, pour into the vacuum the idea of pleasure, in all its manifold, fascinating and increasingly perverted forms.'[10]

What if this prediction were to be right? Would the result of all our scientific progress then still be seen as progress or would it not better be called decline?

Grant's inclination to dissent from our collective faith in scientific progress was greatly strengthened and clarified in the 1960s by his discovery of two rather different European writers who were also great dissenters, Jacques Ellul and Martin Heidegger. There is more direct evidence of the impact of the former, whose book, *The Technological Society*, Grant praised in a review published in 1966.[11] His enthusiasm for Ellul was short-lived, however, and it was with Heidegger's writings on technology that he later felt the deeper affinity.[12] Heidegger's way of showing that technology is not just a collection of techniques but rather something distinct and comprehensive – 'the essence of technology is nothing technological' – reinforced and clarified Grant's fear and suspicion about a mysterious and fundamental error in how most people in modern societies understand their own existence and its relation to the natural order.

In the 1970s Grant regularly had his students read Heidegger's famous essay on 'The Question concerning Technology.'[13] It is a startling expression of some crucial themes that are more soberly stated, with more qualifications or nuances, in Grant's writings from the 1950s to the end of his life. Indeed, Grant's 'Defence of North America' seems to be, on the one hand, a 'Heideggerian' depiction of North American life, but on the other hand, a corrective to Heidegger's (or perhaps Ellul's) 'continental' tendency to misrepresent North America – really the whole of Anglo-American civilization – as 'a society barren of anything but the drive to technology' or 'the pure will to technique.'[14]

It may seem tempting at this point to turn away from Grant to consider Heidegger's essay or indeed all his writings about technology. Would Grant's critique of modernity not be understood best by going to its Heideggerian source? Unfortunately, most would find that source (putting aside for the moment the question of whether it is *the* source) to be more confusing than helpful, and no summary of it that I could provide here would be more than a distraction, for it would have to presuppose a better understanding of Heidegger's larger claims than can be assumed. What Heidegger says about technology, Being, and human existence cannot be reduced to a few easily digestible formulas. Not only are the basic issues rather abstract and subtle, but one is almost compelled, when discussing his analysis of them, to use his own German vocabulary – or makeshift English equivalents to it. This can make Heidegger sound very strange indeed to the English ear. Moreover, his reputation as a 'difficult' philosopher creates its own difficulties. Anticipating difficulties, the English reader, schooled in the deflationary plain-speaking associated with English 'empiricism,' can easily fail to see what is plain and simple in Heidegger. Sometimes the simplest messages are the hardest to grasp.

3 From Education to Indoctrination

George Grant maintained that Canada's disappearance was necessary, but not that it was good. He distinguished between the necessity of events and their goodness. Yet he also maintained, as I indicated earlier, that necessity in human affairs depends on what is thought to be good: we are in a sense compelled to do what we think it would be good to do. There is no contradiction here since what is truly good may not be the same as what we think is good. The basic purpose of education, one can say, is to develop real knowledge of what is genuinely good in order to correct or displace false or inadequate opinions about goodness.

In connection with the smaller events of our lives, we easily make these simple distinctions, but we hesitate to apply them, and sometimes end up in confusion as a result, when we are thinking about politics and morality. Thus a pot boiling over on the stove we can accept as a necessary mishap, given the setting of the gas, without feeling any compulsion to welcome the event as good. Similarly, various kinds of natural turbulence – the famous Lisbon earthquake of 1755 or some more recent natural catastrophe – can be accepted as necessary without our feeling any obligation to call them good. (Those who have read Voltaire's *Candide* will understand that this clarity is a recent achievement: there was a time, not so long ago, when apparently intelligent people felt obliged to deny that natural disasters are really bad, because of their 'optimistic' theory that we live in 'the best of all possible worlds.') Only in connection with the larger pattern of human affairs do we hesitate to make a distinction between necessity and goodness, since the goodness of what must happen in this realm tends to be a matter of faith. If human institutions and the development of society are governed by our pursuit of obvious goods – by our desire for a better, freer, less painful, richer, and more enjoyable life – then surely (how could it be otherwise?) these institutions and social processes must gradually (all things considered) provide a future that will be better, freer, and so on than the past has been. Any persuasive theory or philosophy of history as progress can easily accommodate some temporary setbacks or bumps on the road to that better future, countering any tendency we might have to question the goodness or overall direction of our movement. Or if there is divine providence as commonly understood, that is, if history is the realm within which a loving, omnipotent, and omniscient God shows his care for all his creatures, even a sparrow, then whatever happens, and however difficult it may be to see particular events as good, they must be part of a divine plan for mankind's salvation. If Canada's disappearance is necessary, as Grant claims, can we not then say that it must also be good for it to disappear? Not only is there no stopping progress, but also no point in trying to swim upstream against its course (as Trudeau might have said), for there seems to be no higher standard than the one that history enforces.

To distinguish necessity from goodness as Grant did is to raise difficult questions not just about social mechanisms or divine providence but also about the sources of moral authority and the grounds of our judgments of better and worse. How is one to *know* what is good, apart from what people think is good or what is necessary? What qualifies a person to stand in judgment over history or the development of human society? What makes one person's opinions better than another's? How can the individual escape being subject to the historical and social necessities – the circumstances and forces – that he or she claims to judge? Must our judgments of value not be 'relative' to our circumstances in a way that deprives them of any ultimate validity? Reflecting on these questions, one can see where they point. Grant may have been dismayed by the disappearance of the Canada he loved, one can say, and no one should deny him his right to express his emotions about it ('to cry out at the death or dying of something loved'), but his emotions do not entitle him to pose as an authority, passing an unfavourable value judgment on the new Canada that has replaced the old.

Grant confronted questions and objections of this kind at every stage of his life and in almost all of his writings, but most directly and clearly in his writings about education. These are not as well known as his more obviously political writings, but they need to be taken into account to understand Grant's political thought, for he saw politics as properly subordinate to education.

Subordinating politics to education may sound like the daydream of an academic – someone like myself who has lived too long in an ivory tower. Let the teachers and academic bureaucrats set the taxes the public will have to pay to support their activities! Let the teachers determine what they will teach and let them impose it on their students! Let them call the tune while others pay the piper! Common sense balks at what seems to be a complete inversion of the right and necessary relationship between politics and education. The basic subjects young people are taught, the specialized training they are offered, the costly research that will be funded in institutions of higher learning in an advanced society such as ours – surely these must all inevitably be decided by reference to the needs of society as a whole, as determined by those in positions of authority. The education the educators provide must surely serve the needs of society and of the individual too, of course, but only insofar as individuals are inevitably members of society and require, in a society such as ours, not just some basic 'socialization' but also, generally speaking, some specialized training in order to play independent and responsible roles as adults within the society. Even when the authorities make a sharp distinction between liberal or general education, on the one hand, and professional or vocational training, on the other hand, the less practical 'liberal' kind of education, whatever exactly it may comprise, will necessarily be conducted with an eye to its practical consequences. In a democracy such as ours, general education must be in part education for citizenship and, at its higher levels, for political (or bureaucratic) leadership, on the assumption that the major institutions and overall purposes of the society as a whole are sound. Even if liberal education is understood to be an end in itself and therefore somehow 'above politics,' it will be regarded as complementary to public purposes, helping individuals to relate their particular functions and individual predilections to the general ends that society desires.

As a young man, Grant espoused a view of education not very different from the one I have just outlined, but in the 1960s and 1970s he became increasingly apprehensive about the corruption of common sense by technology. His first significant publication, his 1951 essay on

'Philosophy' for the Massey Commission, provides a baseline for understanding the development of his views about liberal education and the difficulties it faces. In this essay Grant equates genuine education with philosophy and sets it apart from modern science. Philosophy and science refer to quite different intellectual disciplines, he maintains, because they represent quite different approaches to reality. The first is contemplative, the second, essentially active. Philosophy, strictly speaking, is the rational form of the contemplative life. Like science (and unlike mystical and artistic contemplation), philosophy requires careful training in the use of reason. But philosophical reason, as Grant understood it, has a distinctly different aim from that of modern scientific reason. It aspires to grasp, in a rationally justifiable way, the order of the cosmos as a whole and consequently the place that naturally belongs to mankind within that order. It requires that its students learn to think about their world and themselves in the broadest and deepest way. It is more closely related to theology, therefore, than to the kind of 'experimental' reasoning about natural laws found in the modern natural sciences. Science, particularly as it is taught in today's schools and universities, is a collection of specialized disciplines that aim to uncover particular mechanisms of the natural and social world so that we can adapt our behaviour, the better to achieve our goals. It is generally active or interventionist in spirit and narrow in its focus, rather than broad and contemplative. Its slogan, as Grant said, is 'knowledge for power' – in the confident expectation that power will be used for good.[1]

Grant began his essay with the bold declaration, already quoted, that 'the study of philosophy is the analysis of the traditions of our society and the judgement of those traditions against our varying intuitions of the Perfection of God' (4). The function of the philosopher, he said, is to scrutinize and refine the faith by which those dedicated to the practical life live. Only in relation to some overall purpose or vision of the good society, accepted in faith, can the more active members of a society – its judges, doctors, civil servants, scientists, and entrepreneurs, for example – know the limits of their own competence and the relations among their necessarily specialized functions. 'Active men depend upon faith of some sort for their very existence' (8). Their unifying faith can, of course, be more or less rational. Ideally, by purging the irrational elements from the prevailing opinions about goodness by which a society lives, philosophy can give the activities of its members a 'rational groundwork' (11). Thus philosophy, as a comprehensive contemplative discipline, exists not just for the good of those who dedicate themselves to it but for the good of all. And if it is to serve its social or political function, it must resist the lure of technical competence. 'Philosophy is not in essence a technique. Its purpose is to relate and see in unity all the techniques, so that the physicist for instance can relate his activity to the fact of moral freedom, the economist see the productive capacity of his nation in relation to the Love of God' (6).

Grant did not explain what he meant by 'the Love of God' or 'the Perfection of God,' nor did he say anything about the relation between religious faith and political faith. If challenged, he might well have said that 'a fuller and more balanced intuition of God' could be the culmination of a lifetime of philosophical study, but not something that a young man can be expected to hand over, like a mathematical formula or an architectural blueprint, to a royal commission investigating practical ways of promoting 'National Development in the Arts, Letters and Sciences.' Nonetheless, Grant's 1951 essay does make quite clear what he was rejecting, namely, modern scientific secularism or the view that 'salvation is achieved by technique' (7). Likewise, there can be no doubt about the tradition to which he was appealing, namely, the Christian tradition. He showed little sympathy for the 'childish hopes' and 'unbalanced cults' that the practically oriented succumb to, particularly when they are young, if their search for faith is not subject to the 'rational discipline' of philosophy (8). His examples were Marxism and the Jehovah's Witnesses. Both have become more respectable in the past fifty years. If Grant were writing today, he would probably choose other examples, as the reader may wish to do. But he would insist that the larger problem he was pointing to is still with us. Indeed, he would undoubtedly depict it in even starker terms.

From his earliest years, Grant seems to have been struck by the changes going on in higher education, especially the growth of practical technical specialization, which he found deplorable. In 1938, while still an undergraduate at Queen's, he published a favourable review of the 'brilliantly destructive attack' on the egalitarian pragmatism of American higher education by a prominent American educator.[2] In 1951, in his royal commission essay, the challenge was to sustain liberal education in the modern university, since it provides almost the only framework there is in our society for the cultivation of rational contemplation or philosophical reason. 'In the universities, society allows scholars the time and the freedom to contemplate the universe, to partake of the wisdom of the past, to add their small measure to the understanding of that wisdom and to transmit the great tradition to certain chosen members of the younger generation. If the universities are not rich in the practice of philosophy it is unlikely that less favoured parts of the community will be much touched by it' (4). But he thought that it was becoming more and more difficult for the study of philosophy in this sense to flourish in our universities. Not only were they becoming larger and more impersonal, but they were also becoming more deeply involved in specialized practical studies of an unphilosophical character. Writing more than fifty years ago, Grant claimed that universities had become essentially technical schools for the training of specialists. 'They turn out doctors and physicists, economists and chemists, lawyers and social workers, psychologists and agriculturalists, dietitians and sociologists, and these technicians are not being called upon in any systematic way to relate their necessary technique to any broader whole. Even the traditional humane subjects such as history, the classics, and European literature are in many cases being taught as techniques by which the student can hope to earn his living, not as useful introductions to the sweep of our spiritual tradition' (5). The university is now a collection of specialties without a unity, he wrote, and philosophy is treated as just another technical subject confined to a group of specialists, rather than as an activity necessary for all sorts and conditions of men.[3] In short, the modern university allows scholars to exist but does almost nothing to encourage the contemplative life among its faculty and students. Indeed, by promoting an activist conception of reason as if it were the only possible form of reason, they implicitly deny that there can be any such thing as rational contemplation.

In the 1960s, as Grant began to focus with increasing alarm on technology, his writings about education began to sound a darker note. The basic difficulty, as he had recognized from the outset, was not so much the university itself, with its practical mission and bureaucratic divisions and incentives, but rather the modern philosophy that provided the foundation and justification for modern science and politics.[4] It has undermined liberal education by cultivating systematic doubt about the possibility of knowing 'the cosmos as a whole' – knowing its subjective qualitites, one might say, and not just its objective quantities. Indeed, Grant held that modern science has effectively denied that there is any knowable cosmic order within which it would make sense to speak of 'human nature.' This idea dominates his later writings about education, such as 'The University Curriculum.' 'The very idea of human existence having a given highest purpose, and therefore an excellence which could be known and in terms of which all our activities could be brought into some order [has been given up]. It is now generally assumed that the race has meaning (call it if you will purpose) only on the condition that we view ourselves as purposive and that none of these views are truths concerning the nature of things, but only ideologies which we create to justify our man-made purposes.'[5] In 1977 he wrote that people of his own generation who went to university in the 1930s, and who spoke of the universities their children or grandchildren were attending in the 1970s as if they were the same institutions, were the victims of an illusion. 'The names are the same, but they are such different places that they should have different names.'[6]

Grant was cautious when discussing technology or the paradigm of knowledge that now holds sway over all branches of learning. Logic, epistemology, and the history and philosophy of science were not his specialties, and the subtle differences among the specialists make it difficult to state briefly what practically all seem now to accept, namely, that genuine knowledge is attained by using well-defined procedures to bring particular things before us in order to determine their reasons for being the way they are as objects. 'Our paradigm is that we have knowledge when we represent anything to ourselves as object, and question it, so that it will give us its reasons.'[7]

Naive wonder or astonishment or admiration of the beauty of the world finds no refinement, but rather suffocation or denial, within this way of pursuing knowledge. Modern objectifying science recognizes that we can have various emotional reactions to 'the world,' and it can treat these reactions as objects of scientific investigation, but in investigating their causes, it implicitly denies their grounds. The world as a whole is not an object and cannot be known scientifically. As a celebrated Cambridge physicist once said, 'don't let me catch anyone talking about the Universe in my department.'[8]

Since narrow limits have been put on scientific knowledge, there is now widespread agnosticism regarding the character of the whole, and this agnosticism, in turn, has fostered many professions of neutrality regarding different 'visions' or 'interpretations' of it and the moral principles associated with them. If objectively valid judgments must be judgments about objects, known scientifically as isolated aspects or products of a tangle of necessities, then it seems that there can be only hypothetically valid judgments of what human subjects ought to do. ('Stop smoking if you want to avoid lung cancer.') The question of the rightness of our larger purposes is the question of our relation to the whole and cannot be discussed 'objectively.' Science tells us what is, not what ought to be, the scientists patiently explain, so scientific method and its results can evidently have little or no bearing on our ultimate judgments of value. Such judgments must derive from our subjectivity, perhaps having no foundation in the end except 'what we will in power from the midst of chaos.'[9]

The wonderful discoveries of the modern natural sciences give this paradigm its credibility. The increasing affluence it provides keeps all but an infinitesimal minority from challenging its fundamental sound-ness. Its startling effects in the humanities, which it tends to convert into disreputable purveyors of faded visions, meets some resistance among those most directly affected, the professors of the humanities, but in fact their protests have been surprisingly weak.[10] Grant was struck by their willingness to turn their subjects – religion, philosophy, politics, and literature, for example – into collections of objects – monu-ments, texts, paintings, votes – to be investigated historically, using standard procedures to reveal (ideally) the necessary and sufficient conditions for their appearance as objects.

Already in 1951, Grant directed his sharpest barbs at the professional philosophers employed in universities. With rare exceptions, he thought, they were simply partisans of the scientific age and mass sci-entific society. 'The lie that knowledge exists only to provide power has been as much in the soul of philosophers as in the rest of society' (7). He charged academic philosophers in Canada, like their professional col-leagues elsewhere, with making philosophy the servant rather than the judge of the modern scientific project. Wishing to free their subject from its traditional subordination to theology, and impressed by the amazing power of modern applied science, they had become apologists of mod-ern science and scientific specialization.

Grant had little patience with the apparent modesty and claims to neutrality or 'value freedom' of university teachers. Is it too harsh to say that they often combine scepticism with dogmatism by suppressing thought? Their skepticism in principle about all but physical necessities coexists with firm beliefs about many practical matters. The scepticism can support the denial of clerical authority and thus make it easier to accept – it can even seem to justify – popular sovereignty, the rights of individuals, and an undemanding, utilitarian morality. Modern philos-ophy can serve, not just as an interpretation of science, but in practice also as the basis for a political practice. The specialized scientific educa-tion modern universities provide and justify (with the help of their philosophers) works quite well, Grant thought, as a system of political indoctrination.

Grant repeatedly emphasized that every society needs a system of belief, whether true or false, that will bind together the lives of individuals and give them some consistency of purpose. Our public 'binding' or 'religion' Grant called variously 'the religion of democracy,' 'the religion of progress,' 'the religion of humanity and progress,' 'the religion of progress, mastery, and power,' 'secularism,' and 'liberalism.' Apart from his unpublished doctoral thesis, Grant never wrote at length about science and religion or about the possible connections between the traditional Western religions and the new 'religion of democracy' or 'religion of humanity and progress' that he thought was taking its place. Nonetheless, it is perhaps worth considering the possibility that there may be some merit in what he suggested. One must be careful at this point, of course. In a society that prides itself on having separated religion and politics, an academic who reconnects them risks being accused of faults far more grievous than academic crankiness, obscurity, vagueness, or impracticality. But Grant pointed out that it is wrong to characterize technological societies as essentially nihilistic, 'as if people had no sense of what is good.'[11] In fact, many citizens of modern societies obviously have moral values and political ideals that they are determined to pass on to their own and others' children.

The dogmatic quality of any popular religion is particularly clear when one observes it being taught in primary and secondary schools. Commenting in 1963 on a controversy about the place of religion in the schools of Ontario, Grant insisted that the real issue was not whether religion should be taught, but which one should be taught. 'It is perfectly clear that in all North American state schools religion is already taught in the form of what may best be called "the religion of democracy." That the teaching about the virtues of democracy is religion and not political philosophy is clearly seen from the fact that the young people are expected to accept this on faith and cannot possibly at their age be able to prove the superiority of democracy to other forms of government (if indeed this can be done). The fact that the liberals who most object to any teaching about the deity are generally most insistent that the virtues of democracy be taught, should make us aware that what is at issue is not religion in general, but the content of the religion to be taught.'[12]

Teachers, Grant implies, are the priests of this new religion; universities, its seminaries; distinguished professors, its theologians; deans, its bishops; and Nobel laureates, its cardinals. Like other mass religions, it requires state support (taxes and the punishment of heretics) and a steady flow of miracles (new gadgets and wonder drugs) to sustain the faithful. Its most sacred doctrine, he said, is the fact-value distinction.[13]

Grant's dismissive characterization of contemporary general education is obviously vulnerable to some serious objections. First, is the point of the fact-value distinction not to keep teachers from abusing their authority by mixing political preaching with the instruction they provide in science and the humanities? Max Weber, the greatest proponent of the distinction in the social sciences, thought that it was disgraceful when economists and sociologists used their lecterns as pulpits, and he advocated better instruction in logic or methodology – a better understanding of the difference between facts and values – to prevent this abuse.[14] And the result of the relevant instruction he recommended has surely been to silence some of the potential preachers. Indeed, one may well wonder how any preaching at all gets done in the modern secular religion.

Without pretending to settle a difficult question, let me observe from my experience that the fact-value distinction is often treated as a fact from which certain values (like those mentioned earlier) can be deduced – and since they have been deduced, preached. There is a 'tension' here that fascinates a few specialists, but perhaps it is not a serious difficulty in practice, since both the 'facts' and the 'values' may have a deeper source – the vision of a fully modern and enlightened society of tolerant diversity to be created by the technological mastery of human and non-human nature. And should this vision be challenged by some unexpected eruptions of hatred or violence, one can always point to the need that any society has for its value system or even its mythology, and the importance, therefore, of reaffirming our own.

Still, are we not begging a crucial question if we discuss the principles of modern society as though they were the irrational dogmas of a state church? As Grant observed, 'it will, of course, seem unfair to the exponents of secularism that I have called what they advocate a religion. They will deem it unfair because they think that what they advocate is a product of reason alone and therefore should be called philosophy and not religion.'[15]

Grant's way of speaking is obviously contestable. It is on a par with calling the Pope the CEO of the world's largest MNC. Grant defends himself by saying, in effect, that both philosophy and religion are more complicated and have more in common than the usual contrast between them suggests. At the same time, the subtle truths investigated by philosophers and theologians are generally quite different from the simplified dogmas that bind societies together. These dogmas may be more or less false and misleading. Grant clearly and repeatedly stated his fear that the currently dominant 'religion of progress' harboured enormous potential for evil and that it was far inferior to our previous public religions. He seems to have accepted the ancient view that mass 'enlightenment' is simply not a possibility. 'The older tradition says that philosophy and religion fulfil different (albeit related) roles in the lives of human beings and that the practice of both are necessary to the healthy life of a society. It says that not many men will become philosophers; but that all men are inevitably religious. It is on these principles that one is forced to distinguish (even when its proponents do not) between modern philosophy and the modern religion (namely that of progress).'[16] This passage raises questions that go to the very heart of Grant's thought, his study of religion and its relation to politics and philosophy. The particular formulation of the problem quoted here, from an essay published in 1963, relates to issues and influences that will be discussed in Part II below. But before we turn to these matters, something more needs to be said about Grant's treatment of liberalism and conservatism. How well can he sustain what he repeatedly implies, namely, that the dogmas of 'the religion of progress' are simply without any rational foundation?

4 Modern Liberal Theory

George Grant provided his most careful and detailed analysis of modern liberal principles in his 1974 Josiah Wood Lectures at Mount Allison University, which were later published as *English-Speaking Justice*.[1] He begins by insisting that a distinction be made between our basic political practices that can be called liberal, because they protect individual liberty, and the theories of modern liberal philosophers, which are held to clarify, justify, and extend these practices. Grant's objections are directed, not to the practices, but to the theories. Do they clarify and justify or confuse and undermine the political practices of equal liberty or 'political liberalism'?

The crucial practices are those that ensure government by consent of the governed and the protection by law of the rights of the individual, that is to say, the rights of those whose opinions and activities may be unwelcome to those in power. The first requires representative institutions with effective control of government; the second, the rule of law and an independent judiciary. These are vital protections against the ruthless and arbitrary use of power. Liberalism in this generic form, Grant says, 'is surely something that all decent men accept as good – "conservatives" included. In so far as the word "liberalism" is used to describe the belief that political liberty is a central human good, it is difficult for me to consider as sane those who would deny that they are liberals' (4).

The theories are another matter. Modern liberal philosophers aim to defend and perfect the practices of liberty and equality on the basic assumption that human beings are autonomous, that is to say, free individuals who create their own rules of justice. Modern autonomous human beings do not accept any claim that the form or content of justice has been laid down for them by any higher power or authority on whom they depend for their knowledge of right and wrong. Justice is understood to be something strictly human, having nothing to do with obedience to any divine command or conformity to any pattern 'laid up in heaven.' Moral principles, like all other social conventions, are something 'made on earth.' Human freedom requires that the principles of justice be the product of human agreement or consent, that is, that they be the result of a contract, and these principles must therefore be rooted in an understanding of the interests of human beings as individuals rather than in any sense of duty or obligation to anything above humanity. The terms of the contract may well change as circumstances and interests change. But the restraints free individuals accept must always be 'horizontal' in character rather than 'vertical.' According to the theoretical founders of liberalism, as Grant says, 'justice was neither a natural nor supernatural virtue, but arose from the calculations necessary to our acceptance of the social contract' (11).

The specific question addressed in *English-Speaking Justice* is whether the account of reason associated with modern science tends to strengthen or to weaken support for the practical principles of political liberalism. Our dominant form of public self-definition, Grant says, assumes that modern science or technology and modern liberal politics are interdependent and mutually reinforcing products of the modern understanding of knowledge and what it means to be rational. But the identity of scientific progress and political liberalism may be no more than an unjustifiable hope or faith, he suggests. Can it be sustained under close examination? This basic question has a practical or empirical side as well as a theoretical or scholarly one. To answer it with confidence, we would have to consider, for example, the place of representative government in the 'great society' being created by modern technology – a society that seems to be ruled more and more by enormous bureaucracies and specialized tribunals. Apart from a few brief remarks at the beginning of the book, Grant confines his attention to the scholarly side of the problem. He deals with one theory and one practical problem or question of policy. The theory is that of the celebrated Harvard philosopher John Rawls. The practical problem is that of abortion. Before considering what use Grant makes of these examples, it is necessary to have a clear idea of the main elements of Rawls's famous *Theory of Justice*.[2]

The basic purpose in *A Theory of Justice*, as Rawls explains, is the surprisingly modest one of systematizing our already-existing moral intuitions – our unreflective sense of what is right and wrong in dealing with others – so as to reach a more explicit and more coherent set of rules, values, or principles of action. The problem he addresses is how to guide our thinking towards a clearer, more systematic, and therefore more defensible articulation of what we already know or believe, not how to provide our intuitions with any external support. The aim is to reach what he calls a 'reflective equilibrium' of our various and sometimes conflicting intuitions, so as to avoid quandaries and contradictions. As for providing our moral preconceptions with any more basic or more solid 'grounding' or 'justification' of a scientific or metaphysical character, Rawls is in effect saying that that is not possible.[3]

The most important of our strictly moral intuitions is, of course, that we must not, as Kant put it, make favourable exceptions of ourselves. We must choose only those courses of action which accord with rules or maxims of universal validity. That is, we must be willing to consider the interests of others as being on a par with our own. In principle, others may have as much claim for consideration and respect, and deserve as large a share of the goods that social cooperation creates, as we ourselves do. Morality, as we understand it, demands that the basic principles we adopt be chosen in the light of the interests of all others, and not just to serve our own personal interests, as determined by our own particular circumstances, tastes, talents, needs, and so on. Thus, when considering various possible rules or principles, we must evaluate them from a general point of view or, as is sometimes said, from the *moral* point of view.

Rawls says that such an evaluation is best 'modelled' as the process of reaching a basic agreement – a 'social contract' – that will set out the major principles of justice for a society, provided only that the parties to the agreement being negotiated are individuals who are in an 'original position' behind a 'veil of ignorance.' That is, each individual is to evaluate the merits of competing principles of justice, not by determining, first of all, how well they would in fact serve his or her own particular interests and then choosing accordingly (men, for example, choosing masculinist principles and women feminist ones), but rather by considering how well the principles chosen would serve *all* the members of the future society. They are to choose as if they were still ignorant of the roles they are destined to play in the society to be established, or what stations in life they are to occupy, after the contract is signed. (The proposed evaluation must use *interests* as a criterion rather than any principles of fairness or justice because it is precisely the most reasonable principles of justice that are being sought and that have yet to be defined: in the original position, interests are more basic than principles, and one cannot beg the question by assuming the results of the bargaining, as if one already knew, from some source other than reasoning about interests, what the principles of justice should be.) To be moral, as Rawls presents morality, is essentially to be willing to discuss questions about justice or fairness as if one were in the original position, ignorant of what one's own real interests, in the real world, really are, and then willing to accept whatever limitations on one's actions are required by whatever interpretation of the moral point of view has been adopted.

Rawls argues that individuals in the original position, deliberately disregarding their own particular interests as determined by all the contingencies of personal fate, or unaware of these contingencies but aware of how social cooperation can serve everyone's interests and aware, as well, of its specific dangers (tyranny, exploitation, and the like), will see the unique reasonableness of two basic principles of justice.[4] First, the principle of equal basic liberties: each person is to have an equal right to the most extensive basic liberty compatible with a similar liberty for others. And second, the so-called 'difference principle': social and economic inequalities (the differences in income, wealth, social status, and so on that may exist in the future society) are to be limited to those that can reasonably be expected to serve everyone's interests (given their motivating function as incentives for the talented and energetic to serve the lazy and incompetent) and attached to positions and offices open to all (so that talent and willingness to serve others will be the only basis for exceptional rewards, and not race, gender, family ties, or other such 'ascriptive' qualifications). More briefly, 'justice as fairness requires that all primary social goods be distributed equally unless an unequal distribution would be to everyone's advantage.'[5] Or, more pointedly, the natural abilities of individuals are to be regarded as a collective asset 'so that the more fortunate are to benefit only in ways that help those who have lost out.'[6] Thus, whatever institutions the future society – any just society – erects and maintains, and whatever laws or policies it adopts, they must meet three tests. First, they must not violate any of the basic rights of all individuals (the traditional liberal rights to life, liberty, freedom of expression, a fair trial, and the like). Second, they must not provide any unnecessary or unearned advantages to some but must rather provide all with a more or less equal share of the benefits of social cooperation. Finally, they must offer all a meaningful 'equality of opportunity' to secure whatever superior positions may exist and the rewards that go with them. In short, the future just society will be free to adopt a variety of laws and policies (it may decree, for example, that its drivers drive on the right and not on the left), but it will not be free (within the constraints of reason) to violate basic individual rights or to establish any inequalities that are not to the benefit of all.

Rawls moves from his 'original position' to his two basic principles, which are to govern all subsequent legislation, by construing the situation of choice behind the veil of ignorance as a very special kind of bargaining game in which, as he says, 'the parties have no basis for bargaining in the usual sense' because 'no one knows his situation in society nor his natural assets, and therefore no one is in a position to tailor principles to his advantage.'[7] Nonetheless, Rawls maintains, all the parties to his modernized 'state of nature,' considering only abstracted individual interests in general but informed by the most up-to-date knowledge of individual psychology and social mechanisms,[8] will converge, unanimously, on the two principles summarized above, because they offer everyone the best possible chance of securing a fair share of the 'primary goods' that are important to them (essentially life, liberty, income, and status), regardless of their lot in life (male or female, sickly or healthy, quick or dull, lazy or energetic, and so on).

Rawls's derivation of his two basic principle is, as one might expect, controversial. Some have questioned the risk aversion that Rawls attributes to individuals in the original position. Why exactly must they choose according to the very cautious 'maximin' rule? In theory, they could adopt some other criterion, such as maximizing total utility, that might offer better overall outcomes, from which most would benefit individually, even if they all ran a higher risk of being worse off. Others have challenged the assumptions Rawls makes about the kind of knowledge his 'veiled' and 'ignorant' individuals have. It seems clear that the assumptions from which they start and the interests they secure through the principles they adopt are those of modern, university-educated (up to at least Economics 100) 'selves' seeking autonomy and not, for example, those of 'selves' that attach greater value to respect for tradition or deference to authority. In short, Rawls's reasoning is vulnerable to some damaging 'technical' objections, as the subsequent discussion of his book has shown.[9]

Nonetheless, there is no denying that A Theory of Justice is a remarkable achievement, a real landmark in modern moral philosophizing, and Grant made a good choice, three years after it was published, when he used it to clarify his claim about the relation between liberal principles of justice and the modern 'technological' understanding of human reason. This is the basic theme of his 1974 lectures that became *English-Speaking Justice*, and it is important to keep this in mind when reading his criticisms of Rawls in Part II of the book.

Grant's central objection to Rawls's theory is not one of the standard, more technical objections developed in detail in the secondary literature by Rawls's critics. Thus Grant does not challenge the validity of Rawls's derivation of his two principles of justice; he does not dispute his reliance on the maximin rule. Nor does he question how the individuals in the original position, behind their veils of ignorance, acquired the economic, sociological, psychological, mathematical, and historical 'facts' that Rawls assumes they have, or how their reasoning might change if they happened to have other 'facts.' Grant says nothing directly about the kind of self whose rights are protected by the conception of justice Rawls advocates. And he does not raise what is perhaps the most popular objection to Rawls's theory, that his difference principle would mean violating the rights of property and weakening the incentives for economic progress. Rather, Grant focuses on the nature of the basic transition in Rawls's account of justice from a simple, amoral pursuit of self-interest, based on a common-sense understanding of what one's interests are, to morally constrained action under a conception of justice based on the idea that the interests of all deserve equal consideration and respect. In what sense is this step necessary, not for the modern theorist of justice, perhaps, but for those to whom his theory is to apply? What are the reasons for taking it? Crudely, why be moral? In Rawls's reasoning about justice, the problem is never our ignorance or uncertainty about what our real interests are: it is assumed from the outset that everyone wants 'primary goods' and more of them. The problem is how to resolve conflicts about the sharing or distribution of what all want but not all can have. So why not just pursue one's own interests, even if this means depriving others or making them suffer? To be sure, one might be well advised to keep peace with one's neighbours and to secure their cooperation by pretending to accept the constraints modelled by a social contract process. Indeed, it might be advisable to make a big show of putting on the veil of ignorance whenever one talks about right and wrong, and later of prudently respecting any rules of justice that were being effectively enforced, but all the while keeping one's eyes fixed on one's real interest, which would seem to be that of getting not just a fair share of the goods of this life but the largest possible share. 'He who dies with the most toys wins!'

Rawls devotes almost no attention to this problem, and this is a crucial fact about his long and complicated book. He says, in effect, that no real reasons can be given for being moral: it is just a choice that those who want to be moral will make. In *A Theory of Justice* there is thus a huge, almost laughable disproportion between the vast intellectual resources (careful distinctions, alertness to fallacies, and so on) devoted to working out what morality (or justice or fairness) should mean for those who have decided to be moral (or just or fair) according to our modern lights, on the one hand, and the simplistic, almost dismissive comments about the advantages and disadvantages of the moral point of view, on the other hand.[10] A reader able to escape all the trees in order to get some sense of the Rawlsian forest is likely to conclude that morality, at least for Rawls, is essentially an arbitrary choice, praiseworthy in others, perhaps, but of questionable value for oneself.

Grant makes this point more elegantly by comparing Rawls with Locke, Kant, and Plato. For Locke, justice is respect for the rights of individuals, and especially for their property rights, as defined by legislation according to a basic contract. He maintained that justice in this sense can be seen to be in everyone's real interest: each individual has only to reflect on what his real interests really are. They are not, primarily, an interest in being just or fair, and not even an interest in securing a larger share of the benefits of social cooperation, but rather an interest in avoiding violent death, given the fundamental instability of social institutions. Civilized societies are houses of cards created by the agreements that allow particular groups to move out of the state of nature, but these shelters are always in danger of collapsing and plunging their denizens back into that state where life is nasty, poor, brutish, and short. Rawls, by contrast, evinces no awareness of the molten lava, as it were, under the crust of convention. Perhaps it does not really exist, one may say, but for Locke it did, Grant says, and in his early modern account of politics and morality, it provided the ultimate reason for respecting the conventions of contractual justice. 'What holds us in society according to Locke is our consciousness of what we have to lose (life itself) if we do not put up with the convenient rules of the game. The fear of violent death is the reason for setting up those rules and it remains the final reason for staying within them' (21). For Rawls, on the other hand, 'the original position' is not to be confused with any historical or potential 'state of nature.' It is just an imagined abstraction from the way things are, nothing more than a thought experiment to guide us towards fair conventions. It is a state we strive to put ourselves into mentally, if we wish to be moral and to see our choices from the moral point of view, not a state that we ever need to fear falling back into physically, so to speak, and thus not really a motive for respecting the principles of justice, whatever they may be.

This criticism may seem unfair, since Rawls, unlike Locke, makes no appeal to nature as a standard or basis of justice. His theory of justice is, as he says, 'highly Kantian in nature,' meaning that it is an elaboration or clarification of what we think is reasonable rather than of any facts of a scientific character.[11] Rawls, like Kant, conceives moral principles as being essentially the objects of rational choice rather than as inferences from our understanding of nature. But in Kant's writings there is of course an insistence that men *are* free and equal rational beings, not just that they can, if they wish, try to think and act as if they were in an 'original position' of freedom and equality. The 'ontological' affirmations that are fundamental in Kant are absent from Rawls. Justice, for Kant, is an imperative: it is something we are all fitted for, simply as rational creatures, regardless of our various talents, tastes, and circumstances. To simplify, fairness towards others is what we owe ourselves as free and rational beings. For Rawls, by contrast, fair treatment is something we grant others to the extent that we wish to be moral. It is decidedly more 'hypothetical.'[12]

The difference is clarified by what Grant says about the Platonic or Socratic conception of justice. According to this conception, as Grant explains it, justice is something that we recognize to be in our true interest (contrary to appearances) as we discover the powers of our souls and our own deepest desires through the practice of philosophy. 'In philosophy we are given sufficient knowledge of the whole of the nature of things to know what our interests are, and to know them in a scheme of subordination and superordination. In this account, justice is not a certain set of external political arrangements which are a useful means of the realisation of our self-interests; rather it is the very inward harmony of human beings in terms of which they are alone able to calculate their self-interest properly' (44). In Plato's dialogues, especially the *Republic*, justice comes to light as being in a sense a calculation concerning self-interest, but not based on any prior decision to be moral – rather on the interest we all have ultimately in the inward harmony that makes a self truly a self (or to use the older language, a soul truly a soul).

In short, in recommending his modernized liberal conception of justice, Rawls appeals neither to Locke's 'nature' nor to Kant's 'reason,' nor of course to Plato's 'ideas,' but only to 'our intuitions.' And if we are troubled, as we may be, by doubts about the fundamental soundness or validity of those intuitions, then his elaborate reasoning will be, for us, just an elaborate way of avoiding or begging the basic question. The most striking feature of his book will be the complacency it exudes about the moral and other intuitions that prevail in contemporary liberal democracies. And (it will be easy to see) to the extent that we become absorbed in following his elaborate reasoning, we are being encouraged to think not only that self-interest is primary but that we cannot really know anything more about the interests of individuals than what is known to common sense – that different people have different interests not just because of different circumstances but also because of different tastes and opinions about what is good or worth doing, and since none of these opinions can claim to be genuine knowledge, all must be tolerated, provided only that their proponents do no obvious harm to others and refrain from interfering with each other's 'basic liberties.'

Grant is not sounding an alarm because Rawls's book has been published and widely acclaimed. 'One swallow does not make a summer; one academic book does not make an autumn of our justice' (47). The basic question Grant is addressing is, once again, whether the modern technological account of reason, that is, the understanding of reason that underlies technology, must necessarily express itself politically as an ever more scrupulous respect for liberal principles of individual freedom and equality. Or is that account of reason necessarily going to undermine commitment to liberal principles? Political and intellectual histories may suggest that modern science and liberal politics have been mutually supportive; Grant is suggesting that they may no longer have this relationship or may never really have had it. 'Their identity may not be given in the nature of reason itself' (6).

Rawls is Exhibit A in Grant's case for a negative verdict. If his theory is the best that can be done to clarify and sustain justice within the limits of reason as understood today (and the acclaim that greeted its appearance in 1971 and the roughly five thousand books and articles that have discussed it since that time would suggest that it is), then we seem to be at the mercy of 'our intuitions,' without much capacity to say who 'we' are or why we should be bound by even our equilibrated 'intuitions' when they stand in the way of doing what we really want to do, individually or collectively.

Exhibit B is the ruling of the United States Supreme Court in the case of *Roe v. Wade*, the 1973 case in which it was decided that American state governments could not infringe a woman's privacy with respect to reproduction, and thus her right to receive an abortion, during the first six months of pregnancy. Grant insists that the basic question when debating abortion must not be privacy but rather the right to life – whether or when one member of the human species shall have the right to terminate the life of another member. He does not say that there is any absolute 'right to life' (of chickens? of bears?), but he insists that some good reasons must be given for abrogating it for human beings. It is not something that one should be able to choose to do or not to do, at one's own convenience.[13]

Mr Justice Harry A. Blackmun, who wrote the majority decision in *Roe v. Wade*, began his reasoning by endorsing the principle that rights under the constitution are prior to any account of the good. The moral pluralism of a modern society requires that we be officially agnostic regarding disputed claims to knowledge of good and bad. The legal restrictions on abortion that were at issue in the case were the expression, it seemed, of conceptions of justice held by legislators, but challenged by the litigants and by many other Americans. (It was a class-action suit.) The real issue, according to Blackmun, had to be, not the validity of these contested conceptions, but whether the restrictive laws that derived from them infringed the prior right of a pregnant woman to privacy – freedom from state interference – with respect to reproduction. The right to life of the foetus was never the issue, as Grant explains: 'The individual who would seem to have the greatest interest in the litigation, because his or her life or death is at stake, – namely the particular foetus and indeed all future U.S. foetuses – is said by the judge not to be a party to the litigation. He states that foetuses up to six months are not persons, and as non-persons can have no status in the litigation' (70).

Justice Blackmun, in assigning different rights to foetuses and to persons, was invoking an 'ontological' rather than a strictly scientific distinction. (From a strictly scientific standpoint, one could say, foetuses and their mothers and fathers are simply different individual members of the same species.) But having implicitly invoked an ontological distinction, Grant maintains, one can no longer avoid ontological questions. 'What is it about any members of our species which makes the liberal rights of justice their due? The judge unwittingly looses the terrible question: has the long tradition of liberal rights any support in what human beings in fact are? Is this a question that in the modern era can be truthfully answered in the positive? Or does it hand the cup of poison to our liberalism?' (71–2).

Modern scientific reason, Grant is suggesting, cannot deal with what it is about human beings that makes it good that all should have the rights of equal justice. 'To put the matter simply: if "species" is an historical concept and we are a species whose origin and existence can be explained in terms of mechanical necessity and chance, living on a planet which also can be explained in such terms, what requires us to live together according to the principles of equal justice?' (73). Perhaps it would be no less reasonable to go 'beyond freedom and dignity' for the sake of a more elevated, more stable, or more advanced society. This is not, of course, to suggest that societies in the future may somehow dispense altogether with rules of right and wrong. 'Obviously any possible society must have some system of organisation to which the name "justice" can be given' (75). But the prevailing 'system of organisation' – legal justice – may have less and less to do with any 'overriding order which we do not measure and define, but in terms of which we are measured and defined' (74). It may have more and more to do, not with justice as traditionally understood, but with the political experiments and new ways of living that appeal to the talented and energetic.

Grant alludes only once to Rawls in his analysis of *Roe v. Wade* and its implications, but to understand what he is saying, it helps to know a bit about how Rawls deals with abortion. The basic fact is that he is silent on the topic. In *A Theory of Justice* there is no explicit discussion of abortion, one of the most acute and troubling moral controversies of the time, despite the length of the book (more than 607 large pages) and its promise to help its readers to reach a 'reflective equilibrium' in their 'judgements of value.' Rawls touches on the topic only (and unavoidably) in his discussion of 'the basis of equality,' that is, 'the features of human beings in virtue of which they are to be treated in accordance with the principles of justice.'[14] Three brief remarks can be made about his amazingly vacillating analysis of this problem. First, his initial, basic answer is that 'equal justice is owed to those who have the capacity to take part in and to act in accordance with the public understanding of the initial situation.' This is a clear but surprisingly harsh principle, since it excludes a lot of human beings from 'the guarantees of justice,' for example, children. Second, Rawls quickly softens this hard line by shifting from 'the capacity for moral personality' to the presence of 'a potentiality that is ordinarily realized in due course.' This is distinctly better for children (and foetuses) but no improvement for the feeble-minded or those in their declining years. Finally, Rawls says that the vagueness of the idea of a required minimum of 'moral personality,' and whether that minimum is a capacity or a potentiality, is 'best discussed in the context of definite moral problems.' Abortion would seem to provide an excellent 'definite moral problem' to test and refine the theory. Rawls could have seized the opportunity to use his distinctive reasoning about interests, primary goods, original positions, and veils of ignorance to clarify and resolve some seriously conflicting moral intuitions. (Certainly it would have been easy for him to imagine everyone in his imaginary original position insisting on a basic right to life going back to conception.) Instead, he keeps the 'discussion' going on a comfortably high level of abstraction, conceding at the end, rather complacently, the basic deficiency of his whole approach. 'A correct conception of our relations to animals and to nature would seem to depend upon a theory of the natural order and our place in it. One of the tasks of metaphysics is to work out a view of the world which is suited for this purpose; it should identify and systematize the truths decisive for these questions.'[15] But this 'metaphysical' task he evidently did not think was his responsibility, since his business was ethics, not metaphysics.

Grant's purpose in *English-Speaking Justice* was to reveal a problem, not to propose any solutions. The acceptance of abortion by progressive liberals, including the more progressive majority of the American Supreme Court, and their reluctance to be clear about its justification, hiding behind vague talk about 'privacy,' 'persons,' and 'when life begins,' showed how flexible and accommodating 'our intuitions' can be, and how easily the plain meaning of simple words can be put aside, when a scrupulous respect for their meaning would frustrate a powerful personal and social interest.[16]

The conclusion Grant draws is not that ours is a society of terrible injustices (although it may be) but rather that it is becoming harder and harder for us to see what justice requires or why it should be chosen. The practical effects of this increasing darkness may not be immediately apparent – we may be buffered for a long time by our power and the lingering respect for our traditions of justice – but 'theories are at work in the decisions of the world,' as Grant says, and whatever the theories that our leaders accept, they will eventually determine how all of us live. Consequently, when trying to sum up the ideas that now govern our society, it may be better to speak, not of modern liberal theory, but of modern progressivism, for commitment to traditional liberal principles and protections may already have given way to the desire to adapt to the demands of progress, wherever this is deemed necessary or advantageous.

5 Varieties of Conservatism

George Grant's political thought has a complicated relationship to the standard ideological distinctions. Which distinctions? Conservatism, liberalism, and socialism – or, in other words, the familiar view of politics summed up in the idea of a left-right spectrum with liberals in the middle, between conservatives and socialists. (Communists and fascists anchor the left and right 'extremes' of this spectrum.) To the extent that Grant combines a commitment to some elements of liberalism (as we have just seen) with a conservative critique of the modern urban-industrial way of life (big cities, big governments, uprooted populations, secular education, mass media, and the like) and a socialist belief in freedom, equality, and social justice, he can be said to straddle the standard distinctions. This is the interpretation of his political thought suggested by calling him a Red Tory.[1] Alternatively, if he were to deny that there are any real differences between the standard options, he could be said to be collapsing the distinctions that others see as marking important political alternatives. Where others see a range of real choices, and thus the possibility of influencing politics by the choices they make, he would be asserting a 'one-dimensional' lack of choice. This is the interpretation of Grant's thought suggested by calling him a pessimistic technological determinist.[2] Together, the two interpretations raise interesting questions that are best approached by considering the varieties of conservatism and what Grant says about them.

Conservatism is notoriously hard to define or to reduce to any formula: the authorities tend to treat it as an attitude or outlook, or at best an ideology, rather than a principle or theory.[3] Minimally, then, conservatives are those who resist, regret, or reject progress. If they lack any good reasons (a satisfactory principle or theory) for doing so, then it must be because of some personal idiosyncracy. For example, their opposition to women's rights or to the rights of gays and lesbians may spring from their hatred of women or their fear of their own sexuality. Similarly, a gloomy view of politics may reflect nothing more than the resentment often found among classes or ethnic groups that are losing power or prestige.[4] Whether and to what extent such loose generalizations apply to particular individuals may, of course, be difficult to say. Further difficulties arise from the different ways we have of envisioning the future towards which we are now progressing – and therefore the different varieties of conservatism, minimally defined, since they reflect or relate to these different visions.

The variety was hidden for many years by the dominance of a single vision, opposition to which was the main source of unity among conservatives. For almost a century, starting about 1870, the socialist vision – real individual freedom and equality to be achieved by common ownership of the means of production and comprehensive economic planning – had such a broad appeal to virtually all classes of society and seemed to be advancing so inexorably that it created the major left-right division in Western politics. On one side were the socialists of various stripes or colours, the redder ones more radical and revolutionary, the pinker ones more moderate and constitutional; on the other side were their more or less uncompromising opponents – liberal, bourgeois, aristocratic, militarist, fascist, clerical, and so on – united more by their rejection of socialism than by their acceptance of any common principles. To be conservative was simply to oppose socialism.[5] But for at least fifty years, socialism has been losing its unifying power. The Soviet and other experiments gradually discredited the old socialist faith that socialist means would serve socialist ends. After about 1960, socialists in the Western world were generally distinguished from their liberal and conservative opponents only by their 'values' and the interests they served (such as unionized labour), rather than by their old belief in the efficacy of socialist methods (the socialist alternatives to markets and corporations), let alone any lingering faith in the 'historical inevitability' of 'proletarian revolution.'[6] Since 1991 and the collapse of the Soviet empire, not even the old values (or slogans) have been much use in defining the left (or progressive) side of the political spectrum.

As the polarizing power of 'socialism' has waned, the latent conflicts among conservatives have emerged. No classification of the resulting variety of outlooks can be more than a rough approximation to an accurate description, but a few familiar categories – traditional, fiscal, social, and neo – may help to sort out what is involved in Grant's idiosyncratic way of blending ideas from the left and right.

'Traditional' can be used to describe the conservatism that developed more than two centuries ago, in response to the French Revolution. Nineteenth-century conservatives were more or less 'romantic' defenders of the ancien régime – 'throne and altar' – in opposition to its 'radical' critics, who generally espoused more utilitarian principles. The classic expression of this kind of conservatism is Edmund Burke's *Reflections on the Revolution in France*, published in 1790. It can still be used to define a classic kind of conservatism stressing moderation, chivalry, prudence, and an untheoretical approach to politics. Those who are still drawn to Burke's thrilling rhetoric can be called traditional conservatives, though the liberal-democratic vision of the future to which he was opposed is one that his contemporary admirers are likely to accept, prudently, since it is all around them.

'Fiscal' is now the preferred designation for those conservatives who have been the most resolute opponents of socialism and its pale off-shoot, the welfare state. The principles of this conservatism, as explained by economists like Milton Friedman, are those of the liberal political economists of the eighteenth and nineteenth centuries and thus can be called liberal.[7] Fiscal conservatives are the defenders of economic liberty, that is, free enterprise and free markets, despite their potentially disruptive effects. Contemporary commentators who insist that such conservatives are not really conservatives at all, but rather 'neo-liberals,' clearly have a point. There need be nothing very conservative about them, apart from their opposition to liberal and socialist attacks on private property and economic inequality. By contrast, contemporary defenders of the welfare state (since it is now a familiar part of the status quo and since straight socialism no longer needs much opposing) can now appeal to Burke as a patron of their cause.[8] For all these reasons, fiscal conservatives should perhaps be excluded from any attempt to define a genuinely conservative outlook.

'Social conservatives' are defined by their opposition to progressive social morality in all its diverse manifestations, from abortion and euthanasia through recreational drugs, no-fault divorce, feminism, gay rights, pornography, rock music, rap artists, sex education in schools, and welfare mothers. They see themselves as the beleaguered defenders of 'traditional values,' especially the traditional family and traditional conceptions of paternal (or at least parental) authority. The genuineness of their conservatism – their resistance to a currently influential vision of progress as personal liberation – is beyond question, even if the issues that concern them have little to do with either Burke's preoccupations or those of the fiscal conservatives.

Finally, there are the 'neo-conservatives.' The term is often used in Canada – so it *can* be used – to refer to either fiscal or social conservatives, since, as distinct varieties, both these conservatisms are relatively new. But it is more properly used to refer to an outlook shaped by foreign-policy considerations and a familiarity with utilitarian methods of public policy analysis. This latest variant of conservative thinking emerged in the United States in the 1960s and 1970s against the background of Vietnam, draft dodging, détente, desegregation, race riots, and the 'Great Society.' Neo-conservatives took the lead in evaluating the relevant public policies 'realistically' (relying on evidence-based assessments of costs and benefits) rather than 'ideologically' (by their conformity to or departure from any axioms of moral or political theory). At the time, Canadians had almost no interest in the relevant tangle of issues, so until recently there has been almost no understanding here of what Americans know as neo-conservatism. At its heart there is opposition to a vision of 'world peace through world law' that would limit American sovereignty, undermine American power, and expose America's allies to aggression from their neighbours.[9] The threats to American power in the world, domestic as well as foreign, give neo-conservatism its point. Not surprisingly, its proponents can be found among nominal liberals as well as among those who call themselves conservatives.[10]

In *Lament for a Nation* there are two provocative statements about conservatism that help to clarify Grant's broader straddling and collapsing tendencies. The most memorable of these is undoubtedly the flat declaration that begins the sixth chapter of the book: 'The impossibility of conservatism in our era is the impossibility of Canada. As Canadians we attempted a ridiculous task in trying to build a conservative nation in the age of progress, on a continent we share with the most dynamic nation on earth.'[11] Like the related claim about the defeat and disappearance of Canada that was discussed in chapter 1, this statement is hard at first to take seriously.[12] How could Grant possibly have thought that conservatism was impossible, forty years ago, at the very time when socialism was beginning to lose its ideological momentum and when the modern conservative intellectual movement, which has since come to dominate Anglo-American politics, was first gathering steam? But in this case, unlike the earlier one, the puzzle can be quickly solved by making a simple, appealing, and familiar distinction: the conservatism that Grant says is no longer possible is *genuine* or *classical* conservatism, while the new conservatisms that have flourished since the 1960s are really old-fashioned liberalism. Does Grant himself not say as much?

Grant's second provocative statement, which has received relatively little attention, has to do with socialism. It is, he says, 'essentially conservative' (58). Admittedly, this is not how most socialists have thought of their ideology: they have preferred to picture themselves far to the left of the conservatives – as far as possible, within reason, from anything conservative. The reforms they have advocated have been directed to increasing freedom and equality, not bolstering restraints and sustaining privilege. In a society where the means of production were publicly owned and economic relations were rationally planned, they once believed, the restrictions on freedom that conservatives defend and liberals accept would no longer be necessary, for in such a society, with neither scarcity nor class conflict, all desires would be 'socially creative.' But there is confusion in the minds of such socialists, Grant says. They fail to reckon (realistically) with mankind's ineradicable greed. Would the freedom socialists promised not be freedom for greed? 'Yet what is socialism, if it is not the use of the government to restrain greed in the name of social good?' In practice, Grant observes, socialists (like liberals and conservatives) have always advocated restrictions on self-interested freedom. In doing so, he says, they were appealing to 'the conservative idea of social order against the liberal idea of freedom' (57).

Together, Grant's two statements suggest a complete reversal of our usual way of picturing our political alternatives: the so-called conservatives are not really conservatives at all, but rather liberals, while the socialists, who have prided themselves on being far ahead of both liberals and conservatives ideologically, are in reality the only true conservatives. How is one to make sense of such confusing claims?

Grant's remarks about 'the impossibility of conservatism' follow a discussion (at the end of chapter 5) of American conservatism in the early 1960s. Something called conservatism existed in the United States at that time, needless to say, and since then its growing popularity and influence have been crucial facts about American politics, as is well known. But Grant's basic claim had little to do with the fortunes of the politicians Americans call conservative. He thought that these politicians, and the journalists and academics who promoted their cause, were no less liberal fundamentally than their 'liberal' opponents, even if they differed from them on a number of important practical matters. The conservatism of the United States, he said, is an old-fashioned, eighteenth- and nineteenth-century liberalism, an early form of the modern thought that cannot resist the destructive criticism of more radically modern thinkers such as Rousseau and Nietzsche. American conservatives 'stand for the freedom of the individual to use his property as he wishes, and for a limited government which must keep out of the marketplace' (63). In 1963 and 1964, when *Lament for a Nation* was being written, their great representative was a senator from Arizona, Barry Goldwater. He became the Republican presidential candidate in 1964 and was badly beaten by Lyndon Johnson. He and his advisers (including Milton Friedman) appealed to the principles of Locke and the liberal economists of the nineteenth century as the best basis for a progressive society. They attacked social-welfare programs and regulatory legislation for destroying incentives and individual responsibility and for spawning a burdensome bureaucracy. They called for a return to the individualism of the founders of the American regime. 'In this sense, Goldwater is an American conservative. But what he conserves is the liberal philosophy of Locke' (64).

Even this older liberal conservatism (or conservative liberalism) of free enterprise and the constitution, Grant thought, had a dim future in American politics because the United States was not fundamentally a conservative society.[13] Rather it was 'a dynamic empire spearheading the age of progress' (65). For military as well as other reasons, its leaders, even those who call themselves conservatives, are compelled to foster the science that leads to the conquest of nature. 'This science produces such a dynamic society that it is impossible to conserve anything for long. In such an environment, all institutions and standards are constantly changing. Conservatives who attempt to be practical face a dilemma. If they are not committed to a dynamic technology, they cannot hope to make any popular appeal. If they are so committed, they cannot hope to be conservatives' (65). So in practice, conservatives in the United States can be no more than defenders of whatever structures of power are needed to contain, by external force, the tensions generated by a technological society, while sustaining its dynamism. 'They are not conservative in the sense of being the custodians of something that is not subject to change. They are conservatives, generally, in the sense of advocating a sufficient amount of order so the demands of technology will not carry the society into chaos' (66).

In chapter 6, Grant outlines a similar criticism of practical British conservatives and the Canadians who take them as their models. In Britain, too, there are and have been politicians and writers who have called themselves conservative, and there is some reason to think that the conservatism of these British conservatives may once have had more substance – may at one time have been less essentially liberal – than the American variety. Unlike the United States, Britain is a society with traditions from the distant past. Its 'founders' were kings and nobles, partisans of royal authority, not individual rights, and its political institutions, at least on the surface, are monarchical and aristocratic. Unlike the Americans, who have 'no traditions from before the age of progress,' the British are replete with such traditions. At least in the nineteenth century, the British Isles still had 'ways of life from before the age of progress,' and consequently we in Canada saw our connection with Great Britain as 'a means of preserving at every level of our life – religious, educational, political, social – certain forms of existence that distinguish us from the United States' (70). 'Connection' was, in this view, a way of sustaining a conception of society as more than just a contractual arrangement of mutual benefit among consenting adults. British conservatives, and following them, Canadian Loyalists and nationalists, could appeal to these traditions to justify social institutions and restrictions on individual liberty of a more demanding character than 'freedom loving republicanism would allow' (69).

This conservative Canadian nationalism was based on an illusion, however, as Grant explains. British conservatism was never really able to play the role in distinguishing Canada from the United States that conservative Canadians hoped it would. It could not sustain a distinct Canadian identity. 'British conservatism was already a spent force at the beginning of the nineteenth century when English-speaking Canadians were making a nation. By the twentieth century, its adherents in Britain were helping to make their country an island outpost in the American conquest of Europe' (72). In Britain as elsewhere, conservatism has been overwhelmed by Lockean individualism and technological education. The history of British conservatism, Grant says, has been one of 'growing emptiness and ambiguity' (71). For two centuries, Great Britain was the leading imperial power of the West and 'the chief centre from which the progressive civilization spread around the

world' (71). Its real conservatives, despite their appeals to ancient traditions, had less and less influence on their society. The more honest,
Grant says, fought rearguard actions, while the more ambitious twisted
conservatism into a facade for class and imperial interests. 'By the second half of the nineteenth century, appeals to such institutions as the
monarchy and the church become little more than the praising of formal rituals, residual customs, and museums. Politicians from Disraeli
to Macmillan have applied the term "conservative" to themselves; this
was hardly more than a nationalist desire to take as much from the age
of progress as they could' (72).

   One source of this 'emptiness and ambiguity' Grant finds in the writings of the great patron of today's 'traditional conservatives,' namely,
Edmund Burke. Burke was, of course, sharply critical of progressive
theories and the intellectuals who advocated them; he was far more
sympathetic to conservative regrets and resistance than were most
eighteenth-century thinkers and writers; and he was far more respectful of traditional forms than were the liberals (or radical Whigs) of his
day or the socialists of ours. Yet, all that said, Grant held that Burke was
still at bottom a modern progressive thinker and in some ways more
modern than his great authority, John Locke. In *English-Speaking Justice*
Grant says that Burke 'was in practice a Rockingham Whig, and did not
depart from Locke in fundamental matters, except to surround his liberalism with a touch of romanticism. That touch of the historical sense
makes him in fact more modern than the pure milk of bourgeois liberalism.'[14] Earlier, in *Lament for a Nation*, he alluded to Burke only once, to
illustrate his claim that British conservatism 'is less a clear view of existence than an appeal to an ill-defined past' (68). More will have to be
said later about the grounds for this judgment of Burke's standing as a
conservative, but for the present it is enough to say that Grant was not
persuaded, despite Burke's repeated invocations of nature and tradition, that he was an exponent of natural law or divine providence as
traditionally understood. Instead, in Grant's view, he was part of the
radical modern break from the traditional understanding of the rational
basis of political morality. Unlike the classic exponents of natural law
(the Stoics, Thomas Aquinas, Richard Hooker), Burke makes reason relative to circumstances and assumes that it is historically progressive.
He treats those who approach politics in the spirit of 'metaphysics' as
the great enemies of political prudence, and prudence, he says, is 'the
first of all virtues.'[15] Indeed, he goes so far as to suggest that political
science be regarded as an *experimental* science: 'The science of construct-

ing a commonwealth, or renovating it, or reforming it, is, like every other experimental science, not to be taught *a priori*.'[16]

The denial of particular differences, reducing them to empty distinctions, makes sense only in a semantic field where there are other distinctions marking real (or at least more significant) differences. Grant emphasized the similarities among the main modern ideologies to set them all apart from an older way of thinking about politics. This older way is, for Grant, the gold standard of conservatism. He distinguishes the conservatism of practical conservative politicians, who have been preoccupied with fending off the socialist attack on bourgeois civilization and the privileges of its ruling class, from a much earlier way of thinking associated with 'the older aspects of the Western tradition: the Church, constitutional government, classical and philosophical studies' (63). This earlier conservatism, which was never until recently called conservatism, can nonetheless be called 'the organic conservatism that pre-dated the age of progress' (64). Its principles are those of the Western tradition traditionally understood, and thus, obviously, a complex interweaving of many strands over a very long time, not something that is easily or perhaps usefully reduced to a few words. Nonetheless, what Grant means is indicated by the terms used a moment ago, 'natural law' and 'divine providence.' Grant says little about these ideas in *Lament for a Nation*, but enough, particularly in his discussion of French Canada in chapter 6, to make clear what he has in mind. The conservatism that concerns him is the 'ancient doctrine of virtue' according to which 'virtue must be prior to freedom' (74). It is the approach to politics grounded in the teaching of the churches about original sin and in the belief of their theologians that the good life makes strict demands on self-restraint. 'Nothing was more alien to them than "the emancipation of the passions" desired in American liberalism' (69). This conservatism can be described, following Grant, as 'essentially the social doctrine that public order and tradition, in contrast to freedom and experiment, [are] central to the good life' (69). This is the conservatism that must be 'a shadowy voice in a technological civilization' and that must languish as technology increases (71, 73). Its central tenet is perhaps best summed up in a phrase that Grant uses repeatedly, 'the conception of an eternal order by which human actions are measured and defined' (71). Any conservatism lacking such a conception, Grant thought, can be nothing but 'the defence of property rights and chauvinism, attractively packaged as appeal to the past' (71).

Misunderstanding of Grant's meaning sets in when this genuinely old-fashioned conservatism is identified with that of Edmund Burke. Many moderate, flexible, practical conservatives, wishing to distinguish themselves theoretically from their liberal and socialist rivals, but not willing to go back to the Dark Ages or earlier for an authoritative statement of their principles, or even to admit that they really have any, turn to Burke's *Reflections* as the classic statement of a more acceptable modern conservatism. Grant was not among them.

Grant's claims about the impossibility of conservatism and the conservatism of socialism are thus not nearly so strange as they may seem at first glance. Plainly, there are different varieties of conservatism, and some of them are.'ideologically viable' in our time. Grant was by no means denying the possibility of what he could see around him. Nor was he denying that the practically effective 'old-fashioned liberalism' of practical conservatives might sometimes be closer than 'up-to-date liberalism' to the 'genuine conservatism' of Richard Hooker and Thomas Aquinas. Rather he was saying that he could see no way by which the epistemological and metaphysical assumptions that underlie traditional conceptions of natural law – the understanding of nature as a knowable purposive order – could ever again, so long as our society and its education are 'technological,' engage the serious interest and command the respect of many practical men and women. He may of course have been wrong about this, but he was not *obviously* wrong, as it may have seemed at first glance.

If Grant is right, the problem will not be alleviated by any revival of 'Burkean conservatism' or any practical success of 'Red Tories,' for these are the Tories, generally speaking, who pride themselves on being *progressive* conservatives rather than retrograde reformers. For Grant, 'progressive' summed up all those tendencies in thought and action that modern individuals and societies welcome but that he himself questioned and resisted.[17]

An elementary classification of the varieties of conservatism thus helps to clarify the meaning of Grant's lament. The Canadian conservatism that Grant equates with Canadian nationality was essentially the belief that Canada's historic connection with Great Britain, a society 'with ways of life from before the age of progress,' would be 'a means of preserving at every level of our life – religious, educational, political, social – certain forms of existence that [would] distinguish us from the United States' (70). The 'British connection' would make it possible, it seemed, to build a community with 'a stronger sense of the common good and of public order than was possible under the individualism of the American capitalist dream' (lxxiii). Unfortunately, however, the tradition of British conservatism that was the basis for this hope 'was itself largely beaten in Great Britain by the time it was inherited by Canadians' (lxxiii). The Canadians, including his own family, who relied on British traditions as counter-attractions to the American dream did not sufficiently appreciate this. But it was perfectly clear to Grant, as he explained in the Introduction he added to the book in 1970, and from which I have been quoting. His lament was not therefore a lament for the passing of this British dream of Canada. 'It was rather a lament for the romanticism of the original dream. Only a fool could have lived in Toronto in the 1920s and 1930s without recognizing that any British tradition of the common good which transcended contract was only a veneer' (lxxiv). The book was written, Grant says, 'too much from anger and too little from irony' (lxxiii).

Grant's second provocative claim, that the Fabian socialism promoted in Canada by the Co-operative Commonwealth Federation (CCF), forerunner of today's New Democratic Party, was 'essentially conservative,' might also have benefitted from a touch more irony. Its specific justification was the opposition the CCF proclaimed to 'production for profit' rather than 'production for need.'[18] The party was evidently closer on this point to the natural-law condemnation of greed than were the liberal political economists who for the past two centuries had been providing a theoretical justification for self-seeking in a competitive market economy. More broadly, Grant's claim was based on what he says about the historical vision of socialism – that it presupposes a distinction between ways of life in which men and women are fulfilled and others in which they are alienated. Marxism, in particular, is said to include implicitly a doctrine of human good, and therefore to subordinate technological development as a means to the good of humanity as an end. 'Marx is not purely a philosopher of the age of progress; he is rooted in the teleological philosophy that pre-dates the age of progress' (55). According to Grant, North American liberalism better expresses the modern understanding of progress as the will to shape society unhindered by any preconceived notions of good. 'It is the very signature of modern man to deny reality to any conception of good that imposes limits on human freedom. To modern political theory, man's essence is his freedom. Nothing must stand in the way of our absolute freedom to create the world as we want it ... What matters is that men shall be able to do what they want, when they want. The logic of this liberalism makes the distinction between judgements of fact and judgements of value. "Value judgements" are subjective. In other words, man in his freedom creates the valuable. The human good is what we choose for our good' (55). By this stringent standard, Marxism, with its old-fashioned ideas of the perfectibility of man, can be called 'essentially conservative' and therefore can be said to 'block progress.'[19] In practice, however, Marxists in the West have generally put up less resistance to socially progressive reforms (such as abortion on demand) than have the fundamentalists from the religious right.

Finally, there are the neo-conservatives, narrowly understood. Their movement hardly existed when Grant was writing *Lament for a Nation*, and the issues it raises are best considered in connection with what he says, not about conservatism or socialism, but about nationalism and the universal and homogeneous state.

6 Overcoming Nationalism

Sometimes it is necessary to consider Canada alone, in isolation from or in contrast to other countries, in order to understand it, but often it is better to emphasize the common features it shares with other countries, focusing on some larger whole to which it belongs, such as North America or the West. In the writings of George Grant, these two perspectives are complementary, and in *Lament for a Nation* he shifts from one to the other as the argument proceeds. Only with respect to nationalism and globalism is there likely to be some confusion because of the changing frames of reference.

Canada has a distinctive conservatism, but what has been said so far about freedom, science, technology, education, and the shortcomings of modern liberal theory applies equally to Canada and to the United States. The modern scientific view according to which there is no stable order by which we are measured and defined, the view summed up in the phrase 'man's essence is his freedom,' may be even more commonly accepted by Canadians than by Americans.[1] 'Progress as an extension into the unlimited possibility of the future' may have at least as much power to enchant north as south of the 49th parallel.[2] Spiritually, the two societies may be one. But because they are different countries, with different political histories, they diverge politically when they try to come to terms with the practical implications of technology.

Coming to terms with it means containing its dynamism, as already suggested. In this connection, Grant focuses his readers' attention on one political project of enormous and essentially unknown consequences to which a great many citizens and their leaders are now dedicating their best efforts, namely, the overcoming of nationalism, both internally and externally. The result, Grant says, in one of the most important and least understood passages of *Lament for a Nation*, is an 'ineluctable' movement towards a worldwide and uniform society, 'the universal and homogeneous state.'

> The universal and homogeneous state is the pinnacle of political striving. 'Universal' implies a world-wide state, which would eliminate the curse of war among nations; 'homogeneous' means that all men would be equal, and war among classes would be eliminated. The masses and the philosophers have both agreed that this universal and egalitarian society is the goal of historical striving. It gives content to the rhetoric of both Communists and capitalists. This state will be achieved by means of modern science – a science that leads to the conquest of nature. Today scientists master not only non-human nature, but human nature itself. (52)

Grant nowhere fully or systematically explains the meaning of this key statement.[3] The crucial phrase, 'the universal and homogeneous state,' he took from a French philosopher and high civil servant, Alexandre Kojève, whose use of it will be discussed in chapter 12. When trying to describe this new 'goal of historical striving,' Grant wavers between calling it a 'state' and a 'society.' What he had in mind can be quickly clarified by considering two current preoccupations, globalism and terrorism.

Globalism refers not just to the process by which all the peoples of the world are becoming one human society tied together by personal as well as commercial relations that span long distances, crossing old national, ethnic, and racial boundaries, but also to an ideal of global political harmony based on the adoption of common cosmopolitan values.[4] In the meantime, our globalizing society has an obvious need for some overarching political authority (or structure of authorities) and rudimentary laws to resolve its conflicts, from the pettiest economic disputes to the most menacing military confrontations. There is an increasingly clear need, in other words, for effective institutions of international governance, not just to avoid the most destructive effects of interstate rivalry (wars, trade embargoes, and the like), but also to restrict the spread of nuclear, chemical, and bacteriological weapons and to manage the world's economic development in such a way as to minimize the risks associated with pollution and the exhaustion of natural resources. The United Nations is the most familiar but perhaps not the most important response to the demands of our increasingly 'global' world. It can stand, provisionally, for what Grant means by a universal state.

Terrorism – killing, blasting, maiming, and burning, or the threat of it, with a view to coercing a government or political community – is perhaps coeval with human society. In its current use, however, the term refers to the indiscriminate slaughter, by private individuals claiming to represent oppressed racial, ethnic, or religious groups, of civilians who happen to be associated with the major institutions of modern governance – states, corporations, non-governmental organizations, and so on. The traditional expedients of brutal repression (killing, jailing, and torturing terrorists or suspected terrorists or their likely supporters) can temporarily suppress terrorism in this sense, but in the long run it may be impossible to eliminate it entirely without dealing with its root causes, as these are brought to light by practically oriented research in the humanities and social and psychological sciences. Peace in the 'global village' may depend on a host of new developments – better methods for inculcating the values of tolerance and diversity in children, new conflict-resolution protocols, more effective rapid-response teams of soldiers and therapists, more inclusive interpretations of divine revelations, and more effective anger-management drugs with fewer unwanted side effects, for example.[5]

In short, the achievement of a peaceful and productive world society requires not just the overcoming of the potentially explosive rivalries between sovereign nations or states by institutions like the United Nations. It also requires the overcoming of 'internal' rivalries or 'nationalisms' rooted in ethnic, racial, or religious differences and conflicts of interest. These can disrupt even the most progressive societies, as Grant and his early readers could easily see by looking south to the racial turmoil in American cities and as readers today can see by looking across the Atlantic to the problems that Europeans are having with their Muslim minorities. The internal pacification of nations or states would seem to require that they become truly 'open' and inclusive, rather than 'closed' or exclusive, so that all individuals can participate fully in a common society, on a footing of equality. The future universal society will have to be 'homogeneous' in at least one basic sense: it will have to be 'classless' politically, rather than one with a ruling class and those they rule – or even first- and second-class citizens.[6]

Grant's second noteworthy claim – perhaps the most controversial point he makes in *Lament for a Nation* – is that the universal and homogeneous state, were it to come into being, would likely be a tyranny. His defence of Canadian nationalism, he explains, rests on the assumption that a worldwide egalitarian society, far from being the noblest of political goals and the ultimate expression of human freedom, as its partisans believe, would be destructive of human excellence. If it were in fact a noble goal, then Canadian nationalism would be a misguided parochialism. 'The belief in Canada's continued existence has always appealed against universalism ... Only those who reject that goal and claim that the universal state will be a tyranny, that is, a society destructive of human excellence, can assert consistently that parochial nationalisms are to be fought for' (83, 84).

Grant draws back, however, from simply asserting that the universal and homogeneous state, were it to come into being, would be a tyranny.[7] After saying that this was the teaching of the ancient philosophers, represented by Plato and Aristotle, he makes clear, on the penultimate page of the book, how difficult it would be to reach an informed decision about the truth of their teaching: 'To elucidate their argument would require an account of their total teaching concerning human beings. It would take one beyond political philosophy into the metaphysical assertion that changes in the world take place within an eternal order that is not affected by them. This implies a definition of human freedom quite different from the modern view that freedom is man's essence. It implies a science different from that which aims at the conquest of nature' (93-4). Such a vast inquiry, going 'beyond political philosophy,' is obviously impossible in a short writing about Canada, and as for himself, Grant says simply, 'I do not know the truth about these ultimate matters.'

Later we shall have to return to this basic problem and to Grant's suspension of judgment. For the present, in order to make what Grant is suggesting clearer and more easily remembered, it may help to note briefly three rather plebeian but immediately intelligible reasons why a 'universal and homogeneous state' might be regarded as tyrannical. First, it would be very large and hard to control democratically. Its government might seem very remote and alien to most of its 'citizens,' even if all of them were deemed to be 'first class.' Undoubtedly it would suffer from a 'democratic deficit,' and this deficit might well be much more severe than the one that now troubles such a relatively modest aggregation as the European Union. Second, in the education of its citizens, it would have to emphasize technical competence, not just to keep the vast machinery of global commerce and communications running smoothly, but to avoid aggravating any residual ethnic, racial, or religious conflicts that it might inherit from earlier, less enlightened times.

Finally, to the extent that these conflicts threatened to become violent, it would have to deal with them as internal rather than external problems, as if suppressing them were analogous to suppressing property crime or domestic violence. The analogy may be imperfect, however, and the result – given the urgency of suppressing the conflicts – could be that traditional civil liberties would suffer, as recent experience already suggests. For these reasons and others, Grant may have felt that his reservations about global governance – even assuming that the system could be made to work smoothly and would be as free and equal as possible – were more than just the timidity of a conservative with an idiosyncratic fear of progress.

But is there really any alternative to progress in this case? Is it not *necessary*, given our technology? Before considering any of the more refined arguments for and against the universal and homogeneous state, the concept itself requires more clarification. As with any concept, its meaning depends in part on an implied contrast. Against what background do the advocates of this new 'goal of historical striving' recommend it to its potential supporters? What alternative to it would its opponents prefer?

The contrasting state or society could be called partial rather than universal and heterogeneous rather than homogeneous, but this would not make matters much clearer. It is more helpful to use the terms already introduced, 'nations' and 'nationalism,' even though they obviously have a confusing variety of meanings.[8] They are used here to recall a recent but now largely discredited way of thinking about the relations between culturally and politically distinct groups. Rather than thinking of them as cultures or ethnic groups dispersed within a larger whole – at the limit, the universal society of all mankind – one could think of them as distinct societies, each with its own way of life and each naturally isolated from and more or less indifferent to all the others, except where they border on each other and therefore can enjoy some mutually beneficial trade but must also face the possibility of conflicts about boundaries or the sharing of resources. Rather than celebrating the diversity of mankind in a cosmopolitan spirit, each national society could celebrate its own excellence and denigrate the customs and values of all the others. If there were little mixing of the populations of the different nations, such ethnocentrism might hurt the feelings of only a few. Many potential conflicts could be prevented, in principle, by separating the potential antagonists – in the surly spirit of 'good fences make good neighbours.' Those who left home would be accepted elsewhere only as resident aliens, and each nation would be heterogeneous politically insofar as the native-born would have social and political rights denied to the newcomers. The world as a whole would maintain a cultural heterogeneity to the extent that distinct ways of life were upheld on the territories of the different nations. All this is, of course, only an ideal type, to clarify a concept, not a description of any reality that has ever existed, and certainly not of the modern nation-state.

Modern nation-states are generally betwixt and between: they are 'partial' societies but still much larger, more diverse, more advanced, and more interdependent than tribes or ancient cities with their limited hinterlands. Their unity as communities generally involves a large element of make-believe.[9] As a kind of political loyalty or species of political feeling, nationalism falls between cosmopolitanism, on the one side, and localism or provincialism, on the other side. It can be more outward-looking and aggressive, tending to imperialism, or more inward-looking and defensive, closer to xenophobia and isolationism. As a principle rather than just a feeling, nationalism suggests that the world should be organized politically as a plurality of sovereign states, the boundaries of which would correspond more closely than do most today to the boundaries of ethnic or cultural nations.

Grant's *Lament for a Nation* was a lament for the defeat of the Canadian nationalism represented by John Diefenbaker in 1963. His defeat was the most striking evidence of its defeat. What he stood for was definitely a kind of Canadian nationalism, but it was a much more limited and qualified nationalism than the simple model or idealization just outlined. Unlike Grant, he had little or no sympathy for or understanding of the autonomist desires of the Québécois, even though, as Grant explains, 'he was no petty Anglo-Saxon homogenizer who wanted everybody to be the same' (22). Those who wanted to retain 'charming residual customs' would be welcome in the 'One Canada' he advocated, in which, quite rightly, 'individuals would have equal rights irrespective of race and religion [and] there would be no first- and second-class citizens' (21). Both he and his minister of external affairs, Howard Green, looked forward to the creation of international institutions that would be more than just the tools of the most powerful nations, and they used the rhetoric of internationalism to oppose American domination of Canada. They envisioned a Canada that would be an independent agent in the United Nations, using its influence to promote disarmament.[10] They thought that the Cuban missile crisis of 1962 should have been referred to the UN for investigation. Canada's acceptance of nuclear warheads for its BOMARC missiles, they argued, could await a clarification by the North Atlantic Treaty Organization of whether they were really necessary. 'The interests of world peace demanded that warheads should be kept off Canadian soil until it was certain that they were needed' (31). In short, as Grant says, Diefenbaker and Green favoured the 'independent internationalism' that appealed to 'such unimportant groups as the Voice of Women,' who were advocating nuclear disarmament, but that was unacceptable to 'the dominant forces in Canadian life' (32, 36).

Grant contrasts the courage and patriotism of Diefenbaker and Green with the low cunning of Kennedy and Pearson. Kennedy was the 'decisive' practitioner of the new, tougher international morality, with a 'realistic' appreciation of the limited value of NATO and the UN as instruments of the American empire but no patience for the old conventions of national sovereignty. 'In 1962, Kennedy had made it clear that the United States was no longer going to take any nonsense from its allies' (29). He took a tougher line with his European allies than Eisenhower had and he set in motion measures to stop the nonsense among his Vietnamese and Iranian allies. As for Pearson, Grant says that 'he could use the rhetoric of "internationalism" even more effectively than Green, but he knew it for what it was' (32). Both Kennedy and Pearson, in their different ways, can be called nationalists of the American empire. Both were 'internationalists' rather than narrow-minded 'isolationists,' and while it would be too glib to say simply that they promoted the universal but *heterogeneous* state (with the West, from Washington, ruling the East and the South), they both vigorously opposed the more homogenizing ideologies coming from the East. Both embodied what is now recognizable as the distinctively neo-conservative combination of universalist rhetoric (advocating freedom, democracy, and equality for all nations) with a realistic appreciation of the value of nationally organized concentrations of military power.

As a nationalist fearful that the universal and homogeneous state would be a tyranny, no matter whether it arrived under the auspices of the United States or the United Nations, Grant faced the dilemma of having to choose in practice between harder and softer versions of the same thing. The softer was the more remote and theoretical possibility represented by the United Nations. Grant's aversion was directed to the more immediate and realistic threat, so Diefenbaker and Green became the heroes of his book, but the strain of justifying his choice shows at crucial points where he falls silent. What if Lockean liberalism were the conservatism of the English-speaking peoples? Or, more pointedly, is it wise to be as explicit as Howard Green was when he compared Americans to 'the biggest fellow in the school yard' who might be tempted 'to shove everybody else around'? That depends, Grant says, on 'how one interprets the role of the United States in the world, and this question cannot be undertaken here' (29).

anything about what one has done? What is the acclaim of the ignorant multitude (for those who entertain them or serve their material interests) compared to the satisfaction of knowing that one has grasped the insights of the wisest authors of the past and perhaps gone a bit beyond them in one's own thinking? In the *Republic*, Plato has Socrates conclude his description of the philosophic nature with a memorable comparison between the fate of the philosopher in human society and that of someone who has fallen among wild beasts. Being unwilling to join them in their savagery, but unable to dissuade them, he tries to withdraw from the frenzy of those around him. 'As a man in a storm, when dust and rain are blown about by the wind, stands aside under a little wall,' the philosopher tries to protect himself by withdrawing from the storms of political life. 'Seeing others filled full of lawlessness, he is content if somehow he himself can live his life here pure of injustice and unholy deeds, and take his leave from it graciously and cheerfully with fair hope.'[2]

Within religion, that is, Christianity, there is almost as long a tradition of commending those who lead modest lives of quiet contemplation and humble service to others. Of course, this tradition is inter-woven in the history of the church with a long (and not always a pretty) record of close collaboration with those in power, but within the institution there are places for others to practise a more private piety than that of its princes. And these more withdrawn types can claim for their justification some clear scriptural injunctions, such as 'Render to Caesar the things that are Caesar's, and to God the things that are God's' and 'My kingdom is not of this world.'

In the modern world, the two traditions, philosophical and religious, are united in Blaise Pascal, among whose *Pensées* one finds the following quotable fragment: 'We always picture Plato and Aristotle wearing long academic gowns, but they were ordinary decent people like anyone else, who enjoyed a laugh with their friends. And when they amused themselves by composing their *Laws* and *Politics* they did it for fun. It was the least philosophical and least serious part of their lives: the most philosophical part was living simply and without fuss. If they wrote about politics it was as if to lay down rules for a madhouse. And if they pretended to treat it as something really important it was because they knew that the madmen they were talking to believed themselves to be kings and emperors. They humoured these beliefs in order to calm down their madness with as little harm as possible.'[3]

This comparison of kings and their courtiers to madmen was quoted approvingly by no less a person than Pierre Elliott Trudeau, a few years before he 'entered politics.'[4]

Grant's life and writings suggest considerable sympathy for the kinds of quietist disengagement or withdrawal apparently favoured in these familiar quotations, but it would be quite wrong to picture him as cheerfully standing aside in an attitude of bemused superiority to those who seize the opportunities they are given for leadership and responsibility. He had a deep, sustained engagement with Canadian politics, despite being inclined to treat it negatively and even fatalistically, as a misfortune he had to suffer, rather than a blessing. And despite his prominence, he often seemed to deny that he could in any way shape or influence it for the better by his own thought and action. Why then, one may ask, did he not just keep quiet? Why his very public 'pessimism' verging on despair? Why the encouragement of these negative feelings in others?

Grant's teaching and writings have undeniably had some effect on how we Canadians think about our politics. Serious questions can therefore be raised about the justification for his harsh depiction of 'the kind of existence which is becoming universal in advanced technological societies' (78). Does his gloomy analysis of our past and future not risk undermining the loyalty and commitment we must have as citizens to what is good in our liberal-democratic institutions and traditions?

This problem is clearly explained in a recent book about Canadian political thought by one of Grant's students from McMaster in the 1960s, Janet Ajzenstat. She shows that there is a conflict between what he used to say about his love for Canada and what his students actually inferred from his analysis of our political history. 'Grant aroused our passion for Canada,' she says. 'He will be remembered for teaching us to love Canada.' But the Canada he taught his students to love, she says, was not the real country that actually exists today. By appealing to a flattering myth about the Loyalists, he gave Canada a false conservative essence, one that it never really had and certainly does not have today. His deeply conservative Canada – only superficially 'the Canada of his own youth' – was, she says, 'almost entirely fabricated from his imagination and his personal preferences.' It never really existed, but by lamenting its demise – the demise of 'a romantic fiction' – Grant fostered disaffection among his students and readers. He depicted

Canada's future as 'a dreary round of consumerism and pettiness in an environment degraded by the greed and ambition of industrialists.' He encouraged aimless discontent and irresponsible indifference to what is good in our constitution and way of life. 'He taught us to disdain liberal democracy and he offered nothing in its place.'[5]

This is not an indictment to be lightly brushed aside. Perhaps Grant was unwise to write so openly and forcefully about his reasons for taking a bleak or 'pessimistic' view of our future. (If he had been less clear and less eloquent, it would have been much easier to attribute his lamenting to some more personal frustrations, perhaps the decline of his class or even possibly his failure to live up to the political ambitions of his family.) Perhaps he should be blamed for excusing the sin of despair in the name of necessity, as he himself said, or at least for encouraging others to neglect their duties as democratic citizens.[6] This cannot be decided, however, before seeing more clearly and in more detail what Grant said his reasons were for rejecting what he called the dominant world religion, the religion of progress, that is, 'the belief that the conquest of human and non-human nature will give existence meaning' (77). He wrote at length about these reasons, as we have already seen.[7] They led him to side with those who believed 'that this society is quite absurd and that sanity requires one to be either indifferent or hostile to it' (77). But obviously he did not regard the problems we face and the remedies we might adopt as being perfectly clear to untutored common sense: careful thought is required before they can be labelled and any therapy prescribed.

One difficulty in the way of such thought is our loyalty to our own, as Ajzenstat indicates by contrasting love of one's own with love of the good. It was one of Grant's great themes, as she recalls: 'Whatever the assigned text, classroom discussion would come back to questions of friendship, patriotism, the love of "one's own," the love of "the good," love for God. How often, with what ardour, we explored the seeming opposition between love of one's own and love of the good. The love of one's own – personal and private passions, family and tribal affiliations: Does such love lead one by stages to the love of the good absolutely, as Socrates seems to say in the *Symposium*?'[8] Grant, she says, would remind his students that no particular can adequately incarnate the good, the love of which is man's highest end. But he would also ask whether we can ever come to know and to love what is good except in something that is our own – our family, our friends, our part of the world, our traditions. Can a vast abstraction, Goodness, and its close relatives, 'Truth, Beauty, Humanity,' ever have the hold on our hearts that our particular loves have? Perhaps the ascent would be easier if the lower loves were less intense, but real love of one's own country and its way of life is at least some steps removed from the childish absorption in the love of one's own body and its immediate needs that is the most obvious trap. And what could possibly be higher and more deserving of our admiration in the political realm than liberal democracy? Ajzenstat concedes that 'no one reading Grant can fail to benefit from his analysis of moral and religious issues.' But perhaps just because it is so elevated, she says, 'this glorious moral teaching turns to lead when turned into a prescription for Canadian democracy.'[9]

Many readers of Grant's political writings, and especially *Lament for a Nation*, must have wanted to level similar objections to Grant's presentations of Canada's past, with its apparent denial or denigration of the liberal and democratic roots of Canadian politics. What he is lamenting, one sometimes feels compelled to say, is the discrediting of his own preferred construction of our past – a romantically illiberal mythology, according to Ajzenstat – and not *our* way of imagining it, which is altogether more defensible.

To get past this difficulty one must want to see what Grant shows through his debatable, somewhat ironic historical simplifications. One must look in the directions that Grant indicated, towards those landmark figures from which he took his own bearings. And in what one is leaving behind, one must be prepared to recognize some faults or shortcomings where it would have been more agreeable to love wholeheartedly.

PART TWO

Philosophy

The investigation about the things for which you censured me, Callicles, is the finest of all: what sort of man ought one to be and what ought one to pursue and how far, for both an older and a younger man. For if I am doing something incorrectly in the course of my life, know well that I do not make this error voluntarily but through my lack of learning.

Plato, *Gorgias*

We naturally look to others for the clarification of our own insights and observations. What better way is there to deepen one's understanding than by comparing one's own thoughts with those of the most profound and most coherent thinkers one happens to encounter?

To whom did George Grant look? He never wrote about others as I am writing about him, but he called himself a Platonist and clearly felt a particular affinity with three contemporary thinkers of the first rank. Two of these three, Martin Heidegger and Leo Strauss, will figure prominently in the next five chapters. The focus will be on Strauss because he is the easier to understand initially and because Grant wrote a revealing article about him.

Strauss was a political theorist and classical scholar who taught in the University of Chicago from 1949 to 1967. He had been born in Germany in 1899, and his earliest writings, on Jewish religious subjects, were published in German. He lived in England and France on research fellowships from 1932 to 1938, when he emigrated to the United States. During the last twenty-five years of his life (he died in 1973), he published a great deal, but his work was not well known beyond a relatively small circle of his students and their students. His earlier writings were respectfully received by his academic colleagues, and some were even translated into other languages, but they tended to be consigned to an academic limbo as 'controversial' in methods and results. From time to time, his ideas were attacked by other scholars, sometimes rather sharply, but for the most part they were just ignored, and this is especially true of his later writings about Aristophanes, Plato, and Xenophon. Those persuaded by Strauss, on the other hand, have tended to constitute a school – 'the Straussians' – in opposition to conventional scholarship. Among these followers, one sometimes hears a remarkably favourable evaluation of his achievements: that he was the most important philosopher of the twentieth century.

In *Lament for a Nation* Grant makes several provocative references to Strauss. Near the end, for example, there is an arresting tribute to 'the teachings of that wise man.' No one reading the book with any care can fail to sense the significance of such deference, even without knowing what to make of it. Those familiar with Strauss's thought easily see some illuminating parallels between Grant's argument and Strauss's ideas about political philosophy. Some divergences are less striking, but they merit close attention. I shall approach this comparison indirectly, starting, not with an overview of what Strauss wrote, but rather with brief explanations of the main problems Grant addressed in his first book, *Philosophy in the Mass Age*, which was published in 1959 (on the basis of radio talks given the previous year, before Grant seems to have been aware of Strauss), and then in the short book about Nietzsche (again based on radio talks) that Grant published in 1971, *Time as History*. These two books, published six years before and six years after *Lament for a Nation*, show the changes in Grant's thinking that can be associated with his reading of Nietzsche, Heidegger, and Strauss. They will provide the framework needed for a relatively brief presentation of some major themes in Strauss's work. The significance of Heidegger's thought for both Strauss and Grant will be briefly indicated in the last chapter of this part of the book, which will explain the background to Grant's only extended discussion of Strauss, his 1964 essay on 'Tyranny and Wisdom.'

8 Nature and History

George Grant's first book, *Philosophy in the Mass Age,* the most accessible and most immediately revealing of his philosophical writings, was originally a series of radio lectures designed to provide an introduction to philosophy for a general audience.[1] It shows Grant's ability to relate scholarly inquiry to the broader concerns that scholars share with everyone else. An early reviewer praised it for being 'learned but clear,' and it is full of provocative observations on the character of modern life. It is as much an introduction to a kind of sociology as to philosophy.

For Grant, philosophy is fundamentally *moral* philosophy, and by the mass age he means the past few centuries during which a new way of life has gradually come into being in Europe and America. The most important difference between ancient times and the modern urban-industrial world is not, as Grant explains, any objectively definable change in the material circumstances of life (bigger cities and more powerful tools, for example), but rather a new way of thinking about the whole natural order and man's place in it. The book outlines an interpretation of this change to clarify its significance for moral philosophy. Grant's style is familiar and conversational. The ease with which the book can be read is a little deceptive, however, for it is dealing in an original way with questions of profound difficulty. On some points, Grant later changed his mind, but familiarity with his early views is necessary for properly understanding the significance of what he said later. My account of the book can do no more than highlight some key points to keep in mind when reading it.

Grant begins by stating his belief in the reality of moral philosophy, that is, in the decisive importance for how we live of careful thought about the principles governing our choices. He defines his subject as 'the attempt by reflection to make true judgements as to whether actions are right or wrong' (3). It is something we must all do: no one should rely on others to do it for them. Grant is not thinking here primarily about the difficult challenges that those in authority – lawyers and judges, for example – may face when trying to enforce a given code of laws: it may, of course, be necessary for them to reflect on the meaning and purposes of the code as a whole before they can know how to apply its particular provisions in particular cases. But Grant has in mind a much broader and still more fundamental problem of clarification. How should we think of the purposes of human life and our relation to our natural and social environment? Can our judgments of good and bad or right and wrong be grounded in something more solid and stable than our own changing tastes and inherited beliefs?

To think carefully about these questions is the most important task of the philosopher, Grant says, but it is no less a task for each of us. The problem he is addressing is not, as many modern scientists and even philosophers would have it, a time-wasting conundrum that should be left for those with more time than tasks – priests and prophets, for example, or idling academics who claim an authority that professional philosophers do not have and cannot justify. Grant assumes that there is such a thing as moral truth, and it is more than a few loosely defined platitudes, the vague residues of what some Germans have said about duty and some Englishmen about utility. It would be nice if the true principles of moral judgment were immediately apparent to untutored common sense. Then, if any expert guidance were needed in difficult circumstances, it could come from the scientists who extend our vision of the consequences of our possible actions, without claiming any special authority to pronounce on the standards we use when trying to evaluate these consequences. Grant rejects this modern, rather democratic conception of science and philosophy. It is the standards themselves that need clarification, he thinks, and this is a task for philosophy, though not just for those employed as philosophers. 'I would assert that philosophic reflection can lead us to make true judgements about right action. Contemplation can teach us the knowledge of God's law' (xxxi).

This knowledge is important and it will come, not from Scripture, it seems, but from our own reflections on history and society. Grant does not cite the Ten Commandments, nor does he try to deal with the problems of moral philosophy topically or 'analytically.' The analysis of moral concepts outside any clearly defined historical context tends to encourage dogmatism, he says, that is, the easy acceptance of whatever the prevailing moral assumptions happen to be. The challenge of moral philosophy is not just systematization, to reach some kind of synthesis or equilibrium of currently accepted opinions, but rather historical perspective, to gain some understanding of the sources of current opinion as a development from earlier experience. Grant's analysis has a critical edge that reveals his uneasiness about conventional views. 'The historical situation of the West, and of Canadians in particular, calls for the frankest and most critical look at the principles of right in which we put our trust' (4). Admittedly, the historical or sociological approach Grant adopts has a danger of its own: it tends to encourage the relativism that makes moral opinions simply a function of historical circumstances, implicitly denying the possibility of any truth that transcends the conventions of particular societies. But in our present circumstances, this is a less serious problem, he thinks, than that of an unspoken, unthought dogmatism. 'It is indeed true that philosophy stands or falls by its claim to transcend history, but that transcending can only be authentic when it has passed through the forge of historical discipline' (xxx).

Philosophy, as Grant understands it, is thus theoretical or contemplative, but it is also practical and political. 'As we sow in theory so we will reap in action' (96). The task of the philosopher is a public task. Philosophers are society's moral guides or counsellors. They are not hermits, withdrawn from the world, huddling under any walls. Their place is in the thick of the battle, giving directions. Philosophers have important social responsibilities.

Grant's historical account starts from a stark contrast between ancient and modern conceptions of history. He wants to uncover the roots of our modern spirit of practical reform, our dedication to overcoming particular evils such as hunger and disease by gradually building an entirely new kind of society. Most people today, and especially most of those who lead societies like Canada and the United States, take for granted that the chief purpose of life is the making of history. Time is seen as a series of events. It is supremely important how we (or they) shape these events, so that they are shaped as they should be shaped. 'We have taken our fate into our own hands and are determined to make the world as we want it. Man and not God is the maker of history. Unique and irreversible events must be shaped by creative acts of human will' (21–2). Ancient man, by contrast, lacked this sense of 'making history.'[2] Ancient cultures had no sense of their actions as creating a unique series of events of ultimate significance. They had a different relation to the whole realm of the temporal: they saw time not as history but as the moving image of an unmoving eternity. 'They saw events as the pale shadows of divine realities, the temporal as the mere image of the eternal. Therefore, they did not see themselves as making events but as living out divinely established patterns' (15).

The moral principles of ancient societies depended, according to Grant, on the mythic consciousness of archaic religious cultures. For the ancient peoples, all important activities were made holy by religious association and had the character of rituals. 'A human act had meaning in so far as it was thought of as repeating or participating in some divine act which had been performed by a god in the golden age of the past, and which was given men in myth' (17). The particular acts of individuals gained their meanings from being the copies or imitations of divine archetypes, for these were the ultimate reality. The passing events of human life could have meaning and reality only insofar as they repeated and participated in this ultimate reality. The world was a place for the appearance of the divine, and 'human action was the re-creation of the sacred in the world' (18).

Justice, too, for the ancient civilizations, was the living out in time of a transcendent eternal model. The moral codes of particular communities were thought to derive from a supreme law that existed prior to both written human laws and political life. They were seen as the more or less wavering and distorted reflections in time of an unchanging eternal law which enforced limits on human striving. This is the basic idea of natural law, Grant says. In the hands of the ancient philosophers, as they criticized the archaic religious consciousness of their contemporaries and laid the foundations for academic science (or natural philosophy), the idea became a theory of universal order. 'There is an order in the universe which human reason can discover and according to which the human will must act so that it can attune itself to the universal harmony. Human beings in choosing their purposes must recognize that if these purposes are to be right, they must be those which are proper to the place mankind holds within the framework of universal law. We do not make this law, but are made to live within it' (27). The doctrine assumed, in other words, that there is a natural order and a human nature, ultimately the same in all men and women, and our task or destiny as rational creatures is to discover, through reflection, our own proper place within the given structure. The capacity for such reflection – reason – is at first present in us only potentially. It needs to be developed by education, which is the process by which a person comes to think clearly about the various purpose of human life and their wise ordering. 'Wisdom was then the purpose of education. It was the condition which men reached through reason, as they come to know what were the purposes in human life truly worthy of a rational soul' (30).

This theory has been immensely influential, as Grant explains, and it still has its advocates. Its distinction between natural and positive law clarifies our recognition that the laws which legislators enact and courts enforce – positive laws – may have no validity because they diverge too widely from the demands of natural justice. Such laws, from the stand-point of the theory of natural law, are not really laws at all. 'A law is only a law when it is a just law, mirroring the divine law of justice' (31).

The obvious and fateful exception to these generalizations about ancient peoples and natural law is the Jews. As Grant says, they 'discovered the very idea of history' (40). That is, they came to see time as finite, beginning with creation and ending with the end of the world, and they believed that the events between these limits were directly willed by a providential deity with a view to realizing a definite goal or purpose. This goal or purpose – the redemption of the Jewish people through a Messiah – was of course God's choice, not their own. Indeed, mankind, and even the chosen people, were continually falling away from respect for God's purposes and consequently needing to be destroyed or recalled to the path of righteousness by divine wrath. 'The God of the Jewish prophets is no longer an archaic deity who creates archetypal gestures, but a personality who ceaselessly intervenes in history and who reveals his will through particular events. The events of the world take on meaning not only as images of eternal patterns but as concrete expressions of the divine will' (40). These events include the revelation of a divine positive law – a practical code of right conduct – based on the will of God. In short, time is no longer seen as a moving image of eternity, but as a meaningful history, the unfolding of God's purpose in relation to his creation, and it will culminate in the realization of his final purpose, the redemption of his chosen people.

This idea of time as history – 'the idea that the events of human society have a meaning in their totality, as directed towards an end' (41) – first arose within Judaism and was made 'absolute' by belief in Christ as the Messiah. 'Our redemption has been achieved once and for all in His passion and death. This is not going to be repeated an infinite number of times. It was a unique and irreversible event' (42). Christianity, as the form in which biblical religion spread around the world, is thus the most important cause, Grant says, of the destruction of the old religious cultures and the coming to be of modern historical man, imbued with the idea of time as history. And thus it is also the deepest source of modern secular culture as a whole.

This sounds paradoxical – to say that Christianity is the source of secularism – because we tend to identify religion with Christianity and secularism with the rejection of religious belief. 'We identify the old world with Christianity. It therefore seems contradictory to say that Christianity has been the chief cause of the destruction of the traditional religious cultures' (40). In fact, the standard way of accounting for modernity is by citing the recovery of ancient thought during the Renaissance and the subsequent break, in the Reformation, with a long-established religious tradition. But Grant is saying, in effect, that there is a fundamental continuity between the Christian faith of the Middle Ages and modern secular culture. To be sure, there are some obvious and important differences. On the one hand, there is the belief in divine providence and a divinely ordained process of salvation, culminating in the Kingdom of God, and on the other hand, our distinctively modern and secular sense of human independence and utter responsibility. We have taken our fate into our own hands, as Grant says. History is something *we* make, and we are truly responsible for what we make of it – the Kingdom of Man or hell on earth. Our task, we say, is to ensure that humanity stays on the progressive path and avoids falling back into the barbarism and superstitions of earlier times. But underlying this difference is a more basic similarity: both before and after the Renaissance and Reformation, European man understood time as history. And Grant's claim is supported by a massive historical fact: modern society is in its origin *European* society, and the radical difference between Europe and the high cultures of the East, which did not give rise to what we call modernity, is that European civilization was penetrated, not just by Greek philosophy, but also by the Jewish religion in the form of Christianity.

Grant's elaboration of this account – his explanation of its underlying logic and its implications for moral philosophy – is both simple and hard to grasp. The 'mediating term,' he says, between the old providential view of history as God's mighty acts and the modern progressive understanding of history as a human creation is 'freedom' or 'subjectivity.'

Here we touch one of the crucial nodes in Grant's thought – the problem of the meaning of freedom. What he says in 1959 is by no means his first or last word on the subject. In earlier chapters we have already had occasion to consider Grant's rejection of the view that freedom is the ability to get what one wants when one wants it. In subsequent chapters I shall try to clarify more fully the implications of his view that it also involves our ability to reflect on what we should want. For the time being, let me simply repeat some of the things Grant says in *Philosophy in the Mass Age* about 'the freedom of the spirit.'

Humanity's awareness of its essential freedom, and its ability to act on this awareness, is a gradual development, he says. Human beings at first think of themselves as objects among the other objects that make up the world. They do not see that their consciousness or subjectivity sets them apart from the natural objects, such as stone or trees, which simply are whatever they are. Human beings, because of the way they are aware of themselves, can act with a view to the future, can stand above themselves, as it were, and make themselves what they are not. Their future projects can negate their present selves. Thus the logic of spirit – of free spiritual being – is different from the logic of identity proper to nature, and history is ultimately to be understood as the emergence of spirit out of nature.[3] As Grant explains this basic point, the 'I' that thinks about the objects it encounters in the world is not itself an object but a subject with its own mysterious being. 'The more we think about the "I" the more mysterious this subjectivity will appear to us. On the one hand we can never escape it, it is implied in all we think and do and are. On the other hand, though we can never escape ourselves, we can never completely come upon ourselves. When we think about ourselves, we turn ourselves into an object thought about, but there is always the "I" who is doing the thinking about the "I." We can think about ourselves thinking about ourselves, and we can think about ourselves thinking about ourselves thinking about ourselves. But what we really are can never become an object for ourselves' (63–4).

This mysterious subjectivity underlies our private judgment of our own thoughts and actions – what we call our conscience. It means that we are always observing ourselves from some higher perspective and always, in a sense, negating ourselves. 'We are always a project to ourselves, in that in any given situation we can negate what we are in the name of what we ought to be' (64). Moreover, from this moral point of view, above what we have done, we see that praise or blame is deserved only if what we have done somehow expresses who we are. We cannot rightly be praised or blamed for anything we were compelled to do by outside forces or perhaps even for whatever we may have done accidentally, with no conscious intention or awareness of what we were doing. Further, obedience to externally imposed law, from fear of punishment, is at odds with the relation that should exist, ideally, between our actions and our judgment of them. Only obedience that is freely chosen is meritorious and consistent with the dignity of a rational creature. Hence the law itself must somehow be the expression of our freedom if it is to merit our obedience. We must freely choose the law we freely choose to obey. In whatever ways the positive laws of our society may have come into being – and different societies have obviously had different histories – the laws produced by historical processes must ultimately become ones that would be freely chosen by rational human beings. Freedom can no longer be understood simply as freedom from impediments that keep us from what we want, that is, as the power to secure the objects of our desires, since freedom must also be the freedom of self-legislation. A free society can no longer be one that just leaves its members a wide latitude of choice; it must be one that offers them the chance to use their reason in their own government.

To say 'no longer' may suggest a recent development, but Grant traces the intellectual process he is describing far into the past. As noted above, he believed that Christianity had played a vital role in the emergence of this deeper understanding of human freedom. The fundamental difference between subjects and objects was first clearly understood in the ancient world, in Plato's doctrines of the soul and knowledge. 'In the *Republic* the morality and religion of the archaic world as found in Homer and Hesiod is made wonderfully explicit, but it also most stringently criticized and in that criticism transcended' (20). The rational consciousness developed by philosophers made it impossible for them to remain within mythic religion. But their freedom and subjectivity were then seen as special attainments of the privileged few who had the leisure and the natural gifts to escape the religious myths and images that held others in their grip. Only with Christianity did the awareness develop that *all* are free.

For many centuries, this radical insight was contained within the hierarchical and authoritarian forms of the ancient world. Even though Christianity can be characterized as a revolt in the name of freedom against servitude, for many centuries the Christian church modelled itself on the political institutions of the Roman empire, making most believers the spiritual slaves of a clerical elite. With the Protestant Reformation, however, the difference between lay and clerical orders was finally overcome, and at least within the religious sphere, the equal freedom of all was finally recognized. Once affirmed in the religious sphere, it inevitably began to affect all aspects of life – politics, art, and science. The age of natural hierarchies had to end and that of democracy and individual liberty to begin. Henceforth the individual would accept – should accept – only such laws and doctrines as he could regard as his own.

This new view of man's essential freedom or autonomy – the overcoming of the old sense of being simply an object dependent on a creator – strips away the old excuses for stoically accepting the evils and suffering of life.[4] Men and women can no longer in good conscience simply 'refuse history.' They can no longer see themselves as creatures with a pre-determined place in a cosmic order, and moral wisdom can no longer be understood as knowing and accepting that place. Humanity has attained a more radical sense of its own freedom than the ancient philosophers had been able to articulate. We are now our own creators, undeniably and without qualification the makers of our own laws and values, responsible for what we make of ourselves in time, even if we are as yet unaware of our freedom – even if, as Marx put it, the history we make happens behind our backs. Wisdom is now identified with criticism of the old 'metaphysical' doctrines and the deceptive political 'ideologies' that denied oppressed and oppressors alike a clear consciousness of their situation and its responsibilities. More abstractly, wisdom is now a form of human consciousness, the understanding of history as a human creation, as man's being in time. Under this new dispensation, the basic principle of right action shifts from what is natural to what is freely chosen and progressive.[5]

Grant has a chapter on Marxism to illustrate at a high level the critical, rebellious attitude fostered by modern moral philosophy. Among North American academics and journalists in the 1950s, there was a tendency to ridicule Marx as a crude ideologist and bumbling economist. By contrast, Grant presents him as 'a social theorist of the first rank, who reveals to us the diverse currents that make up the progressivist river' (51). He is at bottom a philosopher of history, Grant says. He shows how spirit, as labour, realizes itself in the world, in relation to a nature it must dominate. For Marx, human freedom consists ultimately of this domination, by virtue of which evil will one day be overcome in the world. Thus Marx puts science and technology at the centre of history, as the means for mankind's redemption from pain and work.

Not surprisingly, his theory has had great appeal for scientists and intellectuals, for it has given them a clear account of the universal moral significance of their work.

Grant's presentation of Marxism is surprisingly positive, but it points to one major shortcoming of Marx's thought. Marx does not truly understand the freedom of the spirit, he says. Man is more than simply an object in the world, and ultimately he cannot find satisfaction in the attainment of any finite object of desire, even the communist society of the future, as envisioned by Marx.[6] Man reaches for the infinite with desires (for better or worse) that go beyond liberation from scarcity and class domination. Important as these finite goals are, they are not the limit of human aspiration, and a society that offers nothing more will invite negation as surely as capitalist society does. Lacking an adequate understanding of freedom, Marxism tends to become a species of practical materialism that implicitly in theory and quite obviously in practice denies the full meaning of human freedom and equality. Indeed, by priding itself on its atheism, it denies, in effect, that freedom must find its completion in the recognition of a spiritual order that overcomes the distinction between subject and object or mind and the world.

Grant's discussion of our own society is no less critical: he finds here a practical materialism and dedication to finite goals at least as intense as that of the Marxists in Russia and China. Moreover, in American pragmatism he finds a philosophy that is every bit as this-worldly as Marxism but that expresses the history-making spirit even better than Marxism does because it says nothing whatever about any final necessary outcome. 'In pragmatism man is entirely open to make the world as he chooses and there is no final certainty. Everything is dependent on how man uses his practical freedom' (83). Nonetheless, Grant affirms that more adequate conceptions of spiritual law and freedom than pragmatism provides still have some hold in our midst. Thus the hope that we can reasonably entertain for our society is that the achievements of the age of progress will be put at the service of a human freedom that is more than just getting whatever one wants when one wants it, or in other words, a freedom that will find itself completed and not denied by a spiritual order.

The task of the philosopher in the mass age, Grant concludes, is to 'think together' the apparently contradictory truths of acceptance and rebellion that have made themselves explicit in history. These are the truths, on the one hand, of natural law ('that man lives within an order which he did not make and to which he must subordinate his actions'), and, on the other hand, of the history-making spirit ('that man is free to build a society which eliminates the evils of the world') (70). The challenge is to think these different truths in their unity. How can there be a limiting natural law that recognizes the freedom of the spirit? How can men do what they must do to eliminate evil and suffering if they are restrained by ancient standards of right and wrong? But how can they find any lasting satisfaction in the attainment of finite goals if this achievement entails the loss of any clear sense of the categorical limits on human action?

In Grant's treatment of these difficult questions there is no suggestion that the task of philosophy, as he understands it, is beyond the power of any thinker. In his view, the truths to be reconciled are not simply contradictory propositions – one or the other or both necessarily false. The problem is not to choose between ancient and modern philosophy, but rather to synthesize their apparently conflicting insights and experiences. Grant draws back from suggesting that Hegel has already achieved such a synthesis (98–9), but the assumptions Grant adopts and the goal he has in view are clearly 'Hegelian.'

Moreover, Grant's account of modernity is distinctly 'idealistic.' The explanation for modernity and the remedies for its ills are to be found, fundamentally, not in the study and modification of material conditions, as Marxists think, but rather in the realm of the spirit. Specifically, modernity is to be attributed, ultimately, to the radicalization and 'secularization' of biblical religion in the form of Christianity: this is more important than the development of particular industrial or commercial techniques and more important than even the rebirth of classical science or philosophy in the Renaissance. The implication is that the remedies for modern ills may be found in a return to classical thought and to its sense of limit or dependence. But Grant rejects any idea of simply reviving any earlier way of thought, whether that be Roman Catholic orthodoxy or ancient metaphysics. 'Reactionary experiments are always vain,' he had declared at the outset (8). In a period such as our own, when the meaning of our lives has become obscure and we sense the lack of any general rules or principles to guide us among the innumerable possibilities open to us, the search must be for a new authentic meaning that does justice to the new situation we find ourselves in. There can be no simple return in faith to the teachings of the past. To be effective with those who more and more doubt the reality of absolute limits on our history-making responsibilities, the affirmations of faith have to be recast in new and more resonant terms. The moral law must be reformulated 'in a way that does not override but fully recognizes the freedom of the spirit' (96). Even if it were possible somehow to turn the clock back, it would not be desirable to do so, because the modern understanding of the freedom of the spirit is a real advance over the ancient conception of a substantial soul. The history-making spirit, for all its dangers and limitations, is a higher standpoint than that of natural law.

9 Enlightenment and Nihilism

What does it mean to say that history is a higher standard than nature? What would it mean to say that history is the *only* standard from which we can judge what is good and bad, or better and worse, in human thought and action? Is Grant perhaps embracing 'historicism'? At the end of *Philosophy in the Mass Age*, one is left pondering these questions – if one puts aside, at least temporarily, Grant's hesitant hope for a synthesis of nature and history.

'Historicism' is a troublesome word with a variety of elusive meanings, easily confused, and the most important thing it denotes can appear in a variety of forms. The doctrine that attracted Grant in the 1950s and that he rejected in the 1960s held (to simplify drastically) that our moral and political understanding is gradually perfected by the cumulative experience we call history.[1] Over a long period of time, we as a species gradually attain a clearer and more coherent understanding of right and wrong or good and bad. As a race, we learn from our successes and failures, and thus our present understanding is in principle superior to that of any earlier time. The basic truths of ethics or morality are not equally accessible in principle to all people at all times, for they are not simply innate. Nor do we get our knowledge of them from the teachings of prophets who were granted special divine revelations at particular times in the past. Rather, we are the beneficiaries of a long process of intellectual and moral improvement. We can see that our current beliefs about politics and morality are superior to those that prevailed in the past, and through the study of our own history we can see how we gained our superior knowledge or insight. The absolute standards we naturally seek are in this sense inherent in the historical process by which truth, beauty, and goodness have gradually become clearer and clearer to us. They are relative to this process and its goal, but not, so to speak, absolutely relative.

This qualified historicism can be radicalized by dropping the assumption that the historical process somehow guarantees progress. We could cease to 'believe in progress' in the sense of necessary improvement. Progress could become, not just something more challenging, requiring real thought and effort, but something altogether more dubious. We could assume, provisionally, no more than that our standards of justice and morality do *not* come to us from any external source – not from nature, not from history as an intelligible process directed to a definite end, and not from divinity. There are no laws written in the stars, we could say, and no real Enlightenment or scientific revolution (just shifts from one paradign to another), and certainly no revelations more credible than the Book of Mormon or L. Ron Hubbard's *Scientology*.

Where then would we stand? Our current intuitions about fairness or about the just and the unjust would now be seen simply as our own creations or 'social constructions.' Although they evidently come to us out of our past experience, which we call our history, we would now assume that there is no way of getting outside this history to see it 'under the aspect of eternity,' for we are always within its limits, shaped by it, both in thought and action, in ways that we cannot clearly see or fully understand. We could have no assurance, therefore, that our present standards are in principle superior to those of the past. (We would also be relieved of any worry that they might be inferior to those that prevailed in the past or that may prevail in the future. For all we can know, we may be living at the absolute peak of human moral achievement.) To be sure, we can trace sequences of events from the past to the present and even a bit into the future, if we are clever, but perhaps we deceive ourselves if we think that any sequence we trace is the sequence that would be seen by an omniscient observer on some distant star, for whom all is equally present. Our tracings are necessarily always partial and retrospective. We may not know the future meaning of our own present actions any more than our ancestors could see the meaning of their actions from our perspective.

This more radical doctrine, no matter how plausible it may seem or how vulnerable to peremptory objections it may be, has no more standing at this point than that of an assumption. But the questions it raises are not ones that are easily answered. Clearly it would be a mistake to think that its truth or falsehood could be determined by some straightforward 'empirical research' – by gathering more historical facts, per-haps, or by examining the machinery of the brain more carefully. The questions are not empirical in this familiar sense, but rather conceptual, metaphysical, or ontological. And let us put them aside for a while. In Grant's terms, they come down to the question whether we are ulti-mately 'our own' and thus in the last analysis the source of our own laws or standards, for which we are ultimately responsible (they some-how reveal who we are), or whether we are not our own but rather sub-ject to an eternal standard by which we are measured and defined.

The historicist assumption or working hypothesis I have just sketch-ed is sometimes invoked to justify what is commonly called moral rela-tivism – the relaxed, easy-going attitude towards questions of ethics or morality associated with the rejection of 'absolutism.' We know too much about our past and have become too sophisticated (we could con-tinue) not to see the relation between the old moral 'absolutes' and the practical needs of simpler, poorer societies. The old 'deadly sins' no longer seem to us, in our different circumstances, so deadly. Indeed, the very word 'sin' may bring a smile to our lips. We no longer believe the old stories about a grumpy Patriarch with his heaven for saints and hell for sinners. We understand the practical purposes those stories once served and why so many people back then were willing to believe them. They may still be good for the kids, but we ourselves don't need them any longer. We have learned to relax and enjoy life; we are putting away the old moral straightjackets, 'one size fits all,' and are gradually forget-ting all the crazy demands of the old god for pointless suffering – his lik-ing for poverty, chastity, and obedience, for example, and all his 'higher demands' and 'ascetic virtues.' The virtues we celebrate make some demands, but not such onerous ones. We are challenged to be our own authentic selves, even when that means defying social conventions and confronting the anger of conformists. Of course, there must be some standards to which we can appeal when others demand that we justify our choices, but these can be chosen for the occasion, and authenticity itself can have a prominent place among them. They can change as our tastes and circumstances change, adapting to whatever goals we have set ourselves. They need not derive from any fixed standard of human perfection. Indeed, they can even accommodate, as Rawls imagined, 'someone whose only pleasure is to count blades of grass in various geo-metrically shaped areas such as park squares and well-trimmed lawns.'[2] In short, they can take human beings as they are, sometimes obsessively counting their blades of grass or wriggling their toes in warm mud or their fingers in warm apple pies, but generally aiming to make love, not war, and to live well, enjoying good food, good company, and good conversation.

Moral relativism or radical historicism can appear in a harsher guise as well. In principle, 'history' could liberate those with a taste for ruling from bothersome 'higher demands' to be truthful, tolerant, compassionate, and caring, for the history that has given us our current mix of more or less coherent 'values' is open (we have assumed) to more than one interpretation. Progress or decline? Perhaps, under the aegis of the old 'higher values,' humanity has gradually been making itself morally weaker and uglier rather than finer and nobler, even by its own relative, historical standards. Mass enlightenment may be producing nihilism, the devaluation of the highest values. If the truth of human being is history or change, and if humans are truly historical or 'evolving' beings with no fixed nature, could they not be evolving down, so to speak, as well as up? If we can no longer trust any metaphysical or scientific guarantees that the escalators will always go up, if neither God nor Nature nor History is any longer underwriting the future of mankind, then perhaps we should take more seriously our own responsibility to create a better human being in the future. To be sure, the absence of any divinely or naturally set limits on human action may mean that everything the soft contemporary relativists want to do is in a sense permitted, but that does not mean that *we* have to let them do whatever they would like. Perhaps we should embrace the challenge of doing with them whatever we think is necessary to breed a higher, nobler, stronger human being. Perhaps, when trying to decide what is right and wrong, or better and worse, we should look neither to the old 'absolute standards of right and wrong' nor to the present pleasures and pains of those directly under our authority, but simply to the future strength and greatness of mankind.

That Grant had some understanding of the appeal of this harder or harsher relativism is shown by one of the most revealing of his early writings, the talk he gave to the Couchiching Conference in 1955 on 'The Minds of Men in the Atomic Age.'[3] It is a scornful rejection of the complacent, onwards and upwards, bigger and better salves and bromides of the time. Contrary to appearances, he said, things are generally getting worse, not better. Canadians are undeniably wealthier than they used to be, but their obsessive pursuit of material goods is gradually destroying what makes them human. Genuine education is being replaced by technical training, even in our universities, and in our churches, worship is giving way to the cultivation of good feeling, turning the churches themselves into little more than community clubs. 'I do not want to be pessimistic,' Grant concluded, 'but when asked to give a diagnosis, one must be honest.'[4] And being honest meant explaining his reasons for the arresting statement he had made at the beginning of his talk, when launching his assault on the complacency of his audience: 'I can imagine a prosperous society, without war, of healthy animals adjusted to worshipping their machines, which could be so disgusting that one could will that it should be destroyed.'[5]

Grant's most careful and provocative discussion of radical historicism is the little book he published from his 1969 Massey Lectures, *Time as History*. Its main theme, as its title suggests, is 'what it means to conceive the world as an historical process, to conceive time as history and man as an historical being.'[6] This way of conceiving the temporality of our lives – giving a point or direction to 'the fact that existing is a coming to be and a passing away' (13) – can be called 'historicism,' he says, and it is our modern fate. In all our studies, in the natural as well as in the social sciences and humanities, and therefore in all our practical activities as well, the basic assumption that now prevails is that things must be known in their genesis or development, through an analysis of changes. But Grant himself does not try to define 'time as history' historically, that is, by tracing the development of historical consciousness. He does not do what he did ten years earlier, in his lectures introducing moral philosophy. Instead, he focuses on the thought of one thinker, Friedrich Nietzsche, in whose writings he finds the conception of time as history most luminously articulated. 'Nearly a hundred years ago Nietzsche thought the conception of time as history more comprehensively than any other modern thinker before or since. He did not turn away from what he thought. That is, for good or ill, he accepted "en pleine conscience de cause" that temporality enfolds human beings and that they experience that temporality as history. Yet he also understood, better than any other thinker, the profundity of the crisis that such a recognition must mean for those who have accepted it' (32). It means, for those who have accepted it, that they must abandon the traditional idea that mankind can attain knowledge of eternal realities, including fixed, absolute, or eternal standards of right and wrong. They must accept that even the meaning of progress will change from one era to another. Earlier thinkers lacked this radical sense of the dependence of our thinking on 'history.' They tried to cover over the radical contingency of human existence in time, claiming in various now discredited ways to have attained a sure knowledge of eternal verities. The outstanding and immensely influential example of this is Plato, who can be said to have postulated a fixed universe of unchanging beings, the forms or ideas, to provide a metaphysical foundation for the optimistic moral rationalism he had learned at the feet of Socrates.[7]

In trying to follow Nietzsche's thought about the limitations and deformities of human reason as it struggles to escape its inescapable destiny, we begin to see clearly what it is to live in this era. Nietzsche shows – and he is the first to show – how the effects of our deepening historical consciousness are to be recognized in every realm of existence. 'His thought does not invent the situation of our contemporary existence; it unfolds it' (34). By its unfolding or uncovering, it leads us to speak in new ways, as Grant explained in a later writing about Nietzsche. 'When we speak of morality as concerned with "values," of politics in the language of sheer "decision," or artists as "creative," or "quality of life" as praise and excuse for the manifold forms of human engineering, we are using the language first systematically thought by Nietzsche.'[8]

Historicism encourages historical scholarship – detailed investigations of the past – as one might expect, but to think historically is to be oriented not to the past, as one might at first suppose, Grant says, but to the future. 'Those who study history are concerned with the occurrences of passed time; those who conceive time as history are turned to what will happen in the future' (16). To abandon the idea of an unchanging fundamental reality – to accept the finality of becoming – is inevitably to encourage speculation about what the future holds and to motivate attempts to make it fit our desires. We take our bearings from imagined futures that seem desirable, and this is necessarily associated with striving for mastery and the cultivation of the kind of precise scientific knowledge that can increase our power to shape the future. 'The more we are concentrated on the future as the most fascinating reality, the more we become concentrated on that side of our existence which is concerned with making happen' (19–20). But our desirous and carefully observant 'technological' reasoning about how to produce the future states we desire, again contrary to what one might at first expect, is not so characteristic of our historical consciousness as is *willing*. To desire is to experience dependence on what one desires; while thinking, apart from willing, is contemplation. Both desiring and thinking are involved in willing – desiring in the determination of ends and thinking in the calculation of means. And it is, of course, scientific knowledge in its various forms that has given modern man his unprecedented power to shape the future. (Growing awareness of this mastering potential of progressive science and an increased understanding of its methods explain, more than anything else, Grant says, how the belief in progress gained its hold over the minds of men in recent centuries.) But in willing – in determining to make happen what is to happen – the dependence of desire passes over into the assertiveness of attempted mastery, and there is an end to contemplation: thought about possible consequences is suspended. 'Willing is then the expression of the responsible and independent self, distinguished from the dependent self who desires' (23). Willing requires an active rather than a contemplative or receptive thoughtfulness.

The historical sense is much more than just a wilful orientation to the future, however. It is ultimately the belief or background assumption that everything is always changing, that 'becoming' has displaced any knowable 'being,' and consequently that there is no permanence or eternity – nothing beyond the flow of events in time – in terms of which the changes we observe can be measured or limited or defined. There are just different relative rates of change – in flowers, in our own bodies, in stones, and in stars, for example (37). But there is nothing that is not in flux: even the universe and God have histories, as popular authors tell us. So the historical sense must also influence the responses we give to questions that are inseparable from human action. What is the right thing to do? What shape should the future have? What purposes should be served by our ever more effective science or technology? What are the wilful to will in their increasing mastery of the future?

The early modern thinkers who brought the new natural science to light and who began to trace its implications for politics and religion, and especially those who wrote at the dawn of the historical sense, two centuries ago, took for granted that there was ultimately something permanent to supply the measure or standard of change. There can be no belief in progress, as they propounded it, without some permanent standard of better and worse. 'Because they believed that the process of historical change manifested as a whole the growing power of rationality in the race, and because they assumed that rationality was "good," they could find in history the purpose of their existing. Scientists had increasingly been able to show that the non-human world could be fully explained without any idea of final purpose; but the idea of purpose was retained as the unfolding of rationality among the species, man' (38). Nietzsche's great innovation, Grant says, was to question the goodness of that growing scientific rationality.[9] Can one maintain the traditional exaltation of reason when its nature has been changed in modern science? Reason is no longer understood as our way of participating in the sovereignty of divine wisdom; rather, it is now seen as 'instrumental reason,' no more than a way of understanding and modifying our natural environment. Useful it is, undeniably, but can an instrument of adaptation be the purpose of existence? 'According to Nietzsche, in the light of the historical sense men have to give up belief not only in the transcendent ground of permanence (God is dead), but also in the moral valuations which accompanied the former, particularly the idea that our existing has its crowning purpose in rationality' (39).

To question the traditional valuations, as modern scientists do, quietly and indirectly, and as Nietzsche did openly and polemically, may be of the greatest interest from the standpoint of the philosopher, but it can create grave problems in practical life. Nietzsche pointed out that the growing historical sense of his own time was undermining confidence, particularly among the more sensitive, in those metaphorical 'horizons' – the absolute presuppositions of valuation and axioms of moral debate – within which people had been living and deciding what to do. These were coming to be seen as nothing more than human creations, part of the flux of history. 'They are man-made perspectives by which the charismatic impose their will to power. The historical sense teaches us that horizons are not discoveries about the nature of things; they express the values which our tortured instincts will to create' (40). But how then is one to be resolute in the pursuit of any purposes, if none is sustained in the nature of things, if even 'progress' is ultimately an arbitrary standard rather than a stable basis for human choices? Once we know that all horizons of meaning are historically relative and man-made, they can no longer give us the framework we need in order to decide what is worth doing and to be resolute in our doing of it. The historical sense, as Grant says, 'casts a blight upon living' (39). This may not be immediately apparent, of course. The result may seem for a while like a moral holiday, relief from any demanding moral ideals or codes of conduct, permission to take it easy, to accept human nature as it is, even if this means a slow slipping back into animality. But this is not the end of the matter.

The historical sense also opens the way for an account of justice that carries us, as Nietzsche proclaimed, 'beyond good and evil.' What did he mean by this notorious phrase? What exactly lies beyond the old accounts of what is praiseworthy and contemptible, summed up in his contrast between good and evil (*gut und böse*)? What are we to embrace under the new teaching about good and bad or good and ugly (*gut und schlecht*)? Nietzsche's new teaching obviously has political implications, even when they are not spelled out.[10]

In *Time as History* Grant does not deal with Nietzsche as a political thinker, but in the later writing mentioned a moment ago, 'Nietzsche and the Ancients,' he quotes three unpublished fragments to show that 'his teaching about justice is at the very core of what he is saying.'[11] It becomes clear that justice, for Nietzsche, was 'the building, rejecting, annihilating way of thought which proceeds from the appraisement of value.' It derives from 'a power with all encircling vision, which sees beyond the little perspectives of good and evil, and so has a wider advantage, having the aim of maintaining something which is more than this or that person.'[12] What is given in these quotations, Grant says, is 'an account of justice as the human creating of quality of life.'[13] It amounts to saying that 'politics is the technology of making the human race greater than it has yet been.'[14] And there will inevitably be human beings standing in the way of that great enterprise to whom nothing will be due – other than extermination or enslavement. 'Human beings are so unequal in quality that to some of them no due is owed. What gives meaning in the face of historicism is that willed potentiality is higher than any actuality. Putting aside the petty perspectives of good and evil means that there is nothing belonging to all human beings which need limit the building of the future.'[15]

The great writings of Nietzsche's maturity are his attempt to overcome the dangerous and depressing effects of the historical sense. Grant's polished little chapter on those writings, brief as it is (a mere thirteen pages), provides the best possible stimulus to read what Nietzsche wrote or to recall what one has already read. Grant begins with Nietzsche's conscious parody of the New Testament, at the beginning of *Thus Spake Zarathustra*, and in particular his depiction of the 'last men' – the weak-willed creatures whose petty conceptions of justice and happiness (equal comfort and entertainment for all) are the vulgarized residues of Christianity and the doctrine of progress: 'Because this happiness is to be realized by all men, the conception of its content has to be shrunk to fit what can be realized by all. The sights for human fulfilment have to be lowered. Happiness can be achieved, but only at the cost of emasculating men of all potentialities for nobility and greatness. The last men will gradually come to be the majority in any realized technical society' (44). The counterpoint to the last men are the nihilists – those who have understood that all values, being relative and man-made, cannot provide the fixed standards for action they need, but who, being men of strong will, cannot give up willing. 'They assuage their restlessness by involvement in mastery for its own sake' (47). Their undisciplined and undirected – and, thanks to experimental science or technology, ever more effective, wide-ranging, and disruptive – domination over human and non-human beings promises a global future of violence without end.

The question posed by Nietzsche is whether, without indulging in any fanciful ideas of turning back the clock, there is an escape from a world of last men and nihilists. As Grant says, 'the question is whether there can be men who transcend the alternatives of being nihilists or last men; who know that they are the creators of their own values, but bring forth from that creation in the face of chaos a joy in their willing which will make them deserving of being masters of the earth' (47). For Nietzsche, it seems, the answer lies in redemption from the spirit of revenge by which mankind has been tormented in the past because of the way their instincts have been frustrated by social and natural restrictions. But this redemption is not to be understood as a natural process, with a predictable outcome, like the course of recovery from a disease or the development of society according to any 'iron laws of history.' It must be more like a lucky stab in the dark – no more than the possibility that Nietzsche associates with the appearance of men who have transcended the old alternatives and overcome the spirit of revenge, his infamous 'supermen' (*Übermenschen*). These are the 'blond beasts' whose recovery from the spirit of revenge will mean that their willing, whatever they will, will be creative rather than resentful and destructive. Nietzsche says that the mark of their recovery will be their *amor fati*, that is, their love of fate. But this love will undeniably have to be attained by an act of will in relation to an unchangeable, not even fully knowable past, individual and collective, that has evidently been full of pain and evil. Grant quotes Nietzsche: 'To transform every "it was" into "this is what I wanted" – that alone I could call redemption' (54).

In his final chapter Grant shifts from explaining Nietzsche's understanding of time as history and its potentially paralysing effects on life to an evaluation of his proposed remedy. Very briefly, to simplify some concise but evocative formulations, love of one's fate is perhaps something that can never be *willed*. Must it not be the response to something seen as beautiful? Is not love the response of the needy and desirous person to what is beautiful?

My purpose is not to spare readers the trouble of reading a short and beautifully written little book. Grant's thoughts about loving and desiring are best understood by reflecting on his own words. My aim has been quite limited: to help those reading Grant to pick up the train of thought in *Time as History* that culminates in Grant's statement of what he calls the argument for perfection, 'namely, that human beings are not beyond good and evil, and that the desire for good is a broken hope without perfection, because only the desire to become perfect does in fact make us less imperfect' (60).

A related but subordinate purpose has been to highlight some changes in Grant's thought from the 1950s to the 1970s. Evidently, he moved away from the basic assumption of *Philosophy in the Mass Age*, that historical man and his 'progressive' understanding of morality are best approached historically, by recounting various events that can constitute a history of its development. Instead, he focused on the outcome of the process in the writings of one great thinker, and it yielded a view of our situation that is as bleak as anything Grant ever wrote. There are no longer – as there had been in 1959 – any allusions to the overcoming of the distinction between mind and the world in the Absolute standpoint. Gone is the earlier suggestion that the striving for freedom for all – the recognition of everyone's subjectivity – is somehow the ultimate goal of the historical process. There is no longer any anticipation of any possible 'dawning of the age of reason in North America.' Grant is now dreading the real prospect of centuries upon centuries of the domination of public life by a destructive alliance between those with a trivial view of human happiness, the 'last men,' and their servants and masters, 'the nihilists,' who are unable to believe that any good purpose will be served by their exercise of power, but who are also unable to resist their drive to impose themselves on others. This is the prospect offered by Nietzsche's analysis of our situation, Grant says, and his remedy for it – the overcoming of the spirit of revenge by a new breed of masters who have learned to love their fate despite its being enfolded in time – is one that Grant finds incredible.

With respect to the historical events that have produced this situation and the historical accounts that can give it the appearance of progress, Grant is now much less inclined to generalize. To be sure, we must understand our origins in order to know ourselves and our world, and there is no denying that it was from sources in the ancient world that the modern conception of time as history arose in the West. But these sources have been so overlaid and so obscured by the massive criticism of more recent thinkers, including Nietzsche, and their objections have so penetrated every part of our education, Grant now says, that we cannot hope to reach back easily – as seemed at least possible in the 1950s – to make those remote origins present. Grant's later writings emphasize the difficulty of recovering past thought and of synthesizing it with whatever has been revealed of truth and goodness in more recent times. In *Philosophy in the Mass Age*, he did not assert that he or any other thinker (Hegel being the most relevant possibility) had succeeded in doing this, but the whole presentation of moral philosophy in that book was given its direction by the assumption that such a synthesis was a realistic possibility. In *Time as History*, by contrast, the emphasis at the end is entirely on the difficulties in the way of any 'conservative' appropriation of negated traditions. For example, to think of 'morality' as Grant suggests the ancients did – 'as desiring attention to perfection' – requires that we put aside the modern understanding of it as a self-imposed demand of practical reason, and this is far more easily said than done. Modern assumptions are built into our language and thus into all the readily available and publicly respectable accounts of our tradition. What we most need from ancient authors is thus likely to come to us as apparently unintelligible or arbitrary assertions. There is no easy way to fill the gaps and correct the distortions of the conventional accounts. It requires a kind of 'remembering' that must rely upon scholarship but that will be at odds with the deeply rooted tendency of most scholars to turn the thought of the past into a preparation for the perfected thought of their own time.

By 1970, Hegel had evidently been eclipsed in the background to Grant's thinking by Nietzsche and (less evidently) by those contemporary scholars and thinkers mentioned earlier who offered fundamentally different alternatives to the conventional accounts of the 'progress' or 'modernization' that has produced our modern way of life. In particular, in the 1960s Grant's long-standing reservations about progressive thought had been clarified and reinforced by his discovery of Martin Heidegger and Leo Strauss.

With respect at least to the interpretation of Nietzsche, it is not difficult to demonstrate a connection between Grant and Heidegger. For example, the three fragments about justice that Grant quotes are analysed at length in the lectures on 'Nietzsche's Metaphysics' that are part of Heidegger's *Nietzsche*, and Grant adopts Heidegger's interpretation of these fragments. As Heidegger summed it up, 'justice looks beyond to that sort of mankind which is to be forged and bred into a type, a type that possesses essential aptitude for establishing absolute dominion over the earth.'[16] Yet this is not at all to say that Grant simply took over Heidegger's wide-ranging agreements and disagreements with Nietzsche. These relate to the most fundamental and elusive principles of their thought and are not to be summed up somehow in a sentence or two, the meaning of which will be obvious.[17]

Strauss provides no less of a challenge, and with respect to what Grant wrote about Nietzsche, it is not so easy to show any direct connection. Nonetheless, Strauss is most definitely present in the background to Grant's interpretation, as should not be hard to imagine. There is no denying Strauss's fascination with Nietzsche's writings, as of Grant with those of Strauss. Like Heidegger, Strauss had been, from an early age, deeply influenced by Nietzsche's historicism. Strauss shared the disdain of both his great predecesors for the academic (idealist, materialist, neo-Kantian, etc.) philosophy of the professorial establishment. As a student (as he explained much later), he had also been deeply impressed by Heidegger's independence and seriousness, at the time when he was reviving interest in the question of the meaning of being. Is it right to say, as Nietzsche seems to be saying, that there is no such thing as being, but only becoming? Are we given nothing that simply is without qualification? (Nothing like the Exodus proclamation 'I am that I am'?) Heidegger's reflections led him to become, in Grant's words, 'the consummate historicist,' while Strauss became the great antagonist of historicism.[18]

For the clarification of historicism – of time as history – Grant turned to Nietzsche, saying that he 'thought the conception of time as history more comprehensively than any other modern thinker before or since.' But his own response to Nietzsche parallels that of Strauss, mixing high praise (and scorn for those who would 'inoculate' others against his writings) with a refusal to accept what he taught, even though he could not pretend to base his refusal on any clear and decisive refutation of Nietzsche's claims. Ten years after his Massey lectures, in 'Nietzsche and the Ancients,' he said that one must read Nietzsche if one would understand modernity. 'One must read him as the great clarion of the modern, conscious of itself.'[19] Of course, the modern is not necessarily the good for Grant or for Nietzsche (or Heidegger or Strauss), even if many today treat them as equivalent. So the crucial question is how and to whom Nietzsche should be taught. Grant answered this question as someone within the philosophic and religious tradition that Nietzsche rejected – 'as a political philosopher within Christianity.'[20] From this standpoint, Nietzsche's rejection must itself be rejected. 'The teacher who is within the philosophic and religious tradition, and who also takes upon himself the grave responsibility of teaching Nietzsche, must do so within an explicit understanding with those he teaches that he rejects Nietzsche's doctrine. If I were not afraid of being taken as an innocent dogmatist, I would have written that one should teach Nietzsche within the understanding that he is a teacher of evil.'[21] The justification for this harsh position is the practical danger associated with the diffusion of Nietzsche's relativizing account of justice. The reason for teaching him nonetheless, despite this danger, is the help he can provide in reaching a more satisfactory account of justice. Nietzsche is the great critic of Plato, and with the help of his criticism, one can more easily penetrate to the deepest assumptions of Plato's thought. 'A man with philosophic eros was recently asked the rather silly question: "At what period of time would you best like to have lived?" He answered that he was lucky to have lived in the present period, because the most comprehensive and deepest account of the whole has been given us by Plato, and the most comprehensive criticism of that account has been given us by Nietzsche. In the light of that criticism, one can better understand the depth of the Platonic teaching. That is, one should teach Nietzsche as the great critic of Plato ... His criticism of Plato is root and branch. In the light of it the modern student may break through to what the Platonic teaching is in itself.'[22]

In short, Grant associated 'radical historicism' with Nietzsche rather than with any of the 'softer' modern relativists. He rejected that historicism, without fully spelling out his reasons for doing so, but these reasons appear to be essentially practical rather than theoretical, though it is by no means clear how the distinction should be made here between theory and practice. But Nietzsche may have been pointing in the wrong direction when he said that 'autonomous' and 'moral' are mutually exclusive.[23] Is human freedom rightly understood if it is understood to mean that the finest and noblest human beings should feel liberated to ignore conventional morality, or perhaps even obligated to violate its constraints, for the sake of humanity's future development? Should the best feel bound only by their own commitments to 'higher values' as these have become apparent to them from their imaginative reconstructions of humanity's past and their visionary projections of its possible future? Or is freedom perhaps better understood as something whose attainment requires scrupulous respect for the rights and dignity of others? Could the ancient rationalists have been closer to the truth when they tried to demonstrate the reasonableness of justice as conventionally understood, even from the perspective of those with the highest ambitions and the greatest autonomy? Were they perhaps right to focus, not on humanity's future development, but on its present existence within an eternal order? These are all questions that come to light in a new way in the writings of Leo Strauss.

10 Platonic Political Philosophy

Among the great political thinkers of the twentieth century – Arendt, Berlin, etc. – Leo Strauss is a remote, mysterious, somewhat sinister figure. He is known as a conservative, but his conservatism is hard to pin down. He refuses to be pushed into any of the standard categories. Until recently, his most visible impact was on a few of his own students who have had distinguished academic careers in a variety of disciplines. His writings are either too simple or too complicated to reveal much to most readers. He wrote no big books on big topics that made big splashes and no popular biographies of major modern thinkers. Apart from some topical essays, his writings are very detailed, sometimes rather convoluted commentaries on ancient, medieval, and early-modern philosophers.[1] He was a scholar's scholar, at odds with the modern 'republic of letters,' and he suffered its enmity in return. In recent years, his reputation has been tarnished by the association of some of his students (or students of his students or friends of students of his students) with American foreign policy in the Middle East.[2]

Much about Strauss becomes clearer when his thought is seen as a response to 'historicism.' Strauss wrote very little about Hegel and his successors and gave almost no indication of his interest in their thought, apart from occasional, somewhat oracular references to 'the crisis of the West.' But he laid the responsibility for that crisis – 'the crisis of modern rationalism' – at the feet of 'historicism,' and it is easy to imagine that the questions that Nietzsche, in particular, had posed were never far from his mind. Indeed, much of the difficulty of attaining a clear understanding of Strauss can be traced to the difficulty of seeing his writings, so different in style, as nonetheless a response to those of Nietzsche and Heidegger. The challenge for the interpreter is neither to deny their affinities nor to exaggerate their similarities.[3]

Only those who have felt the force of Nietzsche's observations and arguments (and jokes) are likely to give much thought to how one should respond.[4] For a variety of reasons, he has been easy to dismiss and ignore in the English-speaking world, even though his influence is everywhere. Once discovered, however, the usual ways of brushing him aside – as a mad poet who had no understanding of science, or as a racist and proto-Nazi, or as the kind of amateur philosopher who appeals to high school students and autodidacts – cease to be of much interest. He brings too much out of concealment that others cannot see or dare not say. As Grant put it, 'he articulates what it is to have inherited existence as a present member of western history.'[5] Or in Nietzsche's own words, which Grant quotes, 'after you had discovered me, it was no trick to find me; the difficulty now is to lose me.'[6]

Of course, many of the sharp differences of opinion about Strauss noted a moment ago (and in the introduction to this part of the book) have much simpler explanations than the difficulty of sorting out his ambivalent relation to a paragon of political incorrectness. Strauss developed and expressed many of his ideas through detailed commentaries on the writings of earlier philosophers who are now rarely read with any care except by specialists. The reader of Strauss's works must already have some familiarity with the basic texts being discussed – and these range over the whole history of ancient, medieval, and early-modern thought – before the true character and contribution of Strauss's interpretation can begin to appear, and even then it is hard to separate Strauss's ideas from their scholarly context. For example, when reading his remarkable study of Machiavelli, one sometimes wonders whether one is hearing Strauss speaking, or Machiavelli, or Strauss speaking through Machiavelli. Different reactions to his writings also reflect different presuppositions about the subject matter and methods of philosophy and its relation to the social sciences, as will be explained below. (Was Machiavelli really a philosopher or a social scientist?) But in the end, it is crucial to see the relation of Strauss's writings to the kind of historicism represented by Nietzsche. Strauss's scholarly investigations, despite their extremely academic appearance, touch basic and disturbing political questions in a surprisingly direct way, and this obviously helps to explain both the enthusiasm for his work and the hostility it arouses.

My reason for writing about Strauss in a book about George Grant is to clarify Grant's thinking on the fundamental questions raised in the last two chapters. For example, is there a natural standard of right and wrong, and if so, what is it? How are we to account for the diversity of laws that people have felt obliged to obey and the customs and values they have honoured – what Nietzsche called the thousand and one goals of mankind? Is this diversity not factual disproof of the idea of a universal standard of right and wrong? And how should all the changes in political theory and practice from the ancient world to the present time be understood – as progress or as decline? Should people today be advised to accept the conventions of liberal-democratic societies or should they be urged to rebel against the injustices and mediocrity they see around them?

Grant's connection with Strauss was almost entirely through his writings. He is one of the few who became a 'Straussian' – using that term loosely – without having been his student or the student of a student, but simply from reading his published writings.[7] Grant seems to have been reluctant to write much about Strauss (he wrote one article which will be discussed in detail in chapter 12), and he did not often cite his works, but what he did say about him leaves no doubt about how deeply he felt he was in his debt. His most revealing statement is in the Introduction he added to *Philosophy in the Mass Age* when it was reissued in 1966. There Grant says that the book had been written seven years earlier under the shadow of Hegel. 'I considered Hegel the greatest of all philosophers. He had partaken of all that was true and beautiful and good in the Greek world and was able to synthesize it with Christianity and with the freedom of the enlightenment and modern science.' But reading Strauss had in the meantime shown him how unfounded was Hegel's claim to have preserved the basic truth of ancient moral philosophy ('that we live in an order for which we are not ultimately responsible') together with that of modern thought ('that we are truly and finally responsible for shaping what happens in the world') in a synthesis that was superior to both of its elements.[8] Stating the point more broadly, one could say that Strauss clarified and strengthened Grant's reservations about the modern Anglo-American liberal thought that he had already criticized in journal articles as well as in his first book, and he extended it to cover the German idealists, in whose writings Grant had been schooled. More generally still, Strauss confirmed Grant's belief that the truth of the ancient 'metaphysical' understanding of freedom could not easily be reconciled with the modern liberal-democratic understanding of it as autonomy.

Strauss, like Grant, took his bearings from a basic contrast between ancients and moderns. He maintained that there was a broad agreement among the ancient philosophers that sets them apart from most philosophers of the modern age. Without denying the differences between Plato and Aristotle, for example, Strauss insisted that they both accepted certain fundamental principles that were also accepted by all the major thinkers up to Machiavelli. On the other hand, most modern thinkers, such as Locke and Kant, for example, despite the variety of their doctrines, also shared important common premises that would have been rejected by the ancients and their successors. More important than the undeniable differences among the ancients and among the moderns, then, are the differences that divide the ancients from the moderns, according to Strauss.

His development of this theme is perhaps most easily explained by discussing the ambiguous terms 'natural law' and 'natural rights.' When we speak of what is naturally right or just or of a person's natural rights or basic human rights, we bring to mind the differences that can exist between what is inherently right or just and what the laws or government or social conventions of a given community may require. We imply that what is right and just is not determined entirely by the political or other authorities. Positive law may be unjust, and prevailing customs may violate basic human rights, when judged by a higher standard. When we speak of unjust laws, unjust legal decisions, or unjust customs, we are necessarily invoking, whether we are aware of this or not, some 'natural' standard of right and wrong that we take to be higher than that of positive law and conventional opinion – unless, like John Rawls, we are appealing to the conventional opinions of a community ('our intuitions') against its positive laws. The reasons for invoking 'nature' as a standard, rather than convention, were among the questions that most concerned Strauss. What is the source of its authority?

Strauss's most accessible and certainly his most widely read book, *Natural Right and History*, analyses the emergence of the classic idea of natural right (and with it political science properly understood) out of the conventionalism that had prevailed among Greek thinkers immediately before Socrates. He shows its development in the writings of Plato and Aristotle and, more briefly, in those of their successors, particularly Cicero, Marsilius, and Thomas Aquinas. He contrasts their classic conception with the 'modern natural right' teaching of Hobbes and Locke, and the negative reactions to it – 'the crisis of modern natural right' – represented by Rousseau and Burke. As these groupings may suggest, Strauss presents an unconventional history, bringing together thinkers who are often presented as quite dissimilar (for example, Rousseau and Burke) and emphasizing instead differences that are sometimes minimized (for example, Locke and Aquinas). The analysis concludes (though the book actually begins) with a discussion of those advanced modern thinkers, exemplified by Max Weber, who maintain, and claim to demonstrate, that there is no standard of law and morality higher than the historically given 'ideals' of particular societies or political movements. These are the 'value-free' social scientists whom Strauss berates for their irresponsible relativism and complacency.

The basic problem addressed in *Natural Right and History* is the rejection of natural right by Weber and his predecessors in the name of history or 'the historical sense.' The 'natural right' defended by Strauss is the austere classical doctrine that by no means denies the variety of opinions about right that contemporary historicists (historians, anthropologists, sociologists, and others) like to emphasize. As Strauss uses the term, it refers to a demanding standard of human perfection that many individuals and societies may fail to achieve, or even to comprehend, for easily understandable reasons. The basic claim is a narrow one: for the individual, and thus ultimately for society, there is a natural, not just conventional, standard of right and wrong behaviour and thus of better and worse ways of living. There is a natural hierarchy of human ends and thus a natural order among the good qualities or virtues of a good person – 'a natural perfection of the human soul' – and this natural order provides a permanent if loose standard for legislation.[9] In other words, 'nature' provides a measure, independent of convention, by which laws and conventions and their applications in particular cases can in principle be judged.

'Natural right' in this sense differs from what is commonly meant by both 'natural law' and 'natural rights.' 'Natural law' suggests universally valid rules of action or principles of justice, like the practical social rules of the Ten Commandments. It is *law*, held to be universally recognized as the basis for social peace, and it leaves relatively little latitude for political judgment. 'Natural right' may be said, by contrast, to inhere in concrete decisions that are seen to be just, rather than in general rules that define justice in practice. 'Natural rights' – the most modern of these terms – suggests a shift in orientation or priority from the duties required by 'natural law' to the liberties of free individuals. 'Natural rights,' too, provide a standard of justice independent of and superior to positive law, but the basic idea has changed. The natural standard that the positive law and social conventions must now satisfy, if they are to be reasonable and just, is thought to be respect for the basic or inherent liberty of all individuals apart from or prior to society, a liberty that all are inclined to insist be respected as a condition for their loyalty to it. More broadly, 'natural rights' are the freedoms that all individuals should be given, so that they can live autonomously, in accordance with their own beliefs, interests, tastes, and so on. Rights, in this sense, are liberties; they define the boundaries of the private sphere that public officials, or the state, should never cross. Outside this sphere, rulers have discretion. Within it, each person is as free, in principle, to destroy himself as to perfect himself. The individual has rights, so to speak, to be wrong and to live badly.

To recount a history of changing beliefs is often, as noted earlier, to suggest that the latest stage in the process of development represents the closest approximation to truth or the most adequate account of whatever is in question. In fact, it may be almost impossible to present much earlier beliefs in a modern language without making them seem arbitrary or unintelligible assertions. But this was definitely not Strauss's desire, and it was his genius to give ancient philosophical writings an interpretation that brought them back to life, as it were, and made them the source of a real alternative to modern doctrines.

The interpretation of Platonic dialogues held a central place in Strauss's teaching. His commentaries showed how to understand them, not as poor substitutes for treatises, but as dramatic encounters between interlocutors who are still recognizable types, discussing basic problems of life no different, essentially, from those we face today. Although standard 'metaphysical' topics come up for discussion in these dialogues and his commentaries, the emphasis is on political or 'existential' questions, and the doctrines associated with 'Platonism' in the standard histories of philosophy – in particular, Plato's puzzling doctrine of ideas or forms – get relatively little attention.[10]

An unfamiliar picture of philosophy and the philosophical life gradually emerges from Strauss's various commentaries. The philosopher is Socrates and those who continue his quest for knowledge of 'the human things.' Philosophers are no mere 'underlabourers,' clearing away conceptual brush to speed the progress of the natural and social sciences. Nor are they the builders of comprehensive systems or the propounders of abstruse doctrines about unseen realms of the spirit. Rather they are the persistent investigators of the justifications for common beliefs. They are the first real social scientists, the founders of political science properly understood and still the best models for its true practitioners.

The Socratic philosopher is, as Plato has Socrates say in the *Apology*, a gadfly, pointedly questioning the pieties of his society, revealing the contradictions in its generally accepted beliefs, and clarifying its common purposes. But the object of his persuasion is normally 'the individual,' that is, the potential philosopher, and not the society as a whole or its representative assembly, as shown with special clarity in one of the most appealing of the dialogues, the *Gorgias*. The most important question is how one should live, and the contentious claim is that a certain persistent scepticism can transform one's life by gradually revealing what is truly good and worth pursuing.[11]

Strauss denied that the ancient philosophers were unaware of the facts of diversity and change or development that seem so important to modern philosophers with their 'sense of history.' Even though the ancients had obviously not experienced the horrors of the twentieth century, they knew as much as they needed to know about 'the horrors of history.' They knew as much as Machiavelli did about the differences between public and private morality and between normal and extreme political situations. They were not the dreamy metaphysical innocents that modern historians of philosophy have tended to make of them. They understood, as Strauss said, that 'natural right must be mutable in order to be able to cope with the inventiveness of wickedness.' But unlike Machiavelli, they were willing to leave 'these sad exigencies covered with the veil with which they are justly covered.'[12] Accordingly, they developed an 'art of writing' that allowed them to communicate frankly among themselves and with potential philosophers, but that kept their more radical teachings from disturbing the dogmatic slumbers of careless readers or needlessly provoking the more irascible defenders of established opinion.[13]

Strauss had a shrewd sense of what one can call the sociology of Socratic philosophy.[14] The Socratic philosopher may have little respect for the opinions that prevail among his compatriots; he may be deeply alienated from the enterprises they regard as most important; but, like all men, he needs the society of others and is threatened by the anger and potential hatred of his neighbours, as they may be by his sceptical questioning. For Strauss, the tension between philosophy and the law, including social convention, was a permanent condition. Philosophy seeks truth, but practical cooperation rests on agreement, and political leaders appeal to common opinions. It is not reasonable to expect that politics will ever be the realm of truth rather than opinion, for this would require the philosophic 'enlightenment' of the mass of mankind. Neither the occupations nor the talents of most people make this a reasonable prospect. Rather, if philosophy is to exist, it must be by virtue of an accommodation between the demands of free inquiry and the requirements of institutional stability, and that accommodation must be more on society's terms than on those of the tiny number of philosophers.

The need for such an accommodation gives 'political philosophy' a double meaning for Strauss. On the one hand, the term can refer to the practical political teaching of the philosophers, addressed to the public's 'gentlemanly' leaders, to help them resolve their deadly quarrels, to elevate their practice of virtue, and to cool their superstitious ardours. On the other hand, it can mean the 'politic' presentation of philosophy, that is, 'the political, or popular, treatment of philosophy, or the political introduction to philosophy – the attempt to lead the qualified citizens, or rather their qualified sons, from the political life to the philosophic life.'[15]

The break with classical assumptions that constitutes modernity occurred, according to Strauss, when philosophers ceased to be willing to accept the classic accommodation between enlightening philosophy and unenlightened politics and law, and with it, an essentially unchanging hierarchical social order. The key figure in this revolt of the moderns, as Strauss reconstructs it, was Machiavelli. He complained, in effect, that hitherto the philosophers had only interpreted the world, but the point was to change it. To do so, political philosophers had to abandon their allegiance to 'imaginary kingdoms,' such as Plato's ideal republic, which could never be realized, as Socrates himself seems to say, and which serve only to discourage practical reforms. The philosophers must be bolder in trying to influence those who hold power. They must aim higher, in a sense, than the classical 'utopians,' with their fear of popular passions, had dared to imagine could be possible. Building on the low but solid or at least manageable ground of these popular passions (pride, greed, envy, fear of death, and the like), they must strive to create a new kind of society, one that eventually would be called 'enlightened,' in which human needs would be better satisfied, thanks to the taming of chance or the conquest of nature, and in which the persuasive power of the priests would be put to better use than it had been since Roman times.

Strauss's bewildering book about Machiavelli, *Thoughts on Machiavelli*, is in many ways the manifesto of the school he founded. On its first page it proclaims that 'we ... say that Machiavelli was an evil man.'[16] He was evidently not just an evil man, however, as the book goes on to show, for he was also the founder of modern political philosophy, who effected a break with the whole tradition of political philosophy up to his time. As an analyst of political life, he was both an acute observer and an audacious revealer, as all know who have studied his works with care and sympathy and as those who have the patience to follow Strauss's obscure and convoluted commentary will be shown. Strauss does not really object to Machiavelli's account of the differences between rulers and ruled and the mechanisms or principles of their interaction. On this front, his objection is only that Machiavelli is often given too much credit for originality.[17] His major objection, and his basic reason for treating Machiavelli as a teacher of evil, is his perversion and denial of philosophy as traditionally understood. Machiavelli unscrupulously lent the blessing of philosophy or intellect to what political thugs had always done, and this is objectionable, not so much because it encouraged them to do more of it (they had not been waiting for permission), but because it paralysed their most respectable opponents. Machiavelli's fascinating presentation of the necessity of a strictly political 'virtue' and his enticing invitation to philosophers to use it for the establishment of a new kind of republican society, one that would combine the political excellence of the small republics of the ancient world with the charity or compassion preached by the established religion, transformed the understanding of philosophy. Strauss cannot help but look with a cold eye on the promises that were made and the hopes that were entertained three or four centuries ago for 'new modes and orders,' but he also cannot help but admire the skill with which, as an 'unarmed prophet,' Machiavelli fought 'the powers of darkness' and blazed a trail for 'enlightenment.' He must be called a teacher of evil, Strauss says, but mainly because those who do not take this common opinion seriously enough are unable to do justice 'to what is truly admirable in Machiavelli: the intrepidity of his thought, the grandeur of his vision, and the graceful subtlety of his speech.'[18]

The project Machiavelli inspired drew philosophers into a new kind of esotericism, not as 'seductive' and 'protective' as the old had been, but more manipulative, with a view to transforming the conditions of existence. The transformative ambition and active or manipulative character of modern political thought becomes clearer as the modern project matures and later philosophers, such as Kant, Hegel, and Mill, reveal more openly their desire to make the existing popular faith no longer an otherworldly superstition (or 'positive religion') but a truly moral religion dedicated to promoting the good of a progressive humanity. According to Strauss, this broad movement, initiated by Machiavelli, develops in three distinct stages or 'waves of modernity,' not unlike the 'three waves of paradox' in Plato's *Republic*, each one more fantastic than the last.[19]

The first wave was that of the early moderns up to Montesquieu, who aimed no higher than building stable regimes dedicated, in a utilitarian or bourgeois spirit, to the solid security and comfort of their citizens, or, in short, 'to practical, pedestrian hedonism.'[20] This is the kind of modernity still represented, Strauss thought, by constitutional democracies such as Canada and the United States.

Strauss's second wave was initiated by Rousseau's passionate protest against the degradation of man – the corruption of morality – implicit in any dedication to commerce rather than republican political virtue. The aspiration that defines this second wave is clearest at its beginning and end, that is, in the thought of Rousseau and Marx. Very broadly, they proposed to create societies that would more adequately recognize the fundamental equality of all individuals than was possible given the understanding of natural rights promoted by the early-modern thinkers. In reaction against bourgeois inequality and the Lockean-Hobbesian understanding of nature that gave inequality a modern philosophic justification, they proposed a more radical naturalism, appealing directly to the freedom and equality of primitive man for their standard of justice in civil society. The attainment of justice, insofar as it was attainable (and Rousseau's dreamy escapism obviously differed from Marx's indefatigable conspiring), would depend on the construction of institutions that would automatically yield results that were just for all individuals, that is, would ensure the proper recognition of every person in his or her freedom or autonomy. Marx understood that the attainment of this ambitious goal of a cosmopolitan egalitarian society would depend, ultimately, on the blind selfish passions at work in history, as it had been in the theories of his great preceptors, the classic German idealists, Kant and Hegel.[21] The aim of Marx as an economist was to show what those passions really were and how they worked.

Perhaps the most striking feature of Strauss's narrative account of modern political philosophy is its inclusion of Edmund Burke as an example of the second wave of modernity. Strauss dissented from the standard accounts of Burke's thought which emphasize his rejection of the theories that underlay revolutionary politics. 'His intransigent opposition to the French Revolution must not blind us to the fact that, in opposing the French Revolution, he has recourse to the same fundamental principle which is at the bottom of the revolutionary theorems and which is alien to all earlier thought.'[22] The fundamental principle or premise in question here has to do with the modification of the traditional belief in divine providence, usually described as 'secularization.' According to Burke, processes of historical development not guided by human reason are nonetheless beneficial – the source of a healthy political order – because they are part of a providential order. We know this, not as an article of religious faith, but because providence is amenable to scientific study. In other words, contrary to the traditional view, divine providence is scrutable to sufficiently enlightened minds, and practical politicians can take their bearings from the right historical interpretation of the past, rather than having to rely upon any divine revelation in the form of a higher law. The distinction that Strauss makes here between traditional and 'historicist' political thought derives from the basic distinction he makes between ancients and moderns. In his view, the ancients were the more thorough-going rationalists, while the moderns, including Burke, are the more hopeful as well as the more 'scientific' and 'empirical' thinkers. Among the moderns, Burke is a voice of moderation, and thus in a sense a 'conservative,' but he is still at bottom a modern and in some ways more modern than his more 'unhistorical' predecessors.

The third wave – the wave that bears us today – Strauss credits to Nietzsche and his disgusted reaction to the levelling tendency of modern society. It is distinguished from the second wave by the radicalization of Burke's historicism. Nietzsche denied that the historical process is rational or predictable. The horizons of meaning within which men think and act are simply the creations of great individuals and are not susceptible of rational demonstration or justification. He called for a new age of creativity, dominated by his Supermen (*Übermenschen*), those who would create the new horizons that would give a new and better shape to humanity. 'Nietzsche's call to creativity was addressed to individuals who should revolutionize their own lives, not to society or to his nation. But he expected or hoped that his call, at once stern and imploring, questioning and desirous to be questioned, would tempt the best men of the generations after him to become true selves and thus to form a new nobility which would be able to rule the planet. He opposed the possibility of a planetary aristocracy to the alleged necessity of a universal classless and stateless society.'[23] For obvious reasons, this stern and imploring call reached more receptive ears before 1914 than after 1945. Its meaning – 'relative to history' – had changed with the change in the historical circumstances of its recipients. Many of those who had been most eager to answer the call for a new nobility had shown themselves singularly lacking in that quality.

The crisis of modernity as Strauss presents it is the loss of belief in natural standards of right and justice together with our inability to find any satisfactory substitutes for them in theories about economic development, historical progress, or human creativity. Thus we find ourselves today in the midst of the grandest, most daring political experiments – communism, capitalism, globalism – without any reason to believe that our political scientists – academic, bureaucratic, and democratic – know what they are doing. The experiments are being conducted on the basis of the deepest and most openly proclaimed doubts about the principles that are to guide us towards the goals that we have envisioned. The remedy, according to Strauss, does not lie in trying to harmonize the modern sense of man's freedom and responsibility with the ancient world's sense of dependence and natural limits, as Grant had said in 1959. Rather, we should simply return to the thought of the ancients. This does not require us to return to the ancient polis or an agricultural economy, nor is Strauss suggesting that we replace research institutes and think tanks with visits to a Delphic oracle. As he explained in another context, 'once certain customs, beliefs, or institutions have ceased to be an unquestioned element of human life, no deliberate effort can ever restore their original force. But what holds true of such public things does not apply to insights: those of former thinkers may be forgotten, [but] they can be recovered by unremitting effort.'[24]

My purpose in offering this bird's eye view of Strauss's account of ancients and moderns is, as I have already said, to provide a basis for more clearly understanding some elements of Grant's thought. The point is not to try to determine more precisely the influence of Strauss on Grant. It was obviously considerable, but, barring the discovery of some more detailed explanation by Grant himself of what it was, we cannot go much beyond the account he gave in 1966 from which I have already quoted.[25] And it should be clear that Grant would not have been as immediately receptive to Strauss's influence as he was had he not already been thinking along 'Straussian' lines.[26] The most important point of agreement between them has to do with the existence of an 'objective' overall good that provides public as well as private guidance. Both accepted a classical account of ethics rather than the modern notion of free will. Neither was prepared to accept the 'flattening' of experience – the 'oblivion of eternity' – entailed by the modern conception of human autonomy and contractual justice. It is less clear to what extent and in what ways they agreed or disagreed with respect to the interpretation of Plato. (Can one still be 'within Christianity' if the Plato one loves is the Plato Strauss uncovers in his interpretation of the dialogues?) The greatest clarification may therefore be in connection with those points on which Grant did not simply follow Strauss without demur. Platonic political philosophy, as Strauss explains it, is an austere rationalism that does not try to harmonize divine revelation or prophetic promises with science or philosophy. It does not exclude a priori the possibility of special revelation, but it tends ultimately to undermine belief in it. For a clearer understanding of this point, we must turn back to Strauss's first major publication, his 1930 study of Spinoza's critique of religion, which became available in an English translation only in 1965.

11 Theology and Politics

In 1965, looking back over all his scholarly studies and writing since his youth in the 1920s, Leo Strauss wrote that 'the theological-political problem has remained *the* theme of my investigations.'[1] This somewhat enigmatic but still revealing statement alludes to Strauss's first major publication, a lengthy study of Spinoza's *Theologico-Political Treatise* and to his personal and political reasons for undertaking a detailed study of Spinoza.[2] It testifies to the importance that the study of Spinoza had had in giving a distinctive direction to Strauss's subsequent scholarly work. An examination of these points may provide the best basis for a deeper understanding of Strauss's thought and thus for a clearer view of its significance for Grant and his reservations about it. Unfortunately, the examination must be quite detailed to be of any use. Consequently, this chapter may strike some readers as a needlessly lengthy digression. The next chapter has therefore been written so that this one can be skipped without loss of continuity.

'The theological-political problem' is an unusual but suggestive way of referring to the old and familiar – perhaps, indeed, ageless and inescapable – problem of reason and revelation. Much the same problem could be indicated by speaking of the conflict between science and religion or philosophy and theology or the challenge of free thought or that of scepticism. All of these expressions and other possible combinations of them point to the existence of different and sometimes conflicting sources of knowledge or belief, and they suggest, as well, different ways of life – that of the scientist or other inquirer who asserts a light to question and revise or reject received teachings as against one of respectful adherence to authoritative opinions and submission to those who espouse them.

In 1979, shortly after the death of John Diefenbaker, Grant wrote a brief appreciation of him for the *Globe and Mail*, in which there is a striking passage describing a difference closely related to the difference just indicated: 'Diefenbaker's principles were grounded in primary loyalties, and loyalty is the great virtue for political leaders. That it is a virtue is often denied in modern political thinking. Intellectuals are apt to believe that leaders should have well thought out "philosophies," which have arisen by putting all primary loyalties in question. But this is nonsense for the following reason. The virtue necessary for the political life are not altogether the same as those necessary for the contemplative life. The latter requires that one be open to everything, and this includes putting everything in question.'[3] In short, political action requires a firmer basis and political associations require more stable loyalties than the agreements that may exist for a time among those who scrutinize received opinions in the hope of weeding out unreasonable beliefs. The difference between ways of life that Grant describes is analogous to the familiar distinction between reason and revelation. Revelation can be the basis for stable loyalties (as well as intractable conflicts), while reason is more akin to sceptical questioning.

If we restrict our attention for the present to what is suggested by 'reason' and 'revelation,' we can clarify the problem by invoking two stock figures. On the one hand, simplifying a bit, there is the scoffer or 'free thinker,' exemplified today by the evolutionary biologist Richard Dawkins, who takes pride in having escaped the religious beliefs of his early years and who now puts his trust in the power of ordinary human reasoning, based on experiences accessible to all (or at least all scientists), for guidance in dealing with the challenges we encounter, individually and collectively. Such an unbeliever has little or no interest in the testimony and directives of any prophets or other representatives of religious insight or devotion. He and his fellows openly or covertly dispute the claims of the pious about the existence of an uncanny supernatural realm, the domain of a God or gods who take an interest in human affairs and who reveal themselves or their wishes to selected human beings, demanding human reverence or sacrifices and threatening to administer rewards and punishments in an afterlife, contingent on conformity with or refusal to obey their commands. For them, orthodox religious beliefs and traditional religious practices, far from being the portal to any ancient wisdom, are rather the residues of a simpler, less enlightened age, which now demand criticism and reform. The authority of priests or other religious figures has to be challenged, they believe, for it is only (they maintain, at the extreme) unassisted human reason, as embodied in the latest scientific discoveries and the most advanced philosophical doctrines, that can help us to make sense of our situation as human beings and to reach good decisions about what is ultimately worth doing. Such people can exemplify what is commonly meant today by reliance upon reason alone. On the other hand, there is the stereotype of the conventionally religious zealot, eager to impart his particular faith, impatient with scientific or philosophical objections, uninterested in the customs and beliefs of foreign peoples, and inclined, generally speaking, to be superstitious or dogmatic. The distinguishing marks of this figure are his lack confidence in the power or sufficiency of human reason as we know it, his assumption that mankind stands in need of supernatural assistance in order to settle what is good and lawful, and his conviction that God (or the gods), out of love for mankind, have made available, through the extraordinary experiences and inspired writings of particular prophets and other holy men or women, a sure knowledge of our origins and duties. He may accept the traditional beliefs and practices of his community and thus resist any innovations, or he may be found among the innovators. When he and his fellows are sufficiently numerous, they are likely to demand that orthodox religious devotion be rewarded in this life as an important social virtue and that religious instruction of a doctrinal character be part of the education of the young. (Not for them Jefferson's defiant claim that 'it does me no injury for my neighbour to say there are twenty gods, or no God,' for they know that such neighbours create problems for educators.) Those who have not themselves had any experiences of divine revelation can still share in its benefits, they contend, if they faithfully accept the teachings of those rare individuals to whom genuine revelations have been granted. In the formulation of laws and public policies, they maintain, the priests or other representatives of the correct faith should have a leading role or even an exclusive authority.[4]

To refer to this contrast and the conflicts associated with it as 'the theological-political problem' is to emphasize its close relation to fundamental questions about politics and morality. This relation will of course vary with circumstances, and it is by no means as visible in most Western societies today as it has been at many times and places in the past and as it remains even now in some of the poorer and more backward parts of the world. Nonetheless, even in our own advanced modern societies, rival claims to knowledge and authority, secular and religious, sometimes come into conflict over important practical questions, such as those of gay marriage or abortion. And one need think only of the contemporary Middle East to see that religion and religious differences can play a crucial role in the politics of wealthy societies. In earlier times, of course, questions about reason and revelation sometimes had a direct bearing on basic questions about the legitimacy of particular rulers and the acceptability of different forms of government. Even in tolerant, commercial Holland in the seventeenth century, which was the setting for Spinoza's discussion of philosophy, religion, and politics, the connection between theology and politics was much closer to the surface of everyday life than it usually is today.

Moreover, one should keep in mind that there are other orthodoxies and other forms of 'faith' and 'revelation' than the strictly religious – whatever exactly that is. As calmly unruffled as we Canadians today may be about sexual non-conformity or dissent from political orthodoxy, we have even less difficulty, on the whole, accepting religious diversity and challenges to religious authority. We are certainly more relaxed about denominational differences within Judaism and Christianity than were Spinoza's contemporaries. But this is not to say that we are altogether lacking in basic beliefs or core values. Indeed, our fundamental commitments themselves dictate a certain polite agnosticism or mild-mannered indifference to most of the theological controversies that agitated our ancestors. Religious tolerance is now treated as a cardinal virtue by our political and ecclesiastical authorities. Strong conventional religious beliefs are no bar to offices and honours, particularly when those espousing them show as much commitment to doing good for others in their deeds as in their words, but those who seem too sure of the truth of some questionable religious or political creed are likely to be seen as threats to the established order and frowned upon as 'extremists' or 'fundamentalists.' And needless to say, in other countries – in theocratic Iran, for example, or under a hereditary monarchy like that of North Korea – dissenters from the reigning orthodoxies are dealt with much more harshly than they are here, without the solicitude for the individual rights of dissenters that we have adopted as the best way of confronting the challenge of those who quibble about the truth or falsehood of our most important beliefs. Only those few among us who advocate terrorism or who blatantly preach hatred against identifiable groups must still live in fear – though admittedly not in any great fear – of the penalties of our Criminal Code.

Spinoza's *Theologico-Political Treatise* is perhaps the single most important source of the modern liberal understanding of toleration. His book is a masterpiece of persuasive writing which aims to show, as its subtitle announces, 'that freedom to philosophize can not only be granted without injury to Piety and the Peace of the Commonwealth, but that the Peace of the Commonwealth and Piety are endangered by the suppression of this freedom.' Spinoza held that the political authorities should cease to concern themselves with the defence or promotion of any particular religious orthodoxy. Professions of religious faith and the observance of pious practices should cease to be public obligations: they should be as much matters of private conviction and individual preference as beliefs about rival scientific theories or choices among hobbies and other harmless private pastimes. Only if religious belief were 'privatized' in this way and churches became voluntary associations did he think that there would be any respite from deadly religious quarrels. But before there could be such a displacement of religious doctrine as a basis for law and morality, religious faith itself would have to be revealed as much more questionable than it was generally assumed to be in pre-modern European societies. To discredit belief in religious doctrines, in a context of unquestioned belief, or in other words, to make more insistent and less threatening the natural doubts inseparable from professions of belief in 'things not seen,' was the real challenge that Spinoza faced, and his success in meeting this challenge – his insidiously persuasive encouragement of the most far-reaching disbelief – accounts for the great influence that his book has had and its continuing interest for us.

Behind a veil of respect for religious tradition and the authority of Scripture, Spinoza gives the basic terms of orthodox theology – God, revelation, prophecy, salvation, faith, miracles – radically new meanings consistent with his own naturalistic philosophy. Moreover, he supports his claims with quotations from the Bible while quietly ignoring passages that would tend to discredit his argument. Thus he gradually weans his readers away from their belief that the Bible, or any other similar 'sacred scripture,' could be a source of reliable knowledge of specific duties, as set out, for example, in the Mosaic code of laws or the Sermon on the Mount. He undermines the assumption that different interpretations of any sacred scripture could reasonably be a source of quarrels about what our duties really are. He uses the words of the Bible itself, literally understood, together with the long-standing disagreements between Christians and Jews regarding the meaning of many passages, to destroy belief in its authority as the inspired Word of God and to encourage, instead, not an allegorical or harmonizing interpretation of the problematic passages but the abandonment altogether of the traditional belief in revelation.

Spinoza thus has a double significance in the history of political and religious thought, first of all, as a model of rebellious freedom of thought, and subsequently, as an important source of our new secular orthodoxy. He was an extremely persuasive critic of the traditional reading of the Bible and indeed of the very idea of revealed religion; he was equally one of the most important sources of modern ideas about religious toleration and liberal democracy. On the first score, it is perhaps more difficult for us than it was for Spinoza's contemporaries to see his *Treatise* as a shockingly unorthodox analysis of the scriptural foundations of both Judaism and Christianity. It is a familiar fact, of course, that fourteen years before its publication he was excommunicated by the Jewish community in Amsterdam because of his subversive questioning of accepted doctrine, and later, after the book's appearance, that he was roundly condemned as a dangerous atheist by spokesmen for all the major varieties of European Christianity. But during the eighteenth century, Spinoza began to be seen, as he is often seen today, as the God-intoxicated herald of an edifying liberal interpretation of the Bible, who demonstrated that divine revelation, rightly understood, supports none of the dogmatic and exclusive claims of the warring religious sects that had traditionally appealed to it as the Word of God. Rather, the Bible is a wonderful collection of edifying stories that teach a universal ethic of charity, benevolence, freedom, and toleration.

What most engaged Strauss's interest in Spinoza's *Treatise* was its success in discrediting the very idea of revealed religion as traditionally understood, through its stringent criticism of prophecy and miracles. (As already suggested, Strauss took it for granted that there is a certain relation of mutual support between the Bible, as understood by Spinoza, and modern politics and morality: biblical religion has in fact become a prop for liberal democracy. But how sturdy a prop and of what value?) Strauss focused his attention on Spinoza's attempt, on the basis of a consistent naturalism, to discredit belief in the supernatural and thus the very possibility of a revealed religion. He assumed that the critique of religion pioneered by Spinoza was the inspiration and foundation for the modern liberal theory and practice of religious toleration and the source of the hope that punitive religion could one day be put aside in the building of an enlightened, secular, scientific society.[5] The apparent success of this modern critique has evidently been one of the main reasons for the confidence among the best-known modern philosophers, from the seventeenth century to the present, that their thought represents a decisive advance beyond the doctrines of the ancients and the scholastics. By the time Strauss took up the study of Spinoza, however, there were some important dissenting voices among writers and thinkers who were not at all identified with traditional religious faith. As we have seen, confidence in the superiority of modern rationalism was being shaken by the most modern philosophers, as earlier hopes for secular progress were fading. It was no longer clear that modern liberal principles should be seen as simply superior to the ancient teachings or that modern thought would not itself have to be surpassed, as ancient thought had been by modern thought. It was against this background that Strauss began his study of Spinoza, to determine whether a return to Jewish orthodoxy was possible for someone of 'intellectual probity' or whether the only tenable alternatives would have to be found among 'modern ideas' of one kind or another. A return to orthodoxy would be possible, he explained later, only if Spinoza was 'wrong in every respect.'[6]

Strauss began his study with a lengthy clarification of Spinoza's achievement in laying the foundation of a new kind of biblical study, in which scholars interpret the Bible as a literary document like any other, making it an object of the sciences of culture like all their other objects.[7] Such an approach presupposes a successful critique of the assumption that had guided earlier scholarship, namely, that the Bible is the divinely inspired and preserved record of God's special revelations and is thus quite *unlike* any other book. As Strauss wrote later, 'detached study presupposes detachment, and it is precisely the creation of detachment from the Bible that is Spinoza's primary aim in the *Treatise*.'[8]

Spinoza's critique consisted of two parts, a critique of miracles, as the apparent foundations in experience for the authority of the prophets, and a critique of the prophetic teachings themselves, not just the accounts of natural phenomena that one finds in the sacred books but also the moral insights of their authors. By thus fostering doubt about the credentials of the prophets and the substance of their teachings, Spinoza laid the foundations for an open-minded 'scientific' study of the Bible, using the methods of philology and history to explain some of its puzzling features, such as the inclusion of details about the death of Moses in a book supposedly written by him before his death. More specifically, it was Spinoza's critique of miracles, Strauss maintained, and not any principle of scholarly method he discovered or any hermeneutic genius he possessed, that demanded recognition as the true foundation of Biblical science in the modern sense. What still merited attention, Strauss held, were not Spinoza's achievements as a scrupulous and ingenious interpreter of the Bible, but rather his formidable objections to the very possibility of revelation or of revealed religion as such. As Strauss said of Spinoza's work at the beginning of his study, 'the context to which it belongs is the critique of Revelation as attempted by the radical Enlightenment.'[9]

Now the biblical narratives themselves, it seems, lead one to think that revealed religion can appeal to experience – the experience of miracles that have been observed or reliably reported – as the foundation for faith. The prophets in the past and their sacred writings today address not just believers but also doubters and unbelievers in need of persuasion. The prophets worked miracles and made astonishing predictions as evidence of their divine commission. It seems, therefore, that they were not relying for the justification of their claims on any mysterious gift of faith, granted or withheld by an inscrutable divinity. And the basic question the sacred books raise, according to Spinoza, is whether God can be known from miracles. To affirm that this is possible requires the assumption that miraculous events can be distinguished from the regular course of nature, and this in turn requires the assumption that we are already in possession of reliable knowledge of what can and cannot come to pass as a result of natural causes. Only on the basis of a full knowledge of the limited powers of nature could we be certain that the unusual events said to be miraculous were truly so. As Strauss explains this basic point, 'if anything is to be proven from miracles, then the miracle as miracle must be knowable to reason unguided by faith. Reason must be able to establish that a particular occurrence could not have come to pass as a result of natural causes ... The assumption on which the traditional conception of miracles rests is the possibility of final and conclusive judgments on what is possible within nature.'[10]

The traditional theological explanation of miracles as meaningful interventions by God in the regular course of nature thus rests on a distinction between divine action and natural regularities that Spinoza argued was ultimately untenable. Miracles require a lawful 'nature,' for it is the departure from the expected course of events that is thought to be meaningful, but miracles also require a God who is superior to 'nature': one force or power must be pictured as independent of the other and yet subject to its power. How is this possible, and how is it compatible with the biblical understanding of divine creation ex nihilo? If creation is the fundamental truth, then the idea of a miraculous departure from the natural order is put in doubt, since any natural order that is indeed the creation of an omnipotent and omniscient deity must be expected to be the complete and final expression of the divine will or divine reason. Is it possible to imagine – or rather, is it possible only to *imagine* – a mighty 'master craftsman' who, having created the universe to follow one course of development in time, subsequently 'changes his mind' in response to human pleading or the uncertain unfolding of human events, and thus has to fiddle with the details of his creation, tweaking it in various ways –. for example, making the sun stand still in the heavens for the better part of a day – to get around difficulties that an omniscient creator could have anticipated from the beginning? If not – if all of this is as fanciful as it may seem – then what are we to make of the bewildering number and variety of miracles found in the sacred texts?

Spinoza's basic contention was that the biblical authors had a primitive understanding of natural regularities and were far too ready to interpret rare and unexplained natural phenomena as the deliberate acts of a providential deity partial to their cause. Rather than accepting an unknown 'nature' whose powers – whose regularities and normal patterns of change – were far from being fully known, the biblical writers, unwilling to treat unexpected events as nothing more than challenges to their scientific understanding, assumed that anything at all unusual had to be seen as a wilful intervention by an omnipotent deity in the otherwise perfectly familiar pattern of events. In short, they separated God from nature, despite seeing everything as entirely a divine creation, and then experienced any departure from the most common regularities as the direct expression of an inscrutable divine will. As Spinoza says, 'whatever the Jews did not understand, being at that time ignorant of its natural causes, was referred to God ... Any quality whatsoever whereby one surpassed all others used to be referred to God in olden days, and not only by the Jews but by Gentiles too.'[11]

Strauss provides a clear explanation of the reasoning I have just outlined, but he does not endorse it. In his chapter on 'The Critique of Orthodoxy,' he outlines the basic arguments of Spinoza's *Treatise* in plain language, omitting only the many scriptural quotations and other supporting details of the original and avoiding the impious brio that is the mark of Spinoza's style when he is writing about the Old Testament. But in the book as a whole, this chapter (chapter V) is only the culmination of Strauss's explanation of the philosophical critique of revelation, and by no means the conclusion of his discussion of religion. Indeed, it provides the basis for a reconsideration of the merits of two classics of orthodox faith. In the following two chapters, Strauss directs his attention to those whose teachings Spinoza was criticizing, namely, Maimonides and Calvin, and to the challenge of understanding these earlier authors on their own terms. In these chapters Strauss clarifies two basic objections to Spinoza's critique. First, he shows that the doctrine of creation, far from being incompatible with belief in miracles, as Spinoza would have it, can be seen as the foundation for such a belief. And second, he shows that the relation between miracles and faith can be, as it were, reversed, so that faith, rather than being *based* on belief in miracles, directly observed or reported, can be seen as itself the *basis* for such a belief.

To understand the world as created by a God who is omnipotent wilfulness is to recognize its ultimately mysterious character, and it leaves open the possibility that the Creator, for reasons that are far beyond our understanding, may subsequently seem to act impulsively or capriciously in the ways that we call miraculous. 'Creation of the world is the pre-condition of miracles ... The world is what it is by virtue of having been determined by the will of a being who wills, and who as such can will that the world can be different. Miracles are therefore possible.'[12] Indeed, our bewildered awarenes of astonishing but apparently meaningful phenomena (abrupt changes in fortune, devastating plagues, amazing recoveries, startling coincidences, and the like) is an important argument for the mysterious createdness of the world as opposed to its eternal orderliness. And ultimately, as Calvin, for example, insisted, the so-called miracles of God's making are really no more miraculous than the ordinary working of God's providence in sustaining the familiar processes of nature. 'All events whatsoever are governed by the secret counsel of God,' he wrote. 'God is deemed omnipotent, not because he can act though he may cease or be idle, or because by a general instinct, he continues the order of nature previously appointed; but because, governing heaven and earth by his providence, he so overrules all things that nothing happens without his counsel.'[13] The real issue, then, as Strauss concludes, is not between two rival theoretical positions, one more adequate, the other less so, but between two radically different ways of relating to our social and natural surroundings. 'The issue here is not between a "rational" and an "irrational" *philosophy* but between the unbelieving and the believing manner of experiencing the world.'[14] In short, we are not in the realm of proof and disproof, but of different interpretations of an ambiguous experience, that is, different perspectives on life.

Similarly, Strauss draws from Calvin's *Institutes of the Christian Religion* the most radical, uncompromising statement of his second basic point, that religious faith, or belief in the authority of Holy Scripture, far from resting on the evidence of miracles, can itself be the basis for a belief in miracles. 'For as God alone can properly bear witness to his own words, so these words will not obtain full credit in the hearts of men, until they are sealed by the inward testimony of the Spirit. The same Spirit, therefore, who spoke by the mouth of the prophets, must penetrate our hearts, in order to convince us that they faithfully delivered this message with which they were divinely intrusted.'[15] In short, it is not because we have witnessed miracles that we believe, but rather because we believe that we trust the reports of miraculous events that we have been given.

What follows from these objections is not the *disproof*, that is, the complete discrediting, of Spinoza's critique, but rather the realization that both religious piety and philosophic inquiry must ultimately, according to Spinoza, have the character of faith or belief rather than knowledge. The proponents of orthodox faith, on the one hand, and science or theory as Spinoza understood it, on the other hand, 'stand directly opposed to each other without being able to arrive at agreement or even at mutual toleration.'[16] The problem cannot be avoided or overcome by somehow distinguishing religious from scientific 'truths' or 'language games.' The easy-going compromises according to which religion and science refer to altogether different kinds of experience or realms of being, the natural and the supernatural, so that they can never really come into conflict, regardless of their apparently contradictory assertions, are simply untenable. In fact, religion and science are diametrically opposed positions fighting for the same territory. 'These positions are not defensive positions, impregnable by virtue of a fundamental circle and on that very account inadequate for attack. Rather, the passionate faith in the justice of his cause compels each of the two opponents – it could indeed not be otherwise – to the attack!'[17]

The revelation that Spinoza rejects is admittedly not the same as the religion practised by believers (it might better be called the atheist's version of it), but he is right to think nonetheless that it makes claims to truth that are absolutely incompatible with the scientific or theoretical claims that rationalists such as himself hold to be true. Both are making claims about the 'external' or 'objective' world, not the inner world of our moral consciousness. But Spinoza proves nothing relevant, Strauss insists, in showing that the claims that believers make about miracles are *improbable* or even in establishing that miracles of any kind at all are simply *impossible*, given the philosophic understanding of nature, for it is this understanding of nature (as eternal, uncreated, lawful, etc.) that is ultimately at issue. Spinoza is at most proving something that his opponents would have no inclination to deny, if it were less provocatively stated – for example, 'nothing more than that it is not *humanly* possible that Moses wrote the Pentateuch, and that the text of a book should [have] come down to us through the centuries without any corruption of the text at any single passage.'[18] He is by no means *disproving* the fundamental premises of religious belief. As Strauss declares, 'the assertion that God is omnipotent cannot be refuted ... The assertion that God's wisdom is unfathomable cannot be refuted ... The assertion that God can perform miracles and did perform miracles cannot be refuted ...'[19]

Strauss attributed the enormous influence of Spinoza's *Treatise* and its continuing importance, not to the logical rigour of its main arguments, but to Spinoza's masterful employment of ridicule. His critique, despite its question-begging character, appeals to the prejudices of 'the positive mind.' By this expression, Strauss meant the assumptions about the growth of our knowledge and the gradual perfection of our methods of study that have been commonly accepted among 'enlightened' philosophers and their many followers since the sixteenth century. Thanks to historical progress, it is now widely assumed, we moderns are in possession of a far better understanding of nature and of human psychology than our distant ancestors had in the ancient world. Consequently, what they experienced as miracles, we can now explain scientifically or at least accept as nothing more than challenges to our scientific understanding. And in fact, miracles seem to have largely disappeared from our world – that is, from the modern, Protestant parts of it – presumably because we have become more aware of the lawfulness of nature and more inclined to question the value of the evidence offered for supposedly miraculous events.[20] Modern people are proud of their superior knowledge and thus inclined to contrast their own critical acuity and sober realism with the credulity and superstitions of earlier ages. 'From this point of view,' as Strauss says, 'it is easy to understand how mockery came to play so great a role in critique of religion in the Age of Enlightenment. The Enlightenment, as Lessing put it, had to laugh orthodoxy out of a position from which it could not be driven by any other means.'[21]

Mockery alone is clearly not disproof, however, and no matter how effective it may be in weakening a belief among large numbers of people, it can never suffice to destroy its possibility for any rational person. What Strauss later called 'the irrefutable premise' of all revealed religion – the belief in the existence of an 'omnipotent God whose will is unfathomable, whose ways are not our ways, who has decided to dwell in the thick darkness' – was essentially untouched by Spinoza's critique. To refute this premise, Spinoza would have had to demonstrate that 'the world and human life are perfectly intelligible without the assumption of a mysterious God,' and this he could not do.[22] Orthodox religious belief, as *belief* rather than as a claim to demonstrable *knowledge*, therefore remained a possibility, according to Strauss.

A problem remains, however. *Which* orthodox religious belief? How is one to decide where to put one's trust – in the revelation granted Mohammed, perhaps, or in the one reported more recently (and perhaps more reliably) by Joseph Smith? There are in fact many conflicting claims to revelations from supernatural sources, not all of which can be literally true, even if all can perhaps be given some higher symbolic or allegorical meaning that would somehow resolve their apparent contradictions and show their common 'core values.' And realistically, as Strauss points out, what most believers seem to regard as most important are not the common elements of the various revelations, but the points on which they differ. 'Revealed religion is essentially particular ... Reason is not opposed by the majesty of one single revelation, but by a number of theological systems, each of which is believed by its adherents to be the only true religion, and is defended against all other religions with narrow-minded zeal.'[23]

At the time he was writing his book on Spinoza, Strauss seems to have been interested only in the claims of the revelation said to be the source of his own religious tradition. Subsequently, he avoided directly addressing the problem posed by a plurality of conflicting revelations.[24] The main purpose of his study of Spinoza, as already explained, was to examine the possibility of a return to orthodox Judaism as the solution to the problem of the intellectually honest Jew lost in a secular world that was never religiously neutral, as it sometimes claimed to be, but always more or less openly hostile to Jews and Judaism. The difficulty apparently making such a return impossible was Spinoza's critique of belief in miracles and the importance of this belief for orthodox Judaism. An earlier generation of Jewish thinkers had levelled damaging objections to Spinoza's writings as unfair to Jews and Judaism, objections that Strauss seems to have thought were well justified.[25] But was Spinoza 'wrong in every respect' – that is, was he wrong with respect to miracles? Having established that he was – relying on arguments stated most clearly by Calvin – Strauss could return to his traditional religious beliefs, as could others, if they wished.

The question remains, however, why one might choose to pursue such a course. Possibility is not yet necessity or even probability, let alone obligation. Only in the chapter of *Spinoza's Critique of Religion* devoted to Maimonides does Strauss discuss some of the elements of what later became his distinctive treatment of the relations between reason, science, or philosophy, on the one hand, and dominant political or religious traditions, on the other hand. For Strauss, as for Spinoza, Maimonides represented the medieval 'dogmatic' rather than the more modern 'sceptical' conception of the relation between reason and Holy Scripture. To argue, as Calvin did, that reason must simply subject itself to the supra-rational or contra-rational revelation contained in Scripture is to hold a 'sceptical' view of the powers of unassisted human reason. Maimonides, by contrast, was a theological 'dogmatist' who held that Scripture must be understood in such a way as to remove any apparent conflicts between its teachings and those of reason or science. He was prepared, in other words, to put aside the literal or 'external' meaning of some biblical passages in order to overcome the apparent conflicts between revelation and reasonable belief, without abandoning revelation altogether.[26] For Maimonides, the authority of Scripture rested on historical proofs, that is to say, on the acceptance of a reliable tradition, but its literal meaning was to be considered binding on the faithful only so long as the contrary of what it said had not been proven. 'Everything that in its external meaning disagrees with [a demonstrated truth] must be interpreted figuratively,' he said, 'for it is known that such texts are of necessity fit for figurative interpretation.'[27] The authority of Scripture was thus protected and given a certain priority by making its interpretation subordinate to scientific insight.

Spinoza protested the rather surprising license with which Maimonides, following this rule, sometimes adapted the biblical texts to his preconceived opinions, but the fundamental difference between Maimonides and Spinoza, Strauss explained, was the difference between Spinoza's alienation from the Jewish community and Maimonides' loyalty to it. For Spinoza, philosophy was a matter of escaping from the prejudices of the past and constructing a new community on new principles; for Maimonides, by contrast, it was a matter of protecting and enlightening an existing community. Maimonides' works were not directed to the adherents of another faith or to unbelieving philosophers, but to believers who, because of their own reflections or their exposure to philosophical writings, had fallen into doubt and perplexity. The starting point and foundation for discussion was acceptance of the traditional faith. 'Maimonides is not setting up a pedagogic program by virtue of sovereign philosophy ... As a Jew, born, living and dying with Jews, he pursued philosophy as a Jewish teacher of Jews. His argumentation takes its course, his disputes take place, within the context of Jewish life, and for that context. He defends the context of Jewish life which is threatened by the philosophers in so far as it is threatened by them. He enlightens Judaism by means of philosophy, to the extent that Judaism can be enlightened ... Maimonides' philosophy is based in principle and throughout on Judaism.'[28] Unlike Spinoza, who was an apostate from Judaism living 'cautiously' remote from the multitude, Maimonides was a leader of the Jewish community – 'the philosophically enlightened rabbi, who feels himself responsible for the guidance of the multitude and who enjoys the people's confidence.'[29]

The basic shortcoming of Spinoza's critique of Maimonides, as Strauss presents it, is its failure to grasp what Maimonides' real problem as a philosopher was. It was not to justify revelation, or a theological doctrine of God's nature and providence, in the court of philosophical reason, by prudently interpreting the biblical texts or what earlier commentators had said about them so as to make them more compatible with the teachings of science or philosophy. He did this, but his prior or more fundamental problem was to justify philosophy before the tribunal of religion, that is, in the court responsible for the enforcement of a revealed law. The 'dogmatic' position of Maimonides can be defined, Strauss says, by its relation to two frontiers: 'In the face of orthodoxy [Maimonides] defends the right of reason, in the face of philosophy he directs attention to the bounds of reason.'[30] The second of these frontiers – dividing religious faith from unbelieving philosophy – is the one recognized as important by 'the positive mind.' It is the frontier that divides Spinoza and his successors, even to this day, from Maimonides and his successors. On this frontier, philosophy demands that revealed religion justify itself before the tribunal of unassisted reason and universal humanity. On the other frontier – the most important one in earlier times and still of some interest today – reason or philosophy is required to justify itself in the court of revealed, absolutely binding law. In this court, one might say, philosophy is not sovereign, for religious orthodoxy is.

Strauss devoted his next book, *Philosophy and Law*, to a careful investigation of the origins and distinctive teachings of the medieval rationalists represented by Maimonides.[31] The aim of the book, as he explained in its Introduction, was to 'awaken a prejudice' in favour of this older rationalism as the true natural model of rationalism, in opposition to the prevailing prejudice that the present age represents mankind's highest attainment of rational self-consciousness – a prejudice still firmly held even by those late-modern thinkers who prided themselves on having 'overcome' the 'shallowness' of Enlightenment rationalism. Of course, only through confrontation with Maimonides' genuine teaching could the superiority of his position be tested, and this would require a revival of the old conflicts between religious orthodoxy and the Enlightenment critics of that orthodoxy.[32]

From the standpoint of a revealed religion such as Judaism, the problem of philosophy was its implicit challenge to the authority and sufficiency of an exclusive revelation as a basis for the conduct of life. Revelation confronted the philosopher or potential philosopher within Judaism as a code of laws of divine origin that had to be obeyed. It imposed constraints not just on actions but also on thoughts, through texts that were commonly held to be of unquestionable, unconditional authority because of their supernatural origin. Given such a basis for social life, free rational inquiry, with its potentially disruptive consequences, requires a defence or justification. 'The first and fundamental task of medieval philosophy is the legal foundation of philosophy, that is, first of all, the demonstration that the men suited to philosophizing are obligated and thus authorized to philosophize by the revealed law.'[33]

Strauss traced Maimonides' way of dealing with this problem to Plato and to the Islamic Aristotelians who revived his teaching, in particular al-Farabi and Avicenna. But it was Maimonides' contemporary, Averroes, who provided, in his short *Decisive Treatise* (or Fasl-ul-

Maqal), the clearest systematic discussion of the legal foundations of philosophy in the relevant sense, and it is Averroes' argument that Strauss summarizes in order to explain Maimonides' thought.

The basic question discussed in the *Decisive Treatise* is whether, according to the revealed law of the Muslims, philosophy is forbidden, permitted, or commanded for those qualified to pursue it. This is a legal question, and Averroes, as an imam or jurist, was qualified to give a legal ruling (or fatwa) in response. The question was not whether philosophy is somehow above or independent of the law, but rather where exactly under the law it belongs. The law is sovereign and is assumed to provide all the knowledge needed for living rightly. Philosophy, which is understood to be the rational or scientific examination of the various beings, as exemplified by the writings of Aristotle, and thus to embrace natural science as well as metaphysics, is at best a supplement to the law, like syllogistic logic, which can clarify legal reasoning.

Averroes' argument is, in outline, that the end or goal of the divine law is the happiness of mankind, which consists in the knowledge of God, and this is promoted by philosophy. God is known through his revelation, but also through his creation, or the beings, the knowledge of which is philosophy. Therefore, philosophy has the same end as the law. Of course, the difficulty is that the Prophet – the immediate source of the divine law – sometimes spoke of things in ways that differ from the ways that philosophers such as Aristotle spoke of them. When there are such divergences between the Prophet's statements and the conclusions of demonstrative science, then the sacred texts are in need of interpretation, according to Averroes. That is, the texts should be understood figuratively rather than literally. Indeed, the figurative interpretation of such problematic texts is a *duty* for those suited to philosophy. In other words, the truths revealed in the sacred writings sometimes have an inner meaning that diverges from their apparent outward sense, and this inner meaning must be found in order to overcome the apparent contradictions, not just between philosophy and revelation, but sometimes even within the sacred text itself. Neither the contradictions nor their resolutions need to be widely known, however. Averroes believed that people differ greatly in their natural capacities and innate dispositions. The sacred writings are intended to instruct the multitude and not just the intellectually acute. For the latter, scripture is a challenge to their understanding. 'The reason why the Law came down containing apparent meanings that contradict each other is in order to draw the attention of those who are *well grounded in science* to the interpretation that reconciles them.'[34] Philosophers such as al-Farabi and Avicenna had been charged with unbelief because of their unorthodox treatment of issues such as the eternity of the world and the scope of divine providence. The solution, according to Averroes, was not to forbid philosophizing but to restrict the study of philosophic difficulties and the devising of interpretations to those few who have the talents and dispositions for such potentially disruptive reasoning.

Averroes distinguished three kinds of human beings, depending upon how they could be brought to assent to the truths of the divine law. 'One of them comes to assent through demonstration; another comes to assent through dialectical arguments, just as firmly as the demonstrative man through demonstration, since his nature does not contain any greater capacity; while another comes to assent through rhetorical arguments, again just as firmly as the demonstrative man through demonstrative arguments.'[35] Philosophy is the preserve of those occupying the first grade of 'excellence with respect to assent,' while revelation is adapted in its mode of expression to the multitude who are on the third level.

Averroes offers this rather simple but not unreasonable classification of intellectual aptitudes without apology or regret, and there is no suggestion that any good would come of trying to raise the intellectual level of the multitude so that it could better appreciate dialectical and demonstrative reasoning. The conclusion is instead that philosophers must necessarily adapt themselves, in some respects, to the capacities of the multitude, who will always be ruled – or rule – in accordance with their innate capacities. In short, philosophers need to practise a protective esotericism, proclaiming not their freedom to go wherever their investigations lead them but rather their prior conviction that their inquiries will never do no more than deepen and justify the knowledge accessible to all believers from sources other than philosophical reasoning. The freedom of the philosophers, as Strauss put it, will depend on their bondage. 'Philosophy owes its authorization, its freedom, to the law; *its freedom depends upon its bondage*. Philosophy is not sovereign. The beginning of philosophy is not the beginning simply; the law has the first place.'[36]

The aim of *Philosophy and Law*, as Strauss explained at the very beginning of the book, was to awaken a prejudice in favour of medieval rationalism – best exemplified for Strauss by Maimonides, but whose basic approach or presuppositions had been most clearly explained by Averroes – as 'the true natural model, the standard to be carefully protected from any distortion, and thus the stumbling-block on which modern rationalism falls.'[37] The modern rationalism of the Enlightenment and that of its successors differed from the rationalism Strauss favoured in being more ambitious but less intransigently rational. It aimed to bring, not just a few reclusive philosophers out of the cave and into the light of day, but more or less all of humanity. It strove, not to reach an accommodation with religion and divinely inspired or divinely secured law, but to overcome 'the kingdom of darkness' and to substitute rational laws for the arbitrary restrictions of the past. Its hope was that philosophy would one day fulfil the function of both philosophy and religion, and this hope rested on the assumption, as Strauss had put it in his study of Spinoza, that 'prejudice' is a historical category – that is, that the fight against prejudice was one that could in time result in the triumph of philosophical reason, and not remain, as the ancient philosophers had assumed, an inescapable burden because of the ineradicable power of appearance and opinion.[38] The danger was that, in aiming to replace rather than just to reach a favourable accommodation with popular belief, philosophy itself would begin to take on some of the lineaments of its rival. Would it not eventually have to adapt itself to the capacities of those it proposed to rule? Was there not a real danger that philosophy and philosophers would cease to exist, replaced by intellectuals and propagandists trying to advance the public understanding of science?

These questions may seem remote from the issues raised by Spinoza in his treatise on theology and politics. He was far from being what is today called a public intellectual. Rather he was a master of the 'art of allusive and elusive writing' that has fallen out of favour since the French Revolution. His presentation of Moses as a legislator and Christ as a philosopher showed a good understanding, if not of the Bible, at least of the non-negotiable demands of the authorities under whom he lived. Yet it is Strauss's contention that Spinoza, Machiavelli, and Hobbes were the great pioneers of the specifically modern approach to the theological-political problem and thus ultimately the cause of all the practical and theoretical problems summed up in the phrase 'the crisis of modernity.'

This has been a long digression, and it may be helpful to recall our starting point. In his earliest academic writings, Strauss had examined the problem of reason and revelation from a specifically Jewish perspective. As he explained later, he wrote his book on Spinoza in Germany from 1925 to 1928 when he was 'a young Jew born and raised in Germany who found himself in the grip of the theologico-political predicament.'[39] Germany was then a liberal democracy, but it was unable to make good the promise of liberalism to Jews, the promise of social and political equality on the basis of toleration or the privacy of religion. The Christian majority of the German population, a majority which could neither in principle nor in practice be compelled to act otherwise, refused to grant the Jews this equality. As a result, many German-Jewish youth, including Strauss, turned to Zionism as the only honourable alternative. The pioneers of modern Zionism had defined it as a modern nationalist movement: for them, the Jews were a nation without a state. They thought that the only realistic solution to 'the Jewish problem' was that the Jews become a nation like all other nations, that is, that they establish their own modern liberal secular state in which they would be an overwhelming majority and their dignity would be affirmed. But what exactly was it that constituted the nationality of the Jews if not their religion? Strictly political Zionism as an immediate practical response to the degradation of a community defined by common descent had to embrace cultural Zionism and the Jewish heritage, and this meant that it had to embrace Judaism itself, for the cultural heritage was essentially religious. 'When cultural Zionism understands itself, it turns into religious Zionism.'[40] But is religious Zionism – a return to orthodox Jewish faith and the Jewish way of life – any longer possible for anyone of intellectual probity? Among his contemporaries, Strauss found many, including many Zionists, who believed that such a return was altogether impossible. 'They believe that the Jewish faith has been overthrown once and for all, not by blind rebellion, but by evident refutation.'[41] Their opinion, traced to its ultimate source, was Spinoza's critique of miracles and revelation. Thus the problem represented by Spinoza had to be faced. 'Orthodoxy could be returned to only if Spinoza was wrong in every respect.'[42] Cultural and political Zionism would have a secure foundation only if it could be shown that Spinoza had failed to compel disbelief in the orthodox claims about miracles and revelation. This is what Strauss established in his demonstration that Spinoza's critique depends ultimately on ridicule, and further, that this ridicule, no longer seen with a view to its imagined results, but rather in the light of our experience of its real effects, is now falling flat. Later Strauss broadened and deepened this train of thought.[43]

12 'Tyranny and Wisdom'

I dare do all that may become a man;
Who dares do more is none.

Shakespeare, *Macbeth*, I.vii

George Grant wrote at length about Leo Strauss only once, in 1964, in a scholarly article, 'Tyranny and Wisdom,' which presents unusual difficulties for the reader because of its complex background: not only is Grant commenting on comments on a very detailed commentary on a short but perplexing dialogue by a little-known ancient author, but he is also pointing to the significance of a notoriously obscure and controversial contemporary philosopher.[1] The article repays close attention, however, for it shows Grant's sympathetic understanding of Strauss's thought and his appreciation of his art of writing and it also provides brief indications of some key points on which Grant had far-reaching reservations about Strauss's teaching.

The ancient author was Xenophon, a contemporary of Plato who was once highly esteemed but whose reputation has suffered in recent centuries as philosophers have lost interest in his writings and historians have compared them unfavourably to those of other ancient historians. The attention Strauss devoted to Xenophon, despite his diminished reputation, is one of the clearest and most revealing ways in which he stood apart from the most influential academic philosophers and classical scholars of the past century or more.

The contemporary philosopher, still living when Grant published his article in 1964, was Martin Heidegger. As indicated earlier, Grant regarded him as 'certainly the greatest philosopher of the modern era.'[2]

Strauss, too, held him in high esteem, as we shall see. But it is not easy to grasp his real significance and virtually impossible to explain it in a few words. Any brief explanation must take the existing language as given and will thus tend to force Heidegger into conformity with the common understanding of its terms, even though it was one of his major contentions that these terms convey a fundamentally mistaken or distorted understanding of our existence and its relation to nature or the world. Indeed, he maintained that there is an inherent tendency for human beings to fall into a mediocre 'practical' everyday understanding of life and its possibilities and to conceal the deficiencies of this understanding under a variety of soothing formulas and expressions – reason, progress, history, providence, nature, science, revolution, and the like – that smother our moody, 'ecstatic' awareness of the mysterious whole of time and space within which we find ourselves. Escape from these numbing philosophic (and political) sedatives requires unflinching attention to hard realities, particularly death, but other reminders as well of our 'finiteness,' that is to say, of our limited existence within a whole whose overall character, dimensions, and purposes we can never really know, whatever we may be told by those who claim the authority of science or religion.

Strauss's high regard for Xenophon was once shared by no less a figure than Machiavelli, as he shows in his monumental study of that disreputable predecessor. 'For him the representative par excellence of classical political philosophy is Xenophon, whose writings he mentions more frequently than those of Plato, Aristotle, and Cicero taken together or those of any other writer with the exception of Livy.'[3] But as Strauss points out, Machiavelli refers to only two of Xenophon's works, the short dialogue *Hiero*, which Strauss calls 'the classic defence of tyranny by a wise man,' and *The Education of Cyrus*, which he says 'describes how an aristocracy can be transformed by the lowering of the moral standards into an absolute monarchy ruling a large empire.' What of Xenophon's other works? What light might they throw on his political thought? Strauss maintains that close attention to the relation among all these writings is the key to understanding, not just Xenophon, but also the pivotal figure in the turn from ancient to modern thought, namely, Machiavelli, for 'he may be said to start from certain observations or suggestions made by Xenophon and to think them through while abandoning the whole of which they form a part.'[4]

Strauss wrote four detailed commentaries on Xenophon's writings, in an attempt to restore his standing. The first of these, a commentary on Xenophon's dialogue *Hiero*, was published in 1948.[5] It has an arresting title, *On Tyranny*, and it can be regarded as the first characteristically 'Straussian' book, since it is the first of his large-scale works in which he discusses a fundamental problem of political philosophy indirectly, by commenting on the work of an ancient author.

The dialogue recounts an imaginary conversation between two historical figures, the Syracusan tyrant Hiero I and a visitor to his court, the poet Simonides of Ceos, who had a reputation for wisdom and greed. The poet asks the tyrant to compare the life of a tyrant with that of a private citizen. Who has the more pleasant life? After some hesitation, Hiero explains all the disadvantages of tyranny for the tyrant. He lives in fear; the delicacies he enjoys are not really gratifying; he has no true friends, only flatterers; the honours he receives are hollow; his situation compels him to associate with base and slavish companions while he oppresses or kills the noblest citizens. The real disadvantages of tyranny thus stand in stark contrast to its reputed advantages. It is really a snare, the only escape from which is suicide. Man is evidently not made to rule over others against their will and without the restraint of laws.

Simonides is apparently not impressed, however, by Hiero's litany of complaints. A passion for honour and praise, he suggests, is what distinguishes real men from mere beasts and the vulgar multitude. The burdens of tyranny may be heavy, but its rewards are sweet for real men, since rulers are honoured above all others. Ordinary people are naturally grateful – genuinely grateful – for any attention or marks of esteem they receive from their social superiors, so rulers are in a position to get more real honour (and pleasure) from others than are private citizens. To avoid the hatred of their subjects, tyrants need only delegate to others the actual execution of the harsh measures that are admittedly inseparable from ruling human beings. The conversation between the tyrant and the poet ends with Simonides making a number of practical suggestions for the transformation of Hiero's rule into a more stable if not more lawful rule of willing subjects. By following this advice, it seems, and by directing his attention to the glory and prosperity of his city vis-à-vis other cities – and not just to his own superiority vis-à-vis other citizens – Hiero can reap rewards from tyranny that will more than repay its burdens. In the end the reader is left wondering whether tyranny deserves its ill repute. Neither the tyrant nor his city, it seems, need suffer from tyrannical rule. Autocratic or even somewhat despotic rule may sometimes be defensible. Simonides has the last word about tyranny, and it is a more favourable word than the standard teaching about tyranny associated with the Socratic tradition in philosophy.[6]

In his commentary on the dialogue – his first major contribution to classical scholarship – Strauss does not remonstrate with Xenophon for his urbane presentation of the urbane Simonides. He does not, as it were, bring him up to date by pointing to the horrors perpetrated by more recent tyrants and sternly reminding him of what the highest morality demands, that tyranny be condemned in the strongest possible terms and the tyrant killed, if possible. ('Give me liberty or give me death!') But Strauss also does not leave undisturbed the impression that the inattentive reader may have acquired, that Simonides' last word is Xenophon's last word, or that Simonides' failure to make any moralistic criticisms of tyranny implies any refusal on the part of Xenophon to judge its value. The fundamental problem of tyranny, apart from its murderously undemocratic and unjust character, seems to be shown by the unhappiness of the tyrant. A life devoted to winning the recognition of others, whether as a tyrant or as a legitimate ruler, or perhaps even as a free and equal citizen, may be a life directed to the wrong goal. The pursuit of recognition may be a well of unhappiness. This is the lesson Machiavelli could perhaps have learned from reading Xenophon's other writings more carefully. At any rate, the neglect of what lies beyond politics is what Strauss says is the fundamental shortcoming of Machiavelli's political science: 'Xenophon's thought and work has two foci, Cyrus and Socrates. While Machiavelli is greatly concerned with Cyrus, he forgets Socrates.'[7]

Jumping from Xenophon to Heidegger is not as arbitrary as it might seem on first glance, for Xenophon provides a corrective to the understanding of Socrates and his followers that Heidegger takes over from Nietzsche. As for Strauss and Heidegger, there may be a surprisingly close and complex relation of indebtedness and antagonism between the younger and the older man, but it is hard to say where exactly one should see the points of contact and how they should be put into words. Strauss himself provides minimal assistance.[8] There are allusions to Heidegger scattered throughout his writings, but he seems to have spoken publicly about him at some length on only three occasions.[9] On these occasions he avoided any detailed discussion of specific agreements and disagreements. Instead he mixed very high praise with unblinking recognition of 'the Heidegger problem' – the problem represented by the fact that Heidegger had publicly supported Hitler in

1933 and had played a significant role in legitimizing the Nazi regime.[10] To be sure, Heidegger had withdrawn to his teaching and private life early in 1934, but he never publicly opposed Hitler and he did not later disavow his earlier actions. In short, he had been an 'engaged intellectual,' but for the wrong side, and he did not publicly repent after 1945, apparently refusing the humiliation of those who begged their new masters to be allowed to continue their academic careers. Unlike some followers of Heidegger, Strauss had no inclination to minimize this problem by minimizing Heidegger's involvement with the Nazi party or by separating his thought from his actions. Yet he was also unwilling to let Heidegger's entanglement with tyranny diminish his claims to attention as a philosopher. Indeed, in his longest and most revealing discussion of Heidegger, Strauss concluded a remarkable account of his own youthful impressions of Heidegger's intellectual pre-eminence (too long to quote here) with the following stunning tribute: 'All rational liberal philosophic positions have lost their significance and power. One may deplore this, but I for one cannot bring myself to clinging to philosophic positions which have been shown to be inadequate. I am afraid that we shall have to make a very great effort in order to find a solid basis for rational liberalism. Only a great thinker could help us in our intellectual plight. But here is the great trouble: the only great thinker in our time is Heidegger.'[11]

Strauss went on to explain that the scholar who is not a great thinker (though able to recognize one) can reasonably hope to reach some worthwhile conclusions of his own only by trying to compare the great thinker's thoughts with those of other great thinkers. Freedom in this context can be nothing more than the freedom to choose. But Strauss did not claim at that point (in the 1950s) to be able to offer more than a provisional judgment of Heidegger. 'The more I understand what Heidegger is aiming at, the more I see how much still escapes me. The most stupid thing I could do would be to close my eyes or to reject his work.'[12]

Perhaps it would be equally stupid to close one's eyes, as so many have done, to 'the Heidegger problem.' What should one think about philosophers who consort with tyrants? Is their fawning on those with power a disgrace to philosophy? Heidegger offers a particular instance of what can be called, more abstractly, the problem of tyranny and wisdom.

The challenge facing the reader of *On Tyranny* is given an additional twist by the existence of a lengthy comment on Strauss's commentary that Strauss himself invited. Shortly after the book was published, he sent a copy of it to his friend Alexandre Kojève, who enjoyed at the time a considerable if somewhat hidden prominence in French intellectual life. He was virtually unknown in the English-speaking world (even less well known than Strauss) and he had no standing as a classical scholar. Such fame as he had among French intellectuals derived from his lectures on Hegel at the Sorbonne between 1933 and 1939.[13] But Strauss evidently regarded him as an outstanding representative of modern thought on a high level, and he wanted to know what he would make of his reading of Xenophon's little dialogue. 'I am very anxious to have a review by you because you are one of the three people who will have a full understanding of what I am driving at,' he wrote in his covering letter. The result was Kojève's review essay, 'L'Action politique des philosophes,' which then provided the basis for a 'Restatement' by Strauss, which was published first in French and then separately in English.[14]

Why was Strauss so eager to have Kojève's reaction to his interpretation of Xenophon's unimposing little dialogue? Presumably because he knew that Kojève would understand his intention correctly and challenge his claims in an interesting way. His objections would not be those of a blinkered, nitpicking scholar, but of someone gripped by the basic question being discussed and as keenly aware as Strauss was of the importance of Heidegger – and of the importance, therefore, of 'the Heidegger problem.'

Kojève had been born in Russia in 1902, the child of wealthy parents who lost their property in the revolution. After fleeing Russia in 1920, he had studied in Germany (in Heidelberg, with Karl Jaspers), then settled in Paris, where he pursued his literary and philosophical interests at the Sorbonne. He and Strauss seem to have met in Berlin in the 1920s and to have become friends when Strauss was in Paris on a Rockefeller fellowship in 1932.

Kojève was a Marxist and apparently an ardent admirer of Stalin the statesman, party leader, and military strategist, but not of Stalin the philosopher.[15] In fact, it is said that he offered to be Stalin's chief ideologist with a view to helping him to put the Soviet Union on a sounder ideological footing. He would have been well qualified for the task. He was probably the most interesting of the Marxists who were trying sixty years ago to deal in a genuinely Marxist spirit with the obvious deficiencies of orthodox Marxist theory – deficiencies that were being dramatically demonstrated by the very success of a Marxist revolutionary movement in a backward country that was not ('theoretically') ripe for revolution. Kojève knew that the old incantation that 'everything has to be understood dialectically' was little more than an evasion, a mystifying way of denying the problems illustrated by the Soviet Union. But these problems were fundamental, and they called for a complete recasting of Marx's treatment of theory and practice. The determinism of the orthodox 'materialist' theory had to be supplemented somehow – without exploding Marxism altogether – by the voluntarism associated with the very antithesis of 'scientific socialism,' namely, 'idealism.'[16]

These antitheses – materialism and idealism, voluntarism and determinism – pointed to Heidegger's reflections. What does it mean to be? What does it mean to think? What is human freedom? Questions of this kind had been put aside in Marx's attempt to formulate an evolutionary science of society. Human beings might have a 'species being,' but its description or analysis was not a high priority. Humans, it was assumed, were really just flexible, tool-using animals that had gradually, accidentally changed their own 'natures' as they developed better and better tools, including languages, for satisfying their bodily needs. Their various 'superstructures' of art, religion, and philosophy could be understood as nothing more than by-products of the social 'bases' of their practical cooperation for the production of useful things. 'Mankind must first of all eat, drink, have shelter and clothing, before it can pursue politics, science, art, religion, etc.,' Engels had said, in his short speech at the graveside of his friend Marx, neatly summing up his view of such matters.[17] Marx himself had said that changes in the realm of ideas and values must somehow be explained by changes in the fundamental 'forces of production' and 'relations of production' that determine all other human activity. 'The hand-mill gives you society with the feudal lord; the steam-mill, society with the industrial capitalist.'[18] This is the view, in a nutshell, that 'idealists' of various kinds have found unacceptable, most famously Max Weber in his analysis of the Protestant ethic and the spirit of capitalism. But how is the importance of 'ideas' or 'the spirit' to be made clear? The 'existentialism' of Heidegger's *Being and Time* offered a way of expressing the importance of thought for action without denying the priority of practical engagement with the world as it lies 'ready-to-hand.' Heidegger's analysis avoided any assumption of a fixed human nature or a natural form of human society. It could easily accommodate the idea that human sociability has advanced in scale and complexity, from families to tribes to nations and beyond, as men and women have gradually found better and better ways of bending natural forces to their will or desire, but it went far beyond Marx's 'dialectics.'

Expressed in the vernacular, the crucial claim of the relevant 'idealism' is that ideas are causes and have consequences. But which ideas have what consequences? How should the whole history of human thought be recapitulated in order to clarify the sources of modernity and the nature of 'capitalism' or 'mass scientific society'? What changes in thinking gradually produced our problematic way of life? Weber had attributed a great deal of importance to Calvin's anxiety-producing theology of predestination. Heidegger, in his later writings, traced what he took to be the essence of modernity – 'subjectivism' and 'the will to will' – back to the founding of the Western metaphysical tradition in the writings of Plato and Aristotle. He called for the overcoming of metaphysics, but he seems to have thought that its distinctive experience of being was so deeply rooted in our science and culture that 'only a god can save us.'[19] Strauss, by contrast, had a slightly brighter view of our situation and found a closer and less mysterious source for the distinctive features of modernity. As noted earlier, he attributed our modern republican politics with its familiar practical preoccupations ('the relief of man's estate' and 'comfortable self-preservation') to the 'lowering of the goals' effected by Machiavelli, and he called for a return, not to the outlook of the Greek tragedians and the pre-Socratic philosophers, but to classical political rationalism.

Kojève, for his part, aimed to revitalize the more hopeful, progressive, 'Marxist' view of modernity by returning to the Hegelian source of Marxism. His magnum opus is a Marxist (and Heideggerian) reading of Hegel's *Phenomenology of Spirit* which highlights – indeed, returns obsessively to – the master-slave phase of Hegel's 'dialectical' account of the emergence of spirit out of nature. According to Kojève, humanity emerged from animality when 'the first man' knowingly risked death for the sake of prevailing over the superficially similar but more timorous, not quite human being who became his slave because he was unwilling to risk his life for the sake of his freedom. ('Better led than dead,' he may be imagined telling his chums.) Since that first day, the history of mankind has been a protracted, largely hidden revolt of the enslaved against their enslavement. It has been the gradual vindication of the slaves' desire to be regarded as fully human by their death-defying masters. They win this recognition by gradually subverting and spiritualizing their masters' understanding of mastery, so that brute force eventually gives way to reasoning and consent. The slaves' overcoming of the master-slave distinction, the original rift or defect in the human condition, will be complete, and the intelligible 'teleological' narrative of mankind's presence on earth will come to an end with the creation of a universal society in which all individuals will be satisfied by the recognition they receive as equally free persons. The world-wide socialist or communist society that Stalin may have thought he was founding would perhaps have come as close as any society could to providing all human beings with such recognition.

As Strauss and Kojève pondered Xenophon's dialogue, Hitler and Stalin can never have been far from their minds, and they must have thought frequently of the relations (and hoped-for relations) of philosophers and philosophy to these two great warriors, but their bloody struggles do not figure explicitly in the pristine scholarly analyses. Both Strauss and Kojève treated the dialogue as an invitation to reflect in the most general terms on the relations between philosophy or wisdom, on the one hand, and political power, on the other, without wasting words on the elementary, even puerile distinction between tyrannical power (which must be decried and opposed) and legitimate power (which we are all obliged to commend and support). Strauss emphasized the differences between the ways of life of the philosopher, who seeks truth but who lives with doubt, and the ruler, who seeks honour and who must at least pretend to know things that he does not know. Both lives are characterized by high ambition, or an intense desire for the recognition of one's superiority by others, but the philosopher is content with the admiration of a narrow circle of competent judges, while the ruler, according to Strauss, craves the love of every citizen. Kojève denied this difference and all that follows from it regarding the ranking of the two ways of life. Strauss and Kojève agreed, however, that the relation between philosophers and rulers is generally filled with tension or conflict: both are necessarily involved in educating the young, so they meet as competitors for their loyalty. Strauss stood for the ancient solution to this problem; Kojève for the modern one. Esotericism confronted enlightenment.

Grant plunged into this rather arcane controversy with a synopsis of Kojève's historical account of the relation between philosophy and politics. A glance at the historical record might lead one to think that there is no relation whatsoever between the two: philosophy has never had any impact on politics, and philosophers are therefore right to withdraw into their ivory towers. On closer inspection, however, history reveals some builders of empires and reformers of society who have been deeply influenced by philosophers. Alexander the Great, for example, was indirectly a pupil of Socrates through Aristotle. Jefferson and Madison borrowed from Locke and Montesquieu. More recently, Lenin and Stalin were inspired and guided by Marx, who learned from Hegel, and so on. The shortcoming of ancient philosophy, according to Kojève, was its inability to overcome class conflict. It was capable of overcoming only the 'racial' or 'ethnic' divisions of mankind – by treating them as 'conventional' rather than 'natural.' Nature as understood by the ancients provided no basis for overcoming the differences between different classes. Only the Semitic religions (Judaism, Christianity, Islam), with their idea of a unity based upon a free 'conversion' open in principle to all mankind, could rise above the pagan opposition between mastery and servitude. In recent centuries this essentially religious idea of human unity on the basis of human equality has become the basis for a practical political program. It has been 'brought down to earth' by modern critical philosophy. Great leaders are now in the process of overcoming both national and class divisions, and thus working out mankind's salvation in this world, by constructing a worldwide democratic state to do away with the scourge of war and to guarantee the equality and rights of all individuals.

Public-spirited philosophers today have the task, it would seem, of advising politicians how best to attain this supreme political ideal, the only political order that can fully satisfy every man's (and woman's) desire for recognition. Practising politicians are too busy for much reflection, so they are sometimes baffled by the novelties they confront – things like nuclear and bacteriological weapons, rockets, communication satellites, television, jumbo jets, populist demagogues, HIV/AIDS, recreational drugs, computers, the Internet, and racial conflict. How do these developments fit into history as mankind's achievement of freedom? According to Kojève, rulers need instruction about the 'contradictions' of the historical situations in which they find themselves. Philosophers must guide them in using these contradictions to work towards the overcoming of poverty and oppression. Conversely, philosophers need the political experiments that only audacious rulers can provide. The validity of a philosophic interpretation of a given historical situation is tested by political practice, according to Kojève. 'If philosophers gave Statesmen no political "advice" at all, in the sense that no political teaching whatever could (directly or indirectly) be drawn from their ideas, there would be no historical progress, and hence no History properly so called. But if the Statesmen did not eventually actualize the philosophically based "advice" by their day-to-day political action, there would be no philosophical progress (toward Wisdom or Truth) and hence no Philosophy in the strict sense of the term.'[20]

Grant agreed that Kojève had in fact accurately described the goal towards which contemporary politics is above all directed. 'Indeed the drive to the universal and homogeneous state remains the dominant ethical "ideal" to which our contemporary society appeals for meaning in its activity. In its terms our society legitimizes itself to itself.'[21] Grant follows Strauss, however, in questioning whether Kojève's Hegelian 'ideal' fully deserves the respect it now generally gets. If it does not, then current efforts to realize it can hardly be considered evidence of the impact of *philosophy* on politics. The universal and homogeneous state may still come into being, but philosophers may find themselves at odds with the ideas about human nature that will explain and justify the achievement, as Kojève himself (Strauss says) seems to think. As Strauss puts it: 'This end of History would be most exhilarating but for the fact that, according to Kojève, it is the participation in bloody political struggles as well as in real work or, generally expressed, the negating action, which raises man above the brutes. The state through which man is said to become reasonably satisfied is, then, the state in which the basis of man's humanity withers away, or in which man loses his humanity. It is the state of Nietzsche's "last man." Kojève in fact confirms the classical view that unlimited technological progress and its accompaniment, which are the indispensable conditions of the universal and homogeneous state, are destructive of humanity.'[22] Strauss goes on to say that those who still long for noble action and great deeds may be driven into revolt against such a state, even if their revolt is 'nihilistic' (because not enlightened by any positive goal) or simply 'terroristic,' as we might say today. 'While perhaps doomed to failure, that nihilistic revolution may be the only action on behalf of man's humanity, the only great and noble deed that is possible once the universal and homogeneous state has become inevitable.'[23]

Strauss's deeper objection to Kojève's argument, Grant notes, has to do with the classical assumption 'that it is in thinking rather than in recognition that men find their fullest satisfaction. The highest good for man is wisdom.'[24] This is a teaching that the authorities in a universal and homogeneous state would apparently have to deny and even suppress, in the interest of affirming the equal dignity and political rights of all citizens.[25] Philosophy as the attained wisdom of such a state might well be held in high esteem, but philosophy in the ancient sense of the love of wisdom, involving unsparing criticism of received opinion and hatred of self-deception ('the lie in the soul'), would be persecuted and perhaps destroyed. Thus, on classical assumptions about human nature, Grant concludes (with Strauss), the universal and homogeneous state, were it to be realized, 'would be a tyranny and indeed the most appalling tyranny in the story of the race.'[26]

This harsh conclusion is vulnerable to a simple objection. Not every complaint against those in power, whether locally or universally, is a reason for condemning them as tyrants, and the legitimate complaints may be different in different circumstances. Does tyranny not take different forms in different historical circumstances? Do our criteria for tyranny not change with our changing assumptions about morality and the good, so that they are in a sense 'subjective' and 'relative'? (Americans had different reasons for calling George III a tyrant than they had for calling Stalin one.) Perhaps future men and women should be left free to define tyranny as they see fit. In short, contemporary readers of 'a detailed analysis of a forgotten dialogue on tyranny' are likely to wonder whether it can possibly throw any light on modern, twentieth-century tyranny, let alone the tyrannical possibilities of future centuries. Strauss dealt with this objection or reservation at the outset, by conceding immediately that there is indeed an 'essential difference' between the tyrannies of the ancient world and those contemporary regimes, usually called totalitarian dictatorships, whose tyrannical excesses have surpassed 'the boldest imagination of the most powerful thinkers of the past.' Yet while making this concession, he insisted that 'one cannot understand modern tyranny in its specific character before one has understood the elementary and in a sense natural form of tyranny which is premodern tyranny.'[27] And it should be clear, even from my brief summary of Strauss's commentary, that in it he was able to raise and discuss questions of the greatest practical relevance. The readers of his book and his exchange with Kojève are led to rethink a possible 're-enactment of the age-old drama' of tyranny and wisdom in the new circumstances of democratic constitutionalism, universal empire, popular enlightenment, and the modern natural and social sciences.

Grant did not question the value of what Strauss had done. He did not let the obvious objection – 'how could the ancients understand something which did not exist in their day?' – deflect him from considering the controversy between Strauss and Kojève about the political role and responsibility of philosophers. His summary of their controversy led him to make two critical comments.

First, he observes that Strauss offers little by way of textual evidence to support his contention that the ancient philosophers deliberately and with good reason turned away from the development of a natural science directed to the conquest of nature. Perhaps the ancient philosophers did so without ever having clearly understood what they were doing, or from little more than a dim suspicion (as some Marxists allege) that technological progress would undermine the aristocratic social order favourable to themselves. Perhaps Strauss, eager to construct a consistent alternative to modern thought, read more into the few passages he cited than is reasonable. Grant notes that modern technology has clearly alleviated some suffering, and this has to be taken into account in any evaluation of it, whatever its relation to ancient philosophy. 'No writing about technological progress and the rightness of imposing limits upon it should avoid expressing the fact that the poor, the diseased, the hungry and the tired can hardly be expected to contemplate any such limitation with the equanimity of the philosopher.'[28]

The question Grant is raising in this first objection has far-reaching implications. It is not fundamentally a scholarly question about the evidence bearing on any conjecture that may be advanced about what ancient philosophers may have thought, but rather the more pressing question of what we today should think.

Whatever their reservations about 'historicism' as a philosophical thesis or rule of scientific method, both Grant and Strauss had considerable sympathy for what Nietzsche had said about the character of the modern world. And evidently both of them agreed that the overarching political project of our time is the creation of a peaceful, prosperous, democratic world order that could be the ideal nursery for 'last men.' They connected the development of this 'universal and homogeneous state' with modern science both as the supplier of the necessary means and as the solvent of the old restraints – the idea of an eternal justice – that might stand in the way of quickly and decisively doing whatever might appear to need doing. ('Letting "I dare not" wait upon "I would"/Like the poor cat i' the adage' – who would eat fish but feared to wet his paws.) Both Grant and Strauss deplored the tendency of their contemporaries to downplay or disregard the old tables of virtues and vices. Both were inclined to ridicule their fascination with each new triumph of technology. Both refused to join them in celebrating the softer, more accommodating 'values' currently favoured, such as creativity, tolerance, compassion, and honesty, sincerity, or authenticity.

Grant and Strauss differed, however, with respect to the practical measures that may reasonably be promoted in today's circumstances. The difference is easy enough to see in outline but difficult to describe in detail with any assurance. Very simply, Grant leaned to the left, and Strauss to the right, but the problem is to understand what this means without becoming entangled in the standard disputes about a progressive movement from conservatism through liberalism to socialism. Grant was more willing to speak openly about the banality of existence in modern mass scientific society and to denounce the inordinate rewards it offers its salesmen and technicians, with the corresponding loss of older, less ephemeral and superficial meanings or purposes in the lives of most of its members. He spoke clearly about the relation between the vague malaise that is now widely felt and its source in what has happened to our understanding of reason, science, and politics. Strauss, by contrast, was convinced of the futility of trying to win more than an infinitesimal fraction of any society to the practice of a genuinely philosophic way of life and was therefore much more guarded in his criticism of conventional opinions and practices. If his countrymen wished to believe that all men had been created equal, with inalienable rights to life, liberty, and the pursuit of happiness (however they might conceive it), he was content to appear, in practical contexts, as a good conservative liberal democrat. So far as I know, he never said anything as drastic as Grant said in 1955 in his talk about 'The Minds of Men in the Atomic Age,' that is, that he could imagine 'a prosperous society, without war, of healthy animals adjusted to worshipping their machines which could be so disgusting that one could will that it should be destroyed.'[29] Nonetheless, one senses in Strauss's writings and among those he directly influenced a steelier determination to support whatever can realistically promise to mitigate the softness that Nietzsche despised and ridiculed. With Grant, on the other hand, one senses a greater willingness to let the world be, to see its beauty despite the various pathologies of modern societies, and to identify with those who, despite all the help of our helping professions and the security afforded by our costly social-safety nets, still suffer.

Grant's second critical comment clarifies this difference. At the end of his article, Grant observes that Strauss shows 'a remarkable reticence' when discussing 'the relationship between the history of philosophy and Biblical religion.' More specifically, Strauss says almost nothing about 'the connection between the religion of western Europe and the dynamic civilisation which first arose there, the spread of which has been so rapid in our century.'[30] Hegelian claims to have synthesized Greek and biblical morality – the pride or nobility of the Greeks with the love of justice of the Hebrews – may be hard to defend, and it may be true, as Strauss said, that the proposed synthesis preserves neither of its original elements but sacrifices both to dignify a lax morality. Yet it may also be true that there is an important connection between the biblical understanding of ultimate reality and human destiny, on the one hand, and the orientation of modern science and philosophy to practical reform in the world, on the other hand. Strauss is clearly aware of that possibility, Grant implies, and therefore his reticence on this fundamental point is surprising. Given his intention of restoring classical social science, and his awareness that its eclipse was related to 'the triumph of the Biblical orientation,' it is perhaps untenable, Grant concludes.

A question just beneath the surface here has to do with responsibility for 'nihilism' and 'the crisis of the West.' To what sources prior to Machiavelli should it be traced? Should it be related to ancient philosophy as well as to 'Biblical religion'? Nietzsche and Heidegger treat the two ancient traditions – more specifically, Plato's original teaching and Christian Platonism – as effectively one. In *On Tyranny*, by contrast, Strauss was beginning to make his case that Socratic rationalism was being falsely accused of fostering a dangerously lax, falsely optimistic, essentially plebian ethic or morality, suggesting that the apparently close relation between ancient philosophy and the religious traditions of the West may rest ón a false understanding of the former. What is now often condemned as 'metaphysical' in ancient thought could be a late creation. Perhaps only with the neo-Platonists and the early church fathers did the seductively mystical elements of the Platonic dialogues – the edifying myths and the perplexing Theory of Ideas – begin to prevail over Plato's mischievously subversive reasoning.

A related question has to do with the character of 'Biblical religion.' As Grant points out, it is as much in need of clarification as philosophy itself is. 'Just as philosophy has always been problematic to itself, so equally Biblical religion is not an easily definable entity ... The effort to understand Biblical religion is as much a philosophical task as to understand its relation to the pursuit of wisdom.'[31] What conception of God and of the ultimate ground or character of reality is being conveyed by the biblical narratives? And to what extent is one justified in putting Moses together with Christ under a single rubric? Nietzsche had sharply distinguished the Old Testament, whose strong characters he admired, from the New Testament, in which he saw little more than weak moralizing. He had dismissively characterized Christianity as 'Platonism for the people,' raising a question about its claim to the title of 'Biblical religion.'

Finally, near the end of his summary of Strauss's position, Grant drew attention to a curious omission in the available English version of his 'Restatement.' It had originally been published in a French translation along with Xenophon's dialogue, Strauss's original commentary, and Kojève's response.[32] When an English version of the 'Restatement' was published separately in 1959, and then in the English edition of the French book in 1963, its final paragraph, which alluded to Heidegger in an unflattering way, was omitted. Grant pointed this out and expressed a wish: 'I wish strongly that Strauss would include [this passage] in any reissue of his English essay.'[33]

Why did Grant wish this strongly? The paragraph in question is a summing up of Strauss's disagreement with Kojève's historicism, that is, the latter's view that 'the highest being is Society and History, or that eternity is nothing but the totality of historical, i.e., finite time.' This view implies that human society does more than just provide the conditions (enough food, drink, shelter, and so on) for philosophy but is indeed the source of philosophic insight, and consequently, that man 'must be absolutely at home on earth, he must be absolutely a citizen of the earth, if not a citizen of a part of the inhabitable earth.' In the classical view, by contrast, the being, the understanding of which is the goal of philosophy, is 'essentially immutable,' that is, unaffected by history, and philosophy therefore requires 'a radical detachment from human concerns: man must not be absolutely at home on earth, he must be a citizen of the whole.' This fundamental difference had hardly been mentioned in their discussion, Strauss says, though both he and Kojève had had it constantly in mind. Some basic problems are best approached indirectly, it seems. The final sentence of the paragraph, with its unflattering allusion to Heidegger, suggests as much: 'We both [Strauss and Kojève] apparently turned away from Being to Tyranny because we have seen that those who lacked the courage to face the issue of Tyranny, who therefore *et humiliter serviebant et superbe dominabantur* [themselves obsequiously subservient while arrogantly lording it over others], were forced to evade the issue of Being as well, precisely because they did nothing but talk of Being.'[34]

What exactly was Grant's concern? The paragraph as a whole is essentially a recapitulation of points made earlier, but its final sentence is the only clue that most readers would have that Strauss's elaborate discussion of tyranny and wisdom had something to do with Heidegger. Grant clearly wanted that clue restored, and he seems to have been hinting as well that he wanted a clearer discussion of Heidegger's thought by Strauss, or at least a clearer indication of its importance.[35] He may well have thought that Strauss and Kojève had given too little attention to the novelty of technology that Heidegger was trying to clarify. And he may also have thought that they were too quick to dismiss the religiosity or religious longings that they saw in Heidegger's sometimes rather lugubrious ruminations on Being and beings. The question would be whether, for Strauss, there really was anything beyond politics and philosophy.[36] Could something more be said for a traditional piety than he had said in his early writings? Grant, as we shall see, held that the choice between philosophy and religious belief is wrongly posed if it is made to seem a stark choice between blind Calvinist faith (or other forms of biblical literalism) and a philosophic scepticism not very different at heart from that of Voltaire, even if (with an eye to the servants and the silverware or their contemporary equivalents) it is more cautiously expressed. The further one follows the paths of thought that Heidegger laid down, the clearer this point becomes. The dichotomy between philosophy and revelation favoured by philosophers of a sceptical bent begins to dissolve. The simple 'existentialist' point that living must come before knowing encourages attention to how little we really know and how dependent we are on fundamental experiences of a character that is difficult to put into words.

PART THREE

Religion

Quid sit deus?
　　　Leo Strauss

Religion provides the ground on which the three great contemporaries I have highlighted – Martin Heidegger, Leo Strauss, and Simone Weil – come together, although never in their own lives in an overt confrontation. To bring them into a more articulate relationship of mutual support and antagonism was the deepest tendency of George Grant's scholarship and reflections.

Grant was clearly a religious believer, but it is less clear what he believed. He called himself a Christian, but the term covers a lot of possibilities. What really is Christianity? How should it be understood? Simply calling oneself a Christian leaves open the possibility that one's Christianity is no more than family loyalty and social responsibility, just as it also leaves open many ways in which adherence to the Christian community could be a matter of deeper conviction. So there need be no contradiction between recognizing that Grant was obviously a Christian and saying that his Christianity is something of a mystery. Anyone taking seriously his apparent willingness to 'put everything in question' will eventually have to confront difficult questions about his (and their own) religious beliefs. Although all of Grant's major writings touch on such questions, and although he had little patience with the rituals of 'objectivity' in scholarship, there is little about religion in his published writings that is reliably 'subjective' in the confessional sense. Readers waiting for Grant to put himself into one of their convenient categories are likely to be disappointed. What he says provokes self-examination. Only those prepared to question the usual categories are likely to approach a clear understanding of his religious thought.

The most important clue by far to Grant's personal convictions – more reliable even than his personal correspondence, affected as it may sometimes have been by the anticipated reactions of his correspondents – was his well-known admiration for Simone Weil. In the letter that is called her spiritual autobiography, she wrote that she had lived since birth 'at the intersection of Christianity and everything that is not Christianity.' Recognizing the great difference in their circumstances, I would still suggest that this description may fit Grant almost as well as it fitted her. The next four chapters aim to discern what her life and writings must have meant for him and on this basis to conclude my scattered remarks about his long-standing interest in Heidegger.

At the end, in my final reflections, looking back over the ground we have covered, I shall review the ways that Grant's thought is often summed up and reconsider its relation to Canadian nationalism. We Canadians have been given the easy possibility of using 'America' to stand for all that we fear and reject in modernity, as if it could be easily separated from what we embrace as our own.

13 Making Sense of Religion

George Grant's family belonged to the Protestant branch of the Christian church. Both of his grandfathers were prominent members of their different denominations. As mentioned earlier, George Monro Grant was a Presbyterian minister, for many years the principal of Queen's University, and a prominent representative of liberal Protestantism in nineteenth-century Canada. Sir George Parkin had been raised a Baptist, but in his twenties he had joined the Church of England and soon afterwards had begun to play an important role as a representative of the laity in its deliberations. Grant's parents, William Grant and Maude Parkin, were married in England in an Anglican ceremony in 1911. In Toronto, the family regularly attended a Presbyterian (later a United) church. When Grant was a child, his father was the principal of Upper Canada College, a private boys' school with no formal religious affiliation but with distinctly Tory origins and Anglican associations. It offered religious instruction to its pupils as well as the regular academic curriculum. Grant himself, when attending this school and later as an undergraduate at Queen's, seems to have shown more interest in religion than most of those his age, but there is no indication that he ever considered following in his grandfather's footsteps and studying for the priesthood or ministry.[1] In 1977, in a recorded conversation with students and commentators on his work, Grant said that his parents' fate had been to belong to that large class of people of their generation who continued to regard themselves as Christians but who could no longer really believe that the old doctrines were simply true. 'I had been brought up in Toronto in a species of what I would call secular liberalism – by fine and well-educated people who found themselves in the destiny of not being able to see the Christianity of their pioneering ancestors as true. As a substitute they had taken on the Canadian form of what can best be called English-speaking liberalism.'[2]

The languishing belief that Grant is describing here – the survival of religious faith as a vague belief in 'something higher' or as a social obligation or something 'good for the children' – is still quite common, as anyone attuned to the spiritual climate of upper-middle-class Canada can attest. It fits with our public neutrality towards all particular religions and our official commitment to multiculturalism. These were obviously not topics of much public discussion in the 1920s and 1930s, when Grant was growing up, but one big public event that must have had some echoes in the Grant household was the creation of the United Church of Canada, by legislation of the federal and provincial parliaments, in 1925. This legislation, by resolving the practical disagreements about property between the Presbyterians who supported church union and those who opposed it, consecrated the voluntary merger of most of Canada's Presbyterians with almost all of its Methodists. The merger no doubt made a good deal of sense from many practical angles, but it was not the wider union of Christians that had been seriously discussed from time to time for more than a generation, nor could it avoid raising troubling questions for those with theological scruples. The Presbyterians were originally strict Calvinists, while the Methodists, an evangelical offshoot of the Church of England, tended to favour an Arminian emphasis on free will. As an adult, Grant remarked from time to time how odd it was to encounter apparently religious people who had no interest in theology because they thought it could be of no importance to anyone except the professionals. The United Church may well have symbolized this attitude for him. Certainly its ecumenism was consistent with dedication to something more practical than Byzantine theological strife, namely, the social gospel.

This movement was the most controversial development within North American Protestantism during the first half of the last century and the clearest expression of a broader shift from an 'individualistic' and 'unworldly' to a more 'social' and 'worldly' understanding of Christianity, the one oriented to 'eternity,' the other to 'history.'[3] The classic Canadian statement of the social gospel is *The New Christianity*, a short book published in 1919 by a Methodist minister, Salem Bland.[4] It argues that the churches, if they are to be true to their mission and respond in a genuinely Christian way to the modern world, must align themselves with the modern labour and socialist movements. All true Christians, Bland thought, must join the struggle to overcome the fierce competitiveness and cruel inequalities of liberal-capitalist society. 'In the name of the brotherhood of Christianity, in the name of the richness and variety of the human soul, the Church must declare a truceless war upon this sterilizing and dehumanizing competition and upon the source of it, an economic order based on profit-seeking.'[5] Bland had no doubts, it seems, about the efficacy of the basic socialist remedy for selfish individualism, that is, common ownership of the means of production. In any case, he promoted it vigorously. 'To discredit and attack the principle of public ownership is to discredit and attack Christianity. It would seem to be the special sin against the Holy Ghost of our age. He who doubts the practicality of public ownership is really doubting human nature and Christianity and God.'[6] By means of historical and national comparisons, Bland then drew sharp distinctions between the new Christianity he was advocating and earlier expressions of 'devotion to the Lord Jesus Christ.' Examining the historical record from a racial or national standpoint, he distinguished a primitive, undogmatic, apocalyptic Jewish form of Christianity from a more theological or philosophical Greek or Hellenistic form, which was followed by Latin (more legalistic) and then eventually Teutonic (individualistic) forms. From this national or racial standpoint, the latest development was an 'American' devotion to Jesus, which is more practical, democratic, and this-worldly, since it anticipates the imminent establishment of the Kingdom of God on earth. 'American Christianity believes in the progressive and aggressive amelioration of things. It believes in this life and its glorious possibilities. It is bent on attaining them as no other sort of Christianity ever was before ... It believes that the fulfilment of our Lord's prayer, that God's Kingdom may come and His will be done on earth as it is in heaven, rests with the Church.'[7] Jesus, as the preacher of the prophetic ethical demand for the complete reconstruction of human society on the basis of brotherhood, was essentially an American, at least until such 'a wider Christianity' should develop as would incorporate the insights of God's Asian and African children.

Bland's little book is not a work of detailed scholarship or profound theological reasoning, but it is effective advocacy, directed to the relatively large number of people interested in reading short, clearly written books on religious subjects. And it certainly indicated a trend. For considerably more than a century, influential philosophers and theologians – thinkers of the calibre of Kant and Hegel – had been striving to reduce or eliminate the mysterious or miraculous elements within Christianity, to make it a more 'human' and 'ethical' religion suitable for an enlightened humanity. A tendency had been growing to base religious commitment, not on acceptance of the reports of extra-ordinary events, but rather on the testimony of the believer's own religious consciousness or feeling of dependence. This tendency to 'internalize' the grounds of religious belief and practice grew stronger over many years, and it was compatible with the tendency to make practical forms of brotherly love the evidence of genuine faith – replac-ing involvement in the sacramental life of the church or acceptance of any particular doctrines or even strict adherence to divinely revealed law.

Of course, in the Christian thought of the period, there were many other currents, some of them much more traditionally religious than the social gospel. Some of them – the fundamentalism and Pentecostal-ism that have since become so visible and the Thomist revival that was then gaining strength among Roman Catholics – were probably rather remote from Grant's world as a young man. But there was one current, the neo-orthodoxy or 'crisis theology' of writers like Reinhold Niebuhr and Karl Barth, that he was definitely aware of, though the only hard evidence of his consideration of it is a rather dismissive remark in one of his earliest publications, which suggests that he had little sympathy with its 'realistic' emphasis on the sinfulness of man and the absolute otherness of God.[8] Nonetheless, it offered a prominent alternative to both orthodoxy, with its traditional conception of revelation, and the more conventionally liberal and progressive conception of Christianity represented by Bland. It rejected the long-standing tendency to equate Christianity with Western culture, which had attained its apotheosis in the social gospel. (For Bland, Christ was the direct inspiration for the democratic, scientific, and industrial culture of the West.) Instead, as representatives of a distinctly twentieth-century, post-world-wars movement, the neo-orthodox theologians emphasized how far from authentic Christianity was the life actually being lived by more and more people in modern mass scientific societies.

Very broadly, this is the background against which we can begin to understand the experience that Grant had in December 1941, which was mentioned in the Introduction.[9] Grant was twenty-three at the time and had been under intense pressure from his family to abandon the pacifist stance he had adopted as a teenager and maintained at the out-break of the war. In October, he had enlisted in the merchant marine but then had disappeared from London and was working as a farm labourer in Buckinghamshire, near Oxford. One morning, on his way to work on a bicycle, he had an experience that stayed with him for the rest of his life. 'At the worst stage of the war for me ... I found myself ill, and deserted from the merchant navy, and went into the English countryside to work on a farm. I went to work at five o'clock in the morning on a bicycle. I got off the bicycle to open a gate and when I got back on I accepted God ... If I try to put [this experience] into words, I would say it was the recognition that I am not my own.'[10] Grant does not seem to have been reluctant to share this experience, which he sometimes called a 'conversion,' but he never seems to have described it much more fully than in the passage I have just quoted, even though it seems to have been a turning point in his life.

When Grant returned to Oxford in 1945 to resume his studies, it was no longer with a view to a legal and political career but to study philosophy and theology, so that he might better understand what had happened to him four years earlier. The understanding he sought was not the kind that can be attainable by classifying and comparing the varieties of religious experience, after the fashion of William James. It was rather the kind that required an investigation of the ultimate grounds for any kind of genuinely religious experience whatsoever. What Grant sought was philosophical understanding, not scientific explanation.

Academic philosophy as found in English-language universities around 1950 was not, generally speaking, much help to someone with Grant's interests. The history of philosophy and all the standard topics (such as epistemology, ethics, and metaphysics) tended to be taught from the perspective of schools that were, at best, indifferent to religious institutions and experiences. The schools in the ascendant were the recently refined 'logical' form of nineteenth-century positivism and the new 'ordinary language' philosophy, which had begun in reaction to the pretentious obscurity of the older British 'Hegelians' but which had more recently been inspired by the genius of Wittgenstein. Both gained their force from the sudden advances in the theory of logic that had been made in the late nineteenth century. For a generation or more after the Second World War, Oxford in particular was the Mecca for those who wished to practise 'the analytic way of doing philosophy.' Its adepts tended to focus on clarifying the ordinary uses of language, so that perlocutionary speech acts would not get mixed up with illocutionary ones, or commands confused with requests or descriptions. The 'continental' alternative to analytic philosophy was visible from the British Isles only in the person of Jean-Paul Sartre, a philosophic star of the first magnitude, but one who showed even less respect for religious concerns than was being shown by the leading lights of the Anglo-American world.

There were, of course, dissenting voices and even contemporary schools that kept alive the old tradition of what Grant later called 'rational philosophy,' most notably the modern French Thomists such as Étienne Gilson and Jacques Maritain. Grant also greatly admired a book by the Canadian classicist Charles Cochrane, which analysed the background in Hellenistic philosophy to Augustine's synthesis of Platonism and Christian doctrine.[11] But it was among the spiritual descendants of the once fashionable British philosophers who a century earlier had turned to German idealism for a deeper or more spiritual alternative to their native empiricism (as represented by Bacon, Hobbes, Locke, Hume, Bentham, and the Mills) that Grant found both his mentor, A.D. Lindsay, and the topic for his thesis, John Oman.

Why did Grant choose to write about Oman? In the abstract introducing the thesis, he emphasizes Oman's 'theology of the cross' and his aim of explaining Christianity without presupposing the validity of any traditional metaphysical doctrines.[12] His is a theology adapted, therefore, to addressing a world that is increasingly peopled by scientifically trained non-believers. Their tendency is to deny mankind any special status within a natural order that in principle can be fully explained by laws of cause and effect. Oman, by contrast, clearly challenges the sufficiency of such scientific rationalism. His great theme is our direct awareness of a supernatural environment that is as real and as 'environing' as the natural environment that is the object of scientific inquiry. The more we try to understand human nature, he claims, the clearer it becomes that it is of the essence of humanity to be aware of a dependence on something beyond what can be explained 'naturally.' Oman's most ambitious work, the culmination of his scholarly career, was a lengthy book published in 1931, *The Natural and the Supernatural*, which offers a comprehensive study of our immediate awareness of this 'higher' environment. Oman did not accept the common assumption, even or especially in the theological tradition, that our awareness of the natural environment is a given while that of the supernatural is not, so that the existence of the supernatural must somehow be proven as an inference from the natural (as prophecy is confirmed by miracles or as the existence of God is inferred from features of the world in some of the traditional 'proofs'). For Oman, as Grant said, 'the seat of religion is in the immediate experience of the supernatural.'[13] This experience, he holds, can be analysed under three heads: the holy (a special feeling of awe or reverence which certain ideas or objects evoke); the sacred (the distinctive judgment that something is of absolute worth, that is, not to be compared with and balanced against the value of natural goods such as pleasure or even life itself); and the supernatural (our awareness that behind these feelings and judgments there must be a reality which is their ground). 'The supernatural may therefore be defined as the environment that stirs our sense of the holy and demands to be valued as sacred.'[14] The activity of thinking these experiences together and relating them to our experience of the natural environment is what Oman means by 'theology.' It was the kind of theological thinking Grant had returned to Oxford to do.

Grant's DPhil thesis was begun in England, but most of the reading it required was done while he was teaching at Dalhousie and much of the writing was done during a year's leave that he spent in England in 1949–50.[15] It was not published in his lifetime, even though it is a finished, indeed a polished work of scholarship on a writer of minor but continuing interest.[16] It has none of the usual faults of the genre – excessive length, lack of focus, repetitiveness, vagueness on crucial points, or heaviness of style – and it is indispensable for anyone wishing to understand the starting point of Grant's philosophical and religious reflections. Fortunately, it is now easily available to readers in the first volume of Grant's *Collected Works*, and it can be read with advantage even if one has no prior knowledge of Oman's writings.

To explain Grant's conclusions about the strengths and weaknesses of Oman's theology would require a far more detailed discussion of its elements (and of nineteenth-century German theology) than is possible here. But it may be worth emphasizing that Grant accepts Oman's starting point, that is, religious experiences of an almost ineffable character or a vague awareness, verging on the mystical, of a supernatural environment. He does not suggest that Oman should have begun with the doctrines or other clearly formulated claims of any established religious community. Oman's purpose, at least in *The Natural and the Supernatural*, is clearly not 'apologetic,' and Grant does not suggest that it should be. Further, Grant seems to have no basic objections to Oman's analysis of freedom as the kind of autonomy that we gain, in relation to our own desires and the demands of others, in the discovery that we belong to an environment of absolute value, that is, from a growing awareness of the supernatural. Neither for Oman nor for Grant is morality essentially a matter of clamping rational restraints on our unruly impulses, on the assumption that we already know what reason demands. Rather, it is a matter of expanding our vision of what is truly desirable. As Oman said, 'victory over ourselves ... is not possible by resolution, however courageous, but only by finding a better environment waiting to be possessed. Only as we seek a better country can we leave a worse, even though we must also be ready to go out, not knowing whither we go, as the way of seeking it.'[17] In short, we become free as we begin to follow the absolute claims called 'sacred' against the claims of natural values such as pleasure and social advancement.

But Grant finds less satisfactory Oman's tendency to evade the traditional language and problems of Christian theology, in the interest of appealing to non-Christian readers. In this respect, Oman belongs to the broader trend, noted earlier, that saw Christianity as a worldly religion oriented to history rather than to eternity.[18] Nonetheless, Grant shares Oman's basic assumption about the relation between reason or philosophy, on the one hand, and religion or revelation, on the other. The task of reason is to clarify the more or less vaguely apprehended spiritual truths implicit in our pre-theoretical awareness of a supernatural environment. As Grant put it later, in the provocative first sentence of his controversial essay on 'Philosophy' for the Massey Commission, 'the study of philosophy is the analysis of the traditions of our society and the judgment of those traditions against our varying intuitions of the Perfection of God.'[19]

Grant's memorable formulation took on a deeper meaning in the following years, as he pursued his studies of philosophy and theology. The questions that had most interested him from his youth were at bottom theological rather than just political or philosophical in the generally accepted senses of these terms. The keys to understanding the overall character and direction of his thought can be found, I shall try to show, in the writings of Martin Heidegger and Simone Weil. As already noted, however, neither of these outstanding thinkers is an easily accessible writer. To understand their significance for Grant, it may be helpful to begin by simplifying and exaggerating one of the dualisms – mind and body or spirit and flesh – encountered in any attempt to come to grips intellectually with 'the supernatural.' The problem is to escape the dualistic distinctions, but first their significance must be grasped, and for this purpose it may be excusable to state one of them as crudely and bluntly as possible.

It concerns the difference between a place or object and an attitude or perspective. Is 'the supernatural' to be understood as an 'objective' reality apart from 'the natural' or as a particular 'subjective' response to 'the natural'? On the one hand, it could be understood as something beyond the familiar natural order, but beyond it in the familiar natural way. It could be something nature-like (a collection of objects or the place where they are found), but distinguished from 'the natural' by its remoteness or invisibility or inaccessibility in the normal course of our lives. Much of what we say when we are talking religiously (or about religion) suggests this conception or representation of the supernatural. God is a person (or a group of persons) in heaven, which is above us. We raise our eyes to him, wonder at his power and glory, adore him, plead with him for special favours, fear his righteous anger, and hope eventually to live with him for all eternity. We also direct our prayers to the saints in heaven, and perhaps especially to Mary, the mother of God (the only human being to have been granted the privilege of ascending bodily into heaven), to intercede with her son on our behalf. While we are here below, in 'this world,' this whole supernatural realm is, of course, obscure, but after death – after we have shaken off the burden of our mortal bodies – our real selves, our souls, will be able to ascend to that transcendent realm where all that is supernatural will be clearly visible.

Evidently, an 'objective' understanding of spiritual reality invites the mocking sceptic to repeat the familiar formulas with a subversive purpose. Is there no alternative to this dangerously natural way of understanding the supernatural? Could it not be understood as a different way of experiencing 'the natural' (all the things that make up our everyday world), rather than as a different place or set of objects? Perhaps the transition from the natural to the supernatural is like changing our attitude or perspective or 'Gestalt' and not at all like being transported to some remote location where odd things can be observed (such as disembodied spirits). The 'objects' of supernatural experience could be the same objects perceived by our 'natural' senses, but seen differently because they are seen more spiritually. Perhaps we attain the supernatural, not by rising into the ether, but by coming down to earth from whatever dream-world we may be inhabiting. But how then should we describe this more spiritual or supernatural way of perceiving the everyday world? Should we say that it is like putting on (or taking off) rose-coloured glasses or letting our minds entertain pleasant (or unpleasant) fantasies or giving its sluggish circuitry a little chemical boost? Should we perhaps say that God as spirit is just man when he is in a religious mood? Or perhaps we enter the supernatural realm, not by dreamy mediation or swallowing a pill, but by resolutely choosing new values or deciding to pursue new goals in life. In short, is everything spiritual or supernatural just something 'subjective'? From a religious standpoint, this alternative way of making sense of the supernatural seems no better than the former 'objective' approach. What would it now mean to pray to God or to plead for his intervention in the natural order? How could we make any sense, from this standpoint, of traditional religious imagery and observances? If the 'subjective' understanding of religion were to become common, would it not mean the gradual disappearance of all the traditional beliefs and forms of worship, leaving only the mildest, vaguest, most vaporous residue of 'spirituality,' like the smile of the Cheshire cat?

Oman, in the interest of addressing a scientifically trained and increasingly sceptical public, wished to get away from some of the traditional language of dogmatic Christianity, but he risked turning 'the supernatural' into something merely 'subjective.' He did not play with the distinction between subjects and objects as freely as I have, but neither did he squarely address the question of what would become of traditional Christian beliefs and practices if the more 'objective' interpretations of the supernatural were to be completely discredited and to disappear.

For Grant, the problem Oman was grappling with – how to understand a supernatural environment as neither 'subjective' nor 'objective' – was presented in a more satisfactory way in the apparently unrelated writings of Martin Heidegger, who was searching for an escape from the either/or dualism of knowing 'subjects' and known 'objects' that has fascinated philosophers since Descartes. It is unclear how or when Grant became acquainted with Heidegger as more than just the name of a contemporary German philosopher of dubious repute.[20] In the thesis on Oman, Kierkegaard is mentioned twice, and there are some critical asides directed against 'Barth' and 'Barthian scripturalism.' Grant was certainly aware then of existential theology and the various 'existential' revolts against traditional philosophy. In 1955 he was sufficiently familiar with the writings of the most celebrated post-war existentialist, Jean-Paul Sartre, to give them a strong but qualified endorsement in an important talk on CBC radio.[21] Sometime in the 1950s, probably towards the end of the decade, Grant began to read Heidegger with close attention. Some of his later writings were beginning to become available in English, and it is these that Grant presumably read.[22]

In a lecture Grant wrote for a course on Plato at Dalhousie in 1958 or 1959, there is a remarkable passage describing the impact that Heidegger had made on him at that time. 'What I say now,' he told his students, 'is not for this course or for your understanding at this stage of your lives or perhaps never – but I say it because perhaps someday it may interest one of you.' What he had found in Heidegger's later works that might interest that 'one' was an interpretation of Greek philosophy very similar to 'some of the remarks' he had been making about it in the course. 'What [Heidegger] says at great length and great subtlety is that western thought has floated out upon a great tide of nihilism, and the origin of that nihilism is what happened to philosophy somewhere between the time of Parmenides and Plato. For Parmenides, being and awareness were one, and according to Heidegger human existence was rooted in that oneness; man was deep in Being, drew his life from the appearance of Being, which was truly appearance, not illusion; for the being of Being, which again was at one with Being, [was] not the mere flux which modern interpretations of Heraclitus have led us to think it was.'[23] This is an extremely condensed account of a fundamental – perhaps the fundamental – insight or claim that underlies all of what Heidegger wrote about metaphysics, truth, freedom, history, language, technology, and the relation of being to time. It points to the significance of Heidegger's thought, not just for the standard philosophical topics, but also for Christian theology.

Summaries or compressions, like translations, inevitably modify or distort, and they are sometimes quite misleading. ('Translators, traitors,' as the Italians say.) Any brief explanation of Heidegger's ontology may be worse than useless. Grant himself never tried to put it on the head of a pin. In the lecture just quoted, he was only introducing a name and trying to provoke a little interest. But for that 'one of you' who may be enticed to embark on a study of Heidegger from his own writings, it may be justifiable to say a few more words about what to expect and what it was that Grant was excited to discover.

Heidegger's philosophy is in some ways closer to poetry and religion than to science and mathematics, but his writing, though full of gnomic utterances, is strictly scientific in the sense that it makes no appeal to personal authority or to any extraordinary experiences of revelation or illumination. Heidegger leads his readers on paths of thought that all should be able to follow, though many will naturally lack the patience or determination needed to follow them very far. The persistent ones find themselves being led far away from the standard ways of dealing with the standard philosophical topics, especially epistemology and ethics. Traditional academic reasoning gives way to a much less 'disciplined' exploration of obscure linguistic harmonies and puzzling phenomena at the boundaries of consciousness. The familiar distinction between a rigorous 'reckoning' reasoning directed to the solution of well-defined problems and a more contemplative or meditative thoughtfulness gradually becomes clearer. 'Contemplation' and 'meditation' lose some of their derogatory association with the dreamy absence of any worthwhile thought.

Heidegger is famous, or notorious, for reversing the usual way of thinking about language as something spoken, that is, actively used by human beings. He says instead that 'language speaks, not humans.' In other words, we humans are more passive in relation to our languages than we usually realize: a language speaks through us, and only by attentively listening to what it says can we gain a measure of freedom in relation to it. In the lecture just quoted, Grant went on to indicate how Heidegger's claim about the pre-Socratic experience of Being casts a new light on the traditional language of philosophy. 'What he is saying is that all our traditional separations like subject/object, substance/ accident, etc. – in fact all the words we use to talk about philosophical problems – are so many veils over Being, so many chasms between ourselves and Being. To understand the pre-Socratic insight we must penetrate far into the first roots of our own language, cutting out ruthlessly all the deceiving growth of the centuries. For the pre-Socratics, truth was what Heidegger calls the unhiddenness of Being.'[24] Much of Heidegger's scholarly work was in fact devoted to getting behind the familiar, sedimented meanings of the old words – the big words of the philosophical tradition – to see once again the fundamental experiences that underlay them, in order to escape being simply spoken by the language we speak. In particular, our conventional, essentially 'Platonic' understanding of truth as something that belongs not to Being but to propositions, justified as it may be in many circumstances and applications, may be less profound than the pre-Socratic understanding of truth as 'unhiddenness,' and it may be this shallower understanding that lies at the root of what is now called technology.

Heidegger's writings are pervaded by a fearful awareness of the ways in which our conventionally scientific ways of thinking and speaking are moulding our lives in increasingly disturbing ways. Of course, it is one thing to be dimly aware that there may be something radically wrong with our reasonable, liberal, scientific understanding of things – the reputable routines we follow without much thought in politics, religion, and the sciences – and another thing altogether to find one's way out of the conceptual (or linguistic) labyrinth created by thinkers of the stature of Plato and Aristotle among the ancients and Descartes, Hobbes, Locke, Hume, and Kant among more recent philosophers. Where is one to find the alternative framework – the more 'phenomenological' or 'existential' analysis – that could claim to be more genuinely scientific and objective than what commonly passes today for 'science' and 'objectivity'? Heidegger's great achievement in his early masterwork, *Being and Time*, was to frame (so to speak) such a framework. He called for a revival of inquiry into the most abstract of concepts, being, but one that would employ a new method. He maintained that the proper understanding of any branch of human thought or action, including philosophy and theology, requires that it be brought back ultimately to our own experience of our existence, which is primarily not that of detached observation or disciplined inquiry but rather, to simplify, that of finite beings living with others in a world of common concerns. By failing to face our true situation, we slip into a distorted and perhaps dangerous understanding of what it means to be.

Heidegger's claims about 'the metaphysical tradition,' technology, and the modern understanding of human existence are, of course, contestable. What is clear beyond any doubt is that Grant found his writings immensely illuminating, but he also had deep reservations about them, as did Leo Strauss. The nature of their rather different reservations will be clearer after we have considered the third of Grant's three great contemporaries, Simone Weil.

14 Discovering Simone Weil

Sometime in the early 1970s George Grant wrote down a simple explanation for why he studied the writings of Simone Weil: 'I learn from them. Of all the twentieth century writers, she has been incomparably my greatest teacher.'[1] When Grant wrote this, he was working on a study of her life and writings intended to help others to discover her thought, despite its inherent difficulty, a difficulty increased by the fragmentary and unfinished form of much of what she had written and further complicated by the way in which some of her unpublished writings – in particular, short passages from her notebooks – had been selected and arranged for publication. Unfortunately, the book Grant planned never got much beyond the planning stage; his own writings about Simone Weil are merely short drafts and occasional pieces. But these fragmentary writings – some notes and drafts for the book, an unpublished lecture from about 1970, and two later book reviews – make it possible to see fairly clearly what Grant believed was of crucial importance. It is not something that can be easily conveyed by any short account of Simone Weil's remarkable life and writings.[2]

She was born in 1909 in Paris, the second child of highly educated parents of Jewish ancestry. Her father, Bernard Weil, was a respected physician in general practice who had become an atheist in rebellion against the orthodoxy of his own parents. Her mother, Selma, was part of a prosperous family that had moved from Russia to Belgium, leaving behind their ancestral beliefs and practices.[3] Simone's brother André, three years her elder, was a brilliant student who later became a famous mathematician.[4] She, too, was a brilliant student who attended some of the best French schools and institutions of higher learning. She secured her *baccalauréat* at fifteen, in 1924, with a near perfect grade, and in 1931 completed her formal studies, passing her *agrégation* with flying colours. For the next three years she taught philosophy at three different secondary schools for girls, in Le Puy, Auxerre, and Roanne, but she did not slip easily into a teaching career. Her radical politics, her apparent atheism, and her unorthodox teaching methods alarmed the authorities, and she was relieved of her first two positions. As a student in Paris, she had been convinced by Marxist and pacifist critiques of capitalist society, had joined the syndicalist movement called the Révolution Proletérienne, had collected signatures for various petitions, had participated in some strikes and demonstrations, and had written voluminously on the questions of the day. While teaching philosophy, she did more writing for the radical press and participated in more demonstrations on behalf of strikers and the unemployed. In the summer of 1932 she spent six weeks in Berlin to understand better the political situation there. She gradually became known to a wider circle of radical intellectuals in France and abroad and even drew a rebuke from Leon Trotsky in 1933. A little later she managed to meet him (by arranging for him to stay for a short time in her parents' apartment, where he held secret negotiations with some socialists from Germany), and they had a noisy altercation.[5]

Even more alarming to the school authorities, perhaps, would have been the developments of the next few years, if there had been any hint of them. In 1933 and 1934 Simone Weil was gradually moving away from direct involvement in the political activities of her revolutionary syndicalist friends. A new, more religious phase of her life was beginning, although only gradually at first and even accidentally, one can say, since it does not seem to have been the result of any deliberate search for spiritual grounding or consolation. In the fall of 1934 she completed her longest discussion of social and political matters, her 'Réflexions sur les causes de la liberté et de l'oppression sociale,' which can be seen as a summing up of her involvement in radical politics and an explanation of her reasons for drawing back from direct political action.[6] Earlier she had obtained a year's leave of absence with the intention of gaining some first-hand experience of the iron discipline and exhausting routine of modern factory labour. In December 1934 she began work as a factory hand at an electrical works where she was soon given the task of operating a punch press. At the end of her year of leave, after tormenting employment in three different metal-working factories, physically and spiritually exhausted, having for the first time directly experienced 'the affliction of the oppressed,' she was taken by her parents on a holiday to Portugal. Seven years later, in one of her most important letters, she recounted an incident from that holiday, when she had gone alone to a small fishing village, on the day of the festival of its patron saint: 'It was the evening and there was a full moon. It was by the sea. The wives of the fishermen were going in procession to make a tour of all the ships, carrying candles and singing what must certainly be very ancient hymns of a heart-rending sadness. Nothing can give any idea of it. I have never heard anything so poignant unless it were the song of the boatmen on the Volga. There the conviction was suddenly borne in upon me that Christianity is pre-eminently the religion of slaves, that slaves cannot help belonging to it, and I among others.'[7]

In October she resumed her teaching career, this time at the secondary school in Bourges, but only for the year. In the spring of 1936 she worked for a short time on a farm to understand better the problems of farm labour and then in August, only a month after the beginning of the Civil War, she made her way to Spain to join an anarcho-syndicalist group stationed near Saragossa, one of the cities under the control of Franco's rebellious nationalist forces. In September, because of a serious accident with a pot of boiling oil, she returned to France and was forced to take a sick leave from her teaching position in Bourges. In the spring of 1937, while visiting Milan and Florence, she spent two days at Assisi. 'There, alone in the little XIIth Century Romanesque chapel of Santa Maria degli Angeli, an incomparable marvel of purity where Saint Francis often used to pray, something stronger than I was compelled me for the first time in my life to go down on my knees.'[8] In October she again resumed her teaching career (at the secondary school for girls at Saint-Quentin), but she stayed only until January 1938, when migraine headaches forced her to stop working. In the spring, while spending ten days (from Palm Sunday to Easter Tuesday) at the Benedictine Abbey of Solesmes, famous for its Gregorian plainchant, she experienced one of her most important and difficult-to-explain encounters with the difference between mind and body, an experience that gave a new urgency and direction to her religious and philosophical studies. 'I was suffering from splitting headaches; each sound hurt me like a blow; by an extreme effort of concentration I was able to rise above this wretched flesh, to leave it to suffer by itself, heaped up in a corner, and to find a pure and perfect joy in the unimaginable beauty of the chanting and the words. This experience enabled me by analogy to get a better understanding of the possibility of loving divine love in the midst of affliction. It goes without saying that in the course of these services the thought of the Passion of Christ entered into my being once and for all.'[9] Also in this letter (which is called her Spiritual Autobiography) she describes how she met a young English Catholic who told her of 'those English poets of the XVIIth century who are named metaphysical' and how, when she was later reading the poem by George Herbert called *Love*, 'Christ himself came down and took possession of me.' This was a possibility – 'a real contact, person to person, here below, between a human being and God' – that she says she had never foreseen. 'I had vaguely heard tell of things of this kind, but I had never believed in them. In the *Fioretti* the accounts of apparitions rather put me off if anything, like the miracles in the Gospel. Moreover, in this sudden possession of me by Christ, neither my senses nor my imagination had any part; I only felt in the midst of my suffering the presence of a love, like that which one can read in the smile on a beloved face.'[10]

In June, 1940, the day before the Germans occupied Paris, Simone Weil fled with her family to the south of France. During the next two years she wrote some of her most important texts, most of which remained unpublished in any form for more than a decade. In May and June 1942, she travelled via Casablanca to New York with her parents. In November of that year she managed to make her way back to Liverpool on a Swedish freighter, and then, after two weeks in a detention centre, to London, where she joined the group of Free French around General Charles de Gaulle. (Her travel and her release from detention were assisted by a friend from school days, Maurice Schumann, who was one of de Gaulle's close associates and who later served twice as France's minister of external affairs.) Early in 1943 she quickly wrote a long (book-length) memorandum, later published as *L'Enracinement* (in English, *The Need for Roots*), giving advice on the spirit in which the reconstruction of France should be undertaken, following a victory over the Germans. In August 1943, she died, age thirty-four, of starvation and pulmonary tuberculosis.

This bare outline of Simone Weil's life and work could be summed up by saying that she was a minor revolutionary and then a religious visionary. It provides some justification for thinking of her as essentially a political radical who, from moral or religious motives, dedicated her life to the overthrow of capitalism and the creation of a socialist society that would liberate the oppressed. Whatever reservations those with socialist sympathies may have about such a characterization, its more pertinent shortcoming is the misleading impression it is likely to leave with those who lack any sympathy with radical politics. It may suggest to them that Simone Weil had stronger emotions or moral feelings than powers of thought. Revolutionary syndicalists involved in Trotskyist conspiracies can now be easily dismissed as foolish people who were obsessed with unrealistic, utopian schemes of social betterment. That they had an abundance of idealism may be conceded, and perhaps also that they had a strong sense of social justice, but did their theories not blind them to political realities and the limitations of human nature? And when revolutionary, conspiratorial politics is combined with suggestions of mystical revelations, the impression conveyed is one of even greater eccentricity and impracticality than that of the wildest anarchists or Trotskyists, whose rages against authority may be easier to understand (as well as to condemn) than those of religious zealots. So in turning to the writings of such a mystical revolutionary or revolutionary mystic, one may be expecting to encounter the products of an overheated imagination, very hard to understand, except perhaps from the perspective of abnormal psychology, and very far indeed from the cool reasonableness of modern philosophy and political science.

Grant apparently made his first acquaintance with the writings of Simone Weil in 1952, when he was asked by the CBC to review one of her books. The book was *Waiting on God*, one of the first to provide the reading public with selections from her correspondence and unpublished manuscripts. It had been published in France in 1950, had attracted considerable attention there, and had just been published in an English translation. Grant's comments on it were broadcast on 16 December. The script does not seem to have survived, but whatever Grant thought and said at the time, his reading of the book evidently initiated a prolonged and increasingly intense study of her thought. The reasons why it first engaged his attention must remain a matter of speculation. Nonetheless, one cannot help but notice certain rough parallels between her life and his up to the time of his experience that 'we are not our own' at the farm gate in Buckinghamshire in December 1941. So he must have read with great interest her descriptions of her encounters with the supernatural. And it may have occurred to him that the clarification he had sought by studying Oman might be obtained by studying Simone Weil.

If we now turn to what he wrote about her some twenty or more years later, we see that he emphasizes, not her politics or even the amazing experiences she claimed to have undergone, but her saintliness and her extreme, uncompromising rationalism. In the early 1970s, as noted at the beginning of this chapter, Grant was starting to write a biographical and interpretive guide to her thought.[11] His papers from that period include an undated, two-page typescript, 'Introduction to the Reading of Simone Weil,' that seems to be a draft of the opening paragraphs of an introductory chapter. They begin as follows: 'Simone Weil was both a saint and a philosopher. These terms are used at this point without definition except to say that they are here used as they have been in the past by Christians who paid attention to the works of the Greek philosophers. She was a saint in the sense that she gave herself away to the divine charity. She was a philosopher in the sense that she wrote carefully and clearly about these [those?] matters which in the tradition philosophers have considered the most important.' Grant immediately added that the designation 'philosopher' should perhaps be qualified by saying 'potential,' since she had died at a young age and had been deeply involved since her youth in the turmoil of her violent era, 'so that she had little time for sustained contemplation or writing.' Nonetheless, Grant clearly stood in awe of her scholarly and philosophic achievements. In another fragment from the same period he says, 'From the study of her works there emerges an account of reality which is massively sustained in its consistency. That is to say, writing on a vast range of subjects, she enunciates an account of the whole and the parts that does not seem to me to have internal contradictions.'

Grant's purpose in the book he was starting to write was to persuade others to read her writings; he was most definitely not trying to spare them the trouble of doing so by providing a short, easily digested summary of what she had written. Indeed, Grant repeated his condemnation of the 'impertinent historicist precis written by [modern academics] who think they can say in different (and sometimes fewer) words what wiser men than they have said differently.' The proliferation of such synopses is one of the blights of modern education, he believed, for it means that more and more students now encounter the works of genius, not directly, but as reshaped and rewritten, so to speak, by those of lesser ability. 'God forbid that I should add to such productions or that I should think that I would help in the study of Simone Weil by my synopsis of her work.'[12]

Why then write about Simone Weil at length rather than just urging others to read her, using whatever rhetoric and instruments of persuasion (radio, television, the classroom) might be at one's disposal? Grant answered by pointing, first of all, to the sheer originality of her thought. Many potentially sympathetic readers would not have the patience needed to appreciate her unconventional brilliance without some encouragement and guidance. Simone Weil wrote a great deal about a great many things, but no major work of integration and almost nothing except occasional essays for publication. 'The difficulty can be put in this form,' Grant explained. 'Here is a writer who although she lived only thirty-four years left writings that deal with an immense subject matter. Nearly all the central questions of philosophy, religion and the history of both are commented upon, as well as the most besetting practical problems of the twentieth century. Yet because of the circumstances of her life, her writings on these matters are found in occasional essays, in letters and above all in notebooks which we cannot know if she ever intended to publish. It appears to me indubitable that there emerges from her work an account of what is which is magisterially sustained in its consistency. Yet because of her life and early death, these writings come down to us, almost in the form of extracts, the relation of which to each other may appear disparate.' The reader embarking on the study of her work might thus have great difficulty finding his way among the many collections of writings that have been published under her name. 'There is a need therefore to make a map of her writings as a whole; to state what has been published and what is yet to be published; to state where and when each of these writings were composed and to try and fit them into the body of her life and writings as a whole.'

A second reason for the project was that most readers would need some further help in order to see the real significance of many of the things to be found in Simone Weil's essays, manuscripts, and notebooks. A map, one could say, needs to be supplemented by a guidebook that explains more about 'her life and writings as a whole' than any map alone can. Without a provisional or hypothetical integration of her various writings, readers were likely to overlook some of her most important points or to misunderstand their meaning. The root of the basic difficulty here, Grant thought, was the great difference between her fundamental assumptions and those of almost all other contemporary thinkers. Any reader taking up her works would already have some preconceptions, or provisional interpretive hypotheses, owing perhaps to having seen her described (perhaps on the cover of a book) as a revolutionary who was a mystic (or who became one) or as a Jew who became a Catholic (though not quite, since she refused baptism), or in some other similar way, summed up in some easy-to-remember phrase. This would lead the reader to anticipate some things and to overlook or to be puzzled by others. Only a little attentive reading might be necessary to dispel some of the simpler preconceptions, but others might be much harder to overcome. Grant thought that most readers would encounter her writings within a confusing intellectual framework that they had imbibed, without quite realizing it, from the most influential modern religious and philosophical writers. Thus the second reason he mentioned for writing the book being planned was to help readers to reach a more satisfactory integration of her ideas than they were likely to achieve on their own, within such a confusing framework. His purpose was to help them escape – as he believed she had escaped – the characteristically modern ways of understanding human beings and the world as a whole, and in particular, our modern vision of persons as the creators of value in their freedom. 'To enter into the thought of S.W. – that is to even consider it as possibly true – it is necessary to recognise that her account of morality and indeed of the human conditions in general consciously and explicitly is outside this vision.' And this would mean, for Grant, bringing together the scattered statements on particular topics, such as the thought of Plato, which recur throughout her writings and then trying to state what she was saying about these matters, by relating what she said on one topic to what she said on others. The aim would be to convey an undistorted impression of the systematic character of her thought as a whole.

More specifically, there were two particular difficulties that Grant seems to have thought he might be able to help future readers to overcome. The first was associated with the contemporary understanding of sanctity. The specific difficulty here sprang from the widespread modern admiration of those 'dynamic personalities' that get things done in the world and whose biographies can take shape from the record of their achievements. The saints, by contrast, Grant thought, were those who 'surrender to the good.' Their 'perfecting of the will' is not something that need leave much trace in the world. 'The incidents of action and passion through which the perfection is accomplished are in some sense public and therefore historical; but the movement of the divine love within them is hidden and eternal. If this were not so, the reading of the gospels would be irresistible.' The saints, as Grant repeatedly wrote, 'give themselves away.' Their lives are the opposite of the self-assertion required by life in space and time. 'At the level of history, the saint gives up his personality to that which is not changed by the incidents of history.' Thus a guide to the thought of Simone Weil would have to help readers to avoid the possible misunderstanding of a modern saint that might follow from a common misunderstanding of sanctity itself.

The second difficulty was broader and more elusive as well as more pervasive and was the result of modern historical consciousness. Nothing more can be said about this problem here, except to recall that it is the leading theme of two of Grant's books, *Philosophy in the Mass Age* and *Time as History*, which were discussed in chapters 8 and 9. In these books, Grant contrasted 'time as history,' exemplified first by Judaism and later (and more radically) by Nietzsche, with 'time as the moving image of eternity.' Elsewhere he called Simone Weil's disparate writings 'the supreme statement concerning eternity made in the west in this century.'[13] And he seems to have thought that the most serious difficulty reading Weil, despite the breathtaking clarity of her style, would be due to the 'oblivion of eternity' that had become the fate of Western people, and perhaps especially of those who are, in a sense, the best educated. 'For many readers this will mean that to read her is impossible because she will seem to be talking nonsense. Particulary for intellectuals for whom the modern way of looking at things is not a particular way – but the best way (at least so far) and for some the perfect [way] – [they] will simply not be able to look at her writings with [any] sympathy.'

Grant pondered the task of preparing a comprehensive map and interpretive guidebook knowing that the result could never be entirely satisfactory. 'The synthesizing of works of genius by somebody of lesser capacity can hardly be adequate. What must be avoided at all costs is any hint that by such synthesis anything has been added to the works of genius.' It was worth attempting, nonetheless, he thought, despite the difficulties and pitfalls, because of the rarity of Simone Weil's genius and the importance of her message. 'Somebody who has had the time and opportunity to spend many hours studying these writings may be able to help others who are starting that study.'

It was in this spirit, with this quite limited purpose, that Grant began to write his book about Simone Weil. Why did it never get written – indeed, was never even properly begun? Here one can speculate, though perhaps not very profitably. One reason might be the great difficulty of what Grant was proposing to do. Simone Weil was a person of amazing intellectual accomplishments in the most difficult circumstances. One needs only a nodding acquaintance with her letters and notebooks to know that she thought and wrote at a very high level about a very wide range of very difficult matters. Grant had received as good an education as almost anyone of his generation had in Canada, but it had not given him the grounding in science, mathematics, and the classical languages and literature that Simone Weil had received from her schooling. Nor had Grant taught himself Sanskrit, as she had, in order to gain direct access to the Hindu scriptures. And he had not had to cope with her physical afflictions and had not subjected himself to the painful discipline of factory labour. One does not, of course, have to be a giant to stand on the shoulders of one – gigantic stature may even make it more difficult to do so – but one needs some preparation to scale the heights and to gain a secure footing there. Grant may well have been paralysed by the demands facing anyone trying to do what he was aiming to do.

This is a reasonable conjecture, but there is an additional difficulty, not so obvious or so easily understood, that Grant himself explained and that may have been the most important source of his hesitation and eventual abandonment of his project. To understand this difficulty, there is no substitute for reading Grant's own careful explanation of it, but it can be stated crudely as follows. The truths that we can know may depend on the lives that we lead. There may be an inescapable relation between virtue and access to truth, or sanctity and philosophy. What Simone Weil claimed to know at the end of her life – never claiming more than that it was part of the truth as she knew it – may be accessible only to those whose lives have been like hers, that is to say, lives of sanctity. The highest human life, if Christianity be true, Grant said, is to give oneself away, and he thought that Simone Weil had lived such a life of charity and courage. But he did not think that he himself had done so or that he was capable of doing so. That being so, how could he claim to understand her truth? Or as Grant put it: 'How is one then to give or refuse intellectual assent to doctrines stated by a being who lives on a different level of moral existence from oneself?'[14]

Finally, it is worth noting the position of moral or intellectual authority that Grant had attained in Canadian life by the early 1970s. Admittedly, he was still a controversial figure, and merely an academic; not all Canadians were prepared to defer to his authority; not all, to say the least, knew anything at all about it. Nonetheless, such prominence as he had attained, despite whatever faults or shortcomings he may have had, could well have increased his hesitations about writing at length about such a heterodox writer as Simone Weil. Around 1960, when he embarked on the project, Grant was a different person than when he began the book, in the early 1970s. His own achievements had made it increasingly difficult for him to be the anonymous servant, as it were, of those whom he might persuade to read a little-known author. The danger had grown that whatever he wrote would be taken, not as encouragement to read and modest assistance in doing so, but as the authoritative synopsis, familiarity with which would be sufficient for deciding whether one agreed or disagreed with Simone Weil. Rather than mitigating, he would be aggravating a problem that had been pointed out by T.S. Eliot in a preface he had contributed to *The Need for Roots*, when it was published in English. 'In trying to understand her,' Eliot had warned, 'we must not be distracted – as is only too likely to happen on a first reading – by considering how far, and at what points, we agree or disagree. We must simply expose ourselves to the personality of a woman of genius, of a kind of genius akin to that of the saints.' The danger was that 'many readers, coming for the first time upon some assertion likely to arouse intellectual incredulity or emotional antagonism, might be deterred from improving their acquaintance with a great soul and a brilliant mind.'[15]

Much about George Grant's thought would be clearer if he had written the book about Simone Weil that he long intended to write. Indeed, he may have feared that too much might be revealed about his own thought and not enough about hers, were he to write that book. Nonetheless, the simple fact that Grant seriously intended, for many years, to write at length about Simone Weil is revealing, and something of what he hoped to do can be gleaned from the notes and drafts that he left among his papers at the time of his death. Moreover, near the end of his life he wrote a substantial essay, 'Faith and the Multiversity,' which starts from a remark about faith found in her notebooks and which provides a clear indication of the importance of her thought for his understanding of Christianity. Grant's last book, which contains this essay, will be discussed in detail in the last chapter of this section. Before turning to it, however, it may be helpful to consider briefly four points in Simone Weil's difficult and voluminous reflections on philosophy and religion. I shall follow Grant's suggestions regarding the choice of the points to emphasize, in the hope that this will give readers a little clearer idea of her significance for him.

15 Escaping the Shadows

George Grant's papers pertaining to Simone Weil include another two-page typescript, also undated, which begins with a quotation from a letter she sent to her friend Maurice Schumann in 1942 or 1943: 'I am ceaselessly and increasingly torn both in my intelligence and in the depth of my heart through my inability to conceive simultaneously and in truth of the affliction of men, the perfection of God, and the link between the two.' This sentence, Grant says, can serve as the starting point for his exposition of her thought because it refers to several of the central themes of her writing, '(a) the perfection of God, (b) the affliction of men, (c) the contradiction and (d) love.'[1] In the next few pages, I shall gingerly, like a juggler's apprentice working for the first time with lit torches, outline four basic ideas: perfection, affliction, contradiction, and necessity.

Perfection

It is easy to see that there is suffering and evil in the world, and it is almost as easy to understand that there may be a problem squaring this fact with the existence of a loving and caring omnipotent power, but it is more difficult to know what to make of 'the perfection of God.' For many people today, Grant notes, the phrase has little or no meaning. 'It therefore seems best to begin an account of the thought of Simone Weil by some attempt to state what she means by the perfection of God.'

He then outlines an explanation that starts from the observation that 'human life is in essence the moral life' – that is, a life in which we are frequently compelled to make 'value judgments' about others and also inescapably aware of the possibility that we ourselves could become better or worse than we are. We stand always under our own judgment. Unfortunately, it is not nearly so clear exactly what we should do in order to become better. Moral betterment is often seen, as it was by Kant, as a struggle between our generalizing reason and our particular inclinations or emotions, that is, as a matter of imposing order by universal moral law on a naturally disorderly and generally self-serving assortment of desires and emotional impulses. Plainly there is something attractive about bringing order out of this chaos, by permitting ourselves to do only what everyone else can also be permitted to do, but sometimes (who can deny it?) it is even more attractive to indulge one's selfish inclinations, despite the harm it may do to others. Reason has to clamp tight restraints on passion, it seems; passion naturally protests; and reason sometimes finds a way of bringing what passion seeks under some plausible universal rule – for example, that lying may be permissible or even a duty in some particular circumstances, because it would do more good than harm.

Kant's way may be wrong way, however, to think of morality or moral improvement. For Grant, as for John Oman earlier, it had more to do fundamentally with the purification of our desires and their realization than with the suppression or restriction of the passions according to a rational account of our duties. It is a fact, Grant thought, that we cannot become much better by focusing on our own weaknesses and wayward impulses and resolving to be stronger and straighter. Only by paying attention to and desiring perfection can we make any real progress. This is a point that he finds clearly stated in Simone Weil's writings. For example: 'Only desire directed directly towards the pure good, perfect, total, absolute can place in the soul a little more good than was there before.'[2] Further, as this suggests, it may be a basic mistake to assume that moral value is unthinkable apart from the freely chosen actions of freely choosing agents. (People can be rightly praised or blamed, Kant held, only for what they have freely chosen.) Moral goodness, on this assumption, is something brought into the world by the free wills of rational agents, triumphing over their passions or desires for the sake of something more noble than the objects of those desires. But what is this 'more noble'? To see human beings as essentially free or autonomous in the sense that Kant intended, and therefore to limit genuinely good or moral acts to those that are freely chosen, in opposition to (or at least apart from) any human desire, is not just to liberate human reasoning and willing from any external standard or authority. It is also to obscure, if not to deny, the possibility that our apprehension of a perfection that is not our own creation or possession may be the only effective source of guidance in our reasoning about our purposes and therefore the only source of any real moral improvement. It is to leave unanswered on principle the inescapable question of what reason or motive the conventionally moral person has for submitting to the necessary 'universal' constraints? The pride he or she may take in being able to do so may be dangerously close to the proud independence of those who feel strong enough to give themselves more demanding, less conventionally 'moral' duties.

It may simply be the case, as Grant claims, that 'the moral life is unthinkable without the desire for perfection.' In addition, the desire for perfection can be effective in making us better, Grant thinks, only if it is a desire for something real, that is, only if perfection itself is somehow something to which we are attracted, like other objects of desire, such as the familiar tangible ones (such as good food and fine clothing) and the more elusive intangibles (such as love and respect). Only the desire for something real can draw us away from the vagaries of our own imagination. But this appears to mean that perfection, which seems to be akin to an attribute or quality of tangible things or actions (the perfect meal, the perfect smile), is itself somehow a thing that has a distinct reality or 'exists.'

In his sketch of a starting point for his exposition, Grant goes on to relate Simone Weil's analysis of the moral life to the Platonic tradition in theology. Perfection as the goal of the desire that makes us better brings to mind Plato's (or Socrates') objections to the Homeric gods and his idea of a sovereign goodness that exists 'beyond being.' If we follow up Grant's allusions, we are led to parts of Plato's writings, such as the key passages about the good in the *Republic* (esp. 509B) and in the *Symposium*, that have long been the subject of scholarly dispute. If Grant had focused on the 'idea of the Good' and had identified this 'idea' with God, then asserted its existence, he would have been carried, as we are being carried, into some very deep waters. To pursue this train of thought here may be to invite some serious misunderstandings, but there seems to be no alternative, if we wish to get a better sense of the deeper sources of Grant's political and philosophical thinking.

The question whether something exists – for example, the 'dog' in the joke about the dyslexic agnostic – normally presupposes that we already know *what* something is (its essence) and are uncertain only about whether it *is* (its existence). Thus we can ask whether some particular dog actually exists (assuming we already know what kind of a creature a dog is). Or – a different question, but on the same assumption – is there anything real that corresponds to our conception of a dog? (Nothing real corresponds to our conception of a unicorn.) But it should be obvious that we may be in a much more perplexing situation when we apply (or deny the application of) the word 'exists' to God or to an idea of goodness. How are we to determine simultaneously what the key terms mean and whether they correspond to anything real? It could be that 'exists' has no legitimate application apart from questions about more or less tangible and visible (and definable) material entities like dogs, cats, and unicorns. Of course it is also possible that the word has a legitimate use in an analogous or more extended sense to cover other kinds of 'being,' even that of an immaterial, ineffable, essentially unknowable divinity or the Being that is the source of all distinct and classifiable beings. Nonetheless, it is certainly difficult to know what is being claimed when it is said that God exists – in part because it is all too easy to have a head full of quite strange images of what God must be. A father with a kindly, loving smile, for example, and a long white beard, a bit like a cross between Santa Claus and our own real father, but much bigger, more powerful, less jovial, more mysterious, and somehow far more remote than even the North Pole.

A profession of faith in a received image – more generally, the acceptance or denial of religious dogmas – can certainly have great social and political significance. It can solidify or sunder relationships, consolidate or disrupt churches and empires, even start or stop great wars. But perhaps the ordinary professions of faith have little or no significance, beyond such obviously important practical matters.

Simone Weil distinguished between 'two sorts of atheism, one of which is a purification of the notion of God.'[3] She went on to say that she was absolutely certain that there is a God ('that my love is not illusory') and equally certain that there is not a God ('there is nothing real which bears a resemblance to what I am able to conceive when I pronounce that name').[4] She went so far as to write that 'an imaginary divinity has been bestowed upon man in order that he may strip himself of it.'[5] And earlier she wrote: 'Of two men who have no experience of God, he who denies him is perhaps nearer to him than the other.'[6]

What needs to be put in place of the imaginary divinity, it would seem, is nothing that can be grasped conceptually or defined by its essential attributes. Indeed, it might be better spoken of as something altogether mysterious, not something to be demonstrated, but rather something towards which we ascend through a process of initiation.[7]

Simone Weil seems to have stated without qualification at least one point that is relevant here, namely, that God has to be understood in relation to goodness, and thus as an object of desire, rather than in relation to power and as an object of fear or awe. 'The essential knowledge about God is the good. All the rest is secondary.'[8] It is this point that Grant has in mind when he writes that 'she has placed herself in the Platonic tradition and has excluded those arguments for God's reality which proceed from Aristotle's writing and which are made explicit in their Christian form in Aquinas.' Further, he notes that the reasoning that leads to an awareness of the divine perfection 'is what has been improperly called in the tradition the ontological proof.'

What is this 'Platonic tradition' and what does Grant mean by 'the ontological proof'? To avoid an extended and difficult (and no doubt unconvincing) attempt on my part to recapitulate the long and tangled relationship between Christianity and ancient philosophy, let me simply point to the most famous of the 'lovers of Plato within Christianity,' Augustine, the fifth-century bishop of Hippo in North Africa, and to one of this shorter writings.[9] 'The ontological proof of God's existence' is usually attributed to Anselm, an eleventh-century bishop of Canterbury, and to Descartes, but the reasoning Grant seems to have in mind is much older, and it may be best to examine the looser form of the argument found in Augustine's early dialogue on free will, *De libero arbitrio*. It is one of his most famous and most influential writings. In the course of the dialogue, he demonstrates the existence of God to his interlocutor, Evodius, by reasoning with him about the degrees of perfection that we recognize in the things that we see. Thus inanimate or merely existing things, such as stones, are evidently less perfect than living beings. Further, what has mere life, such as a plant, is less perfect than a living being that understands. The less perfect is made visible by comparison with the more perfect, one could say, for its imperfection is seen in the light of the more perfect. Continuing this progression, Augustine says that the rational human being is still more perfect than the mere beast that has a certain understanding and power of choice, but not the ability to reason. The problem then becomes whether there is any further term in this series, anything more perfect than human reason. If this can be established, the existence of God will be established, it seems. 'What if we should be able to find something which you [Evodius] would not doubt not only exists, but is even more excellent than our reason? Will you hesitate to say that, whatever it is, this is our God?'[10] Augustine's demonstration then proceeds by showing that there is eternal and immutable truth, exemplified by mathematical reasoning but not limited to it, and that this truth is superior to our reason, since reason desires it and is dependent upon it. 'No man passes judgment on truth, and no man judges well without it. For this reason it is clear that the beauty of truth and wisdom is, without doubt, superior to our minds, which become wise only through this beauty and which make judgments, not about it but through it, on other things.'[11]

Grant recognized that not all those able to follow an argument of this kind will necessarily be convinced by it. Even Augustine conceded that it was 'a somewhat tenuous kind of reasoning.'[12] And Simone Weil never, so far as I know, cited or discussed the Augustinian dialogue that I have been quoting. But Grant evidently shared her conviction that reasoning about God's existence must focus on divine perfection rather than divine power. Given the ambiguity of 'exists,' it may be misleading to call such reasoning the ontological proof of God's *existence*, but Grant, like Weil, said that 'it is not only valid, but the only valid proof of god's reality.'[13]

Affliction

Affliction is not a problem in the same way that perfection is, for we easily see that evil and suffering exist in the world. Indeed, we are usually much more aware of the evils in the world – not just our own moral and intellectual shortcomings, but even those of others, to say nothing of the various natural disasters and other misfortunes that befall all of us – than we are of any 'perfection' in the light of which we may be seeing these imperfections. Many are troubled by the apparent contradiction between the obvious fact of evil and suffering and the existence (not so obvious) of a loving and caring Creator. How is one to reconcile the obvious fact with the hypothetical existence? It is hard to make sense of the permanent coexistence of perfection and imperfection. A perfect being (at least from our standpoint) would presumably be one that combined unlimited power with an equally great love for humanity, and if there were such a being, how could there continue to be so much needless suffering among human beings?

Simone Weil was not at all inclined to deny the existence of evil. She seems to have been disposed, on the contrary, to fault others for their tendency to suppress or deny the hard reality of human suffering. To be sure, the more manageable misfortunes that we experience or observe in daily life – the temporary aches and pains, the occasional deprivations and disappointments, the plans gone awry, the minor injuries, the painful misunderstandings, even the costly accidents – all these can fairly easily be assimilated to the working of a larger order whose fundamental goodness is not put in question by their existence. There may be no denying that such things are undesirable, and that the world or human life would be somehow better without hunger pangs, toothaches, and the like, but they can be seen nonetheless as serving some good purpose in the overall economy of life and the universe. They may, for example, be spurs to the development of human intelligence and the productive power of cooperative labour, driving mankind forward on a course of intellectual and moral improvement.

Simone Weil made a distinction between the more bearable kinds of suffering that can be more easily 'explained away' and the most extreme or disabling suffering that she called affliction. For affliction, she said, there must be not just physical pain but also psychological distress and social degradation. Attacks of pain alone, unless frequent or prolonged, can leave the soul unaffected, while misfortunes unaccompanied by pain can too easily be ignored or denied. 'If there is a complete absence of physical pain there is no affliction for the soul, because our thoughts can turn to no matter what object.' For affliction there must be pain combined with actual or potential humiliation. 'Affliction is an uprooting of life, a more or less attenuated equivalent of death, made irresistibly present to the soul by the attack or immediate apprehension of pain.' It necessarily has a social as well as a physical component. 'There is not real affliction unless the event which has seized and uprooted life attacks it, directly or indirectly, in all its parts, social, psychological and physical ... There is not real affliction where there is not social degradation or the fear of it in some form or other.'[14]

Affliction must be distinguished from simpler or less extreme suffering because it has the power to destroy a person's recognition that there is anything good or anything to love. It leaves its victims 'struggling on the ground like a half crushed worm.' It invites the despair so vividly ascribed to Job. The soul of the afflicted person is penetrated by the scorn, the revulsion, and the hatred that it automatically produces in others, and the whole universe is then coloured by the poisoned light of these internalized reactions. The rather academic or even sophistical argument that evil cannot be known except in the light of the good – as the absence of goodness – ceases to carry any conviction. For a time,

God appears to be absent. 'A kind of horror submerges the whole soul. During this absence there is nothing to love. What is terrible is that if, in this darkness where there is nothing to love, the soul ceases to love, God's absence becomes final.'

Why then is there affliction? From a certain perspective, as already suggested, it is easy enough to explain why there is suffering – why human desires remain unfulfilled, why crimes are committed, or even why there are natural disasters. Some suffering can make us more aware of what is good and can motivate us to pursue it, but what is the use of a paralysing suffering that blots out any awareness of anything good? 'It *is* surprising that God should have given affliction the power to seize the very souls of the innocent and to take possession of them as their sovereign lord.' This is the great enigma of human life. How can affliction be compatible with God's perfection – his love and his desire to be loved – if it obliterates the awareness of that perfection and may even destroy the capacity for love?

Contradiction

No one who has thought much about the biblical idea of God can have escaped being puzzled if not tormented by 'the problem of evil.' Theologians have long been wrestling with it. How is one to reconcile the idea of infinite power and goodness with the undeniable fact of human suffering and evil? Even for Thomas Aquinas, the contradiction constituted an obvious objection to belief in the very existence of God. 'The word "God" means that He is infinite goodness. If, therefore, God existed, there would be no evil discoverable; but there is evil in the world. Therefore God does not exist.'[15] Aquinas then dismissed this objection rather abruptly by quoting Augustine's claim, in another of his writings, that there is a difference between real evil and what merely appears to us as evil, from our limited perspective, but that is really a source of good, within the providence of an infinitely wise and powerful God. 'Since God is the highest good, He would not allow any evil to exist in His works, unless His omnipotence and goodness were such as to bring good even out of evil.'[16]

It may be well to pause at this point to consider another possible solution to the problem – a less peremptory, more Scripturally based resolution of the apparent contradiction between an omnipotent God's loving goodness and the presence of evil in the world – one that was proposed by Augustine in his dialogue on free will. This solution is to attribute the evil, not to God, but to human wilfulness, or rather to Adam's misuse of the freedom that God had given him and then to man's corrupt nature since that original sin. The dialogue starts from this problem or question: 'Tell me, please, whether God is not the cause of evil.'[17] How can he not be, if he is the all-powerful and all-knowing Creator (out of nothing) of all that exists? Augustine gradually brings his troubled but tractable interlocutor, Evodius, to agree that if there is to be praise and blame, there must be not only right and wrong actions to be praised and blamed, but also the freedom to choose to do one or the other. 'It would not be just to punish evil deeds if they were not done willfully.'[18] Evil deeds must be the result of *choosing* to compete for temporal goods (the objects of our lust, or libido, and desire to possess, or *cupiditas*) rather than the spiritual goods (the virtues, truth, a good will) that are common possessions, since they can be shared without loss and cannot be taken from us by fate (once attained they are ours eternally). This is a choice that it must always be within our power to make, Augustine says. It is inconceivable that the Eternal Good or God, the existence of which has been established with the argument outlined earlier, would ever force an evil choice on us. Nor can the temporal goods themselves do so, for, being of a lower order of dignity than the rational mind, they are weaker than it is and cannot compel it to turn towards them. So it must be the free mind itself that is responsible for wrong choices when such choices are made. 'It is as you say,' Evodious concedes. All sins must be the result of 'turning away from divine things that are truly everlasting, toward things that change and are uncertain.' And this incorrect 'turning' can have no other cause than 'the free choice of the will.'[19] But why, Evodius wonders, did God give mankind this free will, since if he had not been given it, he would not be able to go astray? Augustine replies that this is a great mystery, because what we mean by God is mysterious, but it suffices to say that man must have a free will if, by living rightly, he is to merit the happiness that is the reward waiting for those who choose well. 'What was not done by will would be neither evildoing nor right action. Both punishment and reward would be unjust if man did not have free will. Moreover, there must needs be justice both in punishment and in reward, since justice is one of the goods that are from God. Therefore, God must needs have given free will to man.'[20]

Augustine insists that the soul's turning away from shared and immutable goods towards the transitory goods of a lower rank that are privately possessed is not a movement natural to it, like that of a stone when it falls to the earth by the necessity of its own nature. It must rather be regarded as voluntary, so that those who succumb to temptation can rightly be blamed, while those who aspire to higher things can be praised and rewarded. If men did not freely choose, not just what they do, but also what they desire, it would make no sense to reward those who resist the lure of temporal goods and seek the higher ones nor to admonish and punish those who do the opposite. 'Yet he who thinks that we should not be so admonished ought to be banished from the company of men.'[21]

That there is something mysterious about evil choices may already be clear, without delving any deeper into Augustine's fascinating analysis of their basis, and one may also be ready to concede that it makes no sense to attribute evil to the goodness of a Creator. It would make only a little more sense, as Augustine explains, to look for the causes of the will as a cause. Such an inquiry, once properly launched, would be an endless search for the causes of the causes. The point of treating the will as a cause is to put an end to such questioning. 'Either the will is the first cause of sin, or else there is no first cause' and then also no real sin. 'Sin cannot rightly be imputed to anyone but the sinner, nor can it rightly be imputed to him unless he wills it.'[22]

Nevertheless, even if Evodius falls silent at this point, one may still wonder whether it is within the power of the will to choose its understanding of what is good and worth pursuing. Are not all choices made in the light of one's understanding of what is good? Is anyone ever wilfully ignorant? Do we not all want to root out those 'lies in the soul' that keep us from seeing what is truly good for ourselves?

Simone Weil's approach to these difficulties, though perhaps not immediately persuasive or simply unobjectionable, is less evasive and ultimately less perplexing. It does not simply deny that what seems to be evil really is evil. One can say that she even accentuates the difficulty by focusing on the most serious, degrading, and destructive suffering, which she calls affliction, and only then denies that there is any way that the problem can be brushed aside. No mental gymnastics are going to get us past the obvious gap or contradiction between the benevolent omnipotence that we postulate as the object of our love and desire and the particular evils that we see being imposed by human actions as well as by natural forces. Must we not deny either the existence of evil or the existence of God? There is no easy way to make the evils of the world part of our familiar inherited notions of divine power and benevolence. The contradiction is palpable and must be faced. In particular, we must be leery of those who too quickly find good reasons for the suffering of others.[23]

To begin to understand Simone Weil's thinking, one must be prepared to question the common assumption that the holding of contradictory ideas is always evidence of a discreditable intellectual weakness. This assumption underlies the many fruitless attempts people make either boldly to deny contradictions or cleverly to hide them under plausible fictions. To be sure, contradictions are always evidence of the limitations of our intellectual powers, and these limitations can often be overcome by making the effort to think and speak more clearly, but sometimes, Simone Weil thought, contradictions are imposed on us by reality, that is, by the inability of human intelligence, however refined and methodical, to get beyond incompatible truths, none of which should be denied or suppressed. In these cases, no ingenious attempt to preserve the appearance of consistency will do any good; only patient attention to the contradictory truths may eventually lead to illumination.[24]

The first entry in Simone Weil's last notebook, the London notebook from 1943, begins as follows: 'The proper method of philosophy consists in clearly conceiving the insoluble problems in all their insolubility and then in simply contemplating them, fixedly and tirelessly, year after year, without any hope, patiently waiting.' This is a state, she explains, of extreme humiliation, since it is an admission of powerlessness, and few are able to sustain it for long, but it is the condition of going beyond the limits of natural understanding. 'There is no entry into the transcendent until the human faculties – intelligence, will, human love – have come up against a limit, and the human being waits at this threshold, which he can make no move to cross, without turning away and without knowing what he wants, in fixed, unwavering attention.'[25] Simply to declare that there are mysteries and thus a need for faith is not to cross the threshold. What kind of faith, one wonders. The uncritical acceptance of familiar formulas can be a way of turning away from difficulties in order to get on with one's everyday life. Nor is it much help to furrow one's brow as if to squeeze an answer out of one's brain. 'Impossibility – that is, radical impossibility clearly perceived, absurdity – is the gate leading to the supernatural. All we can do is to knock on it. It is another who opens.'[26]

People are often drawn away from the necessary attentive waiting by comforting fictions that seem to resolve the disturbing perplexities. 'The imagination filling up the void' is a phrase that recurrs in Simone Weil's writings. 'The void' is her vivid term for a painfully disoriented lack of intelligible meaning or purpose for the actions we must perform. Soldiers who invent victories in order to endure the prospect of a meaningless death provide a clear illustration of what she means: 'Although we may stand to gain nothing by victory, we can bear to die for a cause which is going to triumph, but not for one which is going to be defeated. For something absolutely deprived of force, it would be superhuman; Christ's disciples. The thought of death calls for a counterweight, and this counterweight – apart from grace – cannot be anything but a lie.'[27] Generalizing the point, one can say that imagination tempts us with the prospect of mastering all the mysteries of existence and even of gaining secure possession of a known future in which all our desires will be satisfied. Among the more common and more important forms of such imaginative reconciliation with painful necessity, Simone Weil would include, it seems, belief in the immortality of the soul and in the providential ordering of human history. 'We should set aside the beliefs which fill up voids, soften bitterness. The belief in immortality ... The belief in the providential ordering of events.'[28] Our aim, she suggests, should not be to defend these consoling products of the imagination, but rather to accept the void in the hope of living in truth.

The recognition of contradictions can be a first step. To face a contradiction is to gain a certain liberation from illusion and to experience an unwelcome but inescapable necessity. 'Contradiction alone makes us experience the fact that we are not All. Contradiction is our wretchedness, and the feeling of our wretchedness is the feeling of reality. For our wretchedness is not something we concoct. It is something truly real. That is why we must love it. All the rest is imaginary.'[29] 'Contradiction is the lever of transcendence.'[30] Even pain, accepted in the right spirit, can be a liberating contact with reality. 'Pain keeps us nailed to time, but acceptance of pain carries us to the end of time, into eternity.'[31]

Simone Weil had no doubt that it was better to live with pain and contradictions, uncomfortably aware of our own limitations and dependence, than to indulge in the fiction that only our lack of power stands between us and all that we desire. 'We must touch impossibility in order to emerge from the dream state. There is no impossibility in dreams, all there is in dreams is simply impotence.'[32]

Necessity

Simone Weil's picture of our situation seems to resemble Plato's in at least one crucial respect, that there is a great distance, even an infinite distance, mediated somehow by intellect, between the ultimate reality that is pure goodness and the shadowy world of our experience, one of physical forces and necessities that make life a mixture, from the natural standpoint, of good and evil. And even more than Plato, perhaps, she was, despite an important qualification to be discussed below, a physical determinist. Among the illusions she seems to have thought we should abandon were those of free will or free choice of the will as usually understood. Before turning in the next chapter to some of her thoughts about love, we should first take note of her somewhat unorthodox views about necessity.

No one today doubts that much of what we encounter in the world is governed by force or necessity, and modern scientific research is steadily expanding our awareness of natural necessities, many of which we cannot easily see. Simple inanimate objects, such as stones or billiard balls, obviously behave in necessary, lawful, predictable ways. Even when we observe such objects deviating in some way from the simplest laws explaining their behaviour – for example, a stone dropping more slowly through oil or water than through air – we immediately attribute these deviations to other, perhaps more complex regularities, which may as yet be unknown. Living beings, too, we can recognize are subject to inexorable necessities of various kinds – physical, chemical, biological, genetic, social, and psychological. Even the behaviour of the most thoughtful, deliberate human beings can easily be used to illustrate necessary 'reflexive' reactions to external forces. In short, we are compelled to concede that we are not, so to speak, pure spirits. We are at least in part physical mechanisms responding in lawful and predictable ways to the circumstances in which we find ourselves or the 'stimuli' to which we have been exposed – at least up to a point. But is there not a point beyond which we are free, that is, a realm in which the ideas of free will and moral responsibility have their traditional meaning?

Plainly we need not accept all the consequences of the regularities and necessities we discover. These consequences are often contrary to what we judge to be desirable, but by uncovering their causes, we can in many cases employ other regularities and necessities to ward off the effects we wish to avoid. There may be nothing we can do about the weather, but we can keep from being soaked or frozen by constructing shelters that will resist the wind and rain. Injuries due to collisions between bodies moving in necessary or lawful ways can be prevented by erecting barriers and imposing regulations. Sickness and death from known causes can be minimized or eliminated altogether by bringing these causes under our deliberate control. In all these examples and many other like them, not only do we see discrepancies between undisturbed natural regularities and our own good, but also some of the ways in which knowledge of necessary relationships can give us the power to modify our environment to our own advantage. In these examples, we see ourselves standing apart, as it were, from natural necessity as a whole in order to make use of it for our own purposes. We picture ourselves 'conquering nature,' that is, separating ourselves, individually and collectively, from the given web of relationships we observe in order to modify it for our own good, on the basis of our human freedom or free will. And both then seem equally real – nature, with its various necessities, and human freedom, with its power to intervene in and redirect these necessities according to our understanding of what is good.

This separating of human freedom from natural necessity – a setting apart of something truly or essentially human from the natural order – threatens to become untenable, however, on further reflection. We cannot deny, of course, our power, in various circumstances, freely to choose what we think is good, one action rather than another, but it is not so clear that we can freely choose what we think is good, that is, our background understanding of both natural causes and effects and what would be good or bad for ourselves and others. On reflection, these presuppositions of our free choices seem to be more a matter of necessity – of the education we have received, the circumstances in which we have lived, the experiences that have befallen us, and even our genetic inheritance – than of any 'free choices.'[33]

Simone Weil was willing to go very far with the train of thought just outlined, even though it threatens fundamental notions of moral responsibility and the distinction between rational thought and emotional, reflexive reactions. It seems to put not just remote events, such as the motions of the planets and the appearance and disappearance of other heavenly bodies, well beyond our control, but even our own most deliberate decisions and most freely chosen actions. All are apparently being absorbed within a comprehensive 'necessity' that is at odds not just with our immediate experience of free choice but also, perhaps more seriously, with our sense of moral responsibility, since it threatens to induce a dangerous passivity or fatalism. Nonetheless, Simone Weil repeatedly seemed to embrace such a comprehensive, unqualified doctrine of necessity. For example, from her reflections on Marxism: 'The essential contradiction in human life is that man, with a straining after the good constituting his very being, is at the same time subject in his entire being, both in mind and in flesh, to a blind force, to a necessity completely indifferent to the good.'[34] This indifferent necessity is the source of affliction, and there can be no explanation of it that bridges its distance from the good. 'There can be no answer to the "Why?" of the afflicted, because the world is necessity and not purpose. If there were finality in the world, the place of the good would not be in the other world. Whenever we look for final causes in this world it refuses them.'[35] From one of her notebooks, there is the following declaration: 'God has entrusted all phenomena, without any exception, to the mechanism of this world.'[36] Similarly, from her last letter to Father Perrin: 'Mechanical necessity holds all men in its grip at every moment.'[37] And, finally, from her wide-ranging discussion of 'The Pythagorean Doctrine': 'The human will, although a certain sentiment of choice be irreducibly attached to it, is simply a phenomenon among all those which are subject to necessity.'[38] On this view, the things that we encounter in the world, including other human beings, have no choice but to obey the necessities governing their natures. There is no question, from this standpoint, of their being morally good or bad or freely striving to become better or failing to be as good as they should be: they are what they are and not anything else, and often, unfortunately, they are far from being anything that we can understand as good.

In writing this chapter, I have taken up and tried to follow through some suggestions I found in Grant's unpublished papers on Simone Weil. Grant himself never put before his readers a quick synopsis of Weil's thought for their agreement or disagreement. In pursuit of a different goal, I have risked exposing her to quick acceptance or rejection. As mitigation, let me reiterate the advice quoted earlier from T.S. Eliot, but this time in the words of an authority who stands even higher than he in the estimation of most philosophers. In the Preface to his epochal *Phenomenology of Mind*, Hegel warned of the tendency to react defensively, with quick rejection, to any radically new teachings. 'A reception of this kind is usually the first reaction on the part of knowing to something unfamiliar; it resists it in order to save its own freedom and its own insight, its own authority, from the alien authority.' Almost as good a defence, Hegel adds, is too quickly to greet the novelty with too much applause, for this, too, can serve 'to get rid of the appearance that something has been learned and of the sort of shame this is supposed to involve.'[39]

16 'Faith and the Multiversity'

George Grant's last book, *Technology and Justice,* was published two years before his death in 1988. It consists of six essays on diverse topics, but all related to the themes announced in its title, which connect the book as a whole with *English-Speaking Justice.* The first two of the essays are substantially new, though different versions of both had been published previously. The first, 'Thinking about Technology,' is Grant's most carefully qualified explanation of the misunderstanding of technology that he maintained has to be overcome in order to understand the problem it presents for politics and morality.[1] (The misunderstanding is to see technology, not as a paradigm of knowledge, but simply as a means or a collection of instruments or techniques, as I explained briefly in chapter 2.) The second substantially new essay, 'Faith and the Multiversity,' is a discussion of the relation between religious faith and contemporary scientific (that is, technological) education.[2] In the third essay of the collection, 'Nietzsche and the Ancients,' Grant continues the discussion of Nietzsche's value for the understanding of modern society that he had begun in his lectures on *Time as History* and that I have already discussed in chapter 9. The last three essays deal with particular examples of the various effects of technology – on our understanding of research in the humanities, on our ways of dealing with the end of life (a mixture of amazing therapies and prostheses with discreetly veiled euthanasia), and on our difficulty in thinking clearly about abortion.

In this final chapter, I shall focus on the longest and most complex of the six essays, 'Faith and the Multiversity,' in the hope that by separating three major themes within it, the reader may more easily see the essay as a whole and may thus be better able to appreciate the unity of the collection to which it belongs. The specific purpose of the essay, as Grant says, is to clarify the problems faced by religiously inclined students and faculty in most of today's universities. The first topic he deals with (continuing the discussion in the preceding essay) is the relation between technology and justice. The second topic, the discussion of which is intertwined with the first, is the relation between Simone Weil's understanding of faith and the conception of it that students are likely to bring with them to university. The third, dealt with only implicitly, except for an appendix, is Heidegger's thought in relation to Christianity.

The multiversity of Grant's title is the sprawling temple of the modern sciences. Several of these sciences have quite long histories, even in their distinctively modern forms, going back to the sixteenth or seventeenth centuries, and all of them, even the most recently established, such as semiotics or microbiology, have some ancient roots, reaching back to classical Greece and even earlier, long before there were the medieval institutions of higher learning to which our contemporary multiversities like to trace their origins. But it is only in the past fifty years or so that our universities have become 'multiversities,' that is to say, institutions governed by the conception of knowledge exemplified by the most prestigious modern disciplines such as physics and chemistry. These and other progressive modern sciences have provided the demanding paradigm of knowledge that has gradually shaped the practice of teaching and research in the 'softer' social sciences and humanities – and, in doing so, have gradually transformed the universities of the recent past into the multiversities of the present and the foreseeable future.

What is this paradigm of knowledge? Grant does not explain it in much detail. It would be folly, he says, to attempt to summarize in a single paragraph what philosophic scientists and philosophers or logicians have learned when they have turned away from the resolute pursuit of modern scientific knowledge in order to contemplate their own methods and patterns of reasoning, the better to define what they are and what they have been studying. Nonetheless, only by encapsulating in a definition something of what these thinkers have learned can we begin to state what the problem is today in the relation between science and religious faith. The essential feature that Grant abstracts from all the different contemporary expressions of modern scientific reason is the attempt to gain objective knowledge. Modern scientific reason uses a variety of well-defined procedures to bring all the various objects of its interest – 'stones, plants, humans and non-human animals' – under its questioning gaze, so that they can be forced to give their reasons for being the way they are as objects. Needless to say, there is always a subjective interest (some understandable interest of human subjects) in the pursuit of such objective knowledge, but it is assumed that the interest is best served by ensuring that the causal regularities (or patterns of efficient causation) revealed, ideally, by scientific observation and reasoning stand apart from the vagaries of the scientists' personal or 'subjective' preferences. The subject must hold the object at a distance, so to speak, while it subjects it to a rigorous, methodical interrogation. The interrogator must strive to be as cool and dispassionate as possible in order to let the object reveal itself simply as an object. And the results that flow from this scientific attitude and its 'forceful' methods of 'research' are a source of wonder, Grant concedes. 'The necessities that we now can know about stones or societies surely produce in us astonishment. These achievements are not simply practical, but also have theoretical consequences. All of us in our everyday lives are so taken up with certain practical achievements, in medicine, in production, in the making of human beings and the making of war, that we are apt to forget the sheer theoretical interest of what has been revealed about necessity in modern physics or biology.'[3]

In a variety of ways, however, modern science, with its revelation of objective necessities, poses a grave problem for religious faith. As already explained, every scientific advance fosters 'the positive mind' with its inclination to see mysteries as merely challenges for future research. Darwin's theory of evolution by random mutation and natural selection dramatizes the problem by showing how little need there is any longer for the biblical account of creation or indeed, it would seem, for any purposive explanation of natural phenomena. Even more insidiously, however, the modern scientific self-understanding seems to exclude the possibility that we can know the world as inherently good, for good and evil now seem to lie on the subjective side of the subject-object dichotomy. As 'subjects,' we can know only 'objects' and can know ourselves only as we know others as objects. We cannot really *know* good and evil or beauty and ugliness, for they cannot be objects for us. They are just our labels for our 'subjective' reactions to the objects we encounter.

Grant begins his discussion of faith by quoting Simone Weil's definition: 'Faith is the experience that the intelligence is enlightened by love.'[4] In the remainder of the essay Grant explains what this means, starting with a clarification of the meaning of love.

Everyone knows that love can have different meanings in different contexts. Here, as Grant explains, following Simone Weil, it has to do with the beauty of otherness. That there are other persons and a whole world apart from ourselves – this much is an obvious, undeniable fact. Yet we can become so self-centred, so preoccupied with ensuring our own survival or so absorbed in our own pursuits, that we live as if we were refusing our consent to the fact of real otherness, seeing everything external to ourselves as simply subordinate to our desires and purposes. 'When life becomes dominated by self-serving, the reality of otherness, in its own being, almost disappears for us' (38).

What saves us from descent into such solipsistic self-absorption is (to quote Simone Weil now, rather than Grant) the beauty of others and the beauty of the world as a whole. 'Beauty captivates the flesh in order to obtain permission to pass right to the soul.'[5] The flesh is desirous, and its desires usually involve attractive images of future possession and enjoyment, but beauty can arrest the wandering imagination. 'The beautiful takes our desire captive and empties it of its object, giving it an object which is present and thus forbidding it to fly off towards the future.'[6] In the contemplation of what is beautiful, our clamorous craving for things we do not already have is temporarily stilled. 'The beautiful is a carnal attraction which keeps us at a distance and implies a renunciation. This includes the renunciation of that which is most deep-seated, the imagination. We want to eat all the other objects of desire. The beautiful is that which we desire without wishing to eat it. We desire that it should be.'[7] And it is.

To desire that something should be, not because we want to use it or to possess it, but simply because of its beauty, is to love it with a particular purity. It is to recognize its goodness, not for one or another of our limited purposes, but absolutely. To see the beauty of the world in this way – not from any practical point of view, but contemplatively, in a way that provides some respite from practical considerations – is to recognize its essential goodness. And finally, to insist, as Simone Weil does, on the beauty and goodness of the world – using these terms to characterize the whole of the natural order, rather than to distinguish its attractive or useful elements from others that are ugly or noxious – is to suggest that beauty and goodness inhere somehow in the natural order itself rather than, as we like to say, 'in the eye of the beholder.' In short, it is to suggest that beauty and goodness are 'objective' features of the world and not just 'subjective' functions of our various reactions to it.

Grant points to the similarity between Simone Weil's understanding of beauty, love, and goodness and that of Plato. In an appendix he has a brief explanation of why he thinks that we should use Platonic rather than modern language to express our understanding of subjects and objects. Platonism, he says, asserts the primacy of goodness itself – 'the truth that the world proceeds from goodness itself' (70) – and it offers uniquely engaging images of the journey of the mind into knowledge.[8] In the *Gorgias* and the *Protagoras* for example, there are memorable characters who show the appeal of worldly know-how and its limitations. In the *Republic*, there are the arresting images of the sun, the line, and the cave. In the *Phaedrus* there is an amazing depiction of different loves and an illuminating classification of different forms of 'divine madness.' In the *Symposium* there is Diotima's famous 'ladder of love' describing the ascent of the soul from an obsessive love of particular beautiful bodies to an even more intoxicating love of beauty and goodness itself. 'Our various journeys out of the shadows and imaginings of opinion into the truth depend on the movements of our minds through love into the lovable,' Grant says. 'What is given us and draws from us our loving is goodness itself; the perfection of all purposes which has been called God' (73, 74).

Modern technological science greatly increases the difficulty of understanding such allusive 'mystical' language. By restricting knowledge to the demonstrable regularities we discover by holding objects at a distance from ourselves for our questioning, we 'subjectivize' whatever intimations we may have of the beauty and goodness of the world. When we treat anything as if it were simply an object for our inspection and analysis, we obscure its inherent beauty or goodness, suffocating whatever tendency we may have to love it. Even our appreciation of works of art that have been created to enthral us by their beauty – beautiful plays or musical compositions – can suffer from the stifling tendency of academic critics to hold them away from themselves, treating them as objects for specialized explanatory research. In the end, this objectivizing stance can gradually sap even the basic term *good* of any definite meaning, for it comes to be seen as a treacherously deceptive way of referring to what are really just our own preferences or tastes. And if we should try to discover these 'values' by turning in on ourselves, rather than, as Grant would have it, outward, we find ourselves guided by no better standard than our own fluctuating tastes and opinions. 'Only as anything stands before us in some relation other than the objective can we learn of its beauty and from its beauty' (41).

Modern science has this obscuring, stifling, suffocating effect because it implicitly denies the possibility of understanding things through the conception of purpose. Indeed, at the inception of modern scientific research, four centuries ago, the denial was explicit in the influential attacks on Aristotelian philosophy or science by influential writers such as Bacon and Descartes. Their identification of scientific thought with basic doubt undermined the traditional understanding of what is good as what any being is fitted for. If, as they suggested, our real knowledge is limited to temporally organized sequences of objectively (that is, publicly) observable events, without reference to any conception of an overall purpose (or final cause), then we cannot know what any being is really fitted for, since ultimately there is nothing knowable within which anything should fit. We are left with nothing but 'subjective' answers to what is due other beings. To be sure, certain animals can breathe and must do so in order to live, but in what sense exactly is it 'good' for them to do so? (In what sense is it 'good' that the dinosaurs perished and the mammals now flourish?) And what sense can we make of analogous statements about human beings? For example: 'Human beings are fitted to live well together in communities and to try to think openly about the nature of the whole. We are fitted for these activities because we are distinguished from other animals in being capable of rational language. In living well together or being open to the whole in thought we are fulfilling the purpose which is given us in being human, not some other type of animal. Good is what is present in the fulfilment of our given purposes' (42).

Such statements – such 'antique wind' as Grant says elsewhere – presuppose a traditional understanding of the natural order as an eternal framework within which human actions can be measured and defined. To the extent that we accept the modern understanding of nature as the product of necessity and chance – that is, outside any idea of purpose – such statements will have at best an untraditional meaning. They may serve to indicate our own goals or purposes, but these will necessarily be *our own* rather than anything that we have been given. Within the limits of modern scientific and philosophical language, little or nothing can be said about the ultimate cause of being and certainly not enough to endorse the Platonic affirmation that it is beneficence. Nor does modern science hold out any promise that we will discover the right use of our power of choice by extending the frontiers of scientific knowledge.

To affirm that our height as human beings is somehow our knowledge of goodness and that the absence of such knowledge is not ignorance but madness, or the loss of our distinctive nature, is to put oneself altogether outside modern assumptions.

Thus the modern disjunction between love and intelligence – the view that love is blind while intelligence is calculating rather than loving – transforms our understanding of justice. All accounts of justice agree in assuming that it has to do with putting limits on the self-serving actions of individuals that can harm others. The just individual must check his own self-assertive impulses; the potentially unjust individual must be deterred or restrained. But necessary as such inhibitions and constraints undoubtedly are, they are not at first sight beautiful, and modern 'contractual' moral philosophy does not try to beautify what they involve (gossip, propaganda, shaming, flogging, prisons, and even executions). Rather it stresses their rational necessity, if we are to enjoy the advantages of social cooperation. Do unto others as you would have them do unto you, and encourage others to do the same, or else we may all find ourselves in the war of all against all, where life is nasty, poor, brutish, and short. Modern theories of justice, such as those advanced by Hobbes and Locke, put what Grant calls a 'horizontal' limitation on self-assertion, based on the fact of social interdependence. 'The basis of society [in these theories] was the calculation of the social contract wherein sensible human beings calculated that all had to surrender some part of their unlimited desire for freedom in order to enjoy the benefits of settled society' (59). In the most influential pre-modern theories of justice, by contrast, the necessary limits on individual liberty were thought to have a 'vertical' justification – that is, they were thought to derive from what we know about the goodness of the world as a whole and our given place within it, rather than from a prudential reckoning about our interests in relation to those of others. 'What was given in our knowledge of the whole was a knowledge of good which we did not measure and define but by which we were measured and defined' (58–9).

Grant's purpose in presenting this simple contrast is evidently to suggest that something has been lost in the waning of the old account of justice, but he is quick to concede that there is much to be said for its replacement; an essentially hierarchical conception of justice has been replaced by one that is more egalitarian. Does Grant go far enough in his concessions? No doubt many partisans of the progressive modern accounts of justice would favour a stronger assertion of the connection between justice and equality. Some would undoubtedly wish to say that nothing at all has been lost, except a confusing intellectual framework that encouraged the telling of 'noble lies' to bolster unjustly hierarchical social orders. Moreover, the old accounts of justice seem to suggest that perfection consists in accepting evil and suffering rather than in rebelling against oppressive conditions. The old teleological scholastic science, whatever help it may have given people to see their places within an overarching natural order, the goodness of which was accepted on trust, did very little to advance our mastery of natural processes through the uncovering of its mechanisms. Modern science has made it possible to intervene more effectively in these processes to correct the shortcomings of the natural order from our human perspective.

But much of this, I think, Grant would have been willing to concede.[9] He insists only that something has also been lost, namely, the capacity to love justice as what is due each being because of its place in a natural order that we love in response to its beauty, rather than hating or resenting because of its stinginess and cruelty. The more we are drawn into the modern scientific or technological way of thinking, the harder it becomes to think of justice as anything but a painfully necessary part of our roundabout way of collectively wresting what we want from nature. 'What has been lost is the belief that justice is something in which we participate as we come to understand the nature of things through love and knowledge' (60). In the modern accounts, justice is fundamentally something of our own making, to be remade from time to time as enlightened leaders see more clearly than their predecessors could what new restrictions an advancing society requires and what old ones can be lifted because they no longer serve any practical purpose. In the account whose passing Grant is lamenting, we were not in this sense our own.

After reading 'Faith and the Multiversity,' paying attention to the illustrations and qualifications as well as to the major points outlined above, the reader may be surprised to learn what Grant said about this essay in his correspondence from the period when it was being written and revised. In February 1985, he wrote to Joan O'Donovan that 'at the moment I am writing for the first time why I think Christianity is the truth and it is around her [Simone Weil's] writing.'[10] Almost two years later, in a letter of November 1986, just before the publication of *Technology and Justice*, he wrote to another correspondent that he had tried, in the central essay of the collection, 'to express Christianity [around] a wonderful sentence of Simone Weil's that "faith is the experience that the intelligence is illuminated by love."'[11]

These remarks are surprising for two reasons. First, they imply that there is a problem expressing the claim to truth of Christianity, even though a great many Christians, perhaps most, would probably say that they know quite well what the major tenets of their faith are. Indeed, what could faith mean apart from such knowledge? Second, Grant's remarks imply that none of his writings before about 1985 bore directly on this problem, despite the many things he had written about religion, going back to the 1940s.

It may not be surprising that a scholarly, reflective person might find it difficult to describe the meaning of any long-established religious faith, even his or her own. The arguments by which the great religions gained whatever ascendancy they now enjoy in different parts of the world are difficult to reconstruct. They were adapted to the intellectual presuppositions and social circumstances of much earlier times, which have long since ceased to exist. This is indeed the problem that Grant is most obviously addressing in his essay: from the standpoint of contemporary science and its positivist or existentialist interpretations, the basic tenets of the Christian faith, and not just the biblical narratives, may appear to be, not just scientifically, but ethically and metaphysically (not to put too fine a point upon it) of doubtful validity. What could it mean to say that goodness is real and that it is divine? To what extent and for what reasons should people be willing to sacrifice themselves for the good of others? Is the willingness simply to give oneself away a mark of sanctity or of insanity?

The heart of the problem is to clarify the meaning of religious faith in its specifically Christian form. Needless to say, faith is one of the key words in the lexicon of biblical religion. In Paul's letters to the Galatians and the Romans, for example, faith is the name for the relationship to be established with God, not by scrupulous adherence to the requirements of a divinely revealed positive law (human obedience in exchange for divine favours), but rather by a trusting response to the claims of divinity in whatever form they may come to light, no matter how surprising these claims may be. 'Look at Abraham: he put his faith in God, and that faith was counted to him as righteousness' (Gal. 3:6).

In more colloquial language, faith is generally understood to be a kind of belief – 'firm belief that does not rest on logical proof or undeniable evidence,' as a dictionary might explain. Religious faith is typically demonstrated by unquestioning acceptance of statements about wondrous possibilities of a supernatural character, beyond the range of ordinary experience, such as holy men who can walk unharmed through fire, or great prophets who are carried bodily into the heavens on flaming steeds, or wizards who can raise corpses from the dead by saying a few special words, and the like. Faith in this sense is often indistinguishable from loyalty to a community of believers – a 'faith community' – who share common convictions about the supernatural or miraculous. Thus, in the great New Testament letter about faith, the letter to the Hebrews, faith is defined as certainty about unseen realities and it is illustrated by figures from the Old Testament who were steadfast in their devotion to the Hebrew nation. 'Faith gives substance to our hopes, and makes us certain of realities we do not see. It is for their faith that the men of old stand on record' (Heb. 11:1–2). According to the anonymous writer of the letter, it was unwavering dedication to the people of God, even in the most dispiriting circumstances, that won the favour of God for exemplary leaders like Moses and Joshua. 'By faith the walls of Jericho fell down after they had been encircled on seven successive days' (Heb. 11:30). And the models of faith in this letter include, not just individuals such as Abraham and Noah, who had been given more or less direct divine instruction, but even some military and political leaders, such as Samson and Jephthah, whose faith was shown by their ready acceptance of the claims of other human beings. In short, then, willingness to profess the beliefs that the members of a community profess, perhaps especially if these beliefs are likely to seem incredible to outsiders, can be a discriminating test of commitment to the cause of a group, provided the beliefs in question are regarded as important, as they are when they are the faith component of a religion.[12]

From this perspective, the most remarkable feature of Grant's definition of faith, taken from Simone Weil, is the emphasis it puts on experience. An *experience* is the heart of the matter, not loyalty to a group or an attitude of trust or any particular claim to knowledge or profession of belief. Faith is not, in this account, a matter of accepting strange possibilities on the authority of others, with the plea, if challenged, that nothing can be excluded as beyond the power of an omnipotent deity, just as no action can be deemed unreasonable from the standpoint of one whose will is known to be inscrutable. To be sure, the crucial experience – 'that the intelligence is illuminated by love' – is not one that can simply be chosen, as one can choose whether or not to taste a particular dish, but it is open in principle to all, however rare it may be in fact and however difficult it may be to demonstrate it 'objectively.'

Perhaps the relation between love and knowledge is most easily seen by considering what it must mean to love justice and not just to understand it as a rational necessity. As already noted in the last chapter, we find ourselves compelled to make choices between better and worse and therefore to search for a clearer understanding of what is meant by good and bad. Giving others their due may at first appear to be no more than a painful necessity explained by our inescapable interdependence, but if we are to love justice, it must come to be experienced as a loving response to an otherness that we apprehend as beautiful. We must be drawn to an ultimately unrepresentable perfection in our relations with others by our desires rather than in opposition to them; each advance in knowledge of the requirements of justice must be supported by a refinement of desire. 'We can only grow in our knowledge of justice in so far as we love what we already know of it and any new knowledge of justice then opens up the possibility of further love which in turn makes possible fuller knowledge.'[13]

For Grant, the experience of faith in this sense was best exemplified by the life and death of Christ. Before Christ's time and after, there must have been some, perhaps many, whose experiences included intimations of what Christ shows, even though they did not have the benefit of revelation as traditionally understood. Indeed, for Grant as for Simone Weil, the Platonic dialogues and the character of Socrates provided the great philosophic articulations of the relevant experience – that love can be a condition for the attainment of knowledge, not a barrier to be overcome at the outset by systematic doubt, and further, that the beauty that evokes love can be an image of goodness itself. The distinctiveness of Christ's teaching does not lie in any clearer explanation of these basic ideas, but rather in what he shows about the price of goodness in the face of evil. 'What Christianity added to the classical account of justice was not any change in its definition but an extension of what was due to others and an account of how to fulfil that due. Christ added to the two great commandments the words that the second is "like unto" the first. At the height of the Gospels we are shown the moment when a tortured being says of his torturers that their due is to be forgiven' (54).

The contemporary university, with its formal religious neutrality and aggressive pursuit of 'objective' knowledge, does not encourage sympathetic reflection on such a starkly 'vertical' and impractical understanding of justice. The modern pursuit of knowledge rests on assumptions that exclude the possibility that only in loving something might one discover what it really is. Grant accepted Simone Weil's claim that faith is to be understood as the experience that the intelligence is enlightened by love and he faced the challenge of vindicating it as knowledge, so that it would not be dismissed as something merely 'mystical' or 'subjective.'[14] In the notebook where the definition of faith just quoted is found, it is followed immediately by an allusion to the dramatic passage in Plato's *Republic* where the idea of good – goodness itself – is said to be 'beyond being,' surpassing it in dignity and power and requiring a different kind of apprehension and representation. Truth, Simone Weil says, following Plato, can be compared to the light coming from goodness. and it is the function of intelligence to perceive this truth. but the organ by which we see the source of light itself is love, not intelligence, even though it must be by intelligence that we discern the illuminating power of love. 'The intelligence must recognize by those means which are proper to it, namely, verification and demonstration, the preeminence of love. It must only, submit itself when it knows in a perfectly clear and precise manner why. Otherwise submission is an error, and that to which it submits itself, in spite of the label attached, is something other than supernatural love.'[15]

Reducing Grant's thought to simpler formulas than he himself offered is something I have tried to avoid. But in reading what Grant wrote about technology, and in particular this last rather dense but illuminating discussion of its relation to justice, one should try to keep in mind the familiar but elusive difference between two basic human experiences, reasoning and willing. When we reason, whether it be in determining the weight of evidence regarding some generalization or in working out the implications of premises or axioms taken as established, we submit ourselves to the guidance of something external. Reasoning involves the recognition that right and wrong or truth and falsehood are not in the end matters of choosing. Reasoning, despite its directedness and seeking, requires a certain passivity or receptivity. To will, on the other hand, is to experience oneself as free of any external determination, as behaving in a way that can shape the external world rather than just receiving its imprint. In willing we are no longer aware of ourselves as dependent beings; instead, we feel ourselves to be independent or autonomous, essentially active and creative rather than passive and receptive. We encounter the world as an array of objects against our subjectivity, impeding our purposes or ready for our use, rather than as an orderly whole inviting our admiration.[16]

Grant relates this difference to the problem of saying what technology is, where it has come from, and why it may threaten justice. He invites reflection on the possibility that it may be rooted in the Western tendency to make the ultimate reality an inscrutable wilfulness and consequently to give willing a false priority over reasoning in the interpretation of our experience. In this connection he once quoted something Strauss wrote at the end of his study of Machiavelli: 'Modern man as little as pre-modern man can escape imitating nature as he understands nature.'[17] Perhaps as a result, justice has come to be understood among us as a kind of willing – the product of self-assertive limitations on self-assertion – rather than as something that can be desired. To understand justice rightly, however, and to practise it wholeheartedly, one may need to have at least a dim apprehension of it as something desirable and not just obligatory. It may be necessary to see it as having some reality apart from our own painful efforts to uphold just institutions and practices. It may be like those 'forms' or 'ideas' that Plato apparently thought were somehow the ultimate reality: we have an idea of equality that is somehow separate from any physical equalities (in the lengths, weights, and so on of particular objects) that we observe, no matter how carefully measured they may have been, and similarly it may be possible to know justice, not as our own creation, but rather as the measure of all our just or unjust acts and institutions. In short, it may be possible to take seriously 'the conception of an eternal order by which human actions are measured and defined.'[18]

Grant objected to the common use of 'technology' to denote the aggregate of modern tools and techniques that we increasingly fear, even as we celebrate what we can do with them and remind ourselves to do only what is consistent with our 'core values.' He maintained that this familiar way of speaking hides the novelty of our situation. Technology must be understood more deeply as a new union of the arts and sciences that changes our understanding of our purposes as well as our ability to realize them. It is not just an excess of 'instrumental reason' that needs to be balanced by an infusion of 'practical reason' or more 'democratic deliberation' on what we all want to achieve. It is something mysterious, beyond the usual distinction between means and ends. At the beginning of *English-Speaking Justice* Grant says that 'the first task of thought in our era is to think what that technology is: to think it in its determining power over our politics and sexuality, our music and education.'[19] In one of his last writings, the essay on 'Justice and Technology' which was published in 1984, he says that it is an unfathomed 'affirmation concerning what is.'[20] The understanding of it must be inseparable from a comprehensive understanding of what is, or, in other words, an 'ontology.' It is, as Heidegger said, 'nothing technological.'

At the end of his life, as I noted earlier, Grant was hoping to write a lengthy critique of Heidegger's treatment of Platonic philosophy. 'If I can summon the courage I would like to write an account of why his criticism of Plato is not true.'[21] The reader will recall that Grant had a long-standing interest in Heidegger; his study of Heidegger's thought had begun in the 1950s, and by 1984 his intention of writing about him may have gone back more than a decade.[22] The interest was plainly both intense and ambivalent. Students who knew Grant well have told me that he kept a small framed photograph of Heidegger on the mantel over the fireplace in his study. On the days when he was well disposed towards his thought, the photograph was turned to face the room. On those days when Grant was feeling his antagonism to Heidegger – when the modern philosopher was in disgrace with the 'lover of Plato within Christianity' – the photograph was turned to the wall. Unfortunately, Grant did not live to explain and resolve his ambivalence in the writings that he had planned for his retirement. We have nothing from his pen about Heidegger more revealing than 'Faith and the Multiversity,' and yet much can be learned from this essay about what he thought was unsatisfactory in Heidegger's thought.[23]

The great attraction of Heidegger for Grant was evidently his root-and-branch rejection of the basic assumptions – the ontology and epistemology – of modern science or technology. By tracing the modern way of thinking about subjects and objects back to ancient sources, Heidegger was able to clarify what these assumptions are and thus to throw a clearer light on some basic questions about the academic and religious traditions of the West. What exactly is the connection between the understanding of truth institutionalized by ancient philosophers such as Plato and Aristotle, on the one hand, and the modern conception of scientific method and scientific truth, on the other? And is there some deep affinity between biblical religion generally or Christianity specifically (or perhaps only Western Christianity) and the modern sciences that have done so much to transform our world? Heidegger struggled to get beneath the surface of the conventional historical accounts of these affinities and divergences. By doing so he cast a new light on the contemporary form of the old conflict between science or

philosophy and religious faith. He vindicated the legitimacy of meditative reflection in opposition to the ever-expanding claims of calculative
scientific reason. Not surprisingly, then, his thought has attracted the
attention of many theologians, for it seems to provide a way of making
the claims of Christian faith intelligible to today's world.

Heidegger's writings are in fact full of allusions to Christian problems and doctrines, and their tone is often that of religious longing, but
he dealt directly with theology only to separate its tasks sharply from
those of philosophy or 'thinking.' Theology, properly understood, he
maintained, is a historical science that has the task of interpreting a particular faith, that is, a way of life or mode of being that has been shaped
by the acceptance of a particular religious teaching or revelation. Theology is, in short, the hermeneutics of faith, not the defence or articulation of a particular faith by showing its compatibility with any prior
philosophical doctrine.[24] As Heidegger conceded at the beginning of
his *Introduction to Metaphysics*, there can be a Christian theology in the
sense that 'one can thoughtfully question and work through the world
of Christian experience – that is, the world of faith.' But it is a mistake to
confuse this thinking and questioning with philosophy. 'Only ages that
really no longer believe in the true greatness of the task of theology
arrive at the pernicious opinion that, through a supposed refurbish-
ment with the help of philosophy, a theology can be gained or even
replaced, and can be made more palatable to the needs of the age.'[25]

Grant's reservations about Heidegger's thought had to do in part
with his tendency to ridicule Christianity.[26] But a more serious impedi-
ment to the theological 'use' of Heidegger's language may be its tendency to distort the Christian experience that the Christian theologian
would interpret. To be sure, there are some striking similarities between
Heidegger's 'Being' and the God of Christian theologians, and his
'thinking' is explicitly linked to 'thanking' – not just by an accident of
etymology in Germanic languages, but because there is something akin
to prayer in Heidegger's description of meditative reflection. Moreover, his phenomenology of Dasein as human existence in *Being and
Time* – the existential analysis of Division Two – is obviously indebted
to Christian ideas about sin and salvation. Following Heidegger's lead,
then, contemporary theologians can go a long way towards giving a
modern 'existential' articulation to some old religious ideas. Yet, as
Grant points out, the fundamental theme of Heidegger's analysis of our
fundamental awareness of things is the terrifying finiteness of human
life as 'Being-toward-death,' rather than its blessedness because of the

goodness of the divinely created order to which we belong. The clarification of this idea in the Platonic dialogues is what Grant thinks accounts for the close association historically between Platonism and Christianity. 'At the heart of the Platonic language is the affirmation – so incredible to nearly everyone at one time or another – that the ultimate cause of being is beneficence. This affirmation was made by people who, as much as anyone, were aware of suffering, war, torture, disease, starvation, madness and the cruel accidents of existing. But it was thought that these evils could only be recognized for what they were if they were seen as deprivations of good' (42–3).

Of course, the given goodness of all that exists is, as one says, a matter of faith. It is an intuition to be justified by further experience. Doubts may be provoked by particular misfortunes, but these doubts can serve to refine a more intuitive faith. 'We start with trust in our knowledge of those things we are presented with immediately, and doubt is the means of moving to an understanding of what makes possible that trust in an educated human being' (43). The interplay of trust and doubt obviously varies from person to person and from age to age. Insights of the kind that we are concerned with here require a certain openness or receptivity that not all have. 'The philosophy of the dialogues is impregnated with the idea of receptivity, or as was said in the old theological language, grace. What is given us and draws from us our loving is goodness itself; the perfection of all purposes which has been called God' (74). Faith does not require that everyone will 'hunger for the bread of eternity': it requires only that those who do will not be denied it. 'Ask, and it will be given you; seek, and you will find; knock, and it will be opened to you.'

Some Further Reflections

My former speeches have but hit your thoughts,
Which can interpret further.
Shakespeare, *Macbeth*, III.vi

George Grant died in September 1988, six weeks shy of his seventieth birthday. His remains are buried in a small graveyard overlooking Terence Bay, a narrow arm of the Atlantic Ocean not far from Halifax. In 1955 he and his wife Sheila had bought a small property near the lighthouse that marks the entrance to the bay, a kilometre or so beyond a fishing village, also called Terence Bay, where they and their children had spent many vacations. The graveyard lies between the village (now beginning to show signs of the city's sprawl) and the cabin, hidden from the local traffic and cut off by a small hill even from the Anglican church to which it belongs, but with an unobstructed view to the end of the bay and the open sea. It is a rugged spot and rather remote, definitely off the beaten path, but very beautiful.

On Grant's gravestone is carved, after his name and dates, 'Out of the shadows and imaginings into the truth.'[1] What are we to make of this epitaph? It will of course mean different things to different readers, for the meaning of a statement is always in a sense just what different people make of it. It can have as many meanings, perhaps, as there are readers. But there is a primary ambiguity here that invites some further reflections. Does it mean – would Grant have wanted us to think – that in passing from his brief life in this world to his eternal life in the next he was leaving behind all the crazy confusion of our shadowy existence in time and space and entering the dazzling light of eternal Truth? Is the epitaph a declaration of a traditional belief in something hoped for but not seen? Or should it be read as a summation of Grant's experience in this world? Does it mean that Grant's life, seen from the perspective of his last years, had been an ascent from a more confused condition, in which his own imagination and that of others had supplied most of his beliefs, to a clearer comprehension of the human condition and a better understanding of reality?

The most remarkable feature of Grant's writings is their power to point beyond themselves to the most difficult and most important questions that human beings can confront. These are not religious rather than political or political rather than philosophical questions; they cannot be assigned to any single discipline, even the greatest; and they are certainly not the preserve of academics. Grant was a disciplined thinker, but he simply disregarded the usual disciplinary boundaries. He dissented in principle from the modern paradigm of knowledge, with its denial of the possibility of comprehensive understanding and its encouragement, therefore, of ever-increasing specialization. Any exposition of Grant's thought – any attempt to show its breadth and depth – requires that a selection be made of particular topics and that they be arranged in a sequence. Moreover, his thinking obviously changed in some ways from his youth to his maturity and old age: the emphasis shifts in his writing, as it has in this book, from politics through philosophy to religion. But my assumption throughout has been that his thought shows a 'massive consistency' of the kind he found in the thinkers he most admired.

Admittedly, most of his writings catch the attention of most of his readers by what they say about Canadian history and politics, but they leave only their sleepier or more distracted readers confined within the limits of the conventionally political. Grant is opinionated and provocative without being simply partisan or blind to the difficulties of his own position. He relates political strife to perplexing questions about science, religion, and education. Even as he makes unmistakeably clear his disagreements with and lack of respect for some eminent authorities, he defers to the wisdom of others, resisting the temptation to try to improve upon what they said. The contemporary thinkers he held in highest esteem were by no means entirely in agreement with each other, but Grant himself did not presume to go beyond them by offering quick answers to the questions their disagreements raise. There is something cautiously 'agnostic' about his thought.

Grant not only linked politics and philosophy more closely than do most professional philosophers and political scientists; he was also reluctant to make any sharp distinction between the tasks of philosophy and those of theology. He was not among those who have turned away from the ancient idea of a natural theology and embraced instead the more modern – and arguably more biblical – conception of theology as the interpretation of a given historical faith. He had similar reservations about the complementary conception of Leo Strauss, that philosophy is essentially a way of life defined by its opposition to religion. According to Strauss, philosophy, facing the challenge of biblical faith, may not be able to establish its credentials on the basis of reason alone, but its relation to religion is nonetheless inherently antagonistic. The Philosopher is, so to speak, the Free Thinker who more or less openly questions the dogmatic claims of those in authority, and especially those claiming religious authority. For Grant, by contrast, philosophy is related to faith in a friendlier way. It is, as Augustine said, 'faith seeking understanding': it is ultimately the interpretation of experiences of a mystical or religious character, and it has broader social responsibilities. Philosophers, as practitioners of the rational form of the contemplative life, have the task of helping those living other lives to relate their specialized functions to the overall good of society.

Earlier I quoted the phrase that Grant used late in life to describe himself – 'a lover of Plato within Christianity.'[2] This is not a standard category within any familiar system of classification, but rather the name of a problem. How should we understand the relation between Christianity and ancient philosophy? Do they stand directly opposed to each other, struggling for the same territory, or is their relation a more complementary one of mutual correction and support? If religious faith were something essentially irrational, or at least somehow entirely beyond reason, how could its claims be communicated to those who had not already embraced them? How could the conflicting claims of different faiths, or different interpretations of the same faith, be resolved? To the extent that philosophy or unassisted reason must be set in opposition to revelation, how is one to decide between them? If reliance upon reason were itself to be seen as basically a matter of faith – 'putting one's faith in reason' – would reason then cease to be a genuine alternative? Some of the earliest Christian theologians, and in particular Augustine, believed that Platonism, though incomplete, was fundamentally true and that it could be used to explain the 'good news' of the gospels and epistles. More recently, some influential theologians have insisted on a radical separation of philosophy and theology: divine revelation is 'spoiled,' they have said, when it is made to conform to the requirements of any alien system of reasoning. These are questions and problems that occupied Grant from his mid-twenties until the end of his life.

The key to a clearer understanding of Grant's religious thought, I have suggested (admittedly without proof), is his deep and sustained interest in Simone Weil. No sooner is this affinity seen, however, than new difficulties appear: What is one to make of her voluminous, very quotable, but enigmatic writings? Grant himself is not as helpful here as he might have been: apart from pointing to her and insisting on her importance as a thinker, he said surprisingly little about where exactly he thought that importance lay or how it should be explained and defended. He never tried to synthesize and summarize her thought, for easier digestion. Perhaps he thought that only those who had confronted her writings directly would be able to see what it was that held his interest.

At the end of his life, as explained earlier, Grant was planning a book about Heidegger that would have thrown a sharp light on many of the questions raised by his writings. What he would have said in his defence of Platonic philosophy, had he been given the time to complete his final projects, no one can now say with any assurance. Yet the elements of the puzzle that he faced are clear enough – Plato, Nietzsche, Heidegger, Strauss, and Weil. These names can be considered convenient labels for an ancient understanding of good, radical modern historicism, that historicism thought comprehensively, a classically rationalist response to historicism or relativism, and a contemporary Christian Platonism that may circumvent the difficulties of the long history of Christian Platonism stemming from Augustine. It is not easy to keep all of this in mind, but it may be necessary to do so, if one is to have a sense of what Grant hoped he would have the time and the courage to do.

In concluding a guide to his thought, it may be permissible to make a very tentative suggestion about what he may have been intending. Strauss had preceded him in providing an effective Platonic rejoinder to Nietzsche and Heidegger, but his unorthodox (dramatic and 'zetetic') reading of the dialogues tends to eliminate those 'intimations of Christianity' that are so vividly highlighted in Simone Weil's writings. The Platonic teaching Grant would have defended would presumably have been one he learned to see more clearly with the help of both these very different readers, the first alert to difficulties on the surface of the texts and quick to find the solutions lurking between the lines, the other more alive to the broader implications of the leading characters' declarations when they are taken at face value. Grant's challenge, however, was not just to defend his reasons for liking a favourite writer, but to defend that writer's claims in the face of the scorn and antipathy of two of the most influential recent thinkers.

The basic difficulty, as Grant well knew and as he explained at some length in his essay on 'Nietzsche and the Ancients,' is that great thinkers tend to colonize the minds of those who are drawn to their writings. One may have turned to them for assistance in some limited scholarly endeavour or to work out a new articulation and defence of a prior faith, political or religious, but rather than being able to use the thinker for that prior purpose, one can find oneself being used by the language one learns. The very purposes from which one set out may be transformed by what it brings out of concealment. 'Once you discovered me, it was no great feat to find me; the difficulty now is to lose me.'

I doubt that Grant would have offered a straightforward defence of Plato's apparently superfluous (and infinitely regressive?) reduplication of the world – as visible but changing appearances and as intelligible permanent reality – that has often served to define 'Platonism' since the time of Aristotle. Perhaps he would have gone back to the problem of freedom that had been at the focus of his reflections in the 1950s, when he was taking his bearings from Augustine and Kant. There is a passage in 'Faith and the Multiversity' that suggests what I have in mind: 'Whatever we are called to do or to make in the world, the freedom to do and to make cannot be for us the final account of what we are. For Plato freedom is not our essence. It is simply the liberty of indifference; the ability to turn away from the light we have sighted' (75).

My aim in writing this book, as I have repeatedly said, has been to assist the reader of Grant's works, not to provide an executive (or sophomore) summary of their contents. I have tried to get beneath the simplifying labels, keeping in mind the general reader, not the academic specialist.[3] I have thought about the difficulties such a reader is likely to encounter and then tried to show the way around them. Some basic points whose significance could easily be missed, I have highlighted and tried to clarify, by restating them in different words and at greater length. Sometimes I have drawn attention to some of the connections between writings from different periods or on different topics that may be overlooked by readers who lack the time that I have had to read practically everything that Grant wrote and to think in a leisurely way about each text in relation to all the others. Finally, and this has been my most difficult task, I have tried to sketch in some of the background to Grant's thought, following his own indications of the contemporary thinkers he most admired. Without some elementary knowledge of their ideas, a good deal of what he wrote must remain quite obscure.

Much that is important for understanding Grant has necessarily been ignored in this short study.[4] I have not tried to comment on all his writings, and I have perhaps failed to give sufficient attention to some of the shorter and unpublished writings that are now becoming easily available in his *Collected Works*. But for the readers of this book, I suspect that it will be my treatment of *Technology and Empire* as a collection of essays rather than as a book in its own right that will be the most serious omission. It deserves attention as a book. (For example, its title invites comparison with Mackenzie King's much-maligned *Industry and Humanity*.) Among all of Grant's books, it is my own favourite. Its beautifully written essays provide the best examples of Grant's distinctive style, and although they deal with quite different topics, ranging from Ontario's public schools to ancient philosophy, they follow one another with a necessity like that of a musical composition.

The basic theme of the collection is easy enough to appreciate but hard to isolate and explain. In the Preface, Grant says only that its six essays (five of which had previously been published separately) were being published together 'because they are all perspectives on what it is to live in the Great Lakes region of North America' – in other words, in the heartland of the most realized technological society that has ever been. How is this fate to be grasped in thought? All of the essays, with their different topics, throw light on this question; the last of the six, which has the unrevealing (and unappealing) title 'A Platitude,' addresses it most directly.

Grant begins this essay with an arresting variation on the commonplace statement that technological society has both costs and benefits. To understand our fate, it would seem, we need to identify these costs and benefits and then to examine how we are striking the balance between them. Are we getting it right? (Perhaps we should rein in our headlong pursuit of better technology and put a little more money into the arts or spirituality?) It is not difficult to see many important benefits of modern technology, such as material abundance, relief from heavy labour, better health (mental as well as physical), and a longer, more exciting life. Nor is there any difficulty collecting all these benefits under a general term, namely, freedom. Our advanced technology seems to be the highest achievement in mankind's quest for a freer, more equal, and more satisfying way of life. But at what cost? Again there is no difficulty suggesting some possible costs – environmental degradation, for example, or social disintegration and spiritual impoverishment – but it is harder to identify the 'essence' of these costs in any clear or convincing way. Indeed, such 'costs' may have no common features and no solid reality that requires any 'balancing.' Perhaps they are best understood as discrete problems to be solved in the future and thus, in effect, as claims for future benefits – sustainable worldwide development, a stable, well-integrated society, and a deeper, richer spirituality. Are those who speak of 'costs' suffering any real deprivations or are they just showing how hard they are to please? Is technology really depriving us of anything tangible and essential to our happiness or is it just providing what we want a little more slowly than we would like?

Grant says that we have difficulty dealing with questions like these because 'technique is ourselves': we are too close to it and too imbued with its understanding of our own nature (as freedom) and the world (as stuff at our disposal) to think clearly about the possibility that it could be denying us something essential to our well-being. Yet, as members of mass scientific societies that insistently celebrate their amazing technical triumphs, social and political as well as electrical and chemical, we are all likely to feel at times some 'intimations of deprival.' These intimations are precious, Grant says, because they remind us of things that are no longer thinkable in the prevailing language, which has given freedom priority over any conception of goodness. Only by listening for such intimations may we be able to retrieve, at least for our own amendment, if not for the reform of our society, something of what our ancestors knew about 'the beautiful as the image, in the world, of the good.'

Admittedly, as Grant concedes, to speak in such lofty terms of human nature and the good, in the midst of the modern drive to mastery, is just 'to pass some antique wind.' Not polite and not very constructive. Indeed, only when such generalities are made more specific can their real meaning be heard by more than a very narrow circle of cloistered scholars. The earlier essays in *Technology and Empire*, which deal with the overall character of North American society, the question of religion in our schools and universities, the ancient understanding of tyranny, and Canada's relation to modern imperialism, provide examples of the clarification that is needed. But it is of course Grant's *Lament for a Nation* that best exemplifies his ability to makes others share his own intimations. He says there that many of our business and political leaders lost nothing they thought essential to their being in losing their country. His readers, on the other hand (some of whom may be destined for leadership), are reminded of 'the need for roots' – the importance of political loyalties in the economy of the soul – and the void that follows the discovery that 'one's own' politically no longer commands one's allegiance.

Grant is often said to be a pessimistic writer because he found little reason to encourage the beliefs that sustain the faith of others in our present way of life. He did not like the word, since it refers in a confusing way both to an interpretation of the world as a whole – that it is not 'the best of all possible worlds' – and to the gloomy feelings or dispirited expectations of particular individuals in particular circumstances. But his weightier objection had to do with the tendency of some impatient critics to dismiss his unwelcome arguments by explaining them away 'psychologically' (as 'too pessimistic'). He invited such critics to look more closely at our way of life and the language we use to describe it. The two are complementary, since the language helps to constitute the social reality it describes. Nonetheless, we are sometimes uncomfortably aware of discrepancies between what our words, such as 'freedom,' are supposed to mean and what they are being used to cover. We then get a glimpse of how we are being hurried along, from one stage of our history to the next, by something of our own creation – the labyrinth of our increasingly technological moral and political language – that hides the light we seek and leaves us stumbling about in the shadows, disoriented and confused. To be sure, the short-term health of our society may depend on those with practical authority sustaining some belief in progress as understood within modern liberal theory. It may therefore be irresponsible to question too sharply all those ways of speaking that derive from the assumption that man's essence is his freedom. Yet is there really any good alternative to the search for a more natural light than the flickering fluorescent glare of our scientific rationality?

Grant did not hide that his disconcerting interpretation of our condition has its basis in tradition. He did not claim simply to know the truth about the ultimate questions he raised. But by raising them he provided

Canadians of my generation with access to an unorthodox understanding of our tangled political-philosophical-religious tradition from an immediately intelligible starting point, beginning from questions that are inescapably present to thoughtful or perplexed Canadians. One can hope that his writings will continue to engage the interest and guide the reflections of a new generation of Canadians.

Notes

Introduction

1 Grant's sister Alison was in London at the time, as were his mother's sister, Alice, and her husband, Vincent Massey, who was the Canadian high commissioner to Britain from 1935 to 1946. Lester Pearson was Massey's first secretary from 1935 to 1941, and at least once he was dispatched to Bermondsey to check on George. This background is described in detail in William Christian, *George Grant: A Biography* (Toronto: University of Toronto Press 1993), chapters 5–7.

2 George Grant, 'Philosophy,' in *Royal Commission Studies: A Selection of Essays Prepared for the Royal Commission on National Development in the Arts, Letters and Sciences* (Ottawa: King's Printer 1951), 119–33, in *Collected Works* 2:4. For full citations of each of the volumes in Grant's Collected Works, see the Bibliographical Notes.

3 Grant, 'Philosophy,' 20.

4 See John A. Irving, ed., *Philosophy in Canada: A Symposium* (Toronto: University of Toronto Press 1952), especially the Introduction by Fulton H. Anderson. This collection of essays was obviously meant to challenge Grant's account of the state of philosophy in English Canada. In 1948 Grant had published a curtly dismissive review of a major scholarly monograph by Anderson, who was almost a generation his senior. See 'Review of *The Philosophy of Francis Bacon* by F.H. Anderson,' *Dalhousie Review,* 28(3) (1948): 312–13, in *Collected Works*, 1:147–8. The same number of the *Review* contained a laudatory review by Grant of *The Pickersgill Letters: 1934–43*, ed. George Ford, also in the *Collected Works*, 1: 149–50. It begins as follows: 'These are the letters of a young Canadian who in the war of 1939–45 worked gallantly for the French underground and was found at the end of

the war beaten and tortured on a butcher's hook at Buchenwald. They are the record of the pilgrimage of this North American, from the easy hopeful years of the 1930s as a student at the University of Manitoba, to his full decision for prodigious courage before the evil and horror of the war of the 1940s ... Through them and behind them, one can feel as they develop the pulse of a man called by his conscience to a terrible agony.'

5 The problem here is not the difficulty of imagining simple-minded people making big fusses about small or non-existent differences – willing to declare, for example, that they love Geminis and hate Libras. But such loves and hates belong to teenagers on sitcoms, we like to think, not to political philosophers in universities, who are supposed to stand above popular passions and superstitions. What some have wondered is whether a thinker and writer of Grant's apparent stature – someone with his erudition and powers of expression – could have taken seriously the slogans and simplifications of Canadian cultural nationalism. And some have resolved their perplexity by jumping to the conclusion that Grant's views are to be explained 'psychologically.'

6 George Grant, *English-Speaking Justice* (Toronto: Anansi 1998), 72.

7 Christian's *George Grant* is the indispensable source for information about Grant's life. See also the other biographical sources listed in the Bibliographical Notes.

8 A fourth landmark figure, much less well known than the others, is Philip Sherrard. His survey of the political and theological background to the division between Eastern and Western Christianity, *The Greek East and the Latin West: A Study in the Christian Tradition* (London: Oxford University Press 1959), made a deep impression on Grant because, as William Christian explains, it showed him 'a way of accounting for the condition of the modern West without holding Christianity itself responsible' (234). By following Sherrard's distinction between the Eastern (more Platonic) and Western (more Aristotelian) traditions, the perfection of the Gospels could be reconciled with the role that the church had played in the development of modern technological civilization.

9 'Reactions against liberalism emerge on our continent based on local patriotisms and parochialities. These reactions are rarely able to sustain any national control of public policy, partially because the moral language in which they express themselves can easily be shown to be "irrational" in terms of liberal premises, by the dominant classes of our society and their instruments of legitimation. Or again, the language of traditional religion can sustain itself in the public realm only in so far as it responds to issues on the same side as the dominating liberalism. If it does, it is allowed to

express itself about social issues. But if there is a conflict between the religious voices and the liberalism, then the religious voices are condemned as reactionary and told to confine themselves to the proper sphere of religion, which is the private realm.' Grant, *English-Speaking Justice*, 6.

10 Simone Weil, 'Human Personality,' in *Selected Essays, 1934–1943*, ed. Richard Rees (London: Oxford University Press 1962), 26 and 27.

1   Nations and Necessities

1 George Grant, *Lament for a Nation: The Defeat of Canadian Nationalism*, Carleton Library Series 205 (Montreal and Kingston: McGill-Queen's University Press 2005), 85. For information about earlier editions and their pagination, see the Bibliographical Notes.

2 For example, Andrew Potter, who contributed the Introduction to the fortieth anniversary edition cited above. His more optimistic view is developed more fully in Joseph Heath and Andrew Potter, *Rebel Sell: Why the Culture Can't Be Jammed* (Toronto: HarperCollins 2004).

3 The argument that Grant had taken too bleak a view of Canada's situation and future was given its most influential expression in the so-called 'fragment theory' that quickly became one of the staples of Canadian political education. The theory derives from an explanation of 'American exceptionalism' (why the United States has never had a major socialist party) developed by a Harvard political scientist, Louis Hartz, in the 1940s and 1950s. It was adapted by a Canadian political scientist, Gad Horowitz, to explain the presence of a minor socialist party (the CCF/NDP) in Canadian politics. According to Horowitz, both conservatives and socialists think of societies as organic entities, or communities of classes, by contrast with liberals, who think of them as aggregates of individuals. Therefore, any society with a Tory past will generate demands for equality that go beyond the liberal ideal of equality of opportunity. The egalitarian politics of such a society will take a socialist form. This is the potential inherent in Canadian society, because of its 'tory touch' from the past (utramontane Catholicism in French Canada and the Loyalists in English Canada), but which Grant, despite his socialist sympathies, seems to be denying in *Lament for a Nation*, because of his own idiosyncratic pessimism. According to Horowitz, Grant was right to lament the death of what used to distinguish Canada from the United States – its British conservatism – but wrong to deny, in effect, that socialism could replace this source of identity in the future. 'His tory fatalism has sucked the life out of his socialist humanism.' Gad Horowitz, 'Tories, Socialists and the Demise of Canada,' *Canadian Dimension*, 2(4)

(1965): 12–15, reprinted in *Canadian Political Thought*, ed. H.D. Forbes (Toronto: Oxford University Press 1985), 352–9. The quoted remarks are from pages 358 and 359 of the latter source. See also Gad Horowitz, 'Conservatism, Liberalism, and Socialism in Canada: An Interpretation,' in *Canadian Labour in Politics* (Toronto: University of Toronto Press 1968), for the classic statement of the Hartz-Horowitz theory, and 'Two Televised Conversations between George Grant and Gad Horowitz,' in *Collected Works*, 3: 431–52.

 4 At several points Grant refers in general terms (e.g., pp. 6, 9, 40–1, and 44) to decisions taken by Liberal governments in the 1940s and earlier that undermined Canadian independence. He may have had in mind the Canadian-American trade agreement of 1935, which restored the level and structure of tariffs that had existed in 1929, before both governments had increased tariffs and adopted other protective measures in a futile attempt to isolate their countries from the effects of the Great Depression, and then the further agreement of 1938, which began the process of generally lowering tariffs; the Ogdensburg Agreement of August 1940, which set up a Canada-United States Permanent Joint Board of Defence to plan continental defence; the Hyde Park Declaration of April 1941, which encouraged the American buying of armaments in Canada and thus the development of Canadian defence production; and the General Agreement on Tariffs and Trade, signed by twenty-three nations in 1947, which provided the framework for subsequent trade negotiations and tariff reductions.

 5 Diefenbaker and Green were more like Jacksonian Democrats, voicing popular opposition to banks and corporations, though both, and particularly Howard Green, the real hero of the book, harboured some more conservative sentiments.

2   Technology, Freedom, Progress

 1 George Grant, 'In Defence of North America,' in *Technology and Empire* (Toronto: Anansi 1969), 28.
 2 Ibid., 17.
 3 Ibid., 19. Cf. Louis Hartz, *The Liberal Tradition in America: An Interpretation of American Political Thought since the Revolution* (New York: Harcourt, Brace and World 1955), 23.
 4 Grant, 'In Defence of North America,' 27.
 5 Grant's most direct statement is in a talk he did not publish and later repudiated. See 'Two Theological Languages' (1953), in *Collected Works*, 2: 48–59. See also the strong statement about this essay in David Cayley, *George Grant*

in Conversation (Toronto: Anansi 1995), 59–60, which I find hard to reconcile with the impression I get from reading the essay. Also relevant is 'Acceptance and Rebellion,' a manuscript written when Grant was on sabbatical leave in England in 1956–7, in *Collected Works*, 2: 224–93, and the letter he wrote to the president of Dalhousie requesting the leave, reproduced in the editorial introduction to that manuscript, 222–3.

6 In Aristotle's *Politics* 'doing what one likes' is called the democrat's idea of freedom and it is contrasted with a nobler willingness to submit to law (1310a31, also 1317b11). The context of these remarks about freedom is the question of what kind of education conduces to the stability of a democratic regime. In a closely related passage at the end of the *Nichomachean Ethics*, Aristotle says that laws are necessary because most people need externally iposed limits on their pursuit of pleasure, being more or less deaf to the arguments about the nobility of moral virtue. Even paternal authority, or more broadly, social pressure, while it may provide some necessary guidance and restraint for most people, lacks the force or compulsive power that is rquired. 'But the law *has* compulsive power, while it is at the same time a rule proceeding from a sort of practical wisdom and intellect. And while people hate *men* who oppose their impulses, even if they oppose them rightly, the law in its ordaining of what is good is not burdensome' (1180a21–5, trans. Ross). Grant was not inclined to cite 'The Philosopher' as an authority, but his common-sense observations point to a kind of freedom that requires respect for more than just 'technical' (including political) limits on 'doing what one likes.'

7 Grant, 'The Uses of Freedom: A Word and Our World,' *Queen's Quarterly*, 62 (1955): 515–27, in *Collected Works*, 2: 192–3. This essay, which may seem a bit diffuse on first reading, is a fascinating first statement of major themes developed later in *Philosophy in the Mass Age*, *Technology and Empire*, and *Time as History*. See also from the same year 'The Minds of Men in the Atomic Age,' in *Texts of Addresses Delivered at the 24th Annual Couchiching Conference* (Toronto: Canadian Institute on Public Affairs and Canadian Broadcasting Corporation 1955), 39–45, in *Collected Works*, 2: 156–64.

8 David Hume, *Treatise of Human Nature*, II, iii, 3 (ed. Selby-Bigge, 415).

9 Grant, 'The Uses of Freedom,' 199.

10 Ibid., 202.

11 George Grant, 'Review of *The Technological Society* by Jacques Ellul,' *Canadian Dimension*, 3 (3 and 4) (1966): 59–60, in *Collected Works*, 3: 412–17.

12 Thus, in 1969, in the Preface to *Technology and Empire*, he wrote: 'Professor Ellul's definition of "technique" is quoted [in one of the book's chapters], while my criticism of that definition is implied throughout "In Defence of North America," the first essay in the book.'

13 Martin Heidegger, *The Question concerning Technology and Other Essays*,
    trans. William Lovitt (New York: Harper and Row 1977), 3–35. Before this
    translation was published, Grant used one that circulated in mimeograph.
    Grant might not have agreed with Heidegger's highly coloured contrast
    between ancient 'bringing-forth' (*Hervorbringen*) and the modern 'challeng-
    ing-forth' (*Herausfordern*), but, without using the Heideggerian idiom, he
    would almost certainly have agreed with the claim that 'technology is a
    way of revealing' (12) and that it is therefore less an activity of human
    beings than a way in which they themselves are challenged 'to reveal the
    real, in the mode of ordering, as standing reserve' (20, 24, also 19).
14 Grant, 'In Defence of North America,' 16 and 19.

3   From Education to Indoctrination

.1 George Grant, 'Philosophy,' 7. Grant's view of liberal education was similar
    to that of George Wilson, a historian who was the dean of the Faculty of
    Arts and Science at Dalhousie when Grant was hired in 1947. Christian,
    George Grant, 140–1 and 161–2, explains the fundamental difference
    between Grant and Wilson. Some important similarities are suggested
    by Henry Roper, 'The Lifelong Pilgrimage of George E. Wilson, Teacher and
    Historian,' *Royal Nova Scotia Historical Society Collections*, 42 (1986),
    139–51.
 2 George Grant, 'Review of *The Higher Learning in America* by Robert
    Maynard Hutchins,' *Queen's University Journal* (1938), in *Collected Works*,
    1: 6–7.
 3 The best of our universities, Grant said, confer doctorates of philosophy on
    their most assiduous students after they have completed a piece of special-
    ized research, but without requiring that they show in any systematic way
    the connection between their narrow investigations and the ultimate ques-
    tions. 'How can the Ph.D. have any meaning as a degree, or any right to its
    title, if it be granted to students who are not required to show any formal
    understanding of the relation of their subjects to the questions of human
    existence as a whole? ... It has often been the way of modern men to laugh
    at the medieval student for discussing how many angels could stand on the
    point of a needle. Our modern laughter must be humbled by reading theses
    on the excreta of rats for which Ph.D.'s have been awarded.' Grant, 'Philos-
    ophy,' 17.
 4 This is clear in the articles and lectures he wrote on adult education in the
    1950s, which are now easily available in volume 2 of the *Collected Works*,
    particularly 'Philosophy and Adult Education' (66–73), 'Adult Education in

the Expanding Economy' (100–8), and 'The Paradox of Democratic Education' (166–81).

5 George Grant, 'The University Curriculum,' in *Technology and Empire*, 128. Cf. Grant, *Time as History*, ed. William Christian (Toronto: University of Toronto Press 1995), 22–7.

6 George Grant, 'Faith and the Multiversity,' in *Technology and Justice* (Toronto: Anansi 1986), 36.

7 Grant, 'Faith and the Multiversity,' 36.

8 Lord Rutherford, quoted in ibid., 35.

9 Grant, 'The University Curriculum,' 121–2. Cf. Martin Heidegger, *Discourse on Thinking*, trans. John M. Anderson and E. Hans Freund (New York: Harper and Row 1966), 56: 'The approaching tide of technological revolution in the atomic age could so captivate, bewitch, dazzle, and beguile man that calculative thinking may someday come to be accepted and practiced *as the only* way of thinking ... The issue is keeping meditative thinking alive.'

10 Cf. Allan Bloom, *The Closing of the American Mind* (New York: Simon and Schuster 1987).

11 George Grant, 'The Computer Does Not Impose on Us the Ways It Should Be Used,' in Abraham Rotstein, ed., *Beyond Industrial Growth*, (Toronto: University of Toronto Press 1976), 126. Cf. Grant, 'Thinking about Technology,' in *Technology and Justice*, 29–30.

12 Grant, 'Religion and the State,' in *Technology and Empire*, 49.

13 Grant, 'The University Curriculum,' 120. Cf. Cayley, *George Grant in Conversation*, 90.

14 Max Weber, *The Methodology of the Social Sciences*, trans. Edward A. Shils and Henry A. Finch (New York: The Free Press 1949), especially 1–6.

15 Grant, 'Religion and the State,' 58.

16 Ibid., 59. 'Religion means what men bow down to, and the great public religion of this society is the bowing down to technology. It is never easy to discuss the truth or falsity of a society's religion when in the midst of that society.' From John Irwin, ed., *Great Societies and Quiet Revolutions*, 35th Couchiching Conference (Toronto: Canadian Institute on Public Affairs and Canadian Broadcasting Corporation 1967), 71–6, in *Collected Works*, 3: 457. Cf. Grant, *English-Speaking Justice*, 52.

4   Modern Liberal Theory

1 See the Bibliographical Notes for further details on the publishing history of this book.

2 John Rawls, *A Theory of Justice* (Cambridge, Mass.: Harvard University Press 1971), is a 607-page treatise on the principles that should govern a just society. Such a treatise, written by someone who for many years (from 1962 until his death in 2002) taught philosophy at Harvard, perhaps the leading university in the English-speaking world, is, as Grant says, 'a good place to start' in pondering 'what is being spoken about human beings in our contemporary liberalism now that technology is not simply a dreamed hope but a realising actuality' (13). For shorter presentations of Rawls's theory, see his 1958 journal article, 'Justice as Fairness,' in his *Collected Papers*, ed. Samuel Freeman (Cambridge, Mass.: Harvard University Press 1999), 47–72, and his lectures on political philosophy, *Justice as Fairness: A Restatement*, ed. Erin Kelly (Cambridge, Mass.: Harvard University Press 2001).

3 'The test [of a theory of the good] is that it should fit our considered judgments in reflective equilibrium.' Rawls, *A Theory of Justice*, 434. As a master at solving problems by evasion (or at least not stumbling over them), he not surprisingly avoids any explicit discussion of contemporary moral realism or naturalism or, at the other extreme, emotivism or noncognitivism. For other statements having to do with his reliance on prior intuitions, see *A Theory of Justice*, viii–ix, 19–22, 48–52, and 579. At one point Rawls compares his whole 'constructivist' approach with abstracting grammatical rules for a particular language from the use of it by native speakers. 'In this case the aim is to characterize the ability to recognize well-formed sentences by formulating clearly expressed principles which make the same discriminations as the native speaker' (47). The basic reliance on prior intuitions, in the form of a hoped-for 'overlapping consensus,' is even clearer in Rawls's *Political Liberalism* (New York: Columbia University Press 1993), 12–15, 22–7, 44–6, 70–1, 134, 150–4, 156, 223–7, and 369.

4 I follow the simplest statement of the principles that Rawls provides, when he first introduces them. See Rawls, *A Theory of Justice*, 60. There are other, increasingly careful and elaborate formulations at 14–15, 83, 250, and 302–3.

5 Ibid., 150. 'Injustice, then, is simply inequalities that are not to the benefit of all' (62).

6 Ibid., 179.

7 Ibid., 139.

8 The 'veil of ignorance' hides from each individual in the 'original position' only his or her own ultimate social identity, and not any knowledge he or she may happen to have about modern social and economic theory, political history, probability theory, the calculation of expected values, the naturalistic fallacy, bargaining games, Pareto optimality, the maximin principle, and the like. 'It is taken for granted ... that they know the general facts

about human society. They understand political affairs and the principles of economic theory; they know the basis of social organization and the laws of human psychology. Indeed, the parties are presumed to know whatever general facts affect the choice of the principles of justice. There are no limitations on general information, that is, on general laws and theories, since conceptions of justice must be adjusted to the characteristics of the system of social cooperation which they are to regulate, and there is no reason to rule out these facts.' Rawls, *A Theory of Justice*, 137–8. What are ruled out are only prior conceptions of justice (or 'conceptions of the good') and any knowledge of where one will fit in the system of social cooperation being established.

9 For example, Brian Barry, *The Liberal Theory of Justice: A Critical Examination of the Principal Doctrines in A Theory of Justice by John Rawls* (Oxford: Clarendon Press 1973); Robert Nozick, *Anarchy, State, and Utopia* (New York: Basic Books 1974); and Michael J. Sandel, *Liberalism and the Limits of Justice* (Cambridge: Cambridge University Press 1982).

10 Most critics of Rawls take his theory very seriously and deal with it very respectfully. For a relevant exception, see Allan Bloom, 'John Rawls versus the Tradition of Political Philosophy,' in *Giants and Dwarfs: Essays 1960–1990* (New York: Simon and Schuster 1990), 315–45.

11 Rawls, *A Theory of Justice*, viii, pointing to a similar desire 'to generalize and to carry to a higher order of abstraction the traditional theory of the social contract.'

12 See ibid., 251–7, for Rawls's most revealing discussion of Kant. Note (at 253) his oddly evasive remarks about what makes an imperative 'categorical.' Admittedly, the ontological affirmations in question here have to do with a 'noumenal' reality inaccessible on the 'phenomenal' level of mere 'empirical' observation, so the difference between Kant's assertion that human beings *are* rational creatures and Rawls's assumption that they can choose to act as if they were rational is perhaps not as clear as Grant is suggesting.

13 Cf. George Grant, *Philosophy in the Mass Age*, ed. William Christian (Toronto: University of Toronto Press 1995), 31–2. The final essay of Grant's *Technology and Justice*, 'Abortion and Rights,' discusses the question of conflicting rights at greater length.

14 Rawls, *A Theory of Justice*, 504. The following quotations are from 505 and 509. On page 505 the issues is stated as 'what sorts of beings are owed the guarantees of justice.'

15 Ibid., 512. There are some extremely brief but at least explicit remarks about abortion in Rawls's *Political Liberalism*, the book in which he attempts to

make his theory of justice more political and *less* metaphysical. In a footnote (page 243) he expresses his opinion that 'any reasonable balance' of the 'political values' involved 'will give a woman a duly qualified right to decide whether to end her pregnancy during the first trimester.' It is interesting to know that this was Rawls's opinion and that in this respect he did not deviate from the common stereotype of liberal academics, but whatever weight it may carry is the weight of Rawls's social prestige and professorial position, not his reasoning. See also Rawls, *Collected Papers*, 605–6.

16 The interest of individuals in being able to start pregnancies without having to continue them is obvious. The relevant social interest or conception of the good was briefly explained by Justice Blackmun at a press conference in April 1994, after he had submitted his resignation to President Bill Clinton. In response to a question about his historic opinion, he said, 'I think it was right in 1973, and I think it was right today. It's a step that had to be taken as we go down the road toward the full emancipation of women.' Apparently it was the need to defend *Roe v. Wade* in the 1980s that showed Blackmun its significance for women's equality. On the surface, the majority opinion he wrote seems to have more to do with the rights of physicians (to give women the therapy that they think they need) than with those of women (to get the therapy they want). According to his biographer, it was only in 1989 that 'equality as well as liberty entered Blackmun's discourse on abortion ... The result would be a unified jurisprudence of women's rights.' Linda Greenhouse, *Becoming Justice Blackmun: Harry Blackmun's Supreme Court Journey* (New York: Henry Holt 2005), 223–4. Blackmun's press conference remark is at 242.

5   Varieties of Conservatism

1 'Red Tory,' as we have seen, is a term that was coined forty years ago by a political scientist, Gad Horowitz, to describe Grant's political thought. It is now frequently used more loosely to claim membership in or to relegate others to the more progressive wing of the Conservative Party. Used in this way, its meaning is no clearer or more stable than the issues that from time to time define such a position in internal party politics. Thus John Diefenbaker was often said to be a Red Tory, but so too, a little later, were those who pushed him out of the leadership of the party, Robert Stanfield and Dalton Camp. At present, the term is being used by both politicians and journalists to distinguish the 'fiscal conservatives' who are socially progressive from the 'social conservatives' who have retrograde views on abortion and gay rights. In academic writing, the term has retained a clearer and

more stable meaning in connection with the theory that Canadian politics has been influenced by a distinctive mixture of ideas from the left, right, and centre. According to Horowitz, who provided the clearest statement of the theory, there are 'crucial assumptions, orientations and values' that are shared by the tory and socialist minds, so that they can appear, from a certain angle, not as enemies, but rather as two different expressions of the same 'organic' or 'collectivist' way of thinking. (See chapter 1, n.3, above.) At the simplest level, therefore, a Red Tory may be just a Tory who prefers the socialists to the Liberals, or a socialist who prefers the Tories to the Liberals, 'without really knowing why' (though others may suspect that it has something to do with tribal loyalties or antipathies). At the highest level, however, as exemplified by Grant, the Red Tory 'is a philosopher who combines elements of socialism and toryism so thoroughly in a single integrated *Weltanschauung* that it is impossible to say that he is a proponent of either one or the other.' The synthesis transcends the antitheses represented by the spectrum, while somehow remaining on the plane of practical politics. See Horowitz, 'Conservatism, Liberalism, and Socialism in Canada, 23.

2 As Potter does in the fortieth anniversary edition of *Lament for a Nation* published in 2005 (xxiv and l–lvi). Potter cites Horowitz in this connection, implicitly recognizing that straddling may not differ fundamentally from collapsing.

3 The authorities I have in mind include conservatives as well as liberals and socialists. The basic problem is the anti-theoretical stance imposed on conservatives by their opposition to liberal and socialist theorizing. Burke is the classic example of this stance, and the problem is clearly explained by a contemporary conservative theorist who tends to equate modern conservatism with 'the political doctrine of Burke': 'There is a difficulty about treating conservatism as an ideology ... Conservatism is distrustful of, or hostile to, theory. An ideology is a kind of theory. Therefore conservatism would not wish to see itself, or to be seen, as an ideology ... As an ideology conservatism is, then, procedural or methodological rather than substantive. It prescribes no principles or ideals or institutions universally and so falls outside the scope of its own rejection of abstract theory.' Anthony Quinton, 'Conservatism,' in *A Companion to Contemporary Political Philosophy*, ed. Robert E. Goodin and Philip Pettit (Oxford: Basil Blackwell 1993), 247. It may be better, consequently, to regard conservatism, generically, as an attitude or disposition expressed in some recurrent themes and metaphors such as tradition, moderation, human imperfection, organic interdependence, and the utility of religion. For similar comments, see Russell Kirk, *The Conservative Mind from Burke to Santayana* (Chicago: Henry Regnery 1953), 7–8, and

Roger Scruton, *The Meaning of Conservatism* (Harmondsworth, U.K.: Penguin Books 1980), 11–13 and 190–1. For a contrasting view, see John Kekes, *A Case for Conservatism* (Ithaca, N.Y.: Cornell University Press 1998), 2–3 and 46–7.

4 Cf. R.K. Crook, 'Modernization and Nostalgia: A Note on the Sociology of Pessimism,' *Queen's Quarterly*, 73 (1966): 269–84, and Robert Blumstock, 'Anglo-Saxon Lament,' *Canadian Review of Sociology and Anthropology*, 3 (1966): 98–105, both of which discuss *Lament for a Nation*. There is an interesting letter from Grant to Crook in the *Selected Letters*, ed. William Christian (Toronto: University of Toronto Press 1996), 230–3, also in the *Collected Works*, 3: 379–82.

5 Although it might seem, from this limited perspective, that there could be no more possibility of being a Red Tory than of being a square circle, in the real world, below the empyrean of Platonic forms, there is of course no shortage of roundish squares and lumpy circles. Grant's 'An Ethic of Community,' in *Social Purpose for Canada*, ed. Michael Oliver (Toronto: University of Toronto Press 1961), 3–26, in *Collected Works*, 3: 20–47, is his one serious attempt to put socialist egalitarianism on a conservative philosophical footing ('an explicit doctrine of human good' – 38). Though harsh in its condemnation of capitalism and capitalists, it defines the fundamental problem as that of 'mass society' or 'industrialism itself' (24 and 39).

6 In Canadian politics, the classic expression of the socialist disillusionment with classic socialist means is David Lewis, 'A Socialist Takes Stock' (1956), reprinted in Forbes, ed., *Canadian Political Thought*, 290–300. See also Charles Taylor, 'The Agony of Economic Man' (1970), also reprinted in ibid., 406–16.

7 As Milton Friedman clearly recognizes in *Capitalism and Freedom* (Chicago: University of Chicago Press 1962), 5: 'It is extremely convenient to have a label for the political and economic viewpoint elaborated in this book. The right and proper label is liberalism.'

8 Burkean socialism can be illustrated by Bob Rae, *The Three Questions: Prosperity and the Public Good* (Toronto: Viking 1998). Any greater reliance on Burke than this would have to confront the evidence of Burke's acceptance of classic political economy, as shown in C.B. Macpherson, *Burke* (Oxford: Oxford University Press 1980).

9 See John Ehrman, *The Rise of Neoconservatism: Intellectuals and Foreign Affairs, 1945–94* (New Haven, Conn.: Yale University Press 1995); Stefan Halper and Jonathan Clarke, *America Alone: The Neo-Conservatives and the Global Order* (Cambridge: Cambridge University Press 2004); and Francis

Fukuyama, *America at the Crossroads: Democracy, Power, and the Neoconservative Legacy* (New Haven, Conn.: Yale University Press 2006).

10 Michael Ignatieff nicely exemplifies what is meant by neo-conservatism in the strict American sense. His practical utilitarian defence of a moderate amount of torture when necessary to achieve important objectives is in the spirit of neo-conservatism. See Ignatieff, *The Lesser Evil: Political Ethics in an Age of Terror* (Princeton, N.J.: Princeton University Press 2004), 7–10, 18–21, 140–1. Note that the currently controversial forms of 'torture,' such as waterboarding, would seem to fall between Ignatieff's 'permissible' and 'impermissible' categories, where the statesman's guide must be prudence (that god of the lower world, as Burke said).

11 Grant, *Lament for a Nation*, 85.

12 'One of the ridiculous sides of my own life is that when I have proved (at least to my own satisfaction) the impossibility of conservatism as a theoretical stance in the technological society, I find myself being described as a conservative. To those who would think conservatism possible, I would recommend what Nietzsche wrote in *The Twilight of the Idols* under the heading "Whispered to Conservatives."' Grant, 'Revolution and Tradition,' in *Tradition and Revolution*, ed. Lionel Rubinoff (Toronto: Macmillan 1971), 87–8. The reference is to s. 43 of 'Expeditions of an Untimely Man.'

13 American intellectuals, Grant says, are no longer persuaded of the simple truth of Locke, and American voters prefer social welfare – or 'law and order' – to limited government and free enterprise. The result is not outright abandonment of American traditions, but neither is it any clear-headed defence of them. 'Skeptical liberalism becomes increasingly the dominant ideology of those who shape society; and ... this ideology is the extreme form of progressive modernity' (62). The conservative elements of American civilization – 'the Church, constitutional government, classical and philosophical studies' – are becoming ever more 'like museum pieces, mere survivals on the periphery' (63). The point of these observations is to question whether, 'if Lockian liberalism is the conservatism of the English-speaking peoples,' 'the United States must be accepted as the guardian of Western values against the perversions of Western revolutionary thought as they have spread from the East' (61). The reference throughout is to the thesis about 'three waves of modernity' propounded by Leo Strauss, as will be explained briefly in chapter 10.

14 Grant, *English-Speaking Justice*, 49–50. This is essentially the argument of Leo Strauss in *Natural Right and History* (Chicago: University of Chicago Press 1953), 294–323.

15 Edmund Burke, *Reflections on the Revolution in France*, ed. J.G.A. Pocock (Indianapolis: Hackett 1987), 54.

16 Ibid., 53.

17 In *English Speaking Justice* Grant explained briefly why he was not happy with the popular (and therefore, admittedly, unavoidable) antithesis of liberal and conservative. He believed that it is more treacherous – more likely to plunge us into pointless wrangling and confusion – than the less familiar antithesis of progressive and conservative. See *English-Speaking Justice*, 4–5. See also Cayley, *George Grant in Conversation*, 72. The last two chapters of Sherrard, *The Greek East and the Latin West*, offer an example of progressive nationalism in the theological context that was of great interest to Grant.

18 'The CCF is a federation of organizations whose purpose is the establishment in Canada of a Co-operative Commonwealth in which the principle regulating production, distribution and exchange will be the supplying of human needs and not the making of profits.' The Regina Manifesto, first paragraph, in Forbes, ed., *Canadian Political Thought*, 241. The fine print, dealing with how need was to be assessed, is worth reading, however. See League for Social Reconstruction, *Social Planning for Canada* (Toronto: Nelson 1935), 282–3: 'Profit reckoning and the allotment of resources according to comparative returns will be maintained in socialized industry ... The efficiency of a concern and the need for its service will be tested on a profit and loss basis. Generally speaking, enterprises which yield a large profit will be pushed, and those which involve a loss will be eliminated. Labour and investment will be applied where earnings are highest. Industry will be carried on in accordance with a rigorous examination of returns.'

19 From a more practical angle, experience has shown that Soviet-style economic planning was effective in 'blocking progress' by stifling (or distorting) entrepreneurial initiative, diffusing responsibility, and weakening labour discipline ('We pretend to work and they pretend to pay us'), but the possibility of assessing it in this way was not as clear forty years ago as it is today.

6   Overcoming Nationalism

1 Polls sometimes provide the best evidence for testing generalizations about public opinion, but it would be foolish to expect much from asking random samples of Canadians and Americans to agree or disagree with the statement that 'man's essence is his freedom.' A more indirect strategy is necessary. Michael Adams, *Fire and Ice: The United States, Canada and the Myth of Converging Values* (Toronto: Penguin Canada 2004), which analyses Cana-

dian and American responses to simple questions about religion and values, is said to show that Canadians are now distinctly more liberal and progressive than Americans.

2 Grant, *Lament for a Nation*, 56.

3 But see Grant, 'Tyranny and Wisdom,' in *Technology and Empire*, 86–9, and Grant, 'Ideology in Modern Empires,' in *Perspectives of Empire: Essays Presented to Gerald S. Graham*, ed. John E. Flint and Glyndwr Williams (London: Longman 1973), 191.

4 Cf. John Ralston Saul, *The Collapse of Globalism, and the Reinvention of the World* (Toronto: Viking 2005), which highlights the discrepancy between ideal and reality in order to decry 'Globalism' without either opposing the process or disavowing the ideal.

5 In this connection Grant cites (63) an article by Charles W. Bray, 'Toward a Technology of Human Behavior for Defense Use,' *American Psychologist*, 17 (August 1962): 527–41, which deals with the research required to meet the long-range needs of the American Department of Defense. 'The key concept behind the reasoning and conclusions expressed here is that Defense management needs a technology of human behavior based on advances in psychology and the social sciences.' In the author's view, one of the six areas for research deserving special support was the social psychology of persuasion and motivation, because it was both relevant and ready to advance, if given support. In fact, this field does not seem to me to have made much progress since 1962, or indeed since Aristotle, but the same cannot be said about psychopharmacology.

6 Classlessness in this sense is quite consistent with the persistence of economic 'classes' in the sense of economic differences or a 'stratification system,' provided the different levels of income and wealth blend seamlessly into one another and do not correspond to any sharper racial, ethnic, or religious differences.

7 Elsewhere he is not so cautious. 'I am sure that the worldwide universal state would be a tyranny': Larry Schmidt, ed., *George Grant in Process: Essays and Conversations* (Toronto: Anansi 1978), 103. See also the much less qualified statements in 'The Great Society,' in Irwin, ed., *Great Societies and Quiet Revolutions*, 71–76, in *Collected Works*, 3: 455–62.

8 'Nation' and 'nationalism,' even in their basic 'sociological' sense, are used in different contexts with different meanings. They can be used to refer to a scale of political life (between the city or principality, smaller than the nation, and the empire or universal state, larger than the nations it comprises) or to its basis (membership in the nation as against some other qualification for full citizenship, such as residence, property, or aristocratic descent).

9 The obligatory citation here is Benedict Anderson, *Imagined Communities: Reflections on the Origin and Spread of Nationalism* (London: Verso 1983), which Andrew Potter may have had in mind when he said, in his Introduction to *Lament for a Nation*, that Grant showed a 'very crude' and 'inadequately theorized' understanding of nationalism (xlviii and lxii), although the allusion seems to be more directly to the liberal theorists of nationalism such as Will Kymlicka and Yael Tamir. Grant, by contrast, accepted the ancient arguments that the best regime is a 'city' rather than a 'state' or an 'empire.' 'The mark of the city is not that everybody knows everybody else, but that everybody knows everybody else at no more than one remove.' Cayley, *George Grant in Conversation*, 77.

10 James M. Minifie, *Peacemaker or Powder-Monkey: Canada's Role in a Revolutionary World* (Toronto: McClelland and Stewart 1960), was a flash in the pan, but a revealing one, and it can be read today as a useful reminder of the tenor of the debate about nuclear weapons in the early 1960s.

7   What Is Worth Doing?

1 George Grant, 'Canadian Fate and Imperialism,' in *Technology and Empire*, originally published in the radical monthly *Canadian Dimension* in 1967. This essay offers a brief review of the entire argument of *Lament for a Nation* and provides the clearest explanation of Grant's views on the war in Vietnam.

2 Plato, *Republic*, 496d (trans. Bloom).

3 Pascal, *Pensées*, No. 533 (Lafuma, trans. Krailsheimer).

4 Pierre Elliott Trudeau, *Approaches to Politics*, trans. I.M. Owen (Toronto: Oxford University Press 1970), 26.

5 Janet Ajzenstat, *The Once and Future Canadian Democracy: An Essay in Political Thought* (Montreal and Kingston: McGill-Queen's University Press 2003), 105, 109–11. See also the comparable argument of Barry Cooper, 'Did George Grant's Canada Ever Exist?' in Yusuf K. Umar, ed., *George Grant and the Future of Canada*, (Calgary: University of Calgary Press 1992), 151–64.

6 Cf. Grant, *Lament for a Nation*, lxxiv.

7 A valuable supplement to Grant's better-known publications is his talk 'Value and Technology,' in *Conference Proceedings: Welfare Services in a Changing Technology* (Ottawa: Canadian Conference on Social Welfare 1964), 21–9, in *Collected Works*, 3: 227–43.

8 Ajzenstat, *Once and Future Canadian Democracy*, 109. Cf. Grant, 'Canadian Fate and Imperialism,' 68 and 73.

9 Ajzenstat, *Once and Future Canadian Democracy*, 178.

8   Nature and History

1 William Christian's 1995 edition of Grant's *Philosophy in the Mass Age* includes material from the broadcast lectures that was not in the edition published in 1959. Some of the lectures were a recasting of material from a manuscript, 'Acceptance of Evil,' that Grant had written during his sabbatical leave in England in 1956–7. It is now available under the title 'Acceptance and Rebellion' in *Collected Works*, 2: 224–93. This manuscript and the lectures represent the culmination of Grant's studies in what is recognizably a 'first phase' of his work, before the three thinkers to be highlighted in the remaining chapters of this study (Heidegger, Strauss, and Weil) had had much (or any) impact on his thinking and mode of expression. This phase is often described positively, following Grant, as 'Hegelian,' though perhaps, as Christian says in his very helpful Introduction, 'Grant exaggerates the extent to which he was initially indebted to Hegel' (xxi). In what follows, I will try to show what I think can be called Hegelian in Grant's treatment of moral philosophy, without attempting any exposition of Hegel's thought.

2 For his account of the ancients, Grant relies upon the writings of Mircea Eliade, particularly *The Myth of the Eternal Return: Archetypes and Repetition*, trans. Willard R. Trask (New York: Pantheon Books 1954). According to Eliade, the ancient peoples wanted to deny or escape 'history' – the actual occurrences that we call historical – because of its 'terrors.'

3 This 'Hegelian' assumption had in the meantime become one of the fundamental principles of modern existentialism. There are parallel passages in George Grant, 'Jean Paul Sartre,' *Architects of Modern Thought* (Toronto: Canadian Broadcasting Corporation 1955), 65–74, in *Collected Works*, 2: 123–33, and in Cayley, *George Grant in Conversation*, 87–9. For a more extensive discussion of modern subjectivity, see the lecture from a course on Kant in *Collected Works*, 2: 490–9.

4 The contrast between Stoic acceptance and modern rebellion is more clearly developed in 'Acceptance and Rebellion.'

5 John Rawls's elaborate 'modernization' of the idea of a social contract can be seen as an attempt, in the context of mass scientific societies with mammoth bureaucracies and convoluted laws on picayune matters that fill volumes, to construe the situation of the ordinary citizen as one in which he can regard the laws he obeys as being his own, since as a moral being he agreed, behind the veil of ignorance (or with the wool over his eyes?), to whatever would be done in his name to implement 'the two principles of justice.'

6 This willingness, in principle, to be content with a finite object of desire is

Grant's reason for saying, in *Lament for a Nation*, that Marxism is closer to ancient teleological thinking than is modern liberalism, which better expresses the idea of progress as an extension without end of past achievements into the unlimited possibility of the future.

9   Enlightenment and Nihilism

1 Hegel provides a classic statement of the basic idea: 'In philosophy the latest birth of time is the result of all the systems that have preceded it, and must include their principles; and so ... will be the fullest, most comprehensive, and most adequate system of all.' Hegel, *The Science of Logic*, I, 13 (*The Logic of Hegel*, trans. Wallace, 2nd ed., 23).

2 Rawls, *Theory of Justice*, 432.

3 Since 1932, conferences sponsored by the YMCA, the Canadian Institute on Public Affairs, and the CBC have been held annually in August at Geneva Park, on the shore of Lake Couchiching, near Orillia, Ontario. The conferences have brought together academics, bureaucrats, journalists, clergymen, and other concerned citizens to hear talks by well-known speakers on designated themes and then to engage in Round Table discussions. In 1955 the theme was 'Co-existence: Why and How?' Sheila Grant was there and later recalled: 'George's speech was somewhat of a thunderbolt. Not popular. People were having a nice weekend in beautiful surroundings and didn't want to be made uncomfortable. It was appreciated more later. I think it was a far better expression of George's thought than the first chapter of *Philosophy in the Mass Age*.' Quoted in *Collected Works*, 2: 156.

4 Grant, 'The Minds of Men in the Atomic Age,' in *Collected Works*, 2: 163.

5 Ibid., 157.

6 Grant, *Time as History*, 13.

7 'Historicism is the exact opposite of Platonism.' George Grant in David Cayley, *George Grant in Conversation*, 89.

8 Grant, 'Nietzsche and the Ancients,' in *Technology and Justice*, 90.

9 It is worth noting that this was not Nietzsche's own way of describing his significance. 'Have I been understood? – What defines me, what sets me apart from the whole rest of humanity is that I *uncovered* Christian morality ... Blindness to Christianity is the crime *par excellence* – the crime against life.' *Ecce Homo*, trans. Walter Kaufmann (New York: Vintage Books 1969), 332. With an aphoristic writer such as Nietzsche, there is more than the usual danger that quotations taken out of context will be misleading, but see his Zarathustra's long account of his own prophetic mission, 'On Old and New Tablets,' in *Thus Spoke Zarathustra*, III, 12, which concludes, 'This new tablet, O my brothers, I place over you: *become hard*!'

10 Indeed, he says that any philosophy must finally be judged in the light of its political recommendations. And the reader easily sees that Nietzsche is not a 'democratic' thinker. Nowhere else does one encounter more sharply stated objections to democratic government and the ideals of social democracy than in Nietzsche's writings. What is modern government by consent of the governed but an arrangement that compels rulers to pander to the whims and fancies and low desires of the ignorant, lazy, unimaginative masses? This is not the 'elitist' or 'Machiavellian' critique of democratic practice represented by writers like Roberto Michels and Gaetano Mosca. Their 'political sociology' amounts to saying that real democracy, though it would be desirable, is no longer possible because of the national and international scale of political life. Nietzsche's critique is almost the opposite of this: that democracy, as the subordination of the higher to the lower, remains all too possible and needs to be combated, even if 'the people' have little say in day-to-day decision making.

11 Grant, 'Nietzsche and the Ancients,' 92.

12 Grant cites the first collected edition of Nietzsche's *Werke*, the 'Grossoktav-Ausgabe' published by Naumann in Leipzig from 1894. In the more recent and more complete *Kritische Gesamtausgabe* edited by Giorgio Colli and Mazzino Montinari, they are found in Part VII, volume 2 (137 and 186) and volume 3 (395).

13 Grant, 'Nietzsche and the Ancients,' 93.

14 Ibid., 94.

15 Ibid., 94–5. This is the conception of justice that is now unveiling itself in the technological West, Grant says, and he illustrates his meaning by pointing to abortion ('mass foeticide') and 'eugenical experimentation.'

16 Martin Heidegger, *Nietzsche*, III: *The Will to Power as Knowledge and as Metaphysics*, ed. David Farrell Krell (San Francisco: Harper and Row 1987), 245.

17 'What I fear in much North American education is the tendency to put even the very great into neat pigeon holes, and therefore put them safely away. This is part of "technological" training. The thinker in question is placed at our disposal, like standing reserve, and is made accessible to us.' From notes for a lecture on Heidegger at McMaster University in 1978. William Christian and Sheila Grant, ed., *The George Grant Reader* (Toronto: University of Toronto Press 1998), 298.

18 In his conversations with David Cayley, Grant praised Heidegger as 'incomparably the supreme historicist; he has thought it to its absolute depths.' *George Grant in Conversation*, 89. Cf. Schmidt, ed., *George Grant in Process*, 142. It is worth noting that Strauss's harshest attacks on relativism and historicism were directed against secondary figures, namely, Berlin, Collingwood, and Wild.

19 Grant, 'Nietzsche and the Ancients,' 90.
20 Ibid., 92.
21 Ibid., 91.
22 Ibid., 90–1. Cf. Cayley, *George Grant in Conversation*, 84.
23 Nietzsche, *On the Genealogy of Morals*, II, 2. The autonomous individual, celebrated in earlier German moral philosophy, is for Nietzsche *beyond* morality. He is said to be the product of the immense process, 'the whole prehistorical labour,' by which an animal able to make promises has been slowly and painfully bred. Such an animal – 'an autonomous, supramoral individual' – is proudly conscious of the strength and reliability of his *'free will'* and consequently of his ability to live without the 'straightjacket' of customary morality (*die Sittlichkeit der Sitte*), with its supplementary rewards and punishments, because he can be guided by his own 'dominating instinct,' which Nietzsche calls his conscience. Kant had postulated human freedom (and autonomy) as the indispensable metaphysical foundation for any morally praiseworthy action, but Grant came to see his conception of freedom as the denial of his own experience that 'we are not our own' and as the most sophisticated expression of the erroneous view that 'man's essence is his freedom.'

10 Platonic Political Philosophy

1 Strauss's best-known writings deal with ancient and early modern political thought, and they were all published in English. They include *The Political Philosophy of Hobbes* (1936), *Persecution and the Art of Writing* (1952), *Natural Right and History* (1953), *Thoughts on Machiavelli* (1958), *What Is Political Philosophy? and Other Studies* (1959), *The City and Man* (1964), *Liberalism Ancient and Modern* (1968), *The Argument and the Action of Plato's Laws* (1975), and *Studies in Platonic Political Philosophy* (1983). In addition, Strauss published three books on Xenophon and a study of Aristophanes' plays. For a brief account of his work and its impact in political science by one of his students familiar with all the sources, see Thomas L. Pangle, *Leo Strauss: An Introduction to His Thought and Intellectual Legacy* (Baltimore: Johns Hopkins University Press 2006). Among the shorter accounts published during Grant's lifetime, two can be recommended: Allan Bloom's obituary article, 'Leo Strauss: September 20, 1899–October 18, 1973,' in *Giants and Dwarfs: Essays, 1960–1990* (New York: Simon and Schuster 1990), 235–55, and Eugène F. Miller, 'Leo Strauss: The Recovery of Political Philosophy,' in Anthony de Crespigny and Kenneth Minogue, eds., *Contemporary Political Philosophy* (London: Methuen 1976), 67–99.

2 Recently (the summer of 2004), the rather distant and debatable connection of Strauss and some Straussians with a few officials in the Bush administration and some leaders of American neo-conservatism has led to the discovery of Strauss's scholarly work by journalists. Unfortunately, that work does not lend itself to journalistic presentation, so a great deal of what is now more widely 'known' about it, while it may have some basis in fact, is quite misleading. A good example of the genre is Earl Shorris, 'Ignoble Liars: Leo Strauss, George Bush, and the Philosophy of Mass Deception,' *Harper's Magazine* (June 2004). Still more recently (the summer of 2006), two books have been published that offer much more accurate accounts of Strauss's teaching and more balanced discussions of the complex relations between theory and practice in modern regimes. Steven B. Smith, *Reading Leo Strauss: Politics, Philosophy, Judaism* (Chicago: University of Chicago Press 2006), pays more attention to the more remote background to Strauss's thought, while Catherine and Michael Zuckert, *The Truth about Leo Strauss: Political Philosophy and American Democracy* (Chicago: University of Chicago Press 2006), focus more directly on its relation to American politics and the role of political philosophers in government and the universities. Smith concludes that 'nothing more clearly distinguishes Strauss from the foreign policy of neo-conservatism [as represented by Richard Perle and David Frum] than his reflections on the intractability of the problem of evil in political life ... Far from justifying war, Strauss's writings may plausibly provide a stinging critique of current policy' (200–1).

3 On the difficulty of striking the right balance, see the illuminating study by Laurence Lampert, *Leo Strauss and Nietzsche* (Chicago: University of Chicago Press 1996).

4 Until one has seen a good critical response, one may be at a loss to say what should count as such. Clearly it would be no refutation to point to Nietzsche's madness at the end of his life. Such ad hominem arguments may work with those who want to be persuaded, but not with anyone who has been impressed by Nietzsche's thought and who wants clarity about the truth or falsehood of his historicism. Nor would it be enough for such a person to be shown the bad practical consequences of Nietzsche's eloquence (assuming this is possible), for that would be like attacking Einstein's theory of relativity because it may have encouraged the 'relativism' of the intellectually lazy and morally lax. Just as clearly, a good response must not simply beg the questions that Nietzsche raised about 'the metaphysical tradition.' To assume what needs to be proved – in this case, that Socratic philosophy is not to be blamed for any dangerous softening that threatens the future of mankind – is sometimes an effective strategy, but

only as long as it is not easily seen. A good negative response would rather have to be one that accepted the challenge of vindicating the rationalism that Nietzsche attacked or that showed that Nietzsche himself had drawn back from the full implications of his own objections.

5 Grant, *Time as History*, 24.

6 Grant, 'Nietzsche and the Ancients,' in *Technology and Justice*, 83, from *Selected Letters of Friedrich Nietzsche*, trans. Christopher Middleton (Chicago: University of Chicago Press, 1969), 345.

7 In *Lament for a Nation*, Grant cites Strauss's *Natural Right and History, What Is Political Philosophy?* and *The City and Man*. In the Introduction to the 1966 edition of *Philosophy in the Mass Age*, he recommends *What Is Political Philosophy?* and *Thoughts on Machiavelli*. From about 1970 Grant was in regular contact with one of Strauss's students, Howard Brotz, who taught sociology at McMaster. In the 1970s he also met regularly with Allan Bloom, then a political scientist at the University of Toronto and later the author of the 1987 bestseller, *The Closing of the American Mind*, which criticizes American education and popular culture from a Straussian standpoint. But Grant's understanding of Strauss was based mainly on his published works and in particular on those that had been published in English before the mid-1960s.

8 Grant, *Philosophy in the Mass Age*, 36, 120. On the previous page of the new Introduction, Grant had explained that 'the book is therefore permeated with the faith that human history for all its pain and ambiguities is somehow to be seen as the progressive incarnation of reason. What had been lost in the immediacy of the North American technological drive would be regained, and regained at a higher level because of the leisure made possible by technology.' And the Introduction concludes with the following memorable statement about Strauss: 'As the greatest joy and that most difficult of attainment is any movement of the mind (however small) towards enlightenment, I count it a high blessing to have been acquainted with this man's thought.'

9 Strauss, *Natural Right and History* (Chicago: University of Chicago Press 1953), 120–64; 'Natural Law,' in *Studies in Platonic Political Philosophy*, ed. Thomas Pangle (Chicago: University of Chicago Press 1983), 139. Cf. Pangle, *Leo Strauss*, 39–42.

10 A noteworthy exception is Strauss, *The City and Man* (Chicago: Rand McNally 1964), 119–21.

11 The relevant scepticism is not the universal doubt from which Descartes claims to start in his *Meditations*. Rather it is the more selective doubt of those who suspect that particular popular beliefs may have no justification. One does not need to doubt all the claims of astronomers in order to have

doubts about astrology. And there may be more reasons to doubt that 'all men are created equal' than that the external world exists.

12 Strauss, *Natural Right and History,* 160, 161. Strauss continues: 'What cannot be decided in advance by universal rules, what can be decided in the critical moment by the most competent and most conscientious statesman on the spot, can be made visible as just, in retrospect, to all; the objective discrimination between extreme actions which were just and extreme actions which were unjust is one of the noblest duties of the historian.'

13 Strauss, *Persecution and the Art of Writing* (Chicago: University of Chicago Press 1952), is a collection of previously published essays on diverse topics. Its Introduction provides the most programmatic statement of Strauss's thesis about philosophic esotericism.

14 Strauss agreed with the 'Marxists or crypto-Marxists' that one must consider the class bias of the originators of political doctrines, but he did not agree with their analysis of the relevant bias for the ancient philosophers, because the class to which they belonged had not been correctly identified. 'In the common view the fact is overlooked that there is a class interest of the philosophers qua philosophers, and this oversight is ultimately due to the denial of the possibility of philosophy. Philosophers as philosophers do not go with their families. The selfish or class interest of the philosophers consists in being left alone, in being allowed to live the life of the blessed on earth by devoting themselves to investigation of the most important subjects.' *Natural Right and History,* 143. See also Strauss, *Persecution and the Art of Writing,* esp. 7–8 and 18–19.

15 Strauss, *What Is Political Philosophy? and Other Studies* (Glencoe, IL: Free Press 1959), 93–4.

16 Strauss, *Thoughts on Machiavelli,* 9.

17 'Machiavelli does not bring to light a single political phenomenon of any fundamental importance which was not fully known to the classics. His seeming discovery is only the reverse side of the oblivion of the most important: all things necessarily appear in a new light if they are seen for the first time in a specifically dimmed light. A stupendous contraction of the horizon appears to Machiavelli and his successors as a wondrous enlargement of the horizon.' Strauss, *Thoughts on Machiavelli,* 295. What Strauss has in mind as 'the most important' is, in a word, philosophy, as will become clearer in the sequel to this chapter.

18 Strauss, *Thoughts on Machiavelli,* 13. See also 120–2 and 153–5.

19 In Book V, Plato's Socrates is forced to clarify an earlier remark about friends having things in common in the good city that he and his interlocutors are imagining. First, women of the guardian class are to have the same

education as men, including the same athletic and military exercises, and (apart from bearing children) the same responsibilities. Second, the male and female guardians are not to form private families but to live communally, without real property, allowing their coupling to be regulated eugenically and the resulting children to be the common possessions of all the 'parents.' Finally, philosophers are to become the rulers of the city, or those who rule are to become genuine philosophers, so that political power and philosophy will be one. Socrates concedes that his proposals may strike some kibitzers as absurdly impractical, but he reminds his young friends that only the foolish, whose standard is not that of the good, find any amusement in ridiculing anything except the spectacle of folly and wickedness.

20 Strauss, *What Is Political Philosophy?* 48. The title essay of this collection provides Strauss's most concise account of his new narrative of philosophy and politics, but the important differences between the first and second wave are more fully explained in chapters 5 and 6 of *Natural Right and History.*

21 Strauss presents the turn to history and to philosophizing about history that is epitomized by Hegel, not as the discovery of a new aspect or dimension of reality, but as a political necessity, almost a rhetorical expedient. 'Philosophy of history shows the essential necessity of the actualization of the right order. There is no chance in this decisive respect, i.e., the same realistic tendency which led to the lowering of the standards in the first wave led to philosophy of history in the second wave. Nor was the introduction of philosophy of history a genuine remedy for the lowering of the standards. The actualization of the right order is achieved by blind selfish passion: the right order is the unintended byproduct of human activities which are in no way directed toward the right order ... The delusions of communism are already the delusions of Hegel and even of Kant.' *What Is Political Philosophy?* 53–4.

22 Strauss, *Natural Right and History,* 316.

23 Strauss, *What Is Political Philosophy?* 54.

24 Strauss, *What Is Political Philosophy?* 269.

25 But see Cayley, *George Grant in Conversation,* 72–5.

26 'Strauss's writing demands the type of scrutiny and interpretive effort that most readers willingly grant to literature, but expect to be spared in the pages of scholarship. One does not learn from Strauss so much as recognize kinship with him; indeed, it is quite difficult to see what he is getting at without first having got at or at least suspected something similar oneself. The hook with which Strauss draws you in is the thought that you may not

need catching.' G.R.F. Ferrari, 'Strauss's Plato,' *Arion*, Third Series 5(2) (1997): 37.

11 Theology and Politics

1 In the Preface to the publication, in 1965, of the German original of *The Political Philosophy of Hobbes: Its Basis and Genesis*, trans. Elsa M. Sinclair (1936). The remark is quoted from the English translation, 'Preface to *Hobbes Politische Wissenschaft*', in Leo Strauss, *Jewish Philosophy and the Crisis of Modernity: Essays and Lectures in Modern Jewish Thought*, ed. Kenneth Hart Green (Albany: State University of New York Press 1997), 453.

2 Strauss, *Die Religionskritik Spinozas als Grundlage seiner Bibelwissenschaft: Untersuchungen zu Spinozas Theologisch-Politischem Traktat* (1930). An English translation by Elsa M. Sinclair, *Spinoza's Critique of Religion*, was published (by Schocken Books in New York) in 1965. See also Strauss's 1948 essay, 'How to Study Spinoza's *Theologico-Political Treatise*,' in *Persecution and the Art of Writing* (1952), 142–201. On the background to Strauss's study, see his 1965 autobiographical 'Preface to the English Translation' in *Spinoza's Critique of Religion*, 1–31, reprinted in *Liberalism Ancient and Modern* (New York: Basic Books 1968), 224–59. See also his 1962 lecture 'Why We Remain Jews,' in *Jewish Philosophy*, ed. Green, 312: 'I believe I can say, without any exaggeration, that since a very, very early time the main theme of my reflections has been what is called the "Jewish question."' For an illuminating study of Strauss's overall understanding of the theological-political problem and two previously unpublished lectures of great interest, see Heinrich Meier, *Leo Strauss and the Theologico-Political Problem*, trans. Marcus Brainard (Cambridge: Cambridge University Press 2006).

3 Grant, 'A Democrat in Theory and in Soul,' in Christian and Grant, eds., *The George Grant Reader,* 135. In his conversations with David Cayley, Grant was blunter: 'What I admired in Diefenbaker was just the apotheosis of straight loyalty, loyalty without great intelligence, but loyalty ... He hadn't a thought in his head.' Cayley, *George Grant in Conversation*, 99 and 149.

4 True believers come in a variety of denominations, and other relevant types could be defined in the light of other contrasts. It might be possible, for example, to combine rejection of religious teachings with a dim view of human reason, that is to say, with the view that its powers are more limited than generally supposed and that there are more people than usually imagined who are incorrigibly ignorant and superstitious. As will be explained below, Spinoza distinguished 'sceptics,' who distrust human reason and who are therefore inclined to put their faith in claims of divine revelation,

from 'dogmatists,' who subordinate revelation to human reason and who are prepared to amend sacred writings or to interpret them allegorically in order to make them more compatible with current assumptions about scientific truth and human reason.

5 Cf. John Stuart Mill, 'Utility of Religion,' in *Collected Works*, 10: 415: 'The value of religion as a supplement to human laws, a more cunning sort of police, an auxiliary to the thief-catcher and the hangman, is not that part of its claims which the more high-minded of its votaries are fondest of insisting upon; and they would probably be as ready as anyone to admit that, if the nobler offices of religion in the soul could be dispensed with, a substitute might be found for so coarse and selfish a social instrument as the fear of hell. In their view of the matter, the best of mankind absolutely require religion for the perfection of their own character, even though the coercion of the worst might possibly be accomplished without its aid.'

6 Strauss, *Spinoza's Critique*, 15. In his 1962 Preface quoted here, Strauss explains the problem of a return to Jewish orthodoxy, given the unorthodox character of the orthodoxy of his time, which one could say gave Judaism a cultural or historical rather than a miraculous religious identity. Some of Strauss's essays in the 1920s suggest that this was for him personally an acceptable identity. See the 'Zionist Writings' and the review of Freud's *Future of an Illusion* in Leo Strauss, *The Early Writings (1931–1932)*, ed. Michael Zank (Albany: State University of New York Press 2002), 64–137 and 202–12.

7 Spinoza's way of dealing with Scripture is generally recognized today as the most important source of modern biblical scholarship – the so-called 'higher criticism' which treats the Bible, and more specifically the books of the Old Testament, as simply human compositions or compilations, rather than as perfectly preserved records of miraculous events and divinely inspired writings. The reader of Spinoza's apparently respectful treatment of the Bible sooner or later becomes aware that science or philosophy is being elevated above divine revelation as traditionally understood and that religion is being turned into a politically useful ethical culture for those incapable of philosophy. The flavour of his treatment of biblical religion is suggested by the following summary of some key points by a contemporary authority: 'Spinoza went somewhat further [than an earlier sceptical author] in assessing the first alleged inspired teachers, the prophets of ancient Israel ... So-called divine inspiration is analyzed into a form of strictly human manic-depression, and so-called divine history, or Providential history, is analyzed into local political history of the early Hebrews. Their peculiar situation after the escape from Egypt put them into a situa-

tion where they were without laws. Moses gave them laws, and called them God's laws to make sure that the early Hebrews would obey them.' Richard H. Popkin, 'Spinoza and Bible Scholarship,' in Don Garrett, ed., *The Cambridge Companion to Spinoza* (Cambridge: Cambridge University Press 1996), 397.

8 Strauss, *Persecution and the Art of Writing*, 194.

9 Strauss, *Spinoza's Critique*, 35.

10 Strauss, *Spinoza's Critique*, 132–3, citing Spinoza, *Theologico-Political Treatise*, VI, middle (in *Complete Works*, trans. Shirley, 447 and 451–2), and Letter 75.

11 Spinoza, *Theologico-Political Treatise*, I, middle (in *Complete Works*, trans. Shirley, 400). See also ibid., 446 and 448, and *Ethics*, I, Appendix, 241. Spinoza does not rely on Hume's basic argument against belief in miracles, but see the *Theologico-Political Treatise*, 452.

12 Strauss, *Spinoza's Critique*, 186 (cf. 197).

13 Calvin, *Institutes of the Christian Religion*, I, 16 (trans. Beveridge, 173–4).

14 Strauss, *Spinoza's Critique*, 198.

15 Calvin, *Institutes*, I, 7 (trans. Beveridge, 72). Strauss states the same point as follows: 'Man is convinced of the authority of Holy Writ by the inner testimony of the Holy Spirit. The same Spirit that spoke through the mouth of the prophets vouches, by being effective in us, for the truth of Scripture.' *Spinoza's Critique*, 193. Strauss could have cited Hume as well as Calvin: 'The *Christian Religion* not only was at first attended with miracles, but even at this day cannot be believed by any reasonable person without one. Mere reason is insufficient to convince us of its veracity; and whoever is moved by *Faith* to assent to it, is conscious of a continued miracle in his own person, which subverts all the principles of his understanding, and gives him a determination to believe what is most contrary to custom and experience.' *An Enquiry concerning Human Understanding*, X, ii (ed. Selby-Bigge, 131).

16 Strauss, *Spinoza's Critique*, 196.

17 Ibid. That reason and faith could coexist in separate realms was later a key teaching of Immanuel Kant.

18 Ibid., 143.

19 Ibid., 143–4.

20 'To speak more precisely, miracles can be rejected only on the ground that these events are seen as occurring for a state of consciousness which is not capable of strict scientific investigation of experience. So it is not the advancing positive method, proceeding from point to point, but only the reflection of the positive mind on itself, the recognition of the positive mind that it represents a progress beyond the previously prevailing form of consciousness (a finding that first takes the form of the crude antithesis

between superstition, prejudice, ignorance, barbarism, benightedness on the one hand, and reason, freedom, culture, enlightenment on the other) which creates a position impregnable to proof by miracles' (*Spinoza's Critique*, 136, also 162). This distinction provides a basis for understanding how the major miraculous revelation allegedly accorded to Joseph Smith in upstate New York as late as the 1820s could be possible.

21 Strauss, *Spinoza's Critique*, 143. Also 28–9, 162. 'Reports of miracles are not miracles.' G.E. Lessing, 'On the Proof of the Spirit and Power,' in *Philosophical and Theological Writings*, trans. H.B. Nisbet (Cambridge: Cambridge University Press 2005), 84.

22 Strauss, *Spinoza's Critique*, 28–9. Or more strongly: 'It would be needful to prove that in the universe of beings there is no place for an unfathomable God' (206).

23 Strauss, *Spinoza's Critique*, 139. As Strauss said later, 'a victory, not of Jewish orthodoxy, but of any orthodoxy' (30).

24 For example, his 1962 lecture, 'Why We Remain Jews,' in *Jewish Philosophy*, ed. Green, 312, 321.

25 In his 1962 autobiographical Preface, Strauss explains the relation of his own study to the writings of Franz Rosenzweig and Hermann Cohen. Rosenzweig had promoted a return to Jewish life, but within the framework of liberal philosophy, so that, as Strauss put it, the 'public temple' of the sacred law would become 'a quarry or a store-house out of which each individual [would take] the materials for building up his private shelter' (14). Cohen, on the other hand, had objected to the then-current glorification of Spinoza as the greatest founder of liberal religion, insisting instead that he fully deserved the excommunication he had suffered, albeit for reasons quite different from those that had concerned his religious contemporaries in Amsterdam. '[Cohen] condemned Spinoza because of his infidelity in the simple human sense, of his complete lack of loyalty to his own people, of his acting like an enemy of the Jews and thus giving aid and comfort to the many enemies of the Jews, of his behaving like a base traitor. Spinoza remains up to the present day the accuser *par excellence* of Judaism before an anti-Jewish world; the disposition of his mind and heart toward Jews and Judaism was "unnatural," he committed a "humanly incomprehensible act of treason," he was possessed by "an evil demon."' *Spinoza's Critique*, 19. On the importance of Cohen for Strauss, see his 'Introductory Essay for Hermann Cohen, *Religion of Reason out of the Sources of Judaism*,' in *Studies in Platonic Political Philosophy*, ed. Thomas L. Pangle (Chicago: University of Chicago Press 1983), 233–47. See also Strauss, 'Cohen's Analysis of Spinoza's Bible Science,' in Strauss, *Early Writings*, ed. Zank, 140–72.

26 As Strauss explains, 'if the literal meaning were the true meaning of Scripture, many statements made in Scripture would be contrary to truth, and
this would be in conflict with the revealed nature of Scripture.' So they
must have other, more acceptable meanings. Strauss, *Spinoza's Critique*,
295n.224. Strauss summarized Maimonides' hermeneutical principle as follows: 'All passages which contradict rational insight when taken literally
are to be interpreted allegorically' (148). Cf. Moses Maimonides, *The Guide
of the Perplexed*, trans. Shlomo Pines (Chicago: University of Chicago Press
1963), Introduction to Part I, 9–10.

27 Maimonides, *Guide*, II, 25 (trans. Pines, 328).

28 Strauss, *Spinoza's Critique*, 164.

29 Ibid., 171.

30 Ibid., 148.

31 Leo Strauss, *Philosophie und Gesetz* (Berlin, 1935), translated by Eve Adler as
*Philosophy and Law: Contributions to the Understanding of Maimonides and His
Predecessors* (Albany: State University of New York Press 1995).

32 In the Introduction to *Philosophy and Law*, Strauss recapitulates the argument of his book on Spinoza. He specifies that genuine orthodoxy requires
belief in verbal inspiration, miracles, the eternal validity of the revealed
law, and creation ex nihilo (or absolute monotheism). Allegiance to these
doctrines had gradually given way, even among loyal Jews, to the kind of
historicizing and allegorical interpretation already described – what was
believable then is no longer believable now, and something else again may
seem right in the future.

33 Strauss, *Philosophy and Law*, 60.

34 Averroes, 'The Decisive Treatise, Determining What Is the Connection
between Religion and Philosophy,' in *Medieval Political Philosophy: A Source-
book*, ed. Ralph Lerner and Muhsin Mahdi (Ithaca, N.Y.: Cornell University
Press 1963), 170.

35 Averroes, 'Decisive Treatise,' 169.

36 Strauss, *Philosophy and Law*, 88 (emphasis in the original). Also Strauss, *Persecution and the Art of Writing*, 21.

37 Ibid., 21.

38 Strauss, *Spinoza's Critique*, 181.

39 Ibid., 1.

40 Ibid., 6.

41 Ibid., 7.

42 Ibid., 15.

43 Meier, *Leo Strauss and the Theologico-Political Problem*, is the most thorough
and careful study of Strauss's political-theological writings, and it includes,

as an appendix, a previously unpublished 1948 lecture on 'Reason and Revelation' that explains the basic issues in an unusually clear and systematic way. 'A philosophy which believes that it can refute the possibility of revelation – and a philosophy which does not believe that: *this* is the real meaning of la querrelle des anciens et des modernes' (177).

12 'Tyranny and Wisdom'

1 George Grant, 'Tyranny and Wisdom: A Comment on the Controversy between Leo Strauss and Alexandre Kojève,' *Social Research*, 31 (1964): 45–72, reprinted in *Technology and Empire*, 81-109, and in *Collected Works*, 3: 532–57.

2 Grant, *Selected Letters*, 365 (to Peter Self, 1987). See also Grant, *Technology and Justice*, 76 ('the profoundest and most complete modern philosophy – certainly the deepest criticism of ancient thought which has ever been made in the name of modernity'), Schmidt, ed., *George Grant in Process*, 141–2 ('the deepest account of modernity ... the most perfectly thought historicist that I have ever read'), and Cayley, *George Grant in Conversation*, 81 ('the greatest modern philosopher'), 125 ('I have no doubt at all that he is *the* great philosopher of the modern era'), and 128 ('the greatest commentator on Aristotle who has ever lived').

3 Leo Strauss, *Thoughts on Machiavelli* (Glencoe, Ill.: Free Press 1958), 291.

4 Strauss, *Thoughts on Machiavelli*, 293.

5 Leo Strauss, *On Tyranny: An Interpretation of Xenophon's 'Hiero'* (New York: Political Science Classics 1948). The other three commentaries are *Xenophon's Socratic Discourse: An Interpretation of the Oeconomicus* (Ithaca, N.Y.: Cornell University Press 1970); *Xenophon's Socrates* (Ithaca, N.Y.: Cornell University Press 1972); and 'Xenophon's Anabasis,' in *Studies in Platonic Political Philosophy,* ed. Thomas L. Pangle (Chicago: University of Chicago Press 1983), 105–36.

6 Cf. Plato, *Republic,* and Aristotle, *Politics.* This is not to deny that some ancient philosophers as well as some modern ones have been entangled more than just accidentally with notorious tyrants, for example, Edmund Burke with George III.

7 Strauss, *Thoughts on Machiavelli*, 291.

8 In his charming autobiographical reflections, George Steiner, who was an undergraduate at the University of Chicago in the late 1940s and early 1950s, recounts the beginning of an advanced seminar taught by Strauss. 'Enter Leo Strauss. "Ladies and gentlemen, good morning. In this classroom, the name of ... who is, of course, strictly incomparable, will not be mentioned. We can now proceed to Plato's Republic." "Who is, of course,

strictly incomparable." I had not caught the name, but that "of course" made me feel as if a bright, cold shaft had passed through my spine. A kindly graduate student wrote down the name for me at the close of the class: one Martin Heidegger. I trotted to the library. That evening, I attempted paragraph one of *Sein und Zeit.*' George Steiner, *Errata: An Examined Life* (London: Phoenix 1997), 44–5. Steiner later wrote one of the best short introductions to Heidegger's thought.

9 See especially the previously unpublished lecture, 'An Introduction to Heideggerian Existentialism,' in *The Rebirth of Classical Political Rationalism*, ed. Thomas L. Pangle (Chicago: University of Chicago Press 1989), 27–46, and Pangle's explanation (xxix) of the sources from which he assembled this text. Ernst Cassirer, whom Strauss compares unfavourably to Heidegger, was his graduate supervisor, what the Germans would call his Doktorvater. See also 'Kurt Riezler (1882–1955),' in *What Is Political Philosophy?* (1959), 233–60, and 'Philosophy as Rigorous Science and Political Philosophy,' in *Studies in Platonic Political Philosophy*, ed. Pangle, 29–37. Other noteworthy references to Heidegger occur in the 1962 'Preface to the English Translation' of *Spinoza's Critique*, 9–13, and in 'An Unspoken Prologue to a Public Lecture at St. John's College in Honor of Jacob Klein,' in *Jewish Philosophy*, ed. Green, 450.

10 This role, being public, was always known to all those who had much interest in Heidegger's thought, and it was held against him by many from the outset. The controversy came back to life in 1987 with the publication of Victor Farias, *Heidegger and Nazism*, trans. Paul Barrell (Philadelphia: Temple University Press 1989), and then, the following year, the disclosure of some previously unknown details in the biography by Hugo Ott, *Martin Heidegger: A Political Life*, trans. Allan Blunden (New York: HarperCollins 1993).

11 Strauss, 'Introduction to Heideggerian Existentialism,' 29.

12 Ibid., 30.

13 The lectures, edited by Raymond Queneau, were published in 1947 as *Introduction à la lecture de Hegel* and a selection made by Allan Bloom is available in English as *Introduction to the Reading of Hegel*, trans. James H. Nichols (New York: Basic Books 1969). For a clear and concise account, not just of Kojève's theory but also of its origins in the difference between the ancient and modern understanding of nature, see F. Roger Devlin, *Alexandre Kojève and the Outcome of Modern Thought* (Lanham, Md.: University Press of America 2004).

14 The original commentary ('On Tyranny') along with a translation of Xenophon's dialogue, an expanded version of Kojève's article ('Tyranny

and Wisdom'), and Strauss's 'Restatement' were published together in French in 1954 and in English in 1963. References below will be to the edition of *On Tyranny* edited by Victor Gourevitch and Michael Roth (New York: Free Press 1991), which also provides the surviving correspondence between Strauss and Kojève going back to 1932. The sentence quoted is from Strauss's covering letter of 6 December 1948 (239). Strauss's letter of 22 August 1948, which deals with Kojève's recently published *Introduction à la lecture de Hegel*, anticipates some of the key points made in his 'Restatement.'

15 Kojève's Marxism and perhaps ironical Stalinism were well known during Kojève's lifetime, and they seem not to have impeded his ascent to the very highest levels of the French civil service. However, his political leanings were put in a new light in September 1999, when stories appeared in the French press alleging that he had been a Soviet agent for the last thirty years of his life. The stories were based on a dossier that the French secret service (the DST) had apparently received from the KGB. After a brief flurry of interest, the controversy surrounding the allegations dropped from view, and nothing more substantial than the original sketchy reports seems ever to have been published. The most thorough discussion of the whole affair is by an Australian writer, Keith Patchen, in 'Alexandre Kojève: Moscow's Mandarin Marxist Mole in France,' *National Observer*, 58 (spring 2003): 37–48. I am grateful to Thomas Pangle and Bryan-Paul Frost for help on this point.

16 In the English-speaking world, this basic problem was fully recognized only a generation later by the 'new left,' which distinguished itself from the intellectual left of the 1930s and 1940s by its loud disavowal of any admiration for the Soviet Union as a pioneering venture in the building of socialism. For the 'new left' of the 1960s and 1970s, Stalin was just a tyrant like all the other tyrants of the time, and the Soviet Union was no longer the first workers' state but just another capitalist society – a 'state capitalist' one – no less alienating than American capitalism. The most eminent representative of the movement was the 'Frankfurt' philosopher Herbert Marcuse, who blended Marx, Hegel, and Heidegger with a pinch of Freud.

17 Friedrich Engels, 'Speech at the Graveside of Karl Marx,' in *The Marx-Engels Reader*, ed. Robert C. Tucker, 2nd ed. (New York: Norton 1978), 681.

18 Karl Marx, *The Poverty of Philosophy*, chapter 2, Second Observation, in David McLellan, ed., *Karl Marx: Selected Writings* (Oxford: Oxford University Press 1972), 202. I am grateful to Ed Andrew for giving me the source of this remark.

19 In 1966 Heidegger was interviewed by two journalists from the German newsmagazine *Der Spiegel*. The interview was published after his death in 1976. It ends with the sentence quoted.

20 Kojève, 'Tyranny and Wisdom,' 174–5.

21 Grant, 'Tyranny and Wisdom,' 88–9. This seems to be Strauss's view as well, though he never says so so clearly.

22 Strauss, 'Restatement,' 208. Cf. Grant, 'Tyranny and Wisdom,' 92: 'The universal and homogenous state, far from being the best social order, will be (if realized) a tyranny, and therefore within classical assumptions destructive of humanity.'

23 Strauss, 'Restatement,' 209.

24 Grant, 'Tyranny and Wisdom,' 94. See Strauss, 'Restatement,' 189-94, and 209-10.

25 'To retain his power, [the Universal and Final Tyrant] will be forced to suppress every activity which might lead people into doubt of the essential soundness of the universal and homogeneous state: he must suppress philosophy as an attempt to corrupt the young. In particular he must in the interest of the homogeneity of his universal state forbid every teaching, every suggestion, that there are politically relevant natural differences among men which cannot be abolished or neutralized by progressing scientific technology.' Strauss, 'Restatement,' 211.

26 Grant, 'Tyranny and Wisdom,' 95. Cf. Strauss, 'Restatement,' 211.

27 Strauss, 'On Tyranny,' 22–3, and 'Restatement,' 177–8.

28 Grant, 'Tyranny and Wisdom,' 103. Cf. Grant, *Lament for a Nation*, 92.

29 Grant, 'The Minds of Men in the Atomic Age,' in *Collected Works*, 2: 157. Strauss led a retired academic life – not at all that of a 'public intellectual' – so the practical ramifications of his teaching can sometimes be better observed in the mirror (no doubt sometimes a distorting one) provided by his students and their students. In his own writings, political philosophy has essentially a critical or negative function rather than any positive or constructive tasks (apart from safely liberating potential philosophers from the madness of those around them). Its negative 'Socratic' wisdom is meant to protect the prudence of statesmen (and the freedom of philosophers) rather than to offer any positive alternatives to the prevailing illusions (including those of the natural scientists).

30 Grant, 'Tyranny and Wisdom,' 103, 106, 108. Grant adds: 'This is the civilisation which in the opinion of both Strauss and Kojève tends towards the universal and homogeneous state.' The relation between Platonic political philosophy and Christian Aristotelianism is clarified by Clark A. Merrill, 'Leo Strauss's Indictment of Christian Philosophy,' *Review of Politics*, 62

(2000), 77–105. Cf. Grant, *Philosophy in the Mass Age*, 40, and Schmidt, ed., *George Grant in Process*, 142–7.

31 Grant, 'Tyranny and Wisdom,' 106. Cf. Sherrard, *The Greek East and the Latin West*, 27–9, 50–61. The relation between different theological interpretations of the Christian revelation or experience and modern scientific rationalism is the most important theme of the book.

32 See n.13.

33 Grant, 'Tyranny and Wisdom,' 102.

34 The missing paragraph is restored in the edition of *On Tyranny* edited by Gourevitch and Roth, 212. Unfortunately, it is not Strauss's original text, since the editors were unable to locate the English original of the essay and therefore had to retranslate the French translation. In the meantime, a copy of the original has come to light, and I have quoted it from Strauss, *Jewish Philosophy and the Crisis of Modernity*, ed. Green, 471–2. The Latin quotation is from Livy, *History of Rome*, XXIV, 25, viii.

35 All but one of the sources noted above (n.9) were not available to Grant when he was writing 'Tyranny and Wisdom.'

36 In his writings about the theological-political problem, Strauss tended to take for granted the identification of philosophy with science (as its culmination or interpretation) and the separation of science from religion that can easily be illustrated from its history by figures such as Hume, Voltaire, Nietzsche, and Russell. From this angle, philosophers are free-thinking inquirers who challenge the popular beliefs, accepted on trust, which justify and restrain the actions of those in positions of authority. Thus philosophy, on this understanding, is striving not so much for spiritual truths in the religious sense as for rational insight into mundane relationships. It has little use for faith but a great need for enough freedom to express and debate unorthodox opinions. In Strauss's writings, this classical 'zetetic' conception of philosophy is turned against current social and political pieties rather than traditional religious dogmas, but the underlying scepticism is not difficult to see. His purpose in writing about Spinoza and Maimonides, he later explained, had been to determine whether a hard 'external' understanding of the claims of Judaism was tenable, in opposition to the prevailing view at the time that they could be sustained only if they were given an 'internal' interpretation, in accordance with broader trends in German theology. Strauss's conclusion, as already shown, was that the traditional claims as traditionally understood were not incoherent or internally contradictory, even though they were clearly beyond anything that could be rationally demonstrated by any kind of natural theology or scientific study of the historical

record, and thus were threatened, not so much by rigorous reasoning, as by ridicule. Their acceptance required what could be called a Kierkegaardian 'leap of faith,' which Strauss explained by reference to Calvin's *Institutes*. His basic reason for rejecting rationalist theologies, never really spelled out, seems to have been the encouragement they gave to the dissolution of Judaism as a particular faith, with its own distinctive 'external' claims, into a vaguely spiritual 'religion of humanity.' In his later writings about politics and philosophy, particularly in *Thoughts about Machiavelli*, Strauss implicitly put a lot of stress on the potential political utility of religious belief as a support for morality and the authority of rulers. And, in his analyses of the Platonic dialogues, he tended to deny or dismiss the more mystical or spiritual elements of Plato's thought, equating Socratic rationalism, as presented by Plato, with an extremely cautious kind of free-thinking liberation from popular piety, rather than any refinement or elevation of it. Cf. Strauss, *The City and Man*, 61, and 'On the Euthyphron,' in *The Rebirth of Classical Political Rationalism*, ed. Pangle, 206: 'A slight bias in favor of laughing and against weeping seems to be essential to philosophy.'

13 Making Sense of Religion

1 '[Grant] was far more religious as a youth than he let on as an adult.' Christian, *George Grant*, 29. But see Grant's 1942 journal in *Collected Works*, 1: 17–30, for a noteworthy absence of religious reflections where one might well expect to find them.
2 Schmidt, ed., *George Grant in Process*, 62.
3 Cf. Grant, 'Tyranny and Wisdom,' in *Technology and Empire*, 107. For a brief but illuminating examination of the intellectual background to the social gospel in Canada, see A.B. McKillop, 'John Watson and the Idealist Legacy,' *Canadian Literature*, No. 83 (Winter 1979), 72–88.
4 Salem Goldworth Bland, *The New Christianity, or the Religion of the New Age*, intro. Richard Allen (Toronto: University of Toronto Press 1973). Bland (1859–1950) was ordained a Methodist and became a minister of the United Church of Canada in 1925. He taught at Wesley (later United) College in Winnipeg (now the University of Winnipeg) from 1903 to 1917. He was an influential advocate for the establishment of a third party for Canada, the CCF, and in 1934 he was a founder of the Fellowship for a Christian Social Order, which involved such distinguished scholars as Eric Havelock and Gregory Vlastos. In his later years he wrote a regular column, 'The Observer,' for the *Toronto Star*.

5 Bland, *The New Christianity*, 27.
6 Ibid., 28.
7 Ibid., 66. This passage may be compared with a 1915 newspaper column, a rough reworking of the Lord's Prayer, by Bland's student J.S. Woodsworth, also a Methodist minister, who was one of the founders and the first leader of the CCF. See 'Thy Kingdom Come,' in Forbes, ed., *Canadian Political Thought*, 224–6.
8 Grant, 'The Failure of Nerve,' *Food for Thought*, 4(3) (1943): 23, in *Collected Works*, 1: 94–6. In this review (of James Burnham's *The Machiavellians*) there is indirectly a slighting reference to Niebuhr as someone who has forgotten that 'it is easy to despair, but difficult to believe' in 'the goodness of people.' Grant owned (and it is still in his library) a two-volume edition of Niebuhr's Gifford Lectures, *The Nature and Destiny of Man*, inscribed 'GPG Feb 1942' (in volume 1, *Human Nature*, published in 1941) and 'GPG Nov 1945' (in volume 2, *Human Destiny*, published in 1943). Later, and especially in one of his most revealing early writings, 'Two Theological Languages,' he criticized Niebuhr specifically for his conservatism and 'extreme' or 'absurd' biblicism. See Grant, *Collected Works*, 2: 55–6, 87, 488.
9 For the following account of Grant's experience and its relation to his studies, I am relying on Christian, *George Grant*, 81–6 and 111–15.
10 Schmidt, ed., *George Grant in Process*, 62–3. Cf. 1 Cor. 6:19: 'Do you not know that your body is a temple of the Holy Spirit within you, which you have from God. You are not your own.' This phrase occurs frequently in Grant's later writings, for example, *Philosophy in the Mass Age*, 37 and 96. There is a slightly fuller description of the experience in David Cayley, *George Grant in Conversation*, 48–9.
11 Charles Norris Cochrane, *Christianity and Classical Culture: A Study of Thought and Action from Augustus to Augustine* (1944). For Grant's view of this book, see his 1954 broadcast talk, 'Charles Cochrane,' in *Collected Works*, 2: 110–15.
12 'Oman's faith is that Our Lord on the Cross reveals the Father as Love, who demands from men that they take up their crosses in forgiveness. The Father's Love and man's freedom to partake of it are the essence of Christianity. All else is but relative and changing.' Regarding the teaching of Christianity, Grant says that Oman's 'certainty that its truth is not dependent on the approval of metaphysicians is combined with his consciousness that it is his duty to explain to the world in reasonable terms the character of [the] Gospel.' George Grant, 'The Concept of Nature and Supernature in the Theology of John Oman,' in *Collected Works*, 1: 168. Oman lived from 1860 to 1939. He was educated at Edinburgh University and then served for

eighteen years as a pastor in the United Presbyterian Church of Scotland. His first publication, in 1893, was a translation of Schleiermacher's *Reden über die Religion* with a fifty-eight page critical introduction. In 1907 he was appointed to a chair of theology at Westminister College, Cambridge, the theological college for the Presbyterian Church of England. He became its principal in 1922 and held that office until his retirement in 1935.

13 Grant, 'Nature and Supernature,' 183. This was the significance for Oman of Schleiermacher's analysis of the religious consciousness – 'feeling is the pioneer.'

14 Ibid., 232.

15 Grant later emphasized the importance of his association in the late 1940s with James Doull, a friend he had met at Oxford and who had preceded him to Dalhousie. 'I had to teach philosophy when I didn't really know any. Doull, who was my own age and really educated in a way I was not, led me into Kant and Plato. I will never forget once, walking down the street in Halifax, he showed me what the image of the sun in Plato's *Republic* meant. Everything that I had been trying to think came together.' Schmidt, ed., *George Grant in Process*, 64.

16 For a recent study of Oman, see Stephen Bevans, *John Oman and His Doctrine of God* (Cambridge: Cambridge University Press 1992). It has an extensive bibliography.

17 John Oman, *The Natural and the Supernatural* (Cambridge: Cambridge University Press 1931), 304.

18 In later years, when Grant discussed the thesis and his reasons for not publishing it, he emphasized his disagreement with Oman's liberalism and his reluctance to ridicule it. See, for example, the extract from a 1986 letter to Peter Self in *Collected Works*, 1: 167. It is worth noting, however, that the thesis was in some ways the most ambitious and systematic work that Grant ever wrote.

19 Grant, 'Philosophy,' in *Collected Works*, 1: 4.

20 'As a young man I heard such leaders of the analytic school as A.J. Ayer and G. Ryle give a two-evening seminar on Heidegger's thought, in which they mostly ridiculed it as consisting essentially of obvious mistakes in the use of the verb "to be."' 'Confronting Heidegger's *Nietzsche*,' in Christian and Grant, ed., *The George Grant Reader*, 304–5. Grant must be referring to an occasion in 1946–7 or 1949–50.

21 Grant, 'Jean-Paul Sartre,' in *Collected Works*, 2: 123–33.

22 Grant had only 'high school German.' The major items available in English before 1960 were *Existence and Being*, ed. Werner Brock (London: Vision 1949), a collection of four late essays with a long introduction by the editor;

and *An Introduction to Metaphysics*, trans. Ralph Manheim (New Haven, Conn.: Yale University Press 1959), a translation of lectures delivered in 1935. The Macquarrie and Robinson translation of *Sein und Zeit* appeared in 1962. A French translation of the 'Letter on Humanism' with an extensive commentary was published in Paris in 1957.

23 Grant, *Collected Works*, 2: 466–7, and Christan and Grant, eds., *George Grant Reader*, 298. There is a line missing in the text of the *Collected Works*. Grant's handwriting is hard to decipher, and I have transcribed this passage slightly differently. It seems to refer to chapter 4 of Heidegger's *Introduction to Metaphysics* and it borrows from Majorie Grene, *Martin Heidegger* (London: Bowes and Bowes 1957), 101, 106–7.

24 Grant, *Collected Works*, 2: 467.

14 Discovering Simone Weil

1 Grant's writings about Simone Weil consist of two published book reviews ('Pétrement's *Simone Weil*' and 'In Defence of Simone Weil'), a finished but unpublished lecture to the Hamilton Association in 1970 ('Introduction to Simone Weil'), an earlier 1,500-word typescript ('Comments on Simone Weil and the Neurotic and the Alienated'), and about fifty pages of notes and drafts for a book. A selection of these items is to be published in volume 4 of the *Collected Works* being edited by Arthur Davis and Henry Roper. The first three – the reviews and the lecture – are already available in Christian and Grant, eds., *The George Grant Reader*, 237–65, and the page references below are to this source. The notes and drafts will be used extensively in what follows even though no exact references can be given (e.g., for the quotation to which this note is appended), since it is too early to know how they will be presented in the *Collected Works*. For other expressions of Grant's admiration for Simone Weil, see 'Introduction to Simone Weil,' 250; 'In Defence of Simone Weil,' 257; Schmidt, ed., *George Grant in Process*, 65; and Christian, ed., *Selected Letters*, 312, 315, 323, and 381.

2 Many have written about Simone Weil's remarkable life. For the following biographical sketch I have relied upon Simone Pétrement, *Simone Weil: A Life*, trans. Raymond Rosenthal (New York: Pantheon Books 1976), and the 'Chronologies' that are included in the volumes of the *Oeuvres Complètes* (Paris: Gallimard), ed. André Devaux and Florence de Lussy.

3 'I was brought up by my parents and my brother in a complete agnosticism, and I never made the slightest effort to depart from it; I never had the slightest desire to do so, quite rightly, I think.' Simone Weil, *Waiting on God*, trans. Emma Craufurd (London: Routledge and Kegan Paul 1951), 42.

4 'Someone said to me about her brother André that what Einstein is to physics he is to modern mathematics.' Cayley, *George Grant in Conversation*, 174.

5 Trotsky had been expelled from the Soviet Union in 1929 and was living secretly in Paris, in danger of being murdered (as he was eventually, in Mexico) if his whereabouts became known to Stalin's agents. He is said to have remarked to the Weils, as he was leaving their apartment, 'You will be able to say that it is in your house that the Fourth International was founded.' Pétrement, *Simone Weil*, 190.

6 This text, which Simone Weil called her 'grand oeuvre' and which was not published until 1955, forms a little more than half of *Oppression and Liberty* (London: Routledge and Kegan Paul 1958). Grant thought that this collection, which contains English translations of her most characteristic social and political writings, was likely to be the best place for someone unfamiliar with Weil's thought to begin reading. He also recommends *Waiting on God*, the collection of letters and essays he reviewed for CBC. See Grant, 'Introduction to Simone Weil,' 245, 246.

7 Weil, *Waiting on God*, 20.

8 Ibid.

9 Ibid.

10 Ibid., 20–1. The *Fioretti* is 'The Little Flowers of Saint Francis' by Brother Ugolino, who lived a century after the death of Francis.

11 As the dating of these materials seems to me uncertain, I should warn the reader that I nonetheless offer a conjecture at the end of this chapter on the assumption that it is correct. The project had actually begun in the early 1960s. In the summer of 1963, Grant made a trip to Paris to consult unpublished manuscripts and to talk to Selma Weil and Simone Pétrement. See Christian, *George Grant*, 228–32, and Christian, ed., *Selected Letters*, 216–19.

12 The Hamilton lecture, 'Introduction to Simone Weil,' in Christian and Grant, eds., *The George Grant Reader*, 238–53, gives a good idea of the kind of book Grant says he was trying to write. Immediately following the remark quoted at the beginning of this chapter, Grant wrote: 'But such a statement does not justify the writing of a book. Most philosophers have learnt from studying the writings of Plato, but God forbid that all those who have so learnt should write for publication a synopsis of what they have learnt therein. All such synopses are only partial gleanings from the philosopher and are often more concerned with the beliefs of the commentator than the thoughts of the philosopher.'

13 Grant, 'Pétrement's *Simone Weil*,' 254.

14 'It is always a mystery to me that I can hold the truth of what Simone Weil

is saying, when I am totally unable to live it.' Grant, in Christian, ed., *Selected Letters*, 355 (to David Cayley, 1986).

15 T.S. Eliot, 'Preface' to Simone Weil, *The Need for Roots*, trans. A.F. Wills (London: Routledge and Kegan Paul 1952), vi and xi.

15 Escaping the Shadows

1 From the notes and drafts that will be published in volume 4 of the *Collected Works* being edited by Arthur Davis and Henry Roper. As explained in chapter 14, n.1, no precise reference can be given for this quotation or for subsequent ones from these notes and drafts, because it is still unclear how they will be arranged by the editors and on which pages of the volume they will be found. The statement by Simone Weil is in *Seventy Letters*, trans. Richard Rees (London: Oxford University Press 1965), 178. The translation quoted is that of George Grant.

2 Simone Weil, *Pensées sans ordre concernant l'amour de Dieu* (Paris: Gallimard 1962), 136. Grant's translation. See also Weil, *First and Last Notebooks*, trans. Richard Rees (London: Oxford Univeristy Press 1970), 342: 'Essential point of Christianity – (and of Platonism) – : It is only the thought of perfection that produces any good – and this good is imperfect. If one aims at imperfect good, one does evil. One cannot really aim at perfection unless it is really possible; so this is the proof that the possibility of perfection exists in this world.'

3 Simone Weil, *Notebooks*, trans. Arthur Wills (London: Routledge and Kegan Paul 1956), 126. This edition, in two volumes, paginated continuously from 1–331 (volume 1) and 333–648 (volume 2), is a translation of the first French edition of the *Cahiers*, in three volumes, published by Librairie Plon between 1952 and 1955. Earlier she had written, 'For want of a smile from Louis XIVm, we manufacture for ourselves a God who smiles on us' (124). In other words, there are attractive images of God that are very far from making any sense, as the philosophic critics of religious belief have always known. There are helpful syntheses of some of the material from the notebooks in the last two selections ('Fragments, London 1943' and 'Is There a Marxist Doctrine?') in *Oppression and Liberty*, one of the collections of Simone Weil's writings that Grant recommended.

4 Weil, *Notebooks*, 1: 127.

5 Ibid., 229.

6 Ibid., 151.

7 Cf. Sherrard, *The Greek East and the Latin West*, 27–8, 43–6, 51–5.

8 Weil, *Pensées sans ordre*, 47. See also Weil, *First and Last Notebooks*, 157: 'If God should be an illusion from the point of view of existence, He is the sole reality from the point of view of the good. I know that for certain, because it

is a definition. "God is the good" is as certain as "I am."' Cf. Weil, *Note-books*, 1: 304: 'God gives himself to Man under the aspect of power or under that of perfection: the choice is left to Man.'

9 My purpose in turning at this juncture to Augustine is only to indicate a landmark of orthodoxy, one that readers can easily see for themselves, since the dialogue in question is short and easily obtained in translation. I do not mean to suggest that this little dialogue alone contains all of Augustine's teaching or the reasons for Grant's interest in it. Only in Augustine's *Confessions* and in his later anti-Pelagian writings does one find his distinctive emphasis on deep-rooted internal conflicts in the human soul and the growth of freedom in willing through the overcoming of doubt.

10 Augustine, *Free Choice of the Will*, II, 6: trans. Anna S. Benjamin and L.H. Hackstaff (Indianapolis: Library of Liberal Arts/Bobbs Merrill 1964), 49.

11 Ibid., II, 14: 70.

12 Ibid., II, 15: 71.

13 Cf. Grant, *Time as History*, ed. Christian, 60; Weil, *Pensées sans ordre*, 136; Weil, *Intimations of Christianity among the Ancient Greeks*, trans. Elisabeth Chase Geissbuhler (London: Routledge and Kegan Paul 1957), 141. The quotation in the text is from Grant's notes.

14 Simone Weil, 'The Love of God and Affliction,' in *Waiting on God*. The quotations in this paragraph and the next two are all from this source, 64–6.

15 Thomas Aquinas, *Summa Theologica*, I, Q. 2, 3 (*Basic Writings*, trans. Pegis, I, 21).

16 Augustine, *Enchirideon*, xi. Cf. Weil, *Notebooks*, 2: 454.

17 Augustine wrote *De libero arbitrio* around 390, just after his conversion to Christianity. As he explains in detail in his *Confessions*, he was then struggling to escape the dualistic view of reality that provides a relatively simple solution to the problem of good and evil in human life by positing two fundamental principles or realities, one the source of good, the other of evil, and assuming that they are locked in a cosmic struggle for domination, a bit like the Devil and his Creator, but without the assumption that the source of evil is ultimately subordinate to or derived from the good. A scheme of this sort was offered by the Manichaean sect that had attracted Augustine's allegiance in his youth.

The founder of Manichaeism was a third-century Babylonian seer, Mani, who claimed to know that there is a god of light or spirit that is eternally at war, on a footing of equality, with a god of darkness or matter. The world of our experience, he taught, is almost entirely within the realm of matter or darkness. The only evidence we have of the divine light is our own souls, which are particles of light trapped in bodies that are otherwise evil and corrupt. The aim of Mani's teaching was to awaken in each soul an awareness of its divine origin and to show it the way – the way of *gnosis* or enlightenment – to escape the forces of darkness.

A similar but less radical or extreme dualism is a basis for Plato's 'likely story' about the creation of the world in the *Timaeus*. The world of our perception – the world that is always becoming or changing – must have a cause of its orderly motion, and this ultimate cause or creator Plato calls a maker or craftsman (more impressively, in some translations, the Demiurge). In shaping the world, this divine maker looks to the eternal forms or ideas, the intelligible patterns that are then exemplified more or less clearly in the visible and tangible things that we perceive. The forms or ideas are thus somehow prior to the maker or creator, as is the unformed substratum of creation, a chaotic, erratic motion that receives the forming influence of the maker, bringing it into conformity with the forms. The ever-changing things of our world are to be understood by seeing their likeness to the eternal patterns that have guided their making. The goodness of the material world is explained by the perfection of the forms. The evils of the world, on the other hand, are to be attributed to the limited power of the maker and the resistance of the pre-existing chaos to his attempts to bring order out of it.

Finally, among the curious heresies that flourished in the early Christian communities, before the councils of the church had provided clear definitions of the basic truths of the Christian religion, the cosmic dualism of Marcion (died c. 160) is worth noting. Interpreting his sources literally, he contrasted the just and wrathful creator God of the Hebrew scriptures with the previously unknown loving and forgiving God of light and salvation found in the Christian writings, particularly the gospel of Luke and the letters of Paul. He concluded that these were not two revelations of the same divinity but rival gods, the one to be abjured, the other to be adored and imitated through ascetic practices. Marcion's antipathy to the Old Testament resembles that of the Gnostics, but he was apparently (his ideas survive only in the attacks on them of writers such as Tertullian) a scriptural purist, indifferent to the elaborate mythological and allegorical fancies characteristic of Gnosticism. Nonetheless, by the fourth century, the Marcionite churches were being absorbed within the broader current of Manichaeism.

18 Augustine, *Free Choice of the Will*, I, 1: 3.
19 Ibid., I 16: 33–4.
20 Ibid., II, 1: 36.
21 Ibid., III, 1: 88. Augustine may be confusing political and metaphysical necessities.
22 Ibid., III, 17: 126.

23 Cf. Weil, *Notebooks*, 1: 255: 'To manage to love God through and beyond the misery of others is very much more difficult than to love him through and beyond one's own suffering. When one loves him through and beyond one's own suffering, this suffering is thereby transfigured ... But love is unable to transfigure the misery of others ... What saint shall transfigure the misery of the slaves who died on the cross in Rome and in the Roman provinces throughout the course of so many centuries?'

24 'There is a legitimate and an illegitimate use of contradiction. The illegitimate use insists on joining together incompatible thoughts as if they were compatible ... The legitimate use seems to me this, when two incompatible thoughts present themselves to us we must exhaust every recourse of our intelligence to try to eliminate one of the conflicting and incompatible thoughts. If this is impossible – if both insist on imposing themselves on our minds, it becomes necessary to recognize the contradiction as a fact. Then it becomes necessary to use this contradiction as a kind of pincers, to try to enter directly in contact with the transcendent which otherwise is inaccessible to human beings. This is what the doctrine of mystery means.' Grant, Lectures at Dalhousie on Augustine, in *Collected Works*, 2: 489. Cf. Sherrard, *The Greek East and the Latin West*, 165.

25 Weil, *First and Last Notebooks*, 335.

26 Weil, *Notebooks*, 412–13.

27 Weil, *Notebooks*, 1: 166. The specific reference here is to Republican militiamen captured by Franco's forces and imprisoned in Seville with Arthur Koestler, as described in his *Spanish Testament* (1937). The prisoners were subject to summary execution, and every night batches of them were dispatched, without trial, by firing squad.

28 Weil, *Notebooks*, 1: 149. See also *First and Last Notebooks*, 160; *Notebooks*, 2: 468, 492, 582; *Oppression and Liberty*, 173; *L'Enracinement*, 246. Note as well her critical attitude towards the products of the 'secular' imagination. 'It is not religion but revolution which is the opium of the people.' *Notebooks*, 2: 596.

29 Weil, *Notebooks*, 2: 411.

30 Weil, *First and Last Notebooks*, 134.

31 Ibid., 199.

32 Weil, *Notebooks*, 2: 410. 'There is no contradiction in what is imaginary.' *Notebooks*, 1: 329.

33 This is not all all the same as denying that human beings frequently make bad choices, by which they bring misery upon themselves and others and add to the evils that must be attributed to natural causes – fires, floods, droughts, plagues, and the like – quite apart from any human actions.

Human beings frequently or even generally or invariably act from an imperfect understanding of what is good. But the imperfection of human understanding may be as much a part of the natural order as tornadoes and volcanoes. See above, p. 26, for some brief comments on Grant's concise statement in *Lament for a Nation* of the kind of necessity that is relevant in human affairs..

34 Weil, *Oppression and Liberty*, 173. See also *L'Enracinement*, 246.

35 Weil, *On Science, Necessity, and the Love of God*, ed. Richard Rees (London: Oxford University Press 1968), 197. The paragraph concludes with a typical reversal: 'But to know that it refuses, one has to ask.'

36 Weil, *Notebooks*, 2: 361. This note continues: 'And what about inspiration regarded as a phenomenon? There lies the great mystery.'

37 Weil, *Waiting on God*, 40. She adds immediately: 'They only escape from it in proportion to the place held in their souls by the authentically supernatural.' Cf. Weil, *First and Last Notebooks*, 82.

38 Weil, *Intimations of Christianity among the Ancient Greeks*, 181. Also p. 116: 'The recognition of might as an absolutely sovereign thing in all of nature, including the natural part of the human soul, with all the thoughts and all the feelings the soul contains, and at the same time as an absolutely detestable thing; this is the innate grandeur of Greece.'

39 Hegel, *Phenomenology of Spirit*, Preface, trans. A.V. Miller (Oxford: Oxford University Press 1977), 35.

16 'Faith and the Multiversity'

1 The earlier, closely related essay is Grant's 'The Computer Does Not Impose on Us the Ways It Should Be Used.' For the earliest systematic statement of Grant's analysis of the distinctive character of modern knowledge, see his Royal Society address, 'Knowing and Making,' *Transactions of the Royal Society of Canada*, Series IV, 12 (1974): 59–67, in Christian and Grant, ed., *The George Grant Reader*, 407–17.

2 This essay exists under the same title in a shorter and substantially different version that seems to have been prepared for the Sixth International Conference on the Unity of the Sciences in 1977. It was later published in *The Search for Absolute Values in a Changing World* (New York: International Cultural Foundation Press 1978), 1: 183–94, and in *The Compass: A Provincial Review*, 4 (Autumn 1978): 3–14.

3 Grant, 'Faith and the Multiversity,' in *Technology and Justice*, 37–8.

4 Weil, *Notebooks*, 1: 240. See also *Notebooks*, 1: 195, and Weil, *Letter to a Priest*, 58–9. Cf. Schmidt, ed., *George Grant in Process*, 105–7.

5 Weil, *Notebooks*, 1: 317.

6 Weil, *Notebooks*. 2: 553.

7 Ibid., 335.

8 In this Appendix, which is a bridge to the next essay on 'Nietzsche and the Ancients,' Grant briefly states some reasons for accepting the historic connection of Christianity with Platonism rather than following the lead of those Protestant theologians, such as Karl Barth, who have emphasized the contrast between Greek rationalism and biblical faith. Grant also notes how strange is the idea of a free choice about such matters. 'I put the word "use" in quotations marks because philosophy always uses the user rather than he or she using it' (71).

9 Cf. Grant, *Lament for a Nation*, 91–5.

10 Grant, *Selected Letters*, ed. Christian, 347. O'Donovan's study of Grant, *George Grant and the Twilight of Justice*, had been published in 1984 by the University of Toronto Press. In a subsequent undated letter to O'Donovan (late in 1985 or early in 1986), Grant explained that the essay on faith and the multiversity 'is really my answer to what you said so well in criticism of my thought' (353). See also the two letters of February 1978 (299–301).

11 Grant, *Selected Letters*, ed. Christian, 361 (to David Dodds, 1986).

12 Cf. Judges, 12:5–6: 'And the Gileadites took the fords of the Jordan against the Ephraimites. And when any of the fugitives of Ephraim said, "Let us go over," the men of Gilead said to him, "Are you an Ephraimite?" When he said, "No," they said to him, "Then say Shibboleth," and he said, "Sibboleth," for he could not pronounce it right; then they seized him and slew him at the fords of the Jordan. And there fell at that time forty-two thousand of the Ephraimites.'

13 Grant, 'Faith and the Multiversity,' *The Compass*, 4. Also Cayley, *George Grant in Conversation*, 175–9, 184–7, and Larry Schmidt, 'An Interview with George Grant,' *Grail*, 1, no. 1 (1985), 44–5.

14 Cf. Cayley, *George Grant in Conversation*, 175–9, 187.

15 Weil, *Notebooks*, 1: 240. Cf. Plato, *Republic*, 507a–509c. For another significant remark about faith, see Weil, *Notebooks*, 2: 388: 'To have faith in the reality of something – if it is a question of something that can be neither ascertained nor demonstrated – means simply to accord to that thing a certain quality of attention. Faith in the Incarnation represents the fullest possible attention accorded to the fullest possible harmony.' See also Weil, 'The Pythagorean Doctrine,' 196.

16 Cf. Grant, 'In Defence of North America,' in *Technology and Empire*, 35.

17 Grant, 'Tyranny and Wisdom,' in *Technology and Empire*, 99, from Strauss, *Thoughts on Machiavelli*, 298.

18 Grant, *Lament for a Nation*, 71.
19 Grant, *English-Speaking Justice*, 1. The passage continues: 'Moreover we are called to think that technological civilization in relation to the eternal fire which flames forth in the Gospels and blazes even in the presence of that determining power.'
20 Grant, 'Justice and Technology,' in *George Grant Reader*, ed. Christian and Grant, 436.
21 Grant, *Selected Letters*, ed. Christian, 365 (to Peter Self, 1987).
22 Many years ago I heard from a source I can no longer confidently recall (though it was probably Allan Bloom) that Grant's interest in Heidegger had been strengthened by the discussion he had with Leo Strauss when he visited him in 1972. Strauss apparently encouraged him to write about Heidegger's interpretation of Plato. Whether this is an accurate recollection or my memory is playing tricks on me is not of much importance: the significant facts are that a deep interest in Heidegger is apparent in his 1964 essay on 'Tyranny and Wisdom' and that he was planning a book about Heidegger at the end of his life. In his retirement Grant was also hoping to write more about Rousseau's Second Discourse and Céline's last three novels. What the connection may have been in his mind between all these projects is hard to say.
23 But see also Grant, 'Confronting Heidegger's *Nietzsche*,' an unpublished manuscript intended for a collection of essays in honour of James Doull, in Christian and Grant eds., *The George Grant Reader*, 303–11. It will be included in Volume 4 of the *Collected Works* being edited by Arthur Davis and Henry Roper.
24 This was the view of theology being advanced at the time by the most influential German theologians, Karl Barth and especially Rudolf Bultmann, with whom Heidegger was closely associated during his five years at Marburg University. See John Macquarrie, *An Existentialist Theology: A Comparison of Heidegger and Bultmann* (London: SCM Press 1955), and Macquarrie, *Heidegger and Christianity*, the Hensley Henson Lectures 1993–4 (New York: Continuum 1994).
25 Martin Heidegger, *Introduction to Metaphysics*, trans. Gregory Fried and Richard Polt (New Haven, Conn.: Yale University Press 2000), 8. This is the view spelled out more fully in a 1927 lecture on 'Phenomenology and Theology' that was not published until 1970 in German and in English only in *The Piety of Thinking: Essays by Martin Heidegger*, ed. John G. Hart and James C. Maraldo (Indianapolis: Indiana University Press 1976), 5–21. See also 'The Problem of a Non-objectifying Thinking and Speaking in Today's Theology' in the same collection.

26 A good example is provided by the context of the remarks just quoted. Heidegger is explaining that philosophy (or metaphysics) starts from the question 'Why are there beings at all instead of nothing?' That is the first, broadest, deepest, and most fundamental of all questions, he says. It is quite different from the subordinate questions about particular beings asked (and answered) in the specialized sciences. Pondering this obscure primordial question is the particular task and dignity of philosophy and philosophers, according to Heidegger. Good Christians, on the other hand, easily answer this potentially most disturbing of questions by recounting the biblical story of creation. ('In the beginning God created heaven and earth, etc.,' as he puts it.) God, as a being, creates all the other beings, while keeping His own being exempt from questioning. Believers, committed in advance to a doctrine that has been handed down to them, may pretend to question, Heidegger says, but what is really asked in the most basic of all questions is, for them, as St Paul said, foolishness. 'Philosophy consists of such foolishness. A "Christian philosophy" is a round square and a misunderstanding.' Heidegger, *Introduction*, 4–8.

Some Further Reflections

1 There is a picture of the gravestone in Christian, *George Grant: A Biography*, xlvii. Grant associated the Latin phrase – *Ex umbris et imaginibus in veritatem* – with Augustine (see *Philosophy in the Mass Age*, 112), perhaps recalling *The City of God*, XX, 22, 'the good will ... pass from these old shadows of time into the new light of eternity' (trans. Bettenson, 944), but the exact phrase does not seem to occur in Augustine's writings. Cardinal Newman also chose it as the epitaph for his gravestone.

2 Grant, 'Nietzsche and the Ancients,' *Technology and Justice*, 90.

3 'Red Tory' is the most popular of the labels. It was coined to describe Grant, and it nicely captures his paradoxical unconventionality. He was not a liberal, but neither was he a conventional socialist or social democrat (despite his scorn for the rich and powerful), and he was far from being simply an old-fashioned Canadian Tory (despite his British imperialist sentiments). He was somehow a mixture, but on what plane? The term is misleading insofar as it puts too much emphasis on practical politics and not enough on Grant's reservations about 'progressive' opinions. It implies that he can be better understood by comparing him with such exemplary Red Tories as Dalton Camp, Joe Clark, David Crombie, Eugene Forsey, Heath Macquarrie, Hugh Segal, and Robert Stanfield. In fact, Grant's political thought comes into sharper focus only when it is related to the political philosophy

of Leo Strauss. Grant's questions were also Strauss's, and they shared a very similar understanding of and reservations about modern thought, even before Grant discovered Strauss's writings.

4 For example, I may have dealt too briefly and indirectly with Grant's study of Augustine and his admiration for the scholarship and insights of Charles Cochrane and Philip Sherrard. I have said almost nothing about Grant's short-lived enthusiasm for Jacques Ellul's *The Technological Society*, followed by his explicit rejection of his conception of technology. Nor have I given as much attention to Eric Voegelin as he may deserve. Grant sometimes cited his writings favourably, but he never said very much about them, until a short time before his death, when he wrote that he felt himself more in Voegelin's ambiance than in that of Strauss, despite the former's tendency to use 'gnostic' as a term of abuse. (See *Selected Letters*, ed. Christian, 380–1, to David Dodds.) Only in a footnote have I mentioned Grant's great admiration for the last three novels of 'that bastard Céline.'

Bibliographical Notes

These pages are not intended to be an exhaustive bibliography, but only to make conveniently available some basic information that does not fit easily into the endnotes and to offer some suggestions for further reading. There are good bibliographies of Grant's writings in several of the sources listed below. The most complete, by K. Mark Haslett, is in William Christian, *George Grant: A Biography* (Toronto: University of Toronto Press 1993), 450–60. I know of no proper bibliography of the secondary literature, but rather than trying to assemble a complete list, I will offer instead a more selective survey of what I think may be worth the reader's attention.

Grant's Writings

This study has focused on the six short books that Grant published during his lifetime. Since some readers are likely to have different editions of these books than the ones I have cited, it may be helpful for them (for finding quoted passages) and it may be of some interest to others to have some details about the publishing history of these six books.

The first, *Philosophy in the Mass Age*, was based on radio lectures delivered in 1958. It appeared in book form, consisting of a main text (1–112) and a short Preface (v–viii), in 1959 from Copp Clark (Toronto) and in 1960 from Hill and Wang (New York). A new edition from Copp Clark appeared in 1966, with the same text, but without the original Preface and instead a new, lengthier Introduction (iii–ix). The current edition of this book, edited by William Christian, was published by the University of Toronto Press in 1995. It is the one I have cited. As well as the main text (3–103), the original Preface (xxix–xxxi), and the Introduction to the 1966 edition (117–22), it includes some additional material from the broadcast lectures, Grant's answers to questions raised in letters from his listeners (105–16), and a new Introduction by the editor (vii–xxiii).

Grant's second book, *Lament for a Nation*, appeared in 1965 from McClelland and Stewart (Toronto). It consisted then of seven untitled chapters (1–97). It was reissued in 1970 by the same publisher in a smaller format as the Carleton Library No. 50, with the same pagination of the main text and a new 'Introduction to the Carleton Library Edition' (vii–xii). An expanded and reset version of this edition was published by Carleton University Press (Ottawa) in 1994, with Grant's 1970 Introduction (9–14), a Foreword by Peter C. Emberley (15–22), and the main text (23–106). In 1997 this edition was supplemented by an Afterword by Sheila Grant (109–11). The current edition, cited above, is from McGill-Queen's University Press (Montreal and Kingston) and consists of the main text (3–95), Grant's 1970 Introduction (lxix–lxxvi), Emberley's Foreword (lxxvii–lxxxv), Sheila Grant's Afterword (97–9), and a lengthy new 'Introduction to the 40th Anniversary Edition' by Andrew Potter (ix–lxviii). In addition, there is a French translation by Gaston Laurion, *Est-ce la fin du Canada? Lamentation sur l'échec du nationalisme canadien*, with a preface by Jacques-Yvan Morin, published by Hurtubise HMH (Montreal) in 1987.

Grant's third book, *Technology and Empire*, is a collection of six essays, two of them written especially for the volume (the first and last, 'In Defence of North America' and 'A Platitude'), and a one-page Preface. It appeared in 1969 from House of Anansi Press (Toronto) and it is still in print, with a different cover and format, but the same pagination (13–143). It has never been supplemented by any new introductions, prefaces, forewords, or afterwords.

Grant's shortest book, his 1969 Massey Lectures, *Time as History*, was published by the Canadian Broadcasting Corporation in 1971. It consists of five untitled chapters (1–52). A new edition, edited by William Christian, was published by the University of Toronto Press in 1995, and it is this edition that I have cited above. It consists of the main text with chapter titles and additional spoken material from the lectures (3–69), an Appendix, 'Dialogue on the Death of God with Dr. Charles Malik' (71–81), and an 'Editor's Introduction: George Grant's Nietzsche' (vii–xli).

Grant's fifth book, *English-Speaking Justice*, his 1974 Josiah Wood Lectures, was first published in a small format by Mount Allison University (Sackville, N.B.) in 1978. The text, in four Parts, is paginated from 1 to 96, followed by 16 pages of notes (ending on 112). Essentially the same text, but with more complete notes and in a larger format, was published in 1985 by House of Anansi Press (Toronto) and simultaneously by the University of Notre Dame Press in the United States, with the text now occupying 1–89 and the notes, 91–104. The American edition has a brief 'Editorial Introduction' by Stanley Hauerwas and Alasdair MacIntyre. In 1998 Anansi issued a new edition, with identical pagination but with an introductory essay, 'In the Perspective of the Citizen: The Public Philosophy of George Grant,' by Robin Lathangue (vii–xxvi).

Finally, Grant's last book, *Technology and Justice*, consisting of six previously published essays, two of them substantially rewritten, and a two-page Preface, was published by House of Anansi Press in 1986. This original edition is the current edition.

Of course, Grant wrote and published much more than these six books. The most convenient source for his most interesting shorter writings (as well as some excerpts from his books) is *The George Grant Reader*, edited by William Christian and Sheila Grant (Toronto: University of Toronto Press 1998). However, anyone drawn to Grant's thought and intending to study it in depth will want to acquire the four-volume *Collected Works* being published by the University of Toronto Press. It will eventually contain all of his published writings and a selection of unpublished talks, lectures, notes, correspondence, and broadcast transcripts, as well as valuable editorial introductions and explanatory notes. Volume I, edited by Arthur Davis and Peter Emberley, was published in 2000 and covers the period up to 1950. Volume II, edited by Arthur Davis, was published in 2002 and covers the years 1951–9. It includes a large unpublished manuscript, 'Acceptance and Rebellion,' and the original published version of the closely related *Philosophy in the Mass Age* (313–88). Volume III, edited by Arthur Davis and Henry Roper, covers the 1960s and includes *Lament for a Nation* (277–347) and *Technology and Empire* (480–581). It was published in 2005. The fourth volume, which will include *Time as History, English-Speaking Justice*, and *Technology and Justice*, is scheduled to appear in 2008. See also Sheila Grant's collation of her husband's writings on Céline, 'Céline's Trilogy,' in *George Grant and the Subversion of Modernity: Art, Philosophy, Politics, Religion, and Education*, ed. Arthur Davis (Toronto: University of Toronto Press 1996), 11–53.

Recorded interviews, in which Grant explains himself, provide some of the most valuable insights into his thinking. Six have been published. The earliest, with Gad Horowitz, from 1966 and 1969, are in the *Collected Works*, 3: 431–52 and 595–602. In *George Grant in Process*, ed. Larry Schmidt (Toronto: Anansi 1978), there are conversations with several interlocutors at a conference on Grant's thought held in 1977. This transcript (in four parts) is especially interesting because of the sharp exchanges that occurred when some of the participants challenged Grant's claims. Two shorter interviews focusing on religious questions are 'George Grant and Religion: A Conversation Prepared and Edited by William Christian,' *Journal of Canadian Studies*, 26.1 (1991), 42–63, and Larry Schmidt, 'An Interview with George Grant,' *Grail*, 1.1 (1985), 35–47. The longest and most valuable interview, which I have frequently cited above, is David Cayley, *George Grant in Conversation* (Toronto: Anansi 1995), an edited transcript of conversations that extended over five days in 1985.

Finally, for some fascinating insights into Grant's origins, character, and circumstances as well as some unguarded expressions of his political and other opinions, see the *Selected Letters*, edited by William Christian (Toronto: University of Toronto Press 1996).

Writings about Grant

Much of the secondary literature can be found in six edited volumes: *George Grant in Process*, ed. Schmidt; *By Loving Our Own: George Grant and the Legacy of Lament for a Nation*, ed. Peter C. Emberley (Ottawa: Carleton University Press 1990); *'Two Theological Languages' by George Grant, and Other Essays in Honour of His Work*, ed. Wayne Whillier (Lewiston, N.Y: Edwin Mellen Press 1990); *George Grant and the Future of Canada*, ed. Yusuf K. Umar (Calgary: University of Calgary Press 1992); *George Grant and the Subversion of Modernity*, ed. Davis; *Athens and Jerusalem: George Grant's Theology, Philosophy, and Politics*, ed. Ian Angus, Ron Dart, and Randy Peg Peters (Toronto: University of Toronto Press 2006). There are also five articles about Grant in a special number of the *Chesterton Review* (vol. 11, no. 2, 1985). The chapters and articles in these collections cover the full range of Grant's political, philosophical, and religious thought. The most recent of the books became available to me only after I had finished writing this guide.

There are several brief introduction to Grant's thought that are essentially expository rather than critical or comparative and that select points for discussion to fit the interests of particular audiences. Thus Neal G. Robertson, 'George Grant: Intimations of Deprival, Intimations of Beauty,' *Modern Age*, 46.1/2 (2004): 74–83, does a little trimming to fit Grant to the taste of American conservatives but rightly notes that they are likely to find him 'deeply disturbing.' Thomas Schofield, 'Justice and the Insights of Resistance: The Red Tory Jurisprudence of George Grant,' *Buffalo Law Review*, 36 (1987): 763–88, puts aside questions about political philosophy and Christian theology in order to recommend Grant's major writings to American practitioners of critical legal studies. Barry Cooper, 'A Imperio usque ad Imperium: The Political Thought of George Grant,' in *George Grant in Process*, ed. Schmidt, 22–39, surveys much the same ground but from a higher theoretical altitude and a more Canadian angle, ignoring the issues raised in *English-Speaking Justice*. Ian Box, 'George Grant and the Embrace of Technology,' *Canadian Journal of Political Science*, 15.3 (1982): 503–15, offers political scientists a good synopsis of Grant's claims about technology but without paying much attention to either Leo Strauss or Simone Weil. (See the subsequent exchange between William Christian and Ian Box in *Canadian Journal of Political Science*, 16.2 [1983]: 349–59.) Terry Anderson, 'George Grant and Religious Social Ethics in Canada,' *Religious Studies Review*, 6.2 (1980): 118–25, examines Grant from the standpoint of 'a revised and deepened social gospel,' paying particular attention to his observations about Canadian culture and politics. David R. Heaven, 'Justice in the Thought of George Grant,' *Chesterton Review*, 167–81, provides a lucid summary of the major themes in Grant's most important writings about justice. Bruce Ward, 'George Grant and the Problem of Theodicy in Western Christianity,' in *Two Theological Languages*,' ed. Whillier, 94–104, briefly explains the questions raised by Grant's treatment of Christianity in relation to modernity. There is an excellent short survey of Grant's thought for German readers by Till Kinzel, 'George Grant: Ein Kanadisher Philosoph als Antimoderner Kulturkriter,' *Zeitschrift für Kanada-Studien*, 19.2 (1999): 185–200. Unfortunately, there seems to be nothing similar in French, though Gaston Laurion, 'Le prophétisme de George Grant: qu'en va-t-il du Québec?' *Action nationale*, 95.9–10 (2005): 99–109, is a recent appreciation of *Lament for a Nation* from a Quebec perspective.

The Canadianness – or English Canadianness – of Grant's thought and writing has been a theme in much of the writing about him, from a variety of perspectives. The most revealing statement, mixing memoir, tribute, and analysis, is Dennis Lee, 'Cadence, Country, Silence: Writing in Colonial Space,' *boundary 2*, 3 (1974): 151–68. For an interesting reaction to Lee's testimony, equally heartfelt but less favourable to Grant, see Eli Mandel, 'George Grant: Language, Nation, the Silence of God,' *Canadian Literature*, 83 (1979): 163–75. See also the comparison of Grant and Lee by R.D. MacDonald, 'Lee's "Civil Elegies" in Relation to Grant's "Lament for a Nation,"' *Canadian Literature*, 98 (1983): 10–30, and the later talk by Lee, 'Grant's Impasse,' in *By Loving Our Own*, ed. Emberley, 11–39. Grant's distinctive blend of conservative nostalgia and left-leaning satire, not unlike that of Stephen Leacock, is the theme of MacDonald's earlier study, 'The Persuasiveness of Grant's *Lament for a Nation*,' *Studies in Canadian Literature*, 2 (1977): 239–51, which concludes that the book points to 'a more profound conservatism,' beyond the realm of Canadian nationalism.

Grant's reputation as a Canadian nationalist is in some respects undeserved, as I have tried to show and as the attentive reader will soon enough discover, but if any doubts remain, they are removed by Robin Mathews, *George Grant's Betrayal of Canada* (Vancouver: Northlands Publications 2004). For Mathews, nationalism is a firm belief in the existence of fundamental differences between the culture of Canada as a whole and that of the United States, together with an unwavering commitment to the superiority of Canadian values, including 'a sense of itself that rejects ethnicism, race, or country of origin as distinguishing characteristics of "those who belong"' (14). By this standard, Grant was, as Mathews says, an 'enormous failure as a human being,' because – influenced, it would seem, by his 'implacable pessimism' rooted in an acute case of colonial mentality and a failure (or refusal) to understand the 'qualities of Marxism' ('better perhaps characterized as left thought') 'that could be of use to Canadians' – he refused 'to comprehend the meaning of fidelity to Canada' (9 and 29). The reasons for Mathews's dissatisfaction with Grant are less rancorously explained in his first foray into the field of Grant scholarship, 'Nationalism, Technology, and Canadian Survival,' *Journal of Canadian Studies*, 5.4 (1970): 44–9, where Grant's basic error is said to be his failure to see that 'political forms can re-express technology,' so that 'the ethic of technology is dependent upon the ethic of community which controls and employs it.'

The strong reactions to Grant's political writings in the 1960s and later become easier to understand when they are put in their historical context. Ramsay Cook, 'Loyalism, Technology, and Canada's Fate,' in *The Maple Leaf Forever: Essays on Nationalism and Politics in Canada* (Toronto: Macmillan 1971), 46–67, the first comprehensive analysis of

Grant's thought, emphasized its relation to Grant's ancestral Loyalism and the British imperialism of Victorian English Canada. Dennis Duffy, *Gardens, Covenants, Exiles: Loyalism in the Literature of Upper Canada/ Ontario* (Toronto: University of Toronto Press 1982), interprets and expounds the Ontario Loyalist literary tradition, then concludes with a brief but insightful discussion of Grant. (See also Duffy's essay cited below, p. 296.) Carl Berger, *The Sense of Power: Studies in the Ideas of Canadian Imperialism, 1867–1914* (Toronto: University of Toronto Press 1970), provides an excellent account of the imperial federation movement and the important roles played in it by Grant's father and grandfathers, W.L. Grant, George Parkin, and George Monro Grant. (This topic has recently been revisited by William Christian, 'Canada's Fate: Principal Grant, Sir George Parkin and George Grant,' *Journal of Canadian Studies*, 34.4 [1999–2000]: 88–104.) Donald Creighton, *The Forked Road: Canada 1939–1957* (Toronto: McClelland and Stewart 1976), offers a readable history of the years of Grant's early manhood from a perspective similar to his own. Among the books discussing the Diefenbaker government's still controversial 1959 decision to cancel the development of the Avro Arrow, the most useful is probably Greig Stewart, *Shutting Down the National Dream: A.V. Roe and the Tragedy of the Avro Arrow* (Toronto: McGraw-Hill Ryerson 1988). R.C. Davidson, 'Military Integration and George Grant's Lament for a Nation,' in *George Grant and the Future of Canada*, ed. Umar, 123–37, analyses the defence crisis that was the immediate background to *Lament for a Nation*. Gregory A. Johnson, 'The Last Gasp of Empire: The 1964 Flag Debate Revisited,' in *Canada and the End of Empire*, ed. Phillip Buckner (Vancouver: UBC Press 2005), 232–50, provides a brief account of the now generally forgotten 'flag debate.' For a much more detailed historical, heraldic, and political analysis of the debate that came to a head in the summer and fall of 1964, see John Ross Matheson, *Canada's Flag: A Search for a Country* (Boston: G.K. Hall 1980). For nationalism in the 1980s, see Tim Thomas, 'George Grant, The Free Trade Agreement, and Contemporary Quebec,' *Journal of Canadian Studies*, 27.4 (1992–3): 180–96. William Watson, *Globalization and the Meaning of Canadian Life* (Toronto: University of Toronto Press 1998), offers a broader survey and critique Canadian attitudes and public policies from the perspective of a 'continentalist' economist with more than just a casual interest in Grant.

A basic problem in writing about Grant is to know how much attention to give to the local and how much to the universal (or at least extra-Canadian) context of his thought. Which comparisons are the most appropriate? The perennially appealing but fundamentally unilluminating comparison with Harold Innis is briefly examined in R. Douglas Francis, 'Technology and Empire: The Ideas of Harold A. Innis and George P. Grant,' in *Canada and the End of Empire*, ed. Buckner, 285–98. Innis and Grant are two of the thinkers discussed from a post-modern perspective by Arthur Kroker, *Technology and the Canadian Mind: Innis/McLuhan/Grant* (Monteal: New World 1984). Grant and Innis are compared with André Laurendeau, Marcel Rioux, Charles Taylor, and Pierre Elliott Trudeau by James Bickerton, Stephen Brooks, and Alain-G. Gagnon, *Freedom, Equality, Community: The Political Philosophy of Six Influential Canadians* (Montreal: McGill-Queen's University Press 2006), in an attempt to clarify the Canadian understanding of freedom, equality, and community as core values of democratic politics. For a more probing, less schematic comparison with Charles Taylor, see Gregory Millard and Jane Forsey, 'Moral Agency in the Modern Age: Reading Charles Taylor through George Grant,' *Journal of Canadian Studies*, 40.1 (2006): 182–209. Philip A. Massolin, *Canadian Intellectuals, the Tory Tradition, and the Challenge of Modernity, 1939–1970* (Toronto: University of Toronto Press 2001), deals with Grant as part of a larger comparative study of English-Canadian 'critics of modernity' including Harold Innis, Donald Creighton, Vincent Massey, Hilda Neatby, and W.L. Morton. In *Radical Tories: The Conservative Tradition in Canada* (Toronto: Anansi 1982), Charles Taylor (the Toronto journalist, not the McGill philosopher) weaves Grant in and out of a chatty analysis of what is distinctively Canadian about Canadian conservatism (as exemplified by Stephen Leacock, Donald Creighton, W.L. Morton, Al Purdy, Eugene Forsey, Robert Stanfield, and David Crombie). Perhaps Grant's little-known (outside Maritime philosophical circles) friend James Doull provides the most illuminating Canadian comparison. See David G. Peddle and Neil G. Robertson, 'Lamentation and Speculation: George Grant, James Doull, and the Possibility of Canada,' *Animus*, 7 (2002), an electronic journal at www.mun.ca/animus. See also Doull's contribution, 'Naturalistic Individualism: Quebec Independence and the Independence of Canada,' in *Modernity and Responsibility: Essays for George Grant*, ed. Eugene Combs (Toronto: University of Toronto Press 1983), 29–50. For other relevant texts with commentaries from Doull's students and colleagues, see *Philosophy and Freedom: The Legacy of James Doull*, ed. David G. Peddle and Neil G. Robertson (University of Toronto Press 2003).

The originality of Grant's political thought is shown by the difficulty commentators have had assigning him a place on the standard spectrum of ideological possibilities. The problem was apparent from the earliest responses to *Lament for a Nation*, for example, the most perceptive hostile review, F.H. Underhill, 'Conservatism = Socialism = Anti-Americanism,' *Journal of Liberal Thought*, 1.1 (1965): 101–5, and the influential essay by Gad Horowitz, 'Tories, Socialists and the Demise of Canada,' *Canadian Dimension*, 2.4 (May–June 1965): 12–15, which introduced the term 'Red Tory' to finesse the problem of explaining Grant's unusual mixture of conservative cultural criticism and leftist political economy. Yet the problem has remained to motivate an ongoing controversy about whether he really belongs to the left or to the right. Was he more of a Red or more of a Tory? The case for the left interpretation of his thought is well stated by Edward Andrew, 'George Grant on the Political Economy of Technology,' *Bulletin of Science, Technology and Society*, 23 (2003): 479–85. See also Andrew, 'George Grant on Technological Imperatives,' in *Democratic Theory and Technological Society*, ed. Richard Day, Ronald Beiner, and Joseph Masciulli (Armonk, N.Y.: M.E. Sharpe 1988), 299–315, which recasts some of Grant's major themes in his own, academically Marxist style, and Andrew's discussion of Céline, 'George Grant's Céline: Thoughts on the Relationship of Philosophy and Art,' in *George Grant and the Subversion of Modernity*, ed. Davis, 77–105, which strikes some discordant notes. For ambivalent conservative reactions to Grant's unsettling claims about 'the impossibility of conservatism in our era' and 'the futility of conservatism as a theoretical standpoint,' see the essays on his political thought by John Muggeridge, 'George Grant's Anguished Conservatism,' and A. James Reimer, 'George Grant: Liberal, Socialist, or Conservative?' in *George Grant in Process*, ed. Schmidt, 40–8 and 49–57. See also Barry Cooper, 'Did George Grant's Canada Ever Exist,' in *George Grant and the Future of Canada*, ed. Umar, 151–64, and Kenneth Minogue, 'Grant's Technology and Justice: Between Philosophy and Prophecy,' in *By Loving Our Own*, ed. Emberley, 161–74. Janet Ajzenstat, *The Once and Future Canadian Democracy: An Essay in Political Thought* (Montreal: McGill-Queen's University Press 2003), is the most sustained attempt to break out of the one-dimensional view of our politics that generates the need for a category like 'Red Tory.'

For Grant, the question of access to abortion was the touchstone of a conservatism that is more oriented to eternity than to mankind's development in time. For a clear overview of Grant's writings on the topic and a vigorous dissent from the tactics of the pro-life movement that he backed, see Leah Bradshaw, 'Love and Will in the Miracle of Birth: An Arendtian Critique of George Grant on Abortion,' in *George Grant and the Subversion of Modernity*, ed. Davis, 220–39. The distinction between what is morally right and what should be legally enforced is the main theme of James B. Gerrie, 'Technology and Choice: George Grant's Disparate Ethical and Legal Positions on Abortion,' *Journal of Canadian Studies*, 38.3 (2004): 153–70. The best discussion of Grant's reasoning in *English-Speaking Justice* is Samuel Ajzenstat, 'The Place of Abortion in George Grant's Thought,' in *George Grant and the Future of Canada*, ed. Umar, 75–101, which clarifies the limitations of the sharp but sympathetic objections in Clifford Orwin's lengthy review of the book in the *University of Toronto Law Journal*, 30.1 (1980): 106–15. William Mathie, 'Reason, Revelation and Liberal Justice: Reflections of George Grant's Analysis of Roe v. Wade,' *Canadian Journal of Political Science*, 19.3 (1986): 443–66, ignores Rawls and focuses instead on the judicial reasoning of Justice Blackmun, in order to throw light on Grant's disturbing suggestion, in *English-Speaking Justice* and elsewhere, that technological science is making it impossible to think and live the ancient philosophical account of justice as giving each human being his due. An article that demands considerable concentration from the reader, it is nonetheless worth reading, not just for its careful analysis of Blackmun's opinion, but also for its objections to the idea that our current understanding of justice derives from the secularization of the biblical concepts of charity and will. John Badertscher, 'The Prophecy of George Grant,' *Canadian Journal of Political and Social Theory*, 4.1 (1980): 183–9, provides an excellent summary of the different elements of *English-Speaking Justice* and concludes with some pointed objections to Grant's concluding declarations.

Professional philosophers have generally ignored Grant or hidden whatever interest they may have in his thought behind a blizzard of references to others, but there are two exceptions worth noting here. David Gauthier, 'George Grant's Justice,' *Dialogue*, 27 (1988): 121–34, offers an accurate and sympathetic analysis and assessment of *English-Speaking Justice*, relating it to the similar concerns of other contemporary moral theorists, in particular, Alasdair MacIntyre and Bernard Williams. Gauthier concludes that 'no recent work offers a more compelling indictment, in terms that the liberal cannot fail to understand, of our contemporary understanding of justice.' Fred Wilson,

'Socrates' Argument for Immortality: Socrates, Maritain, Grant and the Ontology of Morals,' *Etudes Maritainiennes – Maritain Studies*, 20 (2004): 3–26, goes back to Grant's statement of natural law in *Philosophy in the Mass Age* to clarify the fundamental question at issue, but often begged, in arguments about abortion and euthanasia. Wilson credits Grant with making clear that the metaphysical or ontological issues that divide ancient from modern philosophy remain a problem to this day.

Grant's relation to Leo Strauss is noted by many who discuss his thought, but it remains a matter of scholarly controversy how best to describe their similarities and differences. The uninitiated reader may find Larry Schmidt, 'George Grant and the Problem of History,' in *George Grant in Process*, ed. Schmidt, 130–8, the most helpful introduction to the issues. Yusuf K. Umar, 'The Philosophical Context of George Grant's Political Thought,' in *George Grant and the Future of Canada*, ed. Umar, 1–16, outlines the Strauss-Kojève debate and offers some conjectures about the role it played in Grant's political thought. Two essays by Barry Cooper, 'George Grant and the Revival of Political Philosophy,' in *By Loving Our Own*, ed. Emberley, 97–121, and 'George Grant, Political Philosopher,' *Political Science Reviewer*, 18 (1988): 1–33, emphasize the similarities between Grant and Strauss against a backdrop provided by Hegel, Nietzsche, Kojève, and Voegelin. Wayne Whillier, 'George Grant and Leo Strauss: A Parting of the Ways,' and Ian G. Weeks, 'Two Uses of Secrecy: Leo Strauss and George Grant,' both in *'Two Theological Languages'*, ed. Whillier, 63–81 and 82–93, discuss the differences from a theological angle. Both authors acknowledge the temptation to identify Grant with biblical religion and Strauss with its antithesis, philosophic rationalism, but they both arrive, by somewhat different routes, at a contrary conclusion, namely, that their basic difference is the difference between a faithful Christian and a pious Jew. (Weeks also provides some interesting pointers regarding the sources of Strauss's teaching about philosophic esotericism.) Harris Athanasiadis, 'Political Philosophy and Theology: George Grant, Leo Strauss and the Priority of Love,' *Toronto Journal of Theology*, 20.1 (2004): 23–32, distinguishes Grant's Platonism from Strauss's Aristotelian rationalism. Ian Angus, 'Athens and Jerusalem? A Critique of the Relationship between Philosophy and Religion in George Grant's Thought,' *Journal of Canadian Studies*, 39.2 (2005): 81–104, analyses the difficulties confronting any attempt to synthesize Platonism with Christianity and in doing so clarifies Grant's relation to Strauss. For an early critical appreciation of Grant's work by an American Straussian, see Werner J. Dannhauser, 'Ancients, Moderns and Canadians,' *Denver Quarterly*, 4.2 (1969): 94–8.

Two articles by Lawrence Lampert, 'The Uses of Philosophy in George Grant,' in *George Grant in Process*, ed. Schmidt, 179–94, and 'Zarathustra and George Grant: Two Teachers,' *Dalhousie Review*, 58.3 (1978): 443–57, throw a sharp light on Grant's relations to Nietzsche and Heidegger and thus on the character of his thought as a whole. Peter C. Emberley, 'Values and Technology: George Grant and Our Present Possibilities,' *Canadian Journal of Political Science*, 21.3 (1988): 465–94, examines Grant's writings for the access they provide to Nietzsche's account of nihilism and its implications for our current language of values, values education, and technology. The affinity between Grant and Heidegger based on their common antipathy to urban industrial society is the theme of A. James Reimer, 'Do George Grant and Martin Heidegger Share a Common Conservatism?' in *Chesterton Review*, 183–98. For a wider-ranging discussion of Grant and Heidegger, see Arthur Davis, 'Justice and Freedom: George Grant's Encounter with Martin Heidegger,' in *George Grant and the Subversion of Modernity*, ed. Davis, 139–68. Ronald Beiner, 'George Grant, Nietzsche, and the Problem of a Post-Christian Theism,' in *George Grant and the Subversion of Modernity*, ed. Davis, 109–38, deals with civil religion and Grant's ambivalent relation to Nietzsche's attempt to 'recuperate pagan possibilities' in theocratic regimes that would not be 'clerocracies.' Beiner seems to accept Grant's judgment that Nietzsche saw modernity with great clarity, but he faults him for failing to appreciate his profound contempt for modern, democratic, egalitarian man.

Grant's puzzling interest in the later novels of Céline is examined sympathetically by Gerald Owen, 'Why Did Grant Love Céline?' in *George Grant and the Subversion of Modernity*, ed. Davis, 54–76.

There are two book-length commentaries on Grant's thought, Joan O'Donovan's *George Grant and the Twilight of Justice* (Toronto: University of Toronto Press 1984), and Harris Athanasiadis's *George Grant and the Theology of the Cross* (Toronto: University of Toronto Press 2001). Both approach it from a religious or theological standpoint and both deal with the full range of Grant's writings in chronological order, tracing the various influences on them within a biographical and historical framework. No reader can fail to gain important insights from these systematic scholarly analyses, but both seem to me to pay insufficient attention to Leo Strauss and Simone Weil.

O'Donovan is the most prominent source of the widely held view that Grant's writings fall naturally into three groups, representing three phases in the development of his thought. (See also Frank K. Flinn, 'George Parkin Grant: A Bibliographical Introduction,' in *George Grant in Process*, ed. Schmidt, 195–9, and 'George Grant's Three Languages,' in *Chesterton Review*, 155–66.) For a brief, illuminating explanation of O'Donovan's tripartite dissection – into 'a liberal-synthesizing phase' until 1959, then 'a conservative-polemical phase' in the 1960s, followed by 'a tragic-paradoxical phase' after 1969 – see her article, 'The Battleground of Liberalism: Politics of Eternity and Politics of Time,' in *Chesterton Review*, 131–54, which also offers some indications of how Grant could be compared with Chesterton. Without arguing my reservations or disagreements in detail (I am far from having the necessary background in theology to do so), I have elected to present Grant's thought, even his religious thought, from a more political angle, giving more attention to Strauss and Weil and putting more emphasis on its basic continuity from the 1950s to the 1980s. I have ignored Grant's juvenilia (his 'statesmanly' wartime pamphlets on Canada and the empire) and discounted somewhat his professions of faith in Hegel's eminence as a philosopher, drawing attention instead to his early and persistent fascination with 'existentialist' writers and thinkers (Sartre, Heidegger, Nietzsche, and Strauss). The distinction between Hegelian historicism and radical (Nietzschean) historicism, which I have chosen to highlight, O'Donovan leaves in the shadows.

Athanasiadis, writing more recently, makes extensive use of Grant's notes and unpublished writings to support an interpretation of Grant's thought that is the best counterweight to the one that I have adopted. His central purpose, which gives his survey a clear focus, is to reveal the importance for Grant of Luther's 'theology of the cross.' (See also, on this topic, Sheila Grant, 'George Grant and the Theology of the Cross,' in *George Grant and the Subversion of Modernity*, ed. Davis, 243–62.) Athanasiadis pays more attention to Simone Weil than does O'Donovan, and he provides some helpful summaries of her thought, with numerous references to the sources. He also provides good summaries of the relevant ideas of John Oman, Jacques Ellul, and Philip Sherrard. In his conclusion he faults Grant for not working more closely with other contemporary Protestant theologians who were struggling to affirm similar ideas.

For a sharply critical, even dismissive, but unfortunately rather 'technical' discussion of Grant's early religious thought, see Darren C.

Marks, 'George Grant and the *theologia crucis*: A Theological Modern Agenda,' *Studies in Religion*, 33.3–4 (2004): 381–96, which emphasizes its dependence on that of Oman and Oman's theological liberalism (due to his dependence on Rudolf Otto). As a comment on Grant's later thought, this article is weakened by its tendency to conflate ancient and modern 'Athens' and by its neglect of Simone Weil, but it provides an instructive analysis of the issues discussed in Grant's DPhil thesis. Equally interesting is Kenneth C. Russell, 'The Implications of George Grant's Rejection of Natural Law,' *Science et Esprit*, 50.1 (1998): 29–43, which attributes Grant's grim understanding of technology (as 'an apocalyptic monster deceiving millions with its benefits while leading them into the darkness' and as 'an outlaw force beyond human control' – 33 and 43) to his mistaken rejection (following Luther) of natural theology and, consequently, natural law. Bernard Zylstra, 'Philosophy, Revelation and Modernity: Crossroads in the Thought of George Grant,' in *George Grant in Process*, ed. Schmidt, 148–56, though sometimes misleadingly brief, puts his finger on a major source of the confusion surrounding Grant's religious thought.

Three of Grant's students have written good short accounts of the place Simone Weil held in his teaching. See Lawrence Schmidt, 'George Grant on Simone Weil as Saint and Thinker,' in *George Grant and the Subversion of Modernity*, ed. Davis, 263–81, and Edwin B. Heaven and David R. Heaven, 'Some Influences of Simone Weil on George Grant's Silence,' in *George Grant in Process*, ed. Schmidt, 68–78. Wayne Sheppard, 'The Suffering of Love: George Grant and Simone Weil,' in *Two Theological Languages*,' ed. Whillier, 20–62, is a long essay, the second half of which is more relevant than the first half.

The close relation between theology and politics is emphasized in a curious study by Robert Song, *Christianity and Liberal Society* (Oxford: Clarendon Press 1997), which deals with Grant as one of three 'critics of liberalism' (the other two are Reinhold Niebuhr and Jacques Maritain) who provide the backdrop to Song's discussion of questions like whether Britain should have an American-style bill of rights. A professional theologian's comparison of Grant with Niebuhr and Maritain would be of some interest, but readers expecting this from Song will be disappointed. He deals with each of them in 'self-standing studies' and seems more interested in their shortcomings, as judged from the standpoint of contemporary liberal common sense, than in their insights. Grant is found wanting inasmuch as his criticism of Rawls's more 'metaphysical' contractarian theory (in *A Theory of Justice*, 1971) does not deal with the major innovations Rawls advanced in subsequent publications (especially *Political Liberalism*, 1993), even though, as Song concedes, both theories suffer from the basic shortcomings Grant pointed out (question-begging circularity and political naivety).

Louis Greenspan, 'The Unravelling of Liberalism,' in *George Grant and the Subversion of Modernity*, ed. Davis, 201–19, after balancing Grant's awareness of 'the blessings of the liberal heritage' against his claim that technology now presents it with an insurmountable crisis, concludes by affirming the enduring appeal of liberal principles. Greenspan's topical references help to clarify how Grant's use of 'technology' links the fears aroused by our most disturbing instruments of production and destruction (which in principle we can use well or badly, according to our 'values') to their source, the modern understanding of scientific knowledge from which they flow and which is not in the same sense a matter of choice.

Drawing on Eric Voegelin's account of gnosticism and gnostic politics, Zdravko Planinc, 'Paradox and Polyphony in Grant's Critique of Modernity,' in *George Grant and the Future of Canada*, ed. Umar, 17–45, provides a provocative analysis of the various ways of being a critic of (and within) modernity that can be found in Grant's reading and writing. Planinc's shorthand explanations of the similarities and differences among a wide range of thinkers – Plato, Augustine, Shaftesbury, Burke, Hegel, Nietzsche, Heidegger, Strauss, Weil, and Ellul as well as Grant – raise many interesting questions, including whether there is a fundamental difference between Weil's 'contemplative gnosticism' and 'true Christian Platonism,' but in the end it is unclear whether Planinc thinks that the emphasis should fall on the paradoxical contradictions or the polyphonic harmonies in Grant's work. As he himself says, 'without hearing the voice of Grant's *daimon* in the voices of his polyphony, no particular critique can be understood properly' (42).

Finally, Grant has been well served by his biographer, William Christian, in *George Grant: A Biography* (Toronto: University of Toronto Press 1993), which provides a wealth of information about Grant's life and the circumstances of his thought. For a shorter, more anecdotal study, focusing on nationalism and Canadian politics, see T.F. Rigelhof, *George Grant: Redefining Canada* (Montreal: XYZ Publishing 2001). There are interesting glimpses of the Grant family and of George as a student at Upper Canada College, from the perspective of several contemporaries, in James FitzGerald's *Old Boys: The Powerful Legacy of Upper Canada College* (Toronto: Macfarlane Walter and Ross 1994). For some helpful details on a crucial time in Grant's life, see Peter Brock, 'Six Weeks at Hawkspur Green: A Pacifist Episode during the Battle of Britain,' *Peace and Change*, 28.2 (2003): 271–93. Dennis Duffy, 'The Ancestral Journey: Travels with George Grant,' *Journal of Canadian Studies*, 22.3 (1987): 90–103, offers a short but illuminating account not just of the broad historical context of Grant's writings but also of their relation to major turning points in his life. Some of those who knew Grant well have written brief memoirs that are worth consulting. See especially the second part, 'The Sixties,' of Matt Cohen's *Typing: A Life in 26 Keys* (Toronto: Vintage 2000). See also Louis Greenspan, 'George Grant Remembered,' in *'Two Theological Languages,'* ed. Whillier, 1–5; Nita Graham, 'Teaching against the Spirit of the Age: George Grant and Museum Culture,' in *George Grant and the Subversion of Modernity*, ed. Davis, 285–303; Alex Colville, 'A Tribute to Professor George P. Grant,' in *By Loving Our Own*, ed. Emberley, 3–10; Peter Self, 'George Grant, Unique Canadian Philosopher,' *Queen's Quarterly*, 98.1 (1991): 25–39; and James R. Field, 'History, Technology and the Graduate Student: My Encounter with George Grant,' *Queen's Quarterly*, 100.1 (1993): 215–25. In *Sophia*, 33.3 (1994): 101–8, there is a review of Christian's biography by Ian Weeks that is also in part a memoir. The Introduction to *The George Grant Reader*, ed. Christian and Grant, provides not just a valuable overview of its contents but also some interesting details of Grant's life.

Index

Abraham, 215, 216
Ajzenstat, Janet, 82–4
Alexander the Great, 156
Al-Farabi, 142, 144
Anselm, St, 195
Aquinas, Thomas, 66, 68, 117–18, 195, 198
Arendt, Hannah, 114
Aristophanes, 86
Aristotle, 74, 81, 117, 143, 148, 154, 156, 179, 195, 212, 220, 227, 237n.6, 262n.6
Atwood, Margaret, 22
Augustine, 9, 14, 172, 195–6, 198–200, 225–7, 273nn.9,17, 279n.1
Averroes, 142–4
Avicenna, 142, 144

Bacon, Francis, 172, 212
Barth, Karl, 170, 276n.8, 278n.24
Bentham, Jeremy, 172
Berlin, Isaiah, 114, 152, 181
Blackmun, Harry, 55, 242n.16
Bland, Salem, 168–70, 267n.4
Bloom, Allan, 239n.10, 241n.10, 252n.1, 254n.7, 277n.22
Bultmann, Rudolf, 278n.24

Burke, Edmund, 61, 62, 66, 68, 117–18, 123–4, 243n.3, 245n.10, 262n.6

Calvin, Jean, 136, 137, 140, 154, 266n.35
Calvinists, Calvinism, 28, 163, 168
Canada-United States Permanent Joint Board of Defence, 236n.4
Canadian Broadcasting Corporation (CBC), 6, 7, 12, 176, 184
Castro, Fidel, 25
Céline, 277n.22, 279n.4
Christian, William, 13, 234n.8
Christian Aristotelianism, 265n.30
Christian Platonism, 162, 172, 225, 226, 276n.8
Christians, Christianity, 81, 91–2, 94, 97, 107, 116, 131, 146, 156, 161–2, 165–6, 167–70, 172, 174, 176, 189, 195, 214–15, 220–1, 225, 234n.8
Cicero, 117, 148
Cochrane, Charles Norris, 172, 268n.11, 279n.4
Co-operative Commonwealth Federation (CCF), 69, 246n.18, 268n.7
Coupland, Douglas, 22
Cyrus (Persian tyrant), 150

Darwin, Charles, 209
Dawkins, Richard, 128
De Gaulle, Charles, 25, 183
Descartes, René, 176, 179, 195, 212,
    254n.11
Diefenbaker, John, 10, 24–6, 76, 77,
    128, 236n.5, 242n.1, 257n.3
Disraeli, Benjamin, 66
Doull, James, 7, 14, 269n.15

Eisenhower, Dwight, 77
Eliot, T.S., 190, 205
Ellul, Jacques, 33, 34, 237n.12, 279n.4
Engels, Friedrich, 153
Evodius. *See* Augustine

Francis of Assisi, 182
Franco, Francisco, 182, 275n.27
Free Trade Agreement, 12
Freud, Sigmund, 9, 23, 258n.6,
    264n.16
Friedman, Milton, 61, 64, 244n.7

Gallant, Mavis, 22
General Agreement on Tariffs and
    Trade, 236n.4
George III, 158, 262n.6
Gilson, Étienne, 172
Goldwater, Barry, 64
Grant, George Monro, 5, 69, 167

GRANT, GEORGE PARKIN

  life and career, 5–13, 167–8, 170–1
  as Canadian nationalist, 4, 10–11,
    16, 17, 19–21, 73–8, 82–4, 166
  as critic of modernity, 3, 10, 16, 17,
    27–33
  as Hegelian, 92–5, 97, 99–100, 116,
    161, 249n.1

  as Platonist, 3, 14, 85, 112, 126, 161,
    177–8, 211–13, 217, 219–22, 225
  as Red Tory, 3, 10, 15–16, 17, 59, 68,
    235n.3, 242n.1, 244n.5, 279n.3

'Canadian Fate and Imperialism,'
    79–83
'The Computer Does Not Impose
    ...,' 276n.1
'The Concept of Nature and Super-
    nature in the Theology of John
    Oman,' 173–4
'Confronting Heidegger's
    Nietzsche,' 278n.23
'In Defence of North America,' 27–
    9, 34
English-Speaking Justice, 12, 16, 46–
    58, 66, 207, 219, 246n.17
'An Ethic of Community,' 244n.5
'Faith and the Multiversity,' 12, 15,
    190, 207–22, 227
'Justice and Technology,' 219
'Knowing and Making,' 276n.1
Lament for a Nation, 5, 9, 10, 13, 17,
    19–26, 62–70, 71–8, 79, 86, 230,
    249n.6
'The Minds of Men in the Atomic
    Age,' 102–3, 160, 250n.3
'Nietzsche and the Ancients,' 104,
    107, 111–12, 207, 227
'Philosophy' (Massey Commission
    essay), 7–8, 38–40, 42, 174,
    233n.1
Philosophy in the Mass Age, 8,
    15, 86, 87–98, 99, 109, 110, 116,
    188
'A Platitude,' 228–9
'Religion and the State,' 43–5
Technology and Empire, 12, 15, 228–
    31

Technology and Justice, 12, 15, 207–8, 214
'Thinking about Technology,' 207
Time as History, 12, 15, 86, 103–13, 207
'Two Theological Languages,' 236n.5, 268n.8
'Tyranny and Wisdom,' 86, 147–63, 277n.22
'The University Curriculum,' 40–1
'The Uses of Freedom,' 30–3

Grant, Sheila, 7, 223
Grant, William, 5, 69, 167
Green, Howard, 24, 76, 77, 78, 236n.5

Hegel, G.W.F., 7, 14, 97, 110, 114, 116, 122, 123, 152, 154, 156, 161, 169, 171, 205–6, 250n.1, 256n.21, 264n.16
Heidegger, Martin, 9, 12, 14, 15, 33–4, 85, 86, 110–11, 114, 147, 150–4, 161–3, 165–6, 174, 176–9, 208, 220–1, 226, 238n.13, 239n.9, 264n.16, 277n.22, 278nn.24,26
Heraclitus, 177
Herbert, George, 183
Hesiod, 94
Hiero (Syracusan tyrant), 149
Hitler, Adolph, 150–1, 155
Hobbes, Thomas, 117, 123, 145, 172, 179, 213
Homer, Homeric, 94, 193
Hooker, Richard, 66, 68
Horowitz, Gad, 235n.3, 242n.1
Howe, C.D., 24
Hubbard, L. Ron, 100
Hume, David, 31, 172, 179, 259n.15, 266n.35
Hyde Park Declaration, 236n.4

Ignatieff, Michael, 245n.10
Islam, 156

James, William, 171
Jaspers, Karl, 152
Jefferson, Thomas, 24, 129, 156
Jehovah's Witnesses, 39
Jephthah, 216
Jesus Christ, 145, 162, 169, 170, 183, 217
Jews, Judaism, 85, 91, 92, 130, 131, 132, 133, 135, 139, 140–2, 145–6, 156, 161, 188, 258n.6, 260n.25, 261n.32, 266n.35
Job, 197
Johnson, Lyndon, 64
Joshua, 216

Kant, Immanuel, 14, 48, 52–4, 117, 122, 123, 169, 179, 192, 227, 241n.12, 252n.23, 256n.21, 259n.17, 269n.15
Kennedy, John F., 77
Kierkegaard, Soren, 176, 266n.35
King, Mackenzie, 24, 228
Kojève, Alexandre, 72, 152–9, 162, 163, 264n.15

Lenin, Vladimir Ilyich, 156
Lessing, G.E., 139, 260n.21
Lewis, C.S., 7
Lindsay, A.D., 7, 172
Livy, 148
Locke, John, 52–4, 64, 65, 66, 78, 117–18, 123, 156, 172, 179, 213, 245n.13

Machiavelli, Niccolò, 115, 117, 120, 121–3, 145, 148, 150, 154, 161, 219
Macmillan, Harold, 66

Madison, James, 156
Maimonides, Moses, 136, 140–4, 261n.26, 266n.35
Mani, Manichaeism, 273n.17
Marcion, 273n.17
Maritain, Jacques, 172
Marsilius of Padua, 117
Marx, Karl, 9, 23, 69, 70, 95–6, 123, 153, 154, 156, 205
Marxists, Marxism, 39, 69–70, 95–6, 97, 152–4, 159, 181, 205, 255n.14, 264n.16
Massey, Vincent, 7, 38, 111, 174, 233n.1
Mill, John Stuart, 122, 172, 258n.5
Mistry, Rohinton, 22
Mohammed, 139, 143
Montesquieu, 123, 156
Moses, 133, 138, 145, 162, 216, 258n.7
Muslims, 73, 143

Nazi party, 151
neo-Conservatives, 62, 253n.2
neo-Platonists, 161
Newman, John Henry (Cardinal), 279n.1
New Testament, 107, 162, 215, 216
Niebuhr, Reinhold, 170, 268n.8
Nietzsche, Friedrich, 9, 12, 64, 86, 103–13, 114–16, 124, 150, 159, 160, 161–2, 188, 226, 227, 245n.12, 253n.4, 266n.35
Noah, 216
North American Free Trade Agreement, 12
North Atlantic Treaty Organization, 77

O'Donovan, Joan, 214

Ogdensburg Agreement, 236n.4
Old Testament, 136, 162, 216, 258
Oman, John, 7, 14, 15, 172–4, 176, 184, 192, 268n.12
Ondaatje, Michael, 22

Parkin, Sir George, 5, 69, 167
Parkin, Maude, 5, 167
Parmenides, 177
Pascal, Blaise, 81
Pearson, Lester, 77, 233n.1
Pentecostalism, 170
Perrin, Joseph Marie, 205
Pétrement, Simone, 270n.2, 271n.11
Plato, Platonic, 9, 14, 52–4, 74, 81, 85, 86, 94, 104, 112, 117, 119–21, 126, 147, 148, 154, 161, 177–9, 187, 193, 195, 203, 211–13, 217–21, 225, 226, 227, 266n.35
  Apology, 120
  Euthyphro, 266n.36
  Gorgias, 85, 120, 211
  Phaedrus, 211
  Protagoras, 211
  Republic, 53, 81, 94, 123, 193, 211, 218, 262n.6, 269n.15
  Symposium, 83, 193, 211
  Timaeus, 273n.17
Popper, Karl, 8
Potter, Andrew, 235n.2, 243n.2, 248n.9
Protestants, Protestant Reformation, 92, 94, 138, 153, 167

Quebec, Québécois, 21, 25, 76

Rawls, John, 12, 47–57, 101, 117, 241n.15, 249n.5

Red Tories, 3, 10, 15–16, 59, 68,
    242n.1, 244n.5, 279n.3
Renaissance, 92, 97
Ricci, Nino, 22
Roe v. Wade, 12, 55, 56, 242n.16
Roman Catholics, Catholicism, 23,
    97, 170
Roman empire, 94, 121
Ross, Murray, 9
Rousseau, Jean-Jacques, 64, 117–18,
    123, 277n.22
Russell, Bertrand, 8, 266n.35, 293

Samson, 216
Sartre, Jean-Paul, 14, 171, 176
Schumann, Maurice, 183
Scientology, 100
Sherrard, Philip, 234n.8, 246n.17,
    266n.31, 272n.7, 274n.24, 279n.4
Shields, Carol, 22
Simonides of Ceos, 149, 150
Smith, Joseph, 139, 260n.20
Socrates, 81, 83, 104, 117, 119–21, 150,
    156, 193, 217
Soviet Union, 152, 153
Spinoza, Benedict, 126, 127–46,
    266n.35
Stalin, Joseph, 152, 155, 156, 158
Steiner, George, 262n.8
Stoics, 66, 249n.4
Strauss, Leo, 9, 14, 15, 85–6, 110, 111–

13, 114–26, 127–46, 147–63, 165,
    179, 219, 225, 226, 245n.13, 265n.29,
    266n.35, 277n.22, 279nn.3,4

Thomism, Thomists, 170, 172
Tories, 20, 68
Trotsky, Leon, 181, 271n.5
Trudeau, Pierre Elliott, 36, 82

United Church of Canada, 168
United Nations, 72, 73, 76, 77
Upper Canada College, 5, 167

Vietnam, Vietnamese, 11, 20, 62, 77,
    80, 248n.1
Voegelin, Eric, 279n.4
Voltaire, 35, 163, 266n.35

Weber, Max, 44, 118, 153, 154
Weil, André, 180
Weil, Bernard, 180
Weil, Selma, 180, 271n.11
Weil, Simone, 9, 14, 16, 165–6, 174,
    179, 180–90, 191–205, 208, 209–11,
    214–18, 226
Wittgenstein, Ludwig, 171

Xenophon, 86, 147, 148–50, 152, 162

Zionism, 146